The

Torah

The Five Books of Moses

The Confusion of Tongues, Gustave Dore

The
Torah

The Five Books of Moses

Genesis
Exodus
Leviticus
Numbers
Deuteronomy

King James Bible
Readers' Version

Bart Marshall

REALFACE PRESS

Published by Realface Press
info@realface.com

ISBN: 978-0-9992583-1-6

Also published by Realface Press:

Christ Sutras*: The Complete Sayings of Jesus
from All Sources Arranged into Sermons*,
compiled and composed by Bart Marshall

The Perennial Way*, Extended Edition*,
translated by Bart Marshall

Bhagavad Gita*: The Definitive Translation*,
translated by Bart Marshall

The Triune Self*: Confessions of a Ruthless Seer*,
by Mike Snider

The Conquest of Illusion, by J.J. van der Leeuw,
90th Anniversary Edition, edited by Bart Marshall

Letters of Transmission*: The Enlightenment Method of
Zen Master Alfred Pulyan*, edited by Bart Marshall

After the Absolute, by David Gold with Bart Marshall

Think and Grow Rich, by Napoleon Hill,
80th Anniversary Edition, edited by Bart Marshall

Magic, White and Black, by Franz Hartmann, M.D.,
edited by Bart Marshall

Ashtavakra Gita, translated by Bart Marshall

Verses Regarding True Nature, poems by Bart Marshall

Pearl of the Orient, a screenplay by Bart Marshall

Introduction

The Torah is Judaism's most important text. It contains the first five books of the Hebrew Bible—the Tanakh—which are also the first five books of the Christian Bible. The Tanakh is essentially the same as what Christians call the Old Testament, with slight differences in the order and structure of the included books.

The Torah begins with the creation of the world and ends with the death of Moses. The first full draft of the Torah is believed to have been completed in the 6th or 7th century B.C., and has been revised numerous times over subsequent centuries. Jewish tradition teaches that the Torah is the revelation of God, given to Moses, and written down by Moses. It is the document that contains all the rules by which the Jewish people structure their spiritual lives.

The word *torah* means "to teach," and it can mean different things in different contexts. In its most common usage, *the* Torah refers to the Five Books of Moses: Genesis, Exodus, Leviticus, Numbers and Deuteronomy. But the word *torah* is also sometimes used to refer to the entire Hebrew Bible—the Tanakh, or Written Torah—and sometimes even the entire body of Jewish law and teachings.

Traditionally, each synagogue has a copy of the Torah written on a scroll that is wound around two wooden poles. This is known as a *Sefer Torah* and it is handwritten by a *sofer* (scribe) who must copy the text perfectly. In modern printed form, as in this volume, the Torah is usually called a *Chumash*, which comes from the Hebrew word for the number five.

This book, *The Torah: The Five Books of Moses*, is excerpted from a larger work in progress, *The Holy Bible: King James Readers' Version*. As you will see, it is formatted like an epic poem—which it is—and feels like you are reading the King James Bible—which you are—but more smoothly, and with more immediate understanding. It also contains details and names missing from the King James Version that turn up in other versions of the Bible. Needless to say, I hope it increases your enjoyment and comprehension of this keystone document, whose influence on Western civilization and culture is without equal. No education is complete without reading it. Twice.

Bart Marshall

A Sefer Torah

Table of Contents

The Creation of Light, Gustave Dore

The First Book of Moses Called
Genesis

Chapter 1

In the beginning, God created heaven and earth.   1:1
The earth was void and without form,   1:2
and the nature of the void was darkness.
And upon the face of the formless deep moved the Spirit of God.

God said, "Let there be light." And there was light.   1:3
And God saw that the light was good.   1:4
So he separated the light from the darkness.
He called the light Day, and the darkness he called Night.   1:5
And the evening, and the morning, were the first day.

God said, "Let there be a firmament, and let it divide   1:6
the emptiness into below and beyond."
And there was a firmament. And it divided the emptiness below   1:7
from the emptiness beyond. And it was so.
God called the firmament Sky, and the emptiness   1:8
beyond the firmament he called Heavens.
And the evening, and the morning, were the second day.

God said, "Let the waters below the firmament gather together,   1:9
and let dry land appear." And it was so.
God called the dry land Earth, and the gathering together of the waters 1:10
he called Seas. And he saw that it was good.
God said, "Let the earth bring forth grains yielding seed,   1:11
and herbs yielding seed, and trees yielding fruit
whose seed is in itself." And it was so.
The earth brought forth grains and herbs yielding seed after their kind, 1:12
and fruit trees whose seed is in itself, after their kind.
And God saw that it was good.
And the evening, and the morning, were the third day.   1:13

God said, "Let there be lights in the heavens to divide day from night, 1:14
and let these lights mark days, and seasons, and years.
And let these lights illuminate the earth." And it was so.   1:15
God made two great lights. The greater light he made to rule the day. 1:16
The lesser light he made to rule the night,
along with the stars, which he also made.
God set these lights in the expanse of the heavens to give light to earth, 1:17
and to rule over the day and over the night, and to divide the light   1:18
from the darkness. And he saw that it was good.
And the evening, and the morning, were the fourth day.   1:19

God said, "Let the waters abound with life,   1:20
and let birds fill the sky above the earth."
So great sea creatures appeared, and the waters abounded with every   1:21
kind of life, and all manner of birds appeared, according to their kind.
And God saw that it was good.
God blessed them, saying, "Be fruitful and reproduce.   1:22
Let the seas teem with life. Let the birds multiply on earth."
And the evening, and the morning, were the fifth day.   1:23

God said, "Let the earth bring forth every kind of living being—   1:24
cattle, and creatures that crawl, and beasts of the earth,
each according to its kind." And it was so.
The wild beasts of the earth came forth after their kind,   1:25
and the cattle and livestock after their kind, and everything
that walks and crawls upon the earth after its kind.
And God saw that it was good.
God said, "Let us make man in our image and after our likeness.   1:26
Let him have dominion over the fish of the sea, and the birds of the air,
and the cattle of the land. Let him rule over all the earth
and everything that moves upon it."
So God created man to be like him. In the mold of Himself,   1:27
he created Man. Male and female, he created Divine.

God blessed them, and said to them, "Be fruitful and multiply.   1:28
Replenish the earth and master its ways. Enjoy dominion
over the fish of the sea and the birds of the air,
and over every living thing that moves upon the earth."
God said, "I give you every plant that yields seed on the face of the earth,   1:29
and every tree with fruit that holds seed. This is your food.
And to all the beasts of the earth, and all the birds of the sky, and all   1:30
the creatures that crawl along the ground—to everything that lives and
breathes in Creation—I give every green plant for food." And it was so.
God looked upon what he had created and was well pleased.   1:31
And the evening, and the morning, were the sixth day.

Chapter 2

Thus was the creation of heaven and earth completed,   2:1
along with the foundation of all things that have life.
On the seventh day, God ended his acts of creation.   2:2
On the seventh day, God rested from all his work.
And God blessed the seventh day, and sanctified the rest   2:3
he took from all the work he had done.
These are the origins of heaven and earth, when they were created,   2:4
in the days the Lord God made them.
No herbs or trees yet grew on the earth, for the Lord God   2:5
had not caused it to rain, and there was not a man to till the ground.

But there came up a great mist from the earth,   2:6
that fell and watered the whole face of the ground.

The Lord God formed man from the dust of the ground,   2:7
and breathed the breath of life into his nostrils,
and man became a living being.
The Lord God planted a garden to the east, in Eden,   2:8
and there he placed the man whom he had formed.
From the earth the Lord God made every tree to grow,   2:9
both those pleasing to look at, and those good for food.
And in the middle of the garden, he placed the
Tree of Knowledge of Good and Evil.

A river sprung out of Eden to water the garden,   2:10
and it divided itself into four rivers.
The name of the first river is Pishon, which surrounds   2:11
the whole land of Havilah—where there is gold.
The gold of that land is good. Bdellium and onyx stone are there.   2:12
The name of the second river is Gihon,   2:13
which winds through the whole of Ethiopia.
The name of the third river is Tigris, which flows east of Assyria.   2:14
The fourth river is Euphrates.
The Lord God gave the paradise of Eden to the man   2:15
he had made, to tend it and watch over it.
And God warned the man, saying,   2:16
"Eat freely from every other tree in the garden,
but do not eat from the Tree of Knowledge of Good and Evil.   2:17
For if you eat its fruit, you shall surely sow the seeds of death."

Then the Lord God said, "It is not good that this man called Adam   2:18
should be alone. I will make companions to help him."
So from the dust of the ground the Lord God formed every beast   2:19
of the field and every bird of the air, and he brought them to Adam
to see what Adam would call them. And whatever Adam called
each living creature, that was its name.
Adam gave names to all the livestock, and the birds of the air,   2:20
and every beast. But for Adam, there was no companion to help him.
So the Lord God caused Adam to fall into a deep sleep. And as he slept   2:21
he took one of his ribs, then closed and healed the flesh.
From the rib God took from Adam, he made a woman,   2:22
and God brought the woman to Adam.
And Adam said, "She is bone of my bones, and flesh of my flesh,   2:23
and she shall be called Woman because she comes from Man."
Therefore, a man shall leave his father and his mother,   2:24
and cleave unto his wife, and they shall become one flesh.
Adam and his wife were naked, and they were not ashamed.   2:25

Chapter 3

Now the serpent, who was more cunning than other beasts of the field   3:1
the Lord God had made, said to the woman, "Has God indeed said,
'You shall not eat of every tree of the garden'?"

The woman said to the serpent, "We may eat the fruit   3:2
of every other tree of the garden,
but of the fruit of the tree in the middle of the garden,   3:3
God has said, "Do not eat it nor touch it, lest you die."
And the serpent said to the woman, "You will not die.   3:4
God knows that in the day you eat that fruit your eyes will be opened,   3:5
and you shall be as gods, knowing good and evil."

So when the woman saw that the tree was good for food,   3:6
and that it was pleasing to look at, and thinking it was
a tree to make one wise, she took of the fruit and ate it.
She also gave the fruit to her husband, and he ate it.
And their eyes were opened. They knew that they were naked,   3:7
and they sewed fig leaves together to make themselves aprons.

Then they heard the voice of the Lord God, walking in the garden   3:8
in the cool of the day, and they hid themselves from
the presence of the Lord among the trees of the garden.
God called out to Adam, saying, "Where are you?"   3:9
Adam said, "I heard your voice in the garden,   3:10
and I was afraid because I was naked, so I hid myself."
God said, "Who told you that you were naked?   3:11
Have you eaten the fruit of the tree I told you not to eat?"
Adam said, "The woman you created to be with me   3:12
gave me the fruit of that tree, and I did eat it."
God said to the woman, "What have you done?"   3:13
The woman said, "The serpent beguiled me, and I did eat the fruit."

God said to the serpent, "Because you have done this,   3:14
you are cursed above all cattle, and above every beast
of the field. Upon your belly you shall crawl,
and for all the days of your life you shall eat dust."
To Adam God said, "I will put enmity between you and the woman,   3:15
and between the children of your seed and her seed.
To the woman God said, "Woman, he shall crack your head,
and you shall pierce his heel.
I will greatly multiply your pain giving birth.   3:16
In anguish you shall bring forth children, yet still
you will desire your husband, and he shall rule over you."

God said to Adam, "Because you have listened to the voice of your wife   3:17
and eaten of the tree I warned against, saying, 'You shall not eat of it,'
cursed is the ground for your sake.
You shall labor hard for your food all the days of your life.
The ground shall give you thorns and thistles,   3:18
and you shall eat the wild herbs of the fields.
Only by the sweat of your brow shall you eat bread,   3:19
until the day you return to the ground from which you were formed.
For from dust you came, and unto dust you shall return."

Adam called his wife Eve, for she was the mother of all who would live.   3:20
The Lord God made coats of skins for Adam and Eve, and clothed them.   3:21
God said, "Behold, the man has become as one of us,   3:22
knowing good and evil. Now, lest he reach out
and also eat of the Tree of Life, and live forever,
I shall send him forth from the garden of Eden,   3:23
to till the ground from whence he was taken."
So he drove Man out. And to the east of Eden he placed cherubim,   3:24
and a flaming sword that turned in all directions,
guarding the way to the Tree of Life.

Chapter 4

Adam lay with Eve his wife. She conceived and gave birth to Cain.   4:1
Adam said, "I have begotten a man from God."
Eve bore another child, Abel, the brother of Cain.   4:2
Abel was a keeper of sheep. Cain was a tiller of soil.
And after a time Cain brought some of his harvest   4:3
as an offering unto the Lord.
Abel also brought an offering of the firstborn lambs of his flock,   4:4
and the Lord was pleased with Abel and his offering.
But the Lord had little regard for Cain and his offering.   4:5
Cain became angry, and his countenance fell.
The Lord said to Cain, "Why are you angry? Why has your face fallen?   4:6
If you do what is right you will be accepted. If you do not do what is right,   4:7
sin lies in wait for you. It desires to overtake you. You must rule over it."

Then one day Cain said to Abel, "Let us go into the fields." And when they   4:8
were in the fields, Cain rose up against his brother and killed him.
The Lord said to Cain, "Where is your brother Abel?"   4:9
Cain said, "I do not know. Am I my brother's keeper?"
God said, "What have you done? The voice of your brother   4:10
cries out to me from the ground!
Henceforth you are cursed by the ground that opened its mouth   4:11
to receive your brother's blood from your hands.
When you till the soil, it will no longer yield crops for you.   4:12
You shall be a fugitive wandering upon the earth."
Cain said to the Lord, "My punishment is too great to bear!   4:13
You have driven me from the land and banished me from your presence.   4:14
I shall be a vagabond and a fugitive on the earth,
and whoever finds me will kill me."
The Lord said, "Whosoever slays Cain, vengeance shall be taken upon him   4:15
sevenfold." And the Lord set a mark upon Cain, warning all not to kill him.

So Cain was sent out from the presence of the Lord,   4:16
and went to dwell in the land of Nod, which is east of Eden.
Cain lay with his wife, and she conceived. She bore him a child who they   4:17
named Enoch. Cain built a city and he named it Enoch, after his son.
Unto Enoch was born Irad, and Irad begat Mehujael, and Mehujael   4:18

begat Methusael, and Methusael begat Lamech.

Lamech took for himself two wives.   4:19

One was named Adah, and the other was named Zillah.

Adah bore Jabal, who was the first ancestor of those who live in tents   4:20
and are nomadic herdsmen of cattle.

His brother's name was Jubal, who was the father   4:21
of all who play the harp and organ.

Zillah bore Tubalcain, the instructor of every artisan of brass and iron.   4:22
The sister of Tubalcain was Naamah.

And Lamech said to his wives, Adah and Zillah, "Hear my voice,   4:23
wives of Lamech, and listen to what I say. I have slain a man
for wounding me, and a young man for striking me.

If Cain should be avenged sevenfold, then surely   4:23
Lamech shall be avenged seventy and sevenfold."

Adam lay again with Eve. She bore him a son, and she named him Seth.   4:25
"For God, has given me another son in place of Abel, whom Cain slew."

To Seth was also born a son, who was named Enos.   4:26
Then men began to worship and pray in the name of the Lord.

Chapter 5

This is the book of the generations of Adam.   5:1
In the day God created man, he made man to be like God.

Male and female he created, and he blessed them,   5:2
and he called them "Mankind."

Adam lived a hundred and thirty years, then begat a son   5:3
in his own likeness, after his image, and named him Seth.

Adam lived eight hundred years after he begat Seth,   5:4
and begat more sons and daughters.

All the days of Adam were nine hundred and thirty years. Then he died.   5:5

Seth lived a hundred and five years, then begat Enos.   5:6
Seth lived eight hundred and seven years after he begat Enos,   5:7
and begat more sons and daughters.

All the days of Seth were nine hundred and twelve years. Then he died.   5:8
Enos lived ninety years, then begat Cainan.   5:9
Enos lived eight hundred and fifteen years after he begat Cainan,   5:10
and begat more sons and daughters.

All the days of Enos were nine hundred and five years. Then he died.   5:11
Cainan lived seventy years, then begat Mahalaleel.   5:12
Cainan lived eight hundred and forty years after he begat Mahalaleel,   5:13
and begat more sons and daughters.

All the days of Cainan were nine hundred and ten years. Then he died.   5:14
Mahalaleel lived sixty-five years, then begat Jared.   5:15
Mahalaleel lived eight hundred and thirty years after he begat Jared,   5:16
and begat more sons and daughters.

All the days of Mahalaleel were eight hundred ninety-five years.   5:17
Then he died.

Jared lived a hundred sixty-two years, then begat Enoch.   5:18

Jared lived eight hundred years after he begat Enoch,   5:19
and begat more sons and daughters.
All the days of Jared were nine hundred sixty-two years. Then he died.   5:20
Enoch lived sixty-five years, then begat Methuselah.   5:21
Enoch walked with God for three hundred years   5:22
after he begat Methuselah, and begat more sons and daughters.
All the days of Enoch were three hundred sixty-five years.   5:23
Enoch walked with God until one day he disappeared,   5:24
for God had gathered him unto himself.

Methuselah lived a hundred eighty-seven years, then begat Lamech.   5:25
Methuselah lived seven hundred eighty-two years after he begat Lamech,   5:26
and begat more sons and daughters.
All the days of Methuselah were nine hundred sixty-nine years.   5:27
Then he died.
Lamech lived a hundred eighty-two years, then begat a son.   5:28
He named his son Noah, saying, "This one shall bring us   5:29
comfort and relief from the toil and hard work of our hands,
which we endure because the Lord has cursed the ground."
Lamech lived five hundred ninety-five years after he begat Noah,   5:30
and begat more sons and daughters.
All the days of Lamech were seven hundred seventy-seven years.   5:31
Then he died.
Noah lived five hundred years, then begat Shem, Ham and Japheth.   5:32

Chapter 6

And it came to pass as men began to multiply on earth,   6:1
and daughters were born to them,
that the demigods saw that the daughters of men were fair,   6:2
and they took them as wives, as many as they chose.
The Lord said, "My blessing shall not stay with man forever,   6:3
for he is ruled by his flesh. His days shall be numbered
at one hundred and twenty years."
The Nephilim giants were on the earth in those days, and for a time after.   6:4
These demigods lay with the daughters of men,
and the women bore them children.
The Nephilim were mighty warriors of old, famous heroes of their time.

God saw that the wickedness of man was great, and that every   6:5
imagination and thought of his heart was only of evil.
God repented that he had made man, and it grieved him in his heart.   6:6
And the Lord said, "I will destroy mankind, which I have created,   6:7
and wipe all life from the face of the earth—
men and beasts, and things that creep, and the birds of the air—
for I regret that I have made them."
Only Noah found favor in the eyes of the Lord.   6:8

This is the story of Noah. Noah was a just man, the most perfect   6:9
of his generation, for Noah walked with God.

Noah begat three sons, Shem, Ham and Japheth. 6:10
The earth was evil in the eyes of God, and filled with violence. 6:11
God looked upon the earth and saw that it was corrupted, 6:12
for the way of all flesh is corruption.
And God said to Noah, "The end of all flesh has come. 6:13
The earth is corrupted with the violence of men,
and behold, I will use the earth to destroy them.

"Make an ark of gopher wood. Make many rooms in the ark, 6:14
and seal it with pitch within and without.
Make it like this: The length of the ark shall be three hundred cubits, 6:15
its width fifty cubits, and its height thirty cubits.
Make a large window for the ark, a cubit below the roof. 6:16
Place the door on the side of the ark.
Make the ark with lower, second, and third decks.
For I shall bring a flood of waters upon the earth to destroy 6:17
all mankind and all that breathes with life under the heavens.
Everything on the earth shall die.
But with you, I give my covenant: You shall come into the ark 6:18
with your sons, and your wife, and yours sons' wives with you.
And of every living thing you shall bring two of their kind, 6:19
one male and one female, to keep their kind alive with you.
Of birds after their kind, and of cattle after their kind, 6:20
and of every crawling thing of the earth after its kind—
two of every sort shall come with you, to keep them alive.
Take with you all food you need for your family and for them." 6:21
And Noah did this. He did everything that God commanded. 6:22

Chapter 7

The Lord said to Noah, "Come into the ark, you and all your household. 7:1
For you alone have appeared righteous before me in this generation.
Of every clean beast take seven males and seven females, 7:2
and of beasts that are not clean take two, a male and a female.
Of birds of the air, also by sevens, males and females, 7:3
to keep their seed alive upon the face of the earth.
For in seven days, I will cause it to rain upon the earth 7:4
for forty days and forty nights. And every living thing that I have made,
I will wash from the face of the earth."
Noah did all that the Lord commanded him. 7:5
Noah was six hundred years old when the flood waters were on the earth. 7:6
Noah went into the ark, and his sons, and his wife, and his sons' wives 7:7
went into the ark, because of the waters of the flood.
Clean beasts and unclean beasts, and birds, 7:8
and everything that creeps upon the earth,
went two by two, male and the female, 7:9
into the ark of Noah, made as God had commanded it.
And in seven days, the waters of the flood were upon the earth. 7:10
In the six hundredth year of Noah's life, in the second month, 7:11

on the seventeenth day, the fountains of the deep broke forth
and the windows of heaven opened wide.
And rain was upon the earth for forty days and forty nights. 7:12

On that day Noah, and the sons of Noah— Shem, Ham and Japheth— 7:13
and Noah's wife, and the three wives of his sons went into the ark.
And every beast after his kind, and all the cattle after their kind, 7:14
and everything that creeps upon the earth after its kind,
and every bird after its kind, went into the ark of Noah,
two by two of all flesh, whatever had the breath of life. 7:15
They went in, male and female of all flesh, as God had commanded. 7:16
And the Lord shut them in.
The flood was upon the earth for forty days. 7:17
The waters rose, and lifted the ark up above the ground.
The waters prevailed, and were greatly increased upon the earth, 7:18
and the ark went forth upon the face of the waters.
The waters prevailed exceedingly upon the earth, 7:19
and all the high hills under heaven were swallowed up.
The waters rose up fifteen cubits, covering the mountains. 7:20
All life that had moved upon the earth died—birds and cattle and beasts 7:21
and everything that creeps upon the earth. And every man.
All in whose nostrils was the breath of life on dry land, died. 7:22
Every living thing upon the face of the earth was destroyed— 7:23
men, and cattle, and creeping things, and the birds of the sky—
all removed from the earth. Only Noah,
and those with him in the ark, remained alive.
The waters prevailed on the earth for a hundred and fifty days. 7:24

Chapter 8

God reflected on Noah, and on every living thing—all the animals 8:1
that were with him in the ark. And God made a great wind
blow across all the earth. And the waters began to recede.
The fountains of the deep ceased flowing, the skies closed up, 8:2
and all the rains of heaven stopped.
The waters vaporized from off the earth continuously, 8:3
and after one hundred and fifty days, the waters had abated.
And in the seventh month, on the seventeenth day of the month, 8:4
the ark came to rest on the mountains of Ararat.
The waters decreased continually until the tenth month. 8:5
Then in the tenth month, on the first day of the month,
the tops of mountains were seen.

At the end of forty days Noah opened the window of the ark 8:6
and sent forth a raven, which flew everywhere back and forth 8:7
until the waters were dried up from the earth.
Noah also sent forth a dove, to see if the waters had receded. 8:8
But the dove found no place for the soles of her feet, and she 8:9
returned to the ark. For the waters still covered the face of the earth.

Noah reached out his hand, and brought her back into the ark.
Noah waited seven days, then sent her forth again.   8:10
That evening the dove came back to him and, lo,   8:11
in her beak was an olive leaf she had plucked!
So Noah knew that the waters were abated from the earth.
Noah waited yet another seven days, then again sent forth   8:12
the dove from the ark. And she did not anymore return to him.

In the six hundred and first year, in the first month, on the   8:13
first day of the month, the waters were receded from the earth.
Noah removed the covering of the ark and looked.
And, behold, the face of the ground had appeared!
In the second month, on the twenty-seventh day of the month,   8:14
the earth was dry. God said to Noah,   8:15
"Go forth from the ark with your wife and sons, and your sons' wives.   8:16
Bring forth every living thing that is with you—   8:17
birds and cattle and everything that creeps upon the ground—
that they may be fruitful and multiply upon the whole earth."
So Noah went forth with his sons and his wife, and his sons' wives.   8:18
And every beast, every thing that creeps, every fowl,   8:19
and all the living creatures of earth went forth out of the ark.

Then Noah built an altar to the Lord. And he took some hair   8:20
of every clean beast, and some feathers of every clean fowl,
and he burnt them as offerings on the altar.
The aroma of the burnt offerings was pleasing to the Lord, and he said   8:21
in his heart, "I will never again curse the earth because of what men do.
Though the hearts of men are inclined to evil since their youth, I shall
never again destroy every living creature on earth as I have done.
So long as earth exists, seedtime and harvest, heat and cold,   8:22
summer and winter, and day and night, shall never cease."

Chapter 9

God blessed Noah and his sons, and said to them,   9:1
"Be fruitful and multiply, and replenish the earth.
The fear and dread of you shall be within every beast of the earth,   9:2
within every bird of the air, within all that moves upon the earth,
and within all the fish in the sea. Into your care are they delivered.
Everything that lives and moves shall be meat for you.   9:3
As I gave you the green herbs, I now give you all things for food.
But do not eat raw flesh with the blood of life still in it. That do not eat.   9:4

"For the blood of your lives, I will require blood.   9:5
For every beast that kills man, I will require it.
For every man who kills man, I will require it.
For every man's brother who kills man, I will require the life of that man.
Whosoever sheds a man's blood, by a man his blood shall be shed.   9:6
For God made man in the image of God.
So be fruitful and multiply. Bring forth abundance on the earth."   9:7

God spoke to Noah and his sons, saying, — 9:8
"Behold, I establish my covenant with you, and with your children — 9:9
after you, and with every living creature with you,
the birds, the cattle, and every beast of the earth— — 9:10
with every living thing that comes out of the ark—
I establish my covenant: Never again shall all life be destroyed — 9:11
by the waters of a flood. Never again shall a flood destroy the earth."
Then God said, "Here is the token of the covenant I make between — 9:12
me and you and every living creature for all perpetual generations:
I set my rainbow in the sky, and it shall be a token — 9:13
of this covenant between me and the earth.
When I bring rain over the earth, my rainbow shall be seen in the clouds, — 9:14
and I will remember my covenant between me and you and every living — 9:15
creature, and the waters shall no more become a flood to destroy all life.
And I will reflect upon my token, and remember the eternal covenant — 9:16
I made with every living creature on the earth.
This then shall be my token of the covenant — 9:17
I have established between me and all life on earth."

The sons of Noah who went forth from the ark were Shem, — 9:18
Ham and Japheth. Ham was the father of Canaan.
These were the sons of Noah. From them the whole earth was populated. — 9:19
Noah became a farmer, and he planted a vineyard. — 9:20
He drank the wine, and was sometimes drunk, — 9:21
and one day he lay uncovered in his tent.
Ham saw the nakedness of his father and told his two brothers. — 9:22
Shem and Japheth laid a garment on both their shoulders, walked — 9:23
backwards into the tent, and covered the nakedness of their father.
Since their faces were turned, they did not see their father's nakedness.
When Noah awoke, he found out that Ham had seen his nakedness. — 9:24
He said, "Cursed be Canaan.
He shall be a servant to his brothers' servants. — 9:25
Praise the Lord, God of Shem. Canaan shall be his servant. — 9:26
God shall raise up Japheth, and he shall dwell in the tents of Shem, — 9:27
and Canaan shall be servant to both."
Noah lived three hundred and fifty years after the flood. — 9:28
All the days of Noah were nine hundred and fifty years. Then he died. — 9:29

Chapter 10

These are the generations of Shem, Ham and Japheth— — 10:1
the sons of Noah. Unto them were born sons after the flood.
The sons of Japheth were Gomer, Magog, Madai, — 10:2
Javan, Tubal, Meshech and Tiras.
The sons of Gomer were Ashkenaz, Riphath and Togarmah. — 10:3
The sons of Javan were Elishah, Tarshish, Kittim and Dodanim. — 10:4
From these descended the people of the coastlands and islands, — 10:5
who divided into separate tribes and separate nations.

The sons of Ham were Cush, Mizraim, Phut and Canaan. 10:6

The sons of Cush were Seba, Havilah, Sabtah, Raamah and Sabtecha. 10:7
The sons of Raamah were Sheba and Dedan.

Cush begat Nimrod, who became a mighty warrior. 10:8

He was a great hunter in the eyes of the Lord. Therefore it is said, 10:9
"Like Nimrod, the great hunter in the sight of the Lord."

The kingdom of Nimrod began in the land of Shinar, 10:10
with the cities of Babel, Erech, Accad and Calneh.

He went forth from that land and came to Assyria, 10:11
and he built the cities of Nineveh, Rehoboth, Calah,

and Resen—the great city between Nineveh and Calah. 10:12

Mizraim begat Ludim, Anamim, Lehabim, Naphtuhim, 10:13

Pathrusim, Caphtorim and Casluhim—who begat Philistim. 10:14

Canaan begat Sidon, his firstborn, and Heth, 10:15

and the Jebusite, and the Amorite, and the Girgasite, 10:16

and the Hivite, and the Arkite, and the Sinite, 10:17

and the Arvadite, and the Zemarite and the Hamathite. 10:18
Later, the families of the Canaanites spread far and wide.

The boundaries of the land of the Canaanites extended from Sidon, 10:19
towards Gerar, into Gaza by way of Sodom and Gomorrah,
and into Admah and Zeboim, and even into Lasha.

These were the sons of Ham, after their families, 10:20
after their tribes, and after their nations.

Also unto Shem—the father of the children of Eber, 10:21
the elder brother of Japheth—were children born.

The children of Shem were Elam, Asshur, Arphaxad, Lud and Aram. 10:22

The children of Aram were Uz, Hul, Gether and Mash. 10:23

Arphaxad begat Salah, and Salah begat Eber. 10:24

Unto Eber were born two sons. One was named Peleg, 10:25
for in his days the earth was divided. His brother's name was Joktan.

Joktan begat Almodad, Sheleph, Hazarmaveth, Jerah, 10:26

Hadoram, Uzal, Diklah, 10:27

Obal, Abimael, Sheba, 10:28

Ophir, Havilah and Jobab. All these were the sons of Joktan. 10:29

Their territory extended from Mesha, in the direction of Sephar, 10:30
to the hills in the east.

These were the sons of Shem, after their families, 10:31
after their tribes, and after their nations.

These were the families of the sons of Noah. By these families, 10:32
the nations of earth were formed after the flood.

Chapter 11

At that time the whole earth was of one language. 11:1

As people journeyed from the east, they found a plain 11:2
in the land of Shinar, and they settled there.

They said one to another, "Let us make bricks and burn them until 11:3

they are hard." And so they used bricks for stone, and mud for mortar.
They said, "Let us build us a city, and a tower whose peak   11:4
will reach to heaven. And let us take a name for ourselves,
lest we be scattered abroad upon the face of the earth."

The Lord came to see the city and the tower   11:5
that the children of men had built.
And the Lord said, "The people are united, and they all speak   11:6
one language. This is only the start of what they will do.
Nothing will keep from them from doing what they imagine.
Let us confound their language so that they   11:7
cannot understand one another's speech."
So the Lord confounded them, and they stopped building.   11:8
And they were scattered abroad upon the face of the earth.
Therefore the name of that place is Babel, because there   11:9
the Lord confounded the language of men, and from there
he scattered men across the face of all the earth.

These are the generations of Shem: Shem lived a hundred years,   11:10
then begat Arphaxad two years after the flood.
Shem lived five hundred years after he begat Arphaxad,   11:11
and begat more sons and daughters.
Arphaxad lived thirty-five years, then begat Salah.   11:12
Arphaxad lived four hundred and three years after he begat Salah,   11:13
and begat more sons and daughters.
Salah lived thirty years, then begat Eber.   11:14
Salah lived four hundred and three years after he begat Eber,   11:15
and begat more sons and daughters.
Eber lived thirty-four years, then begat Peleg.   11:16
Eber lived four hundred and thirty years after he begat Peleg,   11:17
and begat more sons and daughters.

Peleg lived thirty years, then begat Reu.   11:18
Peleg lived two hundred and nine years after he begat Reu,   11:19
and begat more sons and daughters.
Reu lived thirty-two years, then begat Serug.   11:20
Reu lived two hundred and seven years after he begat Serug,   11:21
and begat more sons and daughters.
Serug lived thirty years, then begat Nahor.   11:22
Serug lived two hundred years after he begat Nahor,   11:23
and begat more sons and daughters.
Nahor lived twenty-nine years, then begat Terah.   11:24
Nahor lived a hundred and nineteen years after he begat Terah,   11:25
and begat more sons and daughters.
Terah lived seventy years, then begat Abram, Nahor and Haran.   11:26

These are the generations of Terah: 11:27
Terah begat Abram, Nahor and Haran. Haran begat Lot.
Haran died before his father Terah in the land of his nativity,   11:28
in Ur of the Chaldees.

Abram and Nahor took wives. Abram's wife was named Sarai.   11:29
Nahor's wife was Milcah, the daughter of Haran,
who was the father of Milcah and Iscah.
Sarai was barren. She had no children.   11:30
Terah took his son Abram, and Lot, the son of his son Haran, and Sarai,   11:31
his daughter-in-law and wife of his son Abram, and they went forth
from Ur of the Chaldees to go to the land of Canaan, where they came
upon a plain they called Haran, and they settled there.
Terah lived for two hundred and five years, then he died in Haran.   11:32

Chapter 12

The Lord said to Abram, "Leave your country, leave your family,   12:1
leave your father's house. Go to a land that I will show you.
I will make of you a great nation, and I will bless you   12:2
and make your name great, so that you shall become a blessing.
I will bless those who bless you and curse those who curse you.   12:3
In you, all families of the earth shall be blessed."
So Abram departed, as the Lord had commanded, and Lot went with him.   12:4
Abram was seventy-five years old when he left Haran.
Abram took his wife Sarai, and Lot, his brother's son. They gathered   12:5
all their possessions, and their servants, and all the members of their
household that had come to them in Haran, and they went forth to Canaan.
And into the land of Canaan they came.
Then Abram passed through the land of Canaan to Sichem,   12:6
on the plain of Moreh. The Canaanites were then also in that land.
And the Lord appeared to Abram, and said, "I give this land   12:7
to your generations." So Abram built an alter there to the Lord,
at the place where the Lord had appeared to him.

Then Abram moved on, to the mountains east of Bethel,   12:8
and there pitched his tent, with Bethel to the west and Hai
to the east. There he built an altar to the Lord, and he prayed.
Then Abram journeyed on, going toward the south.   12:9
But there was a famine in the land, so Abram went into Egypt   12:10
as a sojourner, the famine in the land was so great.
When he came near to entering Egypt he said to his wife Sarai,   12:11
"You are a fair woman to look upon.
When the Egyptians see you they will say, 'This is his wife,'   12:12
and they will kill me, but they will keep you alive.
Therefore, I pray you, say you are my sister so that they will   12:13
treat me well for your sake, and I shall survive because of you."
When Abram came into Egypt, the Egyptians did look upon his wife   12:14
and behold that she was fair.
When the Pharaoh's officers saw her, they commended   12:15
her to Pharaoh, and Sarai was taken into Pharaoh's house.
And Abram was treated well for her sake. He had sheep,   12:16
and oxen, and asses, and camels, and servants and handmaids.

But the Lord cursed Pharaoh and his house with great plagues   12:17
because of Sarai, Abram's wife.
Pharaoh said to Abram, "What have you done to me?   12:18
Why did you not tell me she was your wife?
Why did you say, 'She is my sister,' so that I might take her as a wife?   12:19
Behold, your wife! Take her and go your way!"
So Pharaoh commanded his men concerning Abram,   12:20
and they sent him away, with his wife and all that he had.

Chapter 13

So Abram went out of Egypt with Sarai his wife, and Lot,   13:1
and all that he had, and headed toward the south.
Abram was very rich in cattle, silver and gold.   13:2
On his journey south he came to Bethel, to the place   13:3
he pitched his tent at the beginning, between Bethel and Hai,
to the place of the altar he made.   13:4
There Abram called on the name of the Lord.
Lot also had many herds and flocks and tents,   13:5
and the land was not able to support them all, so they might live together.   13:6
Their substance was so great they could not dwell on the same land.
And there was strife between the herdsmen   13:7
of Abram's cattle and the herdsmen of Lot's cattle.
And the Canaanites and the Perizzites dwelled then in the land.
So Abram said to Lot, "I pray you, let there be no strife between me and   13:8
you, and between my herdsmen and your herdsmen, for we are brethren.
Is not the whole land before you? Separate yourself from me.   13:9
If you depart to the left, I will go to the right.
If you depart to the right, I will go to the left."

Lot lifted up his eyes and beheld the plain of Jordan. This was before   13:10
the Lord destroyed Sodom and Gomorrah. The plain was well-watered
everywhere, like the Lord's garden, like Egypt as you travel to Zoar.
So Lot chose the plain of Jordan. He journeyed east   13:11
and they separated themselves, one from the other.
Abram dwelled in the land of Canaan. Lot dwelled in the cities   13:12
of the plain and pitched his tent toward Sodom.
Now, the men of Sodom were evil, and sinned greatly before the Lord.   13:13

After he was separated from Lot, the Lord said to Abram,   13:14
"Lift up your eyes, and look from where you are—
to the north, and to the south, and to the east, and to the west.
All the land you see I give to you, and to your children,   13:15
and to their generations forever.
I will make your seed as plentiful as the dust of the earth.   13:16
If the grains of dust of the earth can be numbered,
then your descendants can also be numbered.
Arise. Walk the length and breadth of the land. I give it to you."   13:17

So Abram struck his tent and went to dwell on the plain of Mamre,   13:18
in Hebron, and there built an altar to the Lord.

Chapter 14

In the days of Amraphel king of Shinar, Arioch king of Ellasar,   14:1
Chedorlaomer king of Elam, and Tidal king of nations,
these kings made war with Bera king of Sodom, Birsha king of Gomorrah,   14:2
Shinab king of Admah, Shemeber king of Zeboiim, and Zoar king of Bela.
These latter kings joined forces in the valley of Siddim, the Dead Sea.   14:3
For twelve years they served Chedorlaomer,   14:4
but in the thirteenth year they rebelled.
In the fourteenth year Chedorlaomer and the kings who were with him,   14:5
attacked the Rephaims in Ashteroth Karnaim,
and the Zuzims in Ham, and the Emims in Shaveh Kiriathaim,
and the Horites in Mount Seir, and drove them all   14:6
into Elparan, which is at the edge of wilderness.
As they returned, they came to Enmishpat, which is Kadesh,   14:7
and defeated the whole country of the Amalekites,
and also of the Amorites, who dwelt in Hazezontamar.

Then the king of Sodom, and the king of Gomorrah, and the king of Admah,   14:8
and the king of Zeboiim, and the king of Bela, which is Zoar,
joined battle in the valley of Siddim
with Chedorlaomer king of Elam, and Tidal king of nations, and Amraphel   14:9
king of Shinar, and Arioch king of Ellasar. Four kings against five.
Now, the valley of Siddim was full of tar pits. And the armies of the kings   14:10
of Sodom and Gomorrah fell into them as they fled the battle.
Those who survived, fled to the mountains.
The victors took all the goods of Sodom and Gomorrah,   14:11
and all the provisions, and went their way.
They also took Lot, Abram's brother's son, who lived in Sodom,   14:12
and they took all of his goods.

One who escaped the battle came and told Abram the Hebrew,   14:13
who was living in the plain of Mamre the Amorite,
brother of Eshcol and Aner, who were friends of Abram.
When Abram heard that his brother's son was taken captive,   14:14
he armed his trained servants who were born in his house,
three hundred and eighteen strong, and led them into Dan.
One night he divided his forces and attacked them, and defeated them,   14:15
and pursued them unto Hobah, which is north of Damascus.
He brought back all the goods. He brought back Lot   14:16
and all his goods, and the women also, and the people.
The king of Sodom went out to meet him as he returned   14:17
from the slaughter of Chedorlaomer and the kings who were
with him in the valley of Shaveh, which is the king's dale.
Melchizedek, king of Salem, priest of the most high God,   14:18
brought forth bread and wine.

And he blessed him, saying, "Blessed be Abram of the most high God,	14:19
possessor of heaven and earth.
And blessed be God, who delivered your enemies into your hand."	14:20
Abram gave to the priest king one-tenth of the goods he had recovered.
The king of Sodom said to Abram, "Only return my people.	14:21
Keep my goods for yourself."
But Abram said to the king of Sodom, "I have lifted my hand to the Lord,	14:22
the most high God, the creator of heaven and earth,
that I will not take so much as a thread or a sandal lace that is yours,	14:23
so that you cannot say, 'I have made Abram rich.'
I want nothing but that which the young men have eaten,	14:24
and the share of the spoils to the men who went with me:
Aner, Eshcol and Mamre. Let them keep their portions."

Chapter 15

After these things had come to pass, the word of the Lord	15:1
came unto Abram in a vision, saying, "Fear not, Abram.
I am your shield, and great will be your reward."
Abram said, "Lord God, what can you give me? I am childless	15:2
and the heir of my house is this Eliezer of Damascus.
You have given me no seed. A servant born in my house shall be my heir!"	15:3
The Lord said to him, "He shall not be your heir.	15:4
A son of your own body shall come forth and be your heir."
Then the Lord took Abram outside and said,	15:5
"Look now to the heavens and number the stars if you are able.
This shall be the number of your decedents."
Abram had faith in the Lord and believed him.	15:6
And the Lord regarded Abram's righteousness.
The Lord said, "I am the Lord that brought you out	15:7
of Ur of the Chaldees to give you this land to inherit."
Abram said, "Lord, how can I know that I shall inherit it?"	15:8
The Lord said, "Bring me a heifer three years old, and a she-goat three	15:9
years old, and a ram three years old, and a turtledove and a pigeon."
Abram took him all these. He split each of the livestock in half	15:10
and laid one half by the other. The birds he did not cut in half.
The buzzards came down to feed, but Abram drove them away .	15:11
When the sun was going down, a deep sleep came upon Abram.	15:12
And a terrible darkness fell upon him.
The Lord said to Abram, "Know without doubt that your descendants	15:13
shall be strangers in a land that is not theirs, and they shall
be oppressed as slaves for four hundred years.
But I will judge that nation whom they shall serve,	15:14
and afterward your descendants shall come out with great wealth.
You shall go to your fathers in peace, and you shall live to a good old age.	15:15
And in the fourth generation they shall come again,	15:16
for the iniquity of the Amorites is not yet full measure."

When the sun had set and it was dark, a smoking vessel 15:17
and a flaming torch passed between the halves of the animals.
On the same day, the Lord made a covenant with Abram, saying, 15:18
"To your decedents I give all this land,
from the river of Egypt, to the great river Euphrates:
The land of the Kenites, and the Kenizzites, and the Kadmonites, 15:19
and the Hittites, and the Perizzites, and the Rephaims, and the Amorites, 15:20
and the Canaanites, and the Girgashites, and the Jebusites." 15:21

Chapter 16

Sarai, Abram's wife, could give him no children. 16:1
But she had a handmaid, an Egyptian, whose name was Hagar.
Sarai said to Abram, "The Lord has kept me from bearing. 16:2
I pray thee, go and lie with my maid. It may be that I obtain
children by her." And Abram heeded the voice of Sarai.
So Sarai took Hagar, her maid the Egyptian—after Abram had dwelt 16:3
ten years in the land of Canaan—and gave her to Abram as a wife.
Abram lay with Hagar, and she conceived. And when she saw 16:4
that she had conceived, she began to despise her mistress.
Sarai said to Abram, "This is your fault. I gave my maid 16:5
into your embrace, but when she conceived she began to despise me.
May the Lord judge between you and me!"
Abram said to Sarai, "Look, she is your servant. Do with her as you please." 16:6
And Sarai dealt so harshly with Hagar that Hagar fled from her.

An agent of the Lord found Hagar by a spring in the desert, 16:7
by the spring on the way to Shur.
He said, "Hagar, where have you come from and where are you going?" 16:8
Hagar said, "I flee from my mistress Sarai."
The agent said to her, "Return to your mistress and submit to her. 16:9
I will give you many children, so many they cannot be counted. 16:10
You are now with child, and you shall bear a son, and you shall 16:11
call him Ishmael, for the Lord has seen your sorrow.
He will be a wild mule of a man. He will fight with everyone, and everyone 16:12
will fight with him. And he shall dwell apart from all his brethren."
Hagar named the agent that came to her, The One Who Sees Me. 16:13
And she said to herself, "I have seen the one who sees me."
This spring is now called, Well of the One Who Sees Me. 16:14
It is found between Kadesh and Bered.
Hagar bore Abram a son, and Abram called him Ishmael. 16:15
Abram was eighty-six years old when Hagar bore Ishmael. 16:16

Chapter 17

When Abram was ninety-nine years old the Lord appeared to him 17:1
and said, "I am Almighty God. Walk with me and be perfect.
I will make my covenant between me and you, 17:2
and I will give you many descendants."

Abram fell on his face. God talked with him, saying, 17:3
"This is my covenant with you: You shall be the father of many nations. 17:4
You shall no more be called Abram, for I have made you 17:5
the father of nations. Henceforth, your name shall be Abraham.
I will make you exceeding fruitful. I will make nations after you, 17:6
and kings shall come from you.
I make my covenant between me and you, and with your descendants 17:7
after you, as an everlasting covenant: I will be your God,
and I will be the God of your descendants after you in their generations.
And I will give to you, and to your generations after you, 17:8
this land in which you are now a stranger—all the land of Canaan—
as an everlasting possession. And I will be their God."

God said, "As for you, you shall make a covenant with me 17:9
and keep it, and so shall your descendants keep it.
This is the covenant you shall make and keep, between me and you 17:10
and all your seed after you: Every male among you shall be circumcised.
You shall circumcise the flesh of your foreskin, 17:11
and it shall be a token of the covenant between us.
Every male child born to you and your descendants shall be circumcised 17:12
when he is eight days old, and also every male child born to the servants
of your houses, or born to slaves you bought from another country.
He who is born in your house, he who is now in your house, 17:13
and he who is bought with your money, must be circumcised.
My covenant is made in your flesh as an everlasting covenant.
Any male whose flesh of his foreskin is not circumcised, 17:14
shall be sent off from his people. He has broken our covenant."

God said, "As for Sarai your wife, she shall no longer be called Sarai. 17:15
Her name shall now be Sarah.
And I will bless her, and I will give you a son from her. 17:16
I will bless her exceedingly, and she shall be a mother of nations.
Kings of nations shall come from her."
Abraham fell down laughing, and said to himself, 17:17
"Shall a child be born to a hundred year-old man?
Shall Sarah, who is ninety years old, bear a child?"
Abraham said to God, "If only Ishmael might find your favor!" 17:18
God said, "Sarah shall indeed bear you a son. You shall name him Isaac. 17:19
And I will establish my everlasting covenant with him,
and with his descendants after him.
As for Ishmael, I have heard your prayer. Truly, I have blessed him, 17:20
and I will make him fruitful, and I will give him many descendants.
He shall be the ancestor of twelve tribal chiefs,
and I shall make from him a great nation.
But my covenant I will establish with Isaac, 17:21
who shall be born to Sarah on this same day next year."
Then God stopped speaking, and withdrew from Abraham. 17:22

That very day, Abraham took his son Ishmael, and all who were born | 17:23
in his house, and all who were bought with his money—every male among
those of Abraham's house—and circumcised the flesh of their foreskin.
Abraham was ninety-nine years old when he was circumcised. | 17:24
Ishmael was thirteen years old when he was circumcised. | 17:25
They were both circumcised on that same day. | 17:26
All the men of Abraham's house—those born in the house, | 17:27
and those bought with his money—were circumcised that day.

Chapter 18

One day the Lord appeared to Abraham by the sacred oaks of Mamre, | 18:1
as Abraham sat in his tent door in the heat of the day.
Abraham lifted up his eyes and saw three agents of the Lord | 18:2
standing nearby. When he saw them, he ran from his tent to meet them,
and he bowed before them on the ground.
He said, "O Lord, if I have now found favor in your eyes, | 18:3
I pray you, do not pass me by. I am your servant.
I will fetch water and wash your feet as you rest under the tree. | 18:4
I will bring you bread, and you can be refreshed before continuing | 18:5
your journey. For you have come to the house of your servant."
They said, "Very well. Do as you have spoken."
Abraham hastened into his tent and said to Sarah, "Quickly, take three | 18:6
measures of our finest flour, knead bread and bake it upon the hearth."
Then Abraham ran to the herd and chose a calf, tender and good, | 18:7
and gave it to a young servant, who hastened to prepare it.

Abraham took bread and butter and milk, and the prepared meat, and set | 18:8
it before the men, then stood by them under the tree. And they did eat.
One said, "Where is your wife Sarah?" Abraham said, "She is in the tent." | 18:9
He said, "I will return to you after the time it takes life to grow, | 18:10
and Sarah your wife shall give you a son."
Sarah, who stood in the tent door behind him, heard his words.
Now, Abraham and Sarah were old, and well-stricken with age. | 18:11
And Sarah had ceased to bleed after the manner of women.
So Sarah laughed to herself, saying, "I am old and dried up. | 18:12
Can I enjoy sensual pleasure? With my lord who is also old?"
The Lord said to Abraham, "Why did Sarah laugh, thinking, | 18:13
'Can I really bear a child when I am this old?'
Is anything too difficult for God? At the time appointed, according | 18:14
to the gestation of life, I will return, and Sarah shall give you a son."
Then Sarah denied, saying, "I did not laugh," for she was afraid. | 18:15
The Lord said, "No, you did laugh."

The men got up and headed toward Sodom. | 18:16
Abraham went with them to see them on their way.
The Lord thought, "Shall I hide from Abraham that which I shall do? | 18:17
Seeing that Abraham shall surely sire a great and mighty nation, | 18:18
and that all the nations of the earth shall be blessed in him?

I know him. I know that he will command his children and his household,   18:19
and that they shall keep the way of the Lord, that they shall be just
and righteous so that the Lord may fulfill his promise to Abraham."
So the Lord said to Abraham, "Because the outcry against Sodom   18:20
and Gomorrah is great, and because their sin is grievous,
I go there to judge them, to see whether what they have done   18:21
justifies the cry against them. If it does, or does not, I will know."

The men turned from there, and went toward Sodom.   18:22
But Abraham still went with the Lord.
Abraham said, "Will you destroy the righteous along with the wicked?   18:23
Perhaps there are fifty righteous souls within the city.   18:24
Will you then destroy it all and not spare the place
on account of the fifty who are righteous?
That be far from you, to slay the righteous with the wicked.   18:25
To treat the righteous as the wicked—that be far from you.
Shall not the judge of all the earth do what is right?"

The Lord said, "If I find in Sodom fifty righteous souls   18:26
within the city, then I will spare all the place for their sakes."
Abraham said, "Since I have taken it upon me to speak to the Lord,   18:27
even though I am but dust and ashes:
What if there shall lack five of the fifty righteous.   18:28
Will you destroy all the city for the lack of five?" The Lord said,
"If I find there forty-five righteous men, I will not destroy it."
Abraham spoke again, saying, "What if forty righteous are found there?"   18:29
The Lord said, "I will not do it for the sake of the forty."
Abraham said, "Let not the Lord be angry that I speak, but what if thirty be   18:30
found there?" The Lord said, "I will not do it if I find thirty righteous men."
Abraham said, "I have taken it upon me to again speak to the Lord: 18:31
What if twenty be found there?"
The Lord said, "I will not destroy it for the sake of the twenty."
Abraham said, "O let not the Lord be angry, and I will speak   18:32
but once more: What if only ten shall be found there?"
The Lord said, "I will not destroy it for the sake of the ten."
When the Lord was through talking with Abraham,   18:33
he continued on his way. Abraham returned to his tent.

Chapter 19

The agents of the Lord arrived at Sodom that evening. Lot, who was sitting   19:1
near the gate of Sodom, rose up to meet them and bowed to the ground.
He said, "My lords, I pray you, come to your servant's house. You can wash   19:2
your feet and stay the night, then rise up early and go on your way."
They said, "No, we will pass the night in the street."
But Lot pleaded with them, and they went with him into his house.   19:3
Lot made them a feast, and baked unleavened bread. And they ate.
But before they lay down, the men of the city of Sodom—   19:4
both old and young, from every quarter—surrounded the house.

They called out to Lot, "Where are the men who came to you tonight?   19:5
Bring them out to us, so that we can rape them."
Lot went out to them, and shut the door behind him.   19:6
He said, "I pray you, brethren, do not act wickedly.   19:7
Listen, I have two daughters who are virgins. I pray you, let me   19:8
bring them out to you, and you may do to them as please. But do nothing
to these men, for they have come under the protection of my roof."

The men said, "Stand back! These men came here to visit, and now   19:9
they would be our judge? We will deal worse with you than with them!"
Then they pressed hard against Lot and came near to breaking the door.
But the agents reached out and pulled Lot back   19:10
into the house with them, and shut the door.
Then they struck all the men outside with blindness,   19:11
so that they could not find the door.
The agents said to Lot, "Do you have anyone here besides yourself?   19:12
Sons, sons-in-law, daughters? Whatever you have, get them out of the city.
For we will destroy this place. The cry against Sodom has become   19:13
great before the Lord, and he has sent us to destroy it."
So Lot went to his sons-in-law—who had married his daughters—   19:14
and said, "Get up and get out of this place. The Lord is going to
destroy the city!" But they did not take him seriously.

When morning came, the agents hastened Lot, saying,   19:15
"Get up. Take your wife and the two daughters who are here,
and get out, lest you be consumed in the punishment of this city."
But Lot hesitated, so the men took his hand, and the hands   19:16
of his wife and daughters, and led them forth outside the city.
For the Lord had resolved to be merciful to them.
When the men had taken them outside the city, one said,   19:17
"Go now. Escape with your lives and do not look back!
Do not stop on the plain or in the valley.
Escape to the mountains, lest you be consumed."
Lot said to them, "No, I pray you, my lords.   19:18
Your servant has found grace in your sight, and you have magnified   19:19
your mercy by saving my life. But I cannot make it as far as the
mountains before this disaster overtakes me, and I will die.
Look, there is a city near enough to flee to, and it is a little one.   19:20
I pray you, let me escape to there. It is a small city, right?
There my soul shall live."
So he said to Lot, "Agreed. I will grant you this favor also.   19:21
I will not destroy the city of which you speak.
Go there quickly, for I cannot do anything until you arrive."   19:22
Therefore, the name of the city became Zoar.
By the time Lot entered Zoar, the sun had risen upon the earth.   19:23
Then the Lord rained upon Sodom, and also Gomorrah,   19:24
fire and brimstone from the heavens.
He destroyed those cities, and all the plain, and all the   19:25
inhabitants of the cities, and all that grew in the ground there.

Lot's wife turned around to look back upon all this,   19:26
and she became a pillar of salt.

Abraham got up early in the morning   19:27
and went to the place where he stood before the Lord.
He looked toward Sodom and Gomorrah, and toward   19:28
all the land of the plain, and beheld the smoke
of the country as it burned with the fire of a furnace.
So it was, that when God destroyed the cities of the plain, he remembered   19:29
his promise to Abraham, and brought Lot out of the destruction.
Lot came to fear living in Zoar, so he left Zoar with his two daughters   19:30
and went into the mountains. There he dwelt with his daughters in a cave.
One day the firstborn said to the younger, "Our father is getting old,   19:31
and there are no men to lie with us, in the manner of all the world.
Come, let us make our father drink wine, and we will lie with him,   19:32
that we may preserve the seed of our father."
So they made their father drink wine that night.   19:33
And the firstborn went in and lay with her father.
Lot was not aware of when she lay down or arose.

The next day the firstborn said to the younger, "Last night I lay   19:34
with our father. Let us make him drink wine tonight also, and you
go in and lie with him, that we may preserve the seed of our father."
So they made their father drink wine that night.   19:35
And the younger went in and lay with her father.
Lot was not aware of when she lay down or arose.
Thus were both the daughters of Lot with child by their father.   19:36
The firstborn bore a son, and she named him Moab.   19:37
He is the ancestor of the Moabites unto this day.
The younger also bore a son, and she named him Benammi.   19:38
He is the ancestor of the children of Ammon unto this day.

Chapter 20

Abraham journeyed from there toward the south country.   20:1
He lived between Kadesh and Shur, then sojourned in Gerar.
There Abraham said of Sarah his wife, "She is my sister."   20:2
And Abimelech, king of Gerar, sent for Sarah and took her.
But God came to Abimelech in a dream by night, and said to him,   20:3
"You are a dead man, for the woman you took is another man's wife."
But Abimelech had not yet come to her, and he said,   20:4
"Lord, would you slay a righteous nation?
Did he not say to me, 'She is my sister'? And even she herself said,   20:5
'He is my brother.' It is with the integrity of my heart
and the innocence of my hands that have I done this."
God said to him in the dream, "I know that you did this with integrity   20:6
in your heart, and so I kept you from sinning against me,
and did not let you touch her.
Now return the man's wife to him. He is a prophet. He shall pray for you,   20:7

and you shall live. But if you do not return her,
be certain that death will come to you, and to all in your house.”

Abimelech rose early in the morning and called all his servants,   20:8
and he told them all these things, and they were sore afraid.
Abimelech called Abraham, and said to him, “What have you done to us?   20:9
In what way have I offended you, that you brought upon me and my
kingdom this great sin? What you have done to me ought not be done!
What were you thinking to cause you to do such a thing?”   20:10
Abraham said, “I thought, surely the fear of God is not in this place,   20:11
and they will kill me in order to take my wife.
Also, she is indeed my sister. She is the daughter of my father,   20:12
but not of my mother. And she became my wife.
When God caused me to wander from my father's house I said to her,   20:13
‘This is the kindness you shall show me:
At every place we shall come to, say that I am your brother.’”

So Abimelech took sheep, and oxen, and manservants, and maidservants,   20:14
and gave them to Abraham, and restored to him Sarah his wife.
Abimelech said, “My land is before you. Dwell wherever it pleases you.”   20:15
He said to Sarah, “I have given your brother a thousand pieces of silver   20:16
as proof to all who are with you that you are innocent.
Everyone will know that you have done no wrong.”
So Abraham prayed to God, and God healed Abimelech and his wife   20:17
and maidservants, so that they could again bear children.
For the Lord had closed up all the wombs of the house of Abimelech,   20:18
because of Sarah, Abraham's wife.

Chapter 21

The Lord visited Sarah as he said, and he did for her as he promised.   21:1
Sarah conceived, and bore Abraham a son in his old age,   21:2
at the exact time God had told him.
Abraham named the son whom Sarah bore him, Isaac.   21:3
And Abraham circumcised his son Isaac when he was eight days old,   21:4
as God had commanded him.
Abraham was a hundred years old when his son Isaac was born.   21:5
Sarah said, “God has given me reason to laugh,   21:6
so that all who hear will laugh with me.
Who would have said to Abraham that Sarah should have a child   21:7
at her breast? But I have born him a son in his old age.”

The child grew, and was weaned.   21:8
Abraham made a great feast on the day Isaac was weaned.
And there Sarah saw Hagar the Egyptian,   21:9
who had born a son unto Abraham, mocking.
She said to Abraham, “Cast out this slave girl and her son. For the son   21:10
of this servant shall not share in the inheritance with my son Isaac.”
This distressed Abraham grievously because he was his son.   21:11
God said to Abraham, “Do not be distressed about the boy and your slave.   21:12

Whatever Sarah says, listen to her,
for your descendants shall come through Isaac.
I will also make a nation of Hagar's son, because he too is your seed." 21:13

So Abraham rose up early in the morning, and took bread and a skin 21:14
of water, and gave it to Hagar. Then he put the boy in her shoulder sling
and sent her away. She left, and wandered in the wilderness of Beersheba.
When the water in the skin ran out, she set the child down under a bush. 21:15
And she went a distance away from him, about the length 21:16
of an arrow shot, and sat down. She said, "I cannot watch
the death of my child." And she wailed in grief, and she wept.
God heard the cries of the boy, and the angel of God called to Hagar 21:17
from heaven, and said to her, "What is wrong, Hagar?
Fear not, for God has heard the voice of the boy from the bushes.
Arise, lift up your child and hold him in your arms, 21:18
for I will make of him a great nation."
And God opened her eyes, and she saw a wellspring, and she 21:19
went and filled the skin with water. And she gave the boy a drink.
God remained with the boy, and he grew. 21:20
He lived in the wilderness and became an expert archer.
He dwelt in the wilderness of Paran, 21:21
and his mother took to him a wife out of the land of Egypt.

Abimelech and Phichol, the commander of his army, 21:22
spoke to Abraham, saying, "God is with you in all that you do.
Therefore swear to me by God that you will not deal falsely with me, 21:23
nor with my sons, nor with my sons' sons. But according
to the kindness I have done for you, you shall do for me,
and for this land where you have come to live."
Abraham said, "I do so swear it." 21:24
But Abraham reproved Abimelech because of a well he had dug, 21:25
which Abimelech's servants had violently taken away.
Abimelech said, "I do not know who has done this, and you 21:26
did not tell me about it. I have not heard of it until today."
So Abraham took sheep and oxen, and gave them to Abimelech, 21:27
and both of them made a covenant.
And Abraham set seven of the ewe lambs off by themselves. 21:28
Abimelech said to Abraham, "What is the meaning of these 21:29
seven ewe lambs that you set apart?"
Abraham said, "Accept these seven ewe lambs from me, 21:30
that they may signify your witness that I have dug this well."
Abraham called that place Beersheba, for there they both swore an oath. 21:31
Thus they made a covenant at Beersheba. Then Abimelech and Phichol, 21:32
the commander of his army, returned into the land of the Philistines.
Abraham planted a grove in Beersheba, 21:33
and there called on the name of the Lord, the everlasting God.
Abraham lived in the land of the Philistines for many days. 21:34

Chapter 22

After these things, God put Abraham to the test.   22:1
He said, "Abraham," and Abraham answered, "Here I am."
God said, "Take your son, your beloved son Isaac, and go to   22:2
the land of Moriah. There offer your son as a burnt offering
upon one of the mountains, which I will show to you."
Abraham rose up early in the morning and saddled his ass.   22:3
He took two of his young men, and Isaac his son, and cut wood for the
burnt offering. Then he traveled towards the place God had told him.
On the third day Abraham lifted up his eyes, and saw the place far off.   22:4
He said to his young men, "Stay here with the ass.   22:5
My son and I will go forth and worship, then come back here."
Abraham put the wood for the burnt offering on the back of his son Isaac,   22:6
took the fire and the knife in his hand, and they walked on together.
Isaac said to Abraham, "My father," and Abraham said, "Here I am."   22:7
Isaac said, "We have fire and the wood,
but where is the lamb for the burnt offering?"
Abraham said, "My son, God himself will provide a lamb   22:8
for the burnt offering." And they walked on together.

They came to a place that God showed Abraham,   22:9
and Abraham built an altar there, and arranged the wood.
And he bound Isaac his son, and laid him on the alter of wood.
And Abraham reached out his hand, and took up the knife to kill his son.   22:10
But the angel of the Lord called to him from heaven and said,   22:11
"Abraham, Abraham!" And Abraham said, "Here I am."
He said, "Lay not your hand upon the boy. Do not do anything to him.   22:12
For now I know that you fear God, because you
did not withhold your son, your only son, from me."

Abraham lifted up his eyes and saw a ram caught in a thicket by his horns.   22:13
He took the ram, and offered him up as a burnt offering instead of his son.
Abraham named that place The Lord Will Provide, which is why   22:14
to this day people say, "On the mountain of the Lord, it will be provided."
The angel of the Lord called to Abraham the second time,   22:15
and said, "I swear by my own name that because you have   22:16
not withheld your son, your only son, that I will richly bless you,
and greatly multiply your seed. Your descendants shall be as many   22:17
as the stars in heaven, as many as the sands on the seashore,
and they shall conquer their enemies.
Your descendants shall be a blessing to all the   22:18
nations of earth because you obeyed my voice."
Abraham returned to his men, and they went together   22:19
to Beersheba. And Abraham dwelt at Beersheba.

After these things, Abraham was told,   22:20
"Milcah has borne these children to your brother Nahor:
Huz his firstborn, and Buz his brother, and Kemuel father of Aram,   22:21

and Chesed, Hazo, Pildash, Jidlaph and Bethuel.   22:22
And Bethuel begat Rebekah."   22:23
These are the eight children Milcah bore to Nahor, Abraham's brother.
Nahor's concubine, whose name was Reumah, also bore him   22:24
Tebah, Gaham, Thahash and Maachah.

Chapter 23

Sarah lived to be a hundred and twenty-seven years old.   23:1
These were the years of the life of Sarah.
Sarah died in Kirjatharba, also called Hebron, in the land of Canaan.   23:2
Abraham came to mourn for Sarah, and to weep for her.
Abraham stood up from mourning his dead wife,   23:3
and spoke to the sons of Heth, saying,
"I am a stranger and a sojourner among you.   23:4
Give me a burying place here so that I may bury my dead."
The children of Heth answered Abraham, saying,   23:5
"Hear us, my lord: You are a mighty leader in our midst.   23:6
Bury your dead in whatever sepulcher you choose. None of us shall
withhold from you his sepulcher, so that you may bury your dead."

Abraham bowed down to the people of the land, to the children of Heth.   23:7
And he communed with them, saying, "If you desire to help me   23:8
bury my dead, then listen to me and ask Ephron, son of Zohar,
if he will sell me the cave of Machpelah, which is at the end of his field,   23:9
for the full price of its worth, in your presence,
so that I may have a burial site of my own for my dead."
Now, Ephron the Hittite was there among the children of Heth,   23:10
and Ephron answered Abraham in the presence of the children of Heth,
and everyone at the gate of his city, saying,
"No, my lord, hear me: I give you the field and the cave within.   23:11
In the presence of my people I give it to you. Bury your dead."
Abraham bowed down before the people of the land.   23:12
And he spoke to Ephron in the presence of the people, saying, "If you will   23:13
give me it to me, I pray you, let me pay you the price of the field.
Take it, and I will bury my dead there."
Ephron answered Abraham, saying,   23:14
"My lord, hear me: The land is worth four hundred shekels of silver,   23:15
but what is that between me and you? Therefore, bury your dead."

Abraham took note that Ephron named a price in the presence of the sons   23:16
of Heth, so he weighed out to Ephron four hundred shekels of silver,
at the current rate of exchange.
So the field of Ephron in Machpelah, near Mamre, and the cave therein,   23:17
and all the trees within its boundaries, were officially transferred
to Abraham's possession in the presence of the children of Heth,   23:18
and before all that went in at the gate of his city.
After this was done, Abraham buried his wife Sarah in the cave of the field   23:19
of Machpelah, near Mamre, which is Hebron, in the land of Canaan.

The field and the cave therein, were officially transferred to Abraham 23:20
by the sons of Heth, for his burial property.

Chapter 24

Abraham was old and well-stricken with age, 24:1
and the Lord had blessed Abraham in all things.
Abraham said to the eldest servant of his house, who ruled over 24:2
all that he had, "I pray you, put your hand under my thigh,
and swear by the Lord, God of heaven and earth, that you will not 24:3
choose a wife for my son from the Canaanites among whom I am living.
But that you will go to my country, and my kindred, 24:4
to find a wife for my son Isaac."
The servant said, "What if the woman is not willing to follow me here. 24:5
Should I take your son back to the land from which you came?"
Abraham said, "No. Make sure you never take my son back there again. 24:6
The Lord God of heaven, who took me from my father's house 24:7
and from the land of my brethren, who swore to me, saying,
'To your seed I give this land,' he shall send his angel before you,
and give you a wife for my son from that land.
If the woman is not willing to follow you, then you are released 24:8
from this oath. Only do not ever take my son back there."
And the servant put his hand under the thigh of Abraham, his master, 24:9
and swore to him concerning this matter.

The servant took ten of his master's camels, and other good gifts, 24:10
and departed for Mesopotamia, to the city of Nahor.
There he made his camels kneel down outside the city by a wellspring, 24:11
in the evening, when the women go out to draw water.
He said, "O Lord God of my master Abraham, I pray you, 24:12
show kindness to my master and let me prosper this day.
Behold, I stand here by the well, when the daughters 24:13
of the city come out to draw water.
I shall say to each, 'Let down your pitcher, I pray you, so that I may drink.' 24:14
The one who says, 'Here, drink, and I will give your camels water also,'
let her be the one you have chosen for your servant Isaac.
By this I shall know that you have shown kindness to my master."

Before he had even done speaking, Rebekah— 24:15
daughter of Bethuel, son of Milcah and Nahor, Abraham's brother—
came out, with her pitcher on her shoulder.
She was very fair to look upon, a virgin, never known by any man, 24:16
and she went down to the well and filled her pitcher.
The servant ran to meet her and said, "I pray you, 24:17
let me drink a little water from your pitcher."
She said, "Drink, my lord," and lowered her pitcher to give him a drink. 24:18
When she had done giving him a drink, she said, "I will draw water 24:19
for your camels also, until they have done drinking."
Then she emptied her pitcher into the trough, 24:20

and ran again to the well, and drew water for all his camels.
The servant stood in silence, wondering whether or not 24:21
the Lord had made his journey prosperous.
When the camels had done drinking, the servant gave her a golden earring 24:22
weighing half a shekel, and two bracelets of gold weighing ten shekels.
And he said, "Whose daughter are you? Tell me, I pray you, 24:23
is there room in your father's house for us to lodge the night?"
She said, "I am the daughter of Bethuel, son of Milcah and Nahor. 24:24
We have straw and feed for your camels, and room for you to lodge." 24:25
The servant bowed down his head, and thanked the Lord. 24:26
He said, "Blessed be the Lord God of Abraham, who has not withheld 24:27
his faithfulness and mercy from my master, nor from me,
whom he has led to the house of his brethren."

The woman ran to her mother's house, and told the news of these things. 24:28
Now, Rebekah had a brother, whose name was Laban, 24:29
and Laban ran out to the man at the well.
For when he saw the earring, and the bracelets upon his sister's arms, 24:30
and when he heard Rebekah say, "This is what the man said to me,"
he ran to meet the man, and lo, the man stood with his camels at the well.
Laban said, "Come in, blessed one of the Lord. 24:31
Why are you standing outside? I have made room in the house
for you, and prepared a place for your camels."
So the man came to the house. Laban unbridled the camels, 24:32
and gave them straw and feed, and gave the man water to wash his feet,
and for the men with him to wash their feet.
And a meal was set before him. But he said, "I will not eat until 24:33
I have told you my errand." Laban said, "Speak on."

The man said, "I am Abraham's servant. 24:34
The Lord has blessed my master and he has become great, with flocks 24:35
and herds, silver and gold, servants and maids, and camels and asses.
Sarah, my master's wife, bore him a son when she was old, 24:36
and to this son, Abraham has given all that he has.
And my master made me swear, saying, 'You shall not take a wife 24:37
to my son from the daughters of the Canaanites, in whose land I dwell.
Go to my father's land, and to my kindred, and bring a wife to my son.' 24:38
I said to him, 'What if the woman will not follow me?' 24:39
He said, 'The Lord, before whom I walk, will send his angel with you, 24:40
and prosper your way. And you shall take a wife for my son
who is of my kindred, and of my father's house.
Then you shall be free of your oath to me. If they provide 24:41
no woman for you, you shall also be free of your oath.'
So today I came to the well, and said, 'O Lord God of my master Abraham, 24:42
if it is your purpose to prosper my way,
behold, I stand by the well of water. When a maiden comes forth 24:43
to draw water, and I say to her, "Give me, I pray you,
a little water from your pitcher to drink,"

and she says to me, "Drink, and I will also draw water for your camels," | 24:44
let that woman be the one the Lord has chosen for my master's son.'

"Before I had done speaking in my heart, Rebekah came forth with | 24:45
her pitcher on her shoulder, and she went to the well and drew water.
I said to her, 'Let me drink, I pray you.'
She let down her pitcher from her shoulder, and said, | 24:46
'Drink, and I will give your camels drink also.'
So I drank, and she let the camels drink also.
I asked her, 'Whose daughter are you?' She said, | 24:47
'The daughter of Bethuel, Nahor's son, whom Milcah bore him.'
And I gave her the earring, and the bracelets for her arms.
And I bowed down, and worshipped the Lord, and blessed the | 24:48
Lord God of my master Abraham, who led me in the right way
to bring my master's brother's daughter to his son.
Now, if you will deal kindly and truly with my master, tell me. | 24:49
If not, tell me, so that I may turn to the right or to the left."

Laban and Bethuel answered, saying, "This matter proceeds | 24:50
from the Lord. We cannot speak good or bad about it.
Behold, Rebekah is before you. Take her and go. | 24:51
Let her be your master's son's wife, as the Lord has spoken."
When Abraham's servant heard their words, | 24:52
he worshipped the Lord, bowing himself to the earth.
And the servant brought forth jewelry of silver, and jewelry of gold, | 24:53
and clothing, and gave them to Rebekah.
He also gave her brother and her mother precious things.
And they did eat and drink, he and the men who were with him, | 24:54
and they tarried all night. When they rose up in the morning,
the servant said, "Send me off to my master."
Her brother and her mother said, "Let the girl stay with us a few days, | 24:55
at least ten. After that she shall go."
The servant said, "Do not keep me. The Lord has prospered my journey. | 24:56
Send me off that I may go to my master."
They said, "We will ask the girl and see what she says." | 24:57
So they called Rebekah and asked her, "Will you go now with this man?" | 24:58
She said, "I will go."
So they sent off their sister Rebekah, and her nurse, | 24:59
and Abraham's servant and his men.
And they blessed Rebekah, and said to her, "O sister, be the mother | 24:60
of thousands of millions. Let your seed possess the gates
of those who make war against them."
Rebekah arose with her handmaidens, and they mounted the camels, | 24:61
and they followed Abraham's servant as he went his way.

Now, Isaac came from the land of the wellspring Lahairoi, | 24:62
for he dwelt in the south country.
He was meditating in the field one evening, | 24:63
when he looked up and beheld the camels coming.

When Rebekah saw Isaac, she jumped off her camel.   24:64
She said to the servant, "Who is this man who walks out to meet us?" 24:65
The servant said, "My master's son." So she covered her face with a veil.
The servant told Isaac all things he had done.   24:66
Isaac brought Rebekah into his mother Sarah's tent.   24:67
Rebekah became his wife, and he loved her,
and Isaac was comforted after his mother's death.

Chapter 25

Then Abraham again took a wife, and her name was Keturah.   25:1
She bore him Zimran, Jokshan, Medan, Midian, Ishbak and Shuah.   25:2
Jokshan begat Sheba and Dedan.   25:3
The sons of Dedan were Asshurim, Letushim and Leummim.
The sons of Midian were Ephah, Epher, Hanoch, Abida and Eldaah.   25:4
All these were the children of Keturah.
And Abraham gave all that he had to Isaac.   25:5
To the sons of his concubines Abraham gave gifts. And for the time he yet   25:6
lived, he sent them eastward, away from Isaac, to live in the east country.
The days of Abraham's life were one hundred seventy-five years.   25:7
Then Abraham gave up the ghost and died at a good old age,   25:8
an old man full of years. And he was gathered unto his ancestors.
His sons Isaac and Ishmael buried him in the cave of Machpelah,   25:9
near Mamre, in the field of Ephron, son of Zohar the Hittite—
the field that Abraham purchased from the sons of Heth.   25:10
There, next to his wife Sarah, Abraham was buried.
After the death of Abraham, God blessed his son Isaac,   25:11
and Isaac dwelt by the well Lahairoi.

These are the generations of Ishmael, Abraham's son, whom Hagar   25:12
the Egyptian, Sarah's handmaid, bore unto Abraham:
The names of the sons of Ishmael, by their birth order, were Nebajoth,   25:13
the firstborn, and Kedar, Adbeel, Mibsam,
Mishma, Dumah Massa,   25:14
Hadar, Tema, Jetur, Naphish and Kedemah.   25:15
These were the sons of Ishmael, and these were their names, by their 25:16
villages, and by their settlements—twelve leaders of their nations.
The life of Ishmael was a hundred and thirty-seven years,   25:17
then he gave up the ghost and died, and was gathered unto his ancestors.
Ishmael's descendants dwelt from Havilah to Shur,   25:18
which is before you come to Egypt, as you go toward Assyria,
and he died in the presence of all his brethren.

These are the generations of Isaac, Abraham's son. Abraham begat Isaac.   25:19
Isaac was forty years old when he took his wife Rebekah— the daughter   25:20
of Bethuel the Syrian of Padanaram, and sister to Laban the Syrian.
Isaac prayed to the Lord for his wife, because she was barren.   25:21
The Lord heeded his prayer, and Rebekah conceived.
And there were two children within her, and they struggled   25:22

against each other in her womb. She said, "If it is to be like this,
why did I even conceive?" And she asked this of the Lord.
The Lord said to her, "Two nations are in your womb, and two manner 25:23
of people shall come forth from you. One people shall be stronger
than the other, and the elder shall serve the younger."
When her time to deliver came, there were twins in her womb. 25:24
The first came out red, with hair all over like a garment. 25:25
They named him Esau.

After him came his brother, and his hand took hold of Esau's heel. 25:26
They called him Jacob. Isaac was sixty years old when she bore them.
The boys grew. Esau was a cunning hunter, a man of the field. 25:27
Jacob was a plain man, dwelling in tents.
Isaac loved Esau, and enjoyed eating his venison. Rebekah loved Jacob. 25:28
One day Jacob was cooking soup, and Esau 25:29
came in from the field, and he was feeling faint.
He said to Jacob, "I pray you, feed me with your red soup, for I am faint." 25:30
This is why he was called Edom.
Jacob said, "First, sell me your birthright as firstborn." 25:31
Esau said, "I am about to die, what good is the birthright to me?" 25:32
Jacob said, "Swear to me this day." And he swore to him, 25:33
and he sold his birthright to Jacob for soup.
So Jacob gave Esau bread and lentil soup, and he ate then went his way. 25:34
This is how little Esau valued his birthright.

Chapter 26

There was a famine in the land, a different one from the first famine 26:1
in the days of Abraham. And Isaac set out towards Gerar,
to Abimelech, king of the Philistines.
The Lord appeared to him, and said, "Do not go into Egypt. 26:2
Dwell in the land that I shall tell you of.
Sojourn in this land, and I will be with you, and I will bless you. 26:3
For to you and your descendants, I will give all these countries,
and I will perform the oath that I swore to Abraham, your father.
I will make your seed multiply as the stars of heaven, 26:4
and will give to your descendants all these countries.
And in your seed shall all the nations of the earth be blessed.
Because Abraham obeyed my voice, and kept my charge, 26:5
my commandments, my statutes, and my laws."
So Isaac dwelt in Gerar. 26:6
When the men of the place asked him about his wife, he said, 26:7
"She is my sister," for he feared to say she was his wife, thinking,
"The men here would kill me for Rebekah, because she is very fair."
When he had been there a long time, Abimelech, king of the Philistines, 26:8
looked out a window, and saw Isaac sporting with Rebekah, his wife.
Abimelech called Isaac and said, "She is clearly your wife. 26:9
Why did you say, 'She is my sister'? Isaac said to him,
"Because I thought I would be killed for her."

Abimelech said, "What have you done to us? One of our people could   26:10
easily have lay with your wife, and you would have brought guilt upon us."
And Abimelech charged all his people, saying,   26:11
"Whoever touches this man or his wife shall be put to death."

Isaac sowed seed in the earth, and reaped in that same year   26:12
a hundredfold, for the Lord blessed him.
And Isaac waxed greater, and became richer, and became very great.   26:13
He had possession of flocks, and herds, and many servants.   26:14
And the Philistines envied him.
The Philistines filled up with dirt all the wells that Abraham's   26:15
servants had dug in the days of his father Abraham.
And Abimelech said to Isaac, "Go from us,   26:16
for you have become much mightier than we are."
Isaac departed, and pitched his tent in the valley of Gerar, and lived there.   26:17
And Isaac dug again the wells of water that had been dug in the days   26:18
of Abraham his father, which the Philistines had filled up,
and he gave them the same names his father had given them.
Isaac's servants dug in the valley, and found there a wellspring of water.   26:19
The herdsmen of Gerar argued with Isaac's herdsmen, saying, "The water   26:20
is ours!" So Isaac named the well Esek, for they had quarreled with him.
They dug another well, and they quarreled over that one also,   26:21
so he named it Sitnah.
Then he went away from there and dug another well.   26:22
There was no quarrel over this one, so he named it Rehoboth. He said,
"The Lord has now made room for us, and we shall be fruitful in the land."

He went from there to Beersheba.   26:23
The Lord appeared to him that same night, and said, "I am the God   26:24
of Abraham your father. Fear not, for I am with you, and I will bless you,
and I will multiply your seed for the sake of my servant Abraham."
So Isaac built an altar there, and called on the name of the Lord.   26:25
And he pitched his tent there, and his servants dug a well.
Then Abimelech came to him from Gerar, with Ahuzzath, one of his allies,   26:26
and Phichol, the commander of his army.
Isaac said to them, "Why have you come, seeing that you hate me,   26:27
and have sent me away from you?"
They said, "We now see that the Lord is with you, so we decided,   26:28
let there be an oath between us. Let us make a covenant with you,
that you will do us no harm, as we have not harmed you, and as we have   26:29
done to you nothing but good. And we have sent you away in peace,
and you are now blessed by the Lord."

So Isaac made them a feast, and they did eat and drink.   26:30
They got up early in the morning, and swore one to another.   26:31
Then Isaac sent them away, and they departed in peace.
That same day, Isaac's servants came and told him about the well   26:32
they had dug, and said to him, "We have found water."
Isaac called the well Shebah, which is why   26:33

the name of the city is Beersheba to this day.

Esau was forty years old when he took his wives Judith,   26:34
daughter of Beeri the Hittite, and Bashemath, daughter of Elon the Hittite.

They became a grief of mind to Isaac and Rebekah.   26:35

Chapter 27

When Isaac was old and his eyes were so dim he could not see, he called   27:1
Esau his eldest son, and said, "My son?" And Esau said, "Here I am."

Isaac said, "I am old, and I know not the day of my death.   27:2

Therefore, I pray you, take up your weapons, your quiver and bow,   27:3
and go out into the field and bring back some venison.

Make me savory meat, such as I love, and bring it to me,   27:4
that I may eat, and that my soul may bless you before I die."

Rebekah heard what Isaac said to his son Esau.   27:5
Esau went to the field to hunt for venison, and to bring it back.

Rebekah spoke to her son Jacob, saying,   27:6
"Listen, I heard your father speak to your brother, saying,

'Bring me venison, and make me savory meat, that I may eat,   27:7
and bless you before the Lord before my death.'

Now therefore, my son, listen to me and do what I tell you.   27:8

Go to the flock and fetch me two good kids of the goats.   27:9
I will make them savory meat for your father, such as he loves.

And you shall bring it to your father, that he may eat,   27:10
and that he may bless you before his death."

Jacob said to Rebekah his mother, "But my brother Esau   27:11
is a hairy man, and I have smooth skin.

Perhaps my father will touch me, and I shall seem to him a deceiver,   27:12
and I shall bring a curse upon myself, not a blessing."

His mother said to him, "The curse will fall on me, my son.   27:13
Now obey my voice, and go fetch them to me."

So Jacob fetched them and brought them to his mother,   27:14
and his mother made savory meat, such as his father loved.

And she took her eldest son Esau's best clothes, which were with her   27:15
in the house, and put them on her younger son Jacob.

And she put the skins of the young goats on his arms,   27:16
and upon the smooth part of his neck.

She put the savory meat and the bread she had prepared   27:17
into the hands of her son Jacob.

And Jacob went to his father, and said, "My father."   27:18
Isaac said, "Here am I. Who are you, my son?"

Jacob said, "I am Esau, your firstborn. I have done what you asked of me.   27:19
Arise, I pray you. Sit and eat my venison so that your soul may bless me."

Isaac said, "How is it that you found it so quickly, my son?"   27:20
Jacob said, "Because the Lord your God brought it to me."

Isaac said, "Come near, I pray you, that I may feel you,   27:21
and see whether you be my very son Esau or not."

Jacob went near to Isaac, and his father felt him, and said,   27:22

"The voice is Jacob's voice, but the arms are the arms of Esau."
And he discerned him not because his arms were hairy,
just as were his brother Esau's arms. So Isaac blessed him.   27:23

He said, "Are you my very son Esau?" And Jacob said, "I am."   27:24
Isaac said, "Bring the food near, and I will eat of my son's venison,   27:25
that my soul may bless you." And he brought it near to him, and he did eat.
And he brought him wine, and he drank.
Isaac said to him, "Come near now and kiss me, my son."   27:26
And Jacob came near, and kissed him. Isaac smelled the smell   27:27
of his clothes, and blessed him. He said, "The smell of my son
is as the smell of a field, which the Lord has blessed.
Therefore may God give you the dew of heaven,   27:28
and the fatness of the earth, and an abundance of corn and wine.
Let people serve you, and nations bow down to you. Be lord   27:29
of your brethren, and let your mother's sons bow down to you.
Cursed be all who curse you, and blessed be all who bless you."

As soon as Isaac finished blessing Jacob, and Jacob was scarcely gone   27:30
from the presence of his father, his brother Esau came in from hunting.
Esau also had made savory meat, and he said to his father,   27:31
"Arise and eat your son's venison, that your soul may bless me."
Isaac said , "Who are you?" And Esau said, "I am your firstborn son, Esau."   27:32
Isaac trembled, and said, "Who? Where is he who brought me the venison   27:33
I ate before you came? I blessed him, and it is he who has my blessing!"
When Esau heard the words of his father, he cried out with a great and   27:34
bitter cry, and said to his father, "Bless me, even me also, O my father."
Isaac said, "Your brother came with deceit and has taken your blessing."   27:35
Esau said, "Is he not rightly named Jacob? He has supplanted me   27:36
two times. He took away my birthright as firstborn, and now he has
taken my blessing. Have you not reserved a blessing for me?"
Isaac answered Esau, saying, "I have made him your lord,   27:37
and all his brethren I have given him for servants, and with corn
and wine have I sustained him. What can I do for you, my son?"
Esau said, "Have you but one blessing? Bless me, even me also,   27:38
O my father." And Esau lifted up his voice, and wept.
Isaac answered him, saying, "Behold, your dwelling shall be   27:39
the fatness of the earth, and the dew of heaven from above.
By your sword you shall live, and you shall serve your brother.   27:40
And it shall come to pass when you have dominion,
that you shall break his yoke from your neck."

Esau hated Jacob because of the blessing his father had given him,   27:41
and Esau said to himself, "The days of mourning for my father are at hand.
After that, I will kill my brother Jacob."
These words of Esau's heart were revealed to Rebekah. And she sent   27:42
for Jacob her younger son, and said to him, "Your brother Esau
is comforting himself by planning to kill you.
Therefore, obey my voice. Flee to Haran, to my brother Laban.   27:43

Stay with him until your brother's fury turns away,   27:44
until your brother's anger turns from you, and he forgets what   27:45
you have done to him. Then I will send for you and bring you back.
Why should I be deprived of you both in one day?"
So Rebekah said to Isaac, "I am weary of my life because of   27:46
the daughters of Heth. If Jacob takes a wife of the daughters of Heth,
such as the daughters of this land, what good is my life to me?"

Chapter 28

So Isaac called Jacob, and blessed him, and gave him these orders: 28:1
"Do not take a wife from the daughters of Heth, of Canaan.
Go to Padanaram, to the house of Bethuel, your mother's father,   28:2
and there take a wife from the daughters of Laban, your mother's brother.
And may Almighty God bless you, and make you fruitful,   28:3
and multiply you, that you may become a multitude of people.
And may he give to you the blessing of Abraham, and to your descendants,   28:4
that you may inherit the land wherein you now sojourn,
the land that God gave to Abraham."
And Isaac sent Jacob away, and he went to Padanaram, to Laban,   28:5
son of Bethuel, brother of Rebekah, Jacob and Esau's mother.
Now, Esau knew that Isaac had blessed Jacob and sent him   28:6
to Padanaram to take a wife, and that he ordered him,
saying, "Do not take a wife of the daughters of Canaan."
And he knew that Jacob obeyed his father and mother,   28:7
and was gone to Padanaram.
And Esau also knew that the daughters of Canaan   28:8
were not acceptable to Isaac, his father.
So Esau went to Ishmael, and took Mahalath, the daughter of Ishmael,   28:9
Abraham's son, the sister of Nebajoth, to be his wife,
in addition to the other wives he had.

Jacob went out from Beersheba, and went toward Haran.   28:10
He lighted upon a certain place, and tarried there all night because the sun   28:11
was set. He took stones for his pillows, and lay down in that place to sleep.
And he dreamed that a ladder rose up on the earth, and the top of it   28:12
reached to heaven, and the angels of God ascended and descended upon it.
And the Lord stood above it, and said,   28:13
"I am the Lord God of Abraham your father, and the God of Isaac.
The land whereon you now lie, I give to you and your seed.
Your seed shall be as numerous as the grains of dust of the earth. You   28:14
shall spread abroad to the west, and to the east, and to the north, and to
the south. In you and your seed, all the families of earth shall be blessed.
I am with you. I will guard you wherever you go, and I will bring you back   28:15
to this land. I will not leave you until I have done what I have promised."

When Jacob awoke from his sleep, he said,   28:16
"The Lord is truly in this place, and I knew it not."
He was afraid, and said, "How fearsome is this place!   28:17

This is none other but the house of God, and this is the gate of heaven!"

Jacob arose early in the morning and took the stone he had used | 28:18
for his pillow, and set it as a pillar, and poured oil on top of it.

He called that place Bethel, but the original name of that city was Luz. | 28:19

Jacob made a vow, saying, "If God will be with me, and will keep me | 28:20
in this way that I go, and will give me bread to eat, and clothes to wear,

so that I come again to my father's house in peace, | 28:21
then shall the Lord be my God.

And this stone, which I have set for a pillar, shall be God's house. | 28:22
And from all that you shall give me, I will surely give a tenth to you."

Chapter 29

Jacob went on his journey, and came to the land of the people of the east. | 29:1

He looked, and he beheld a well in the field, and there were three flocks | 29:2
of sheep laying by, for out of that well they watered the flocks.
And a great stone was upon the mouth of the well.

When all the flocks were gathered there, they rolled the stone | 29:3
from the well's mouth and watered the sheep.
Then they put the stone in place again upon the well's mouth.

Jacob said to the shepherds, "My brethren, where are you from?" | 29:4
They said, "We are from Haran."

Jacob asked them, "Do you know Laban, son of Nahor?" | 29:5
And they said, "We know him."

Jacob asked, "Is he well?" And they said, "He is well. | 29:6
And behold, Rachel his daughter comes now with their sheep."

Jacob said, "It is only midday, and not yet time to gather the animals home. | 29:7
Go ahead and water your sheep then set them out to pasture."

They said, "We cannot until all the flocks are gathered together | 29:8
and the stone is rolled from the well's mouth. Then we water the sheep."

While Jacob spoke with them, Rachel came | 29:9
with her father's sheep, for she kept them.

When Jacob saw Rachel, the daughter of Laban, his mother's brother, | 29:10
and saw the sheep of Laban, Jacob rolled the stone
from the mouth of the well and watered Laban's flock.

And Jacob kissed Rachel. And he lifted up his voice, and wept. | 29:11

Jacob told Rachel that he was her father's brethren, | 29:12
that he was Rebekah's son. And Rachel ran to tell her father.

When Laban heard the news of Jacob, his sister's son, he ran to meet him, | 29:13
and embraced him, and kissed him, and brought him to his house.
And Jacob told Laban all that had happened.

Laban said to him, "Surely you are my bone and my flesh." | 29:14
Jacob stayed with him for a month.

Then Laban said to Jacob, "Just because we are related, you should not | 29:15
have to work here for naught. Tell me, what shall your payment be?"

Now Laban had two daughters. The name of the elder was Leah, | 29:16
and the name of the younger was Rachel.

Leah was tender-eyed, but Rachel was beautiful and well-favored. | 29:17

Jacob loved Rachel. And he said, "I will serve you   29:18
seven years for Rachel, your younger daughter."
Laban said, "It is better that I give her to you than to another man.   29:19
Stay here and abide with me."

So Jacob served seven years for Rachel, and they seemed   29:20
to him but a few days, such was the love he had for her.
Then Jacob said to Laban, "My days are fulfilled.   29:21
Give me my wife, that I may go to her."
So Laban gathered together all the men, and made a feast.   29:22
And that night he took Leah his daughter, and brought   29:23
her to Jacob in the dark. And Jacob did lay with her.
And Laban gave Zilpah, his maid, to Leah for a handmaid.   29:24
But in the light of morning, Jacob saw that it was Leah!   29:25
And he said to Laban, "What have you done me?
Did I not serve you for Rachel? Why have you beguiled me?"
Laban said, "In our country, it is not the custom   29:26
to give the younger in marriage before the firstborn.
Fulfill Leah's week of wedding celebration and I will give you Rachel also.   29:27
Then you shall serve me yet another seven years."
Jacob agreed, and he fulfilled her week.   29:28
And Laban gave Jacob his daughter Rachel to be his wife also.
And Laban gave Bilhah, his maid, to Rachel for a handmaid.   29:29
Jacob went to Rachel also, and lay with her. He loved Rachel   29:30
more than Leah, and he served Laban seven more years.

When the Lord saw that Leah was unloved, he opened her womb.   29:31
But Rachel was left barren.
Leah conceived, and bore a son, and she named him Reuben, for she said,   29:32
"The Lord has seen my troubles. Now my husband will love me."
And she conceived again, and bore a son, and she said,   29:33
"Because the Lord heard that I was unloved,
he has given me this son also." And she named him Simeon.
And she conceived again, and bore a son, and she said,   29:34
"Now this time my husband will be joined to me,
because I have born him three sons." Therefore she named him Levi.
And she conceived again, and bore a son, and she said,   29:35
"Now will I praise the Lord." Therefore she named him Judah.
And she stopped bearing children.

Chapter 30

When Rachel saw that she bore Jacob no children, she envied her sister,   30:1
and said to Jacob, "Give me children or I will die."
Jacob became angry with Rachel, and said, "Am I in God's stead?   30:2
It is he who has withheld children from you."
She said, "Here is my maid Bilhah. Lay with her and she shall   30:3
give birth for me. Through her I may also have children."
So she gave him Bilhah as a wife. And Jacob lay with her.   30:4

And Bilhah conceived, and bore Jacob a son. 30:5

Rachel said, "God has judged me fair, and has heard my voice 30:6
and given me a son." Therefore she named him Dan.

Bilhah conceived again, and bore Jacob a second son. 30:7

And Rachel said, "I have wrestled greatly with my sister 30:8
and I have prevailed." And she named him Naphtali.

When Leah saw that she had stopped bearing, 30:9
she took Zilpah her maid, and gave her to Jacob as a wife.

And Zilpah, Leah's maid, bore Jacob a son. 30:10

Leah said, "What good fortune!" And she named him Gad. 30:11

And Zilpah bore Jacob a second son. 30:12

Leah said, "I am happy, for the women will say I am blessed." 30:13
And she named him Asher.

Reuben went out during wheat harvest and found mandrakes 30:14
in the field, and he took them to his mother Leah.
Rachel said to Leah, "I pray you, give me some of your son's mandrakes."

Leah said to her, "Is it a small matter that you have taken my husband? 30:15
Would you take my son's mandrakes also?" Rachel said, "Very well,
give me some mandrakes and he shall lay with you tonight."

When Jacob came in from the field that evening, Leah went to him 30:16
and said, "You must lay with me tonight, for I have paid for you
with my son's mandrakes." So Jacob lay with her that night.

And God heard Leah. She conceived, and bore Jacob a fifth son. 30:17

Leah said, "God has given me what I paid for by giving my maid 30:18
to my husband." And she named him Issachar.

And Leah conceived again, and bore Jacob a sixth son. 30:19

Leah said, "God has given me a good dowry. Now my husband will dwell 30:20
with me, because I have born him six sons." And she named him Zebulun.

And afterwards she bore a daughter, and named her Dinah. 30:21

Then God remembered Rachel, and heard her, and opened her womb. 30:22

She conceived, and bore a son. She said, "God has taken away my shame." 30:23

She named him Joseph, and said, "The Lord shall give me another son." 30:24

When Rachel had born Joseph, Jacob said to Laban, "Send me away, 30:25
that I may go to my own place, and to my own country.

Give me my wives and my children, for whom I have served you, 30:26
and let me go. For you know the service I have done you."

Laban said, "I pray you, if I have found favor in your eyes, stay. For it has 30:27
been revealed to me that the Lord has blessed me because of you."

Then Laban said, "Name your payment and I will give it." 30:28

Jacob said, "You know how hard I have worked for you, 30:29
and how well your livestock has done in my care.

Before I came you had little, and it has now increased 30:30
into a multitude, and the Lord has blessed you since my coming.
When shall I provide for my own house also?"

Laban said, "What can I pay you?" Jacob said, "Pay me no wages, 30:31
but if you grant me one thing, I will continue to shepherd your flock.

I will pass through all your flocks and herds today, taking from them 30:32

all the speckled and spotted cattle, and all the black
and brown sheep, and all the spotted and speckled goats.
These and any offspring like them shall be my payment.
So shall my righteousness answer for me in coming years.   30:33
When you check my flocks, every one that is not speckled or
spotted among the goats, and black or brown among the sheep,
shall be considered stolen by me."
Laban said, "Agreed. We will do as you say."   30:34

So Jacob removed that day all the he-goats that were banded   30:35
and colored, and all the she-goats that were speckled and spotted,
or had some white in it, and all the black and brown among the sheep,
and he gave them into the hands of his sons,
and sent them three days journey away.   30:36
Jacob stayed and shepherded the rest of Laban's flocks.
And Jacob cut young branches of green poplar, and hazelnut,   30:37
and chestnut trees. And he peeled the bark to make
streaks and bands in them, exposing the white of the braches.
And he set the branches he had peeled in the gutters   30:38
of the watering troughs where the flocks came for water,
because they often mated when they came to drink.
And because they looked upon these branches while they mated,   30:39
the females gave birth to banded, speckled, and spotted young.
Jacob kept these lambs as his. And he set the rams to face the   30:40
banded and brown females in the flock of Laban, and he kept
his own flocks by themselves, separate from Laban's.
Whenever the stronger livestock mated, Jacob laid the branches before 30:41
their eyes in the gutters, that they might conceive young
that looked like the branches.
But he did not do this with the feeble livestock.   30:42
So the feebler were Laban's, and the stronger were Jacob's.
And Jacob increased exceedingly, and had many cattle,   30:43
and maidservants, and manservants, and camels and asses.

Chapter 31

Jacob heard that Laban's sons were saying that Jacob had taken   31:1
all that was their father's, and from that gained his wealth.
And Jacob beheld the face of Laban, that it did not favor him as before. 31:2
The Lord said to Jacob, "Return to the land of your fathers,   31:3
and to your kindred, and I will be with you."
So Jacob called Rachel and Leah to the field of his flock,   31:4
and he said to them, "I see your father's countenance, that it does not 31:5
favor me as before. But the God of my father is with me.
And you know that with all my power I have served your father.   31:6
And that your father has deceived me, and changed my wages ten times. 31:7
But God suffered him not to hurt me.
If he said, 'The speckled shall be your payment,' the cattle bore speckled. 31:8
If he said, 'The banded shall be your pay,' the cattle all bore banded.

In this way, God has taken the cattle of your father, and given them to me. 31:9
One day, at the time the cattle conceived, I lifted up my eyes 31:10
and saw in a dream that, behold, the bulls
that mount the cattle were banded, speckled and striped.
And the angel of God spoke to me in the dream, saying, 31:11
'Jacob,' and I said, 'Here I am.'
And he said, 'Lift up your eyes and see—all the bulls 31:12
that mount the cattle are banded, speckled and striped.
For I have seen all that Laban does to you.
I am the God of Bethel, where you anointed the pillar, 31:13
and where you swore a vow to me. Now arise.
Get out of this land, and return to the land of your kindred.'"

Rachel and Leah answered saying, "Is there yet any 31:14
portion or inheritance for us in our father's house?
Are we not counted to him as strangers? For he has sold us, 31:15
and devoured the money he received—which is ours.
All the riches God has taken from our father are ours and our children's. 31:16
So then, whatever God has said to you, do."
Then Jacob rose up, and set his sons and his wives upon camels. 31:17
And he set out with all his cattle, and all the goods and livestock 31:18
he had acquired in Padanaram, to go to Isaac his father in Canaan.
But when Laban went out to shear his sheep, 31:19
Rachel had stolen the idols from her father's house.
Jacob went away without Laban the Syrian being aware of it, 31:20
for he told him nothing of it.
He fled with all that he had. And he passed over the river, 31:21
and headed toward Mount Gilead.

On the third day, Laban was told that Jacob had fled. 31:22
So Laban took his brethren and pursued after Jacob for seven days, 31:23
and they overtook him at Mount Gilead.
And God came to Laban in a dream by night and said, 31:24
"Take heed that you speak neither good nor bad to Jacob."
Laban overtook Jacob. Jacob had pitched his tent on the mount, 31:25
and so Laban and his brethren pitched on the mount.
Laban said to Jacob, "What have you done, that you have stolen away 31:26
unawares to me, and carried away my daughters,
as if captives taken with the sword?
Why did you leave secretly and steal away from me, and not tell me? 31:27
I would have sent you away with joy, songs, tambourines and harps.
You did not even let me kiss my sons and my daughters. 31:28
This was a foolish thing to do.

"It is in my power to do you harm, but the God of your father spoke to me 31:29
last night, saying, 'Speak neither good nor bad to Jacob.'
Now it seems you are going because you long for your father's house. 31:30
But why have you stolen my idols?"
Jacob answered, saying, "I left because I was afraid you might 31:31

take your daughters away from me by force.
But whoever you find with your idols, let him not live.   31:32
Before your brethren, discern what I have that is yours and take it."
For Jacob knew not that Rachel had stolen them.

So Laban went into Jacob's tent, and into Leah's tent,   31:33
and into the tents of the two maidservants, but he found them not.
Then he entered Rachel's tent.
Now, Rachel had taken the images and put them in the camel's furniture,   31:34
and sat upon them. And Laban searched all the tent, but found them not.
She said to her father, "Let it not displease my lord that I cannot   31:35
rise up before you, for the way of women is upon me."
And he searched, but found not the idols.
Then Jacob became angry and confronted Laban, saying,   31:36
"What is my trespass? What is my sin, that you so hotly pursued me?
Now that you have searched all my goods, what have you   31:37
found of yours? Set it here before my brethren and your brethren,
that they may judge between us.
These twenty years I have been with you, your ewes and your she-goats   31:38
have never miscarried, and I have never eaten a ram from your flock.
That which was killed by beasts I did not bring to you,   31:39
but made up for the loss myself. That which was stolen by thieves,
day or night, you demanded compensation from me.
Thus I was. In the day the heat consumed me, and the bitter cold   31:40
I endured by night. Sleep fled from my eyes.
I have been twenty years in your house. I served you fourteen years   31:41
for your two daughters, and six years for your cattle,
and you have changed my wages ten times.
If the God of my father, the God of Abraham and the fear of Isaac, had not   31:42
been with me, you would have sent me away empty-handed. God has seen
my affliction and the labor of my hands, and rebuked you last night."

Laban answered Jacob, saying, "These daughters are my daughters,   31:43
and these children are my children, and these cattle are my cattle,
and all that you see is mine. But what can I do today
for my daughters and the children they have born?
Now therefore come, let us make a covenant, you and me.   31:44
And let something be a witness between you and me."
So Jacob took a stone, and set it up for a pillar.   31:45
And he said to his brethren, "Gather stones." So they gathered stones   31:46
and made a mound. And they ate there by the mound.
Laban called it Jegarsahadutha. But Jacob called it Galeed.   31:47
Laban said, "This mound is a witness between me and you this day.   31:48
Therefore the mound shall be called Galeed,
and also Mizpah. For the Lord watches between me and you   31:49
when we are absent one from the other.
If you mistreat my daughters, or if you take other wives besides them,   31:50
though I am not there to see, God shall be a witness."

Then Laban said, "Behold this mound, and this pillar,   31:51
which I have cast between me and you.
This mound shall be witness, and this pillar shall be witness,   31:52
that I will not pass beyond this mound to you, and you shall not pass
beyond this mound and this pillar to me, for harm.
May the God of Abraham and the God of Nahor, the God of their father,   31:53
judge between us." And Jacob swore by the fear of his father Isaac.
Then Jacob offered sacrifice upon the mount, and called his brethren   31:54
to eat bread. And they ate bread, and they tarried all night in the mount.
Early in the morning Laban rose up and kissed his sons and his daughters,   31:55
and blessed them. Then Laban departed, and returned to his place.

Chapter 32

Jacob went on his way, and the agents of God met him.   32:1
When Jacob saw them, he said, "This is God's host."   32:2
And he named that place Mahanaim.
Then Jacob sent messengers before him to Esau, his brother,   32:3
in the land of Seir, in the country of Edom.
He commanded them, saying, "This is what you shall say to my lord Esau: 32:4
'Your servant Jacob says to you, "I have sojourned with Laban,
and stayed there until now.
I have oxen, asses, flocks, manservants and maidservants, and I have sent   32:5
these messengers to ask my lord if I might find grace in your sight."'
The messengers returned to Jacob, saying, "We went to your brother Esau,   32:6
and he now comes to meet you. There are four hundred men with him."
Then Jacob was greatly afraid and distressed. He divided the people   32:7
with him, and the flocks, and the herds, and the camels, into two bands.
He said, "If Esau attacks one band, the other band shall escape."   32:8
Jacob prayed, "O God of my father Abraham, God of my father Isaac,   32:9
O Lord who said to me, 'Return to your country, and your kindred
and I will deal well with you,'
I am not worthy of the least of all your mercies, or of the faith   32:10
you have shown your servant. For with only my staff
I have crossed over Jordan, and now I have become two bands.
Deliver me, I pray you, from the hand of my brother,   32:11
from the hand of Esau. For I fear that he will come and kill me,
and the mothers, and the children.
It was you who said to me, 'I will surely do good by you,   32:12
and I will make your seed as the sands of the sea,
which cannot be numbered for their multitudes.'"

Jacob slept there that night. Then he chose a gift for Esau   32:13
from that which he had with him:
Two hundred she-goats, twenty goats, two hundred ewes, twenty rams,   32:14
thirty nursing camels with their colts, forty cows, ten bulls,   32:15
twenty she-asses, and ten foals.
And he gave them to his servants, each herd by itself, and said,   32:16
"Go ahead of me, and keep some space between the herds."

He told the first herdsman, "When Esau meets you and asks,   32:17
'Whose servant are you? Where are you going? Whose animals are these?'
You shall say, 'They are your servant Jacob's. They are a present   32:18
sent to my lord Esau. Your servant Jacob is behind us.'"
And Jacob so commanded the second, and the third,   32:19
and all that followed the herds, saying,
"In this manner you shall speak to Esau when you meet him.
And be sure to say, 'Your servant Jacob is behind us.'"   32:20
For Jacob thought, "I will appease him with the gifts that go before me,
and when I come to face him, perhaps he will accept me."
Jacob sent the presents before him, and he stayed the night with his band.   32:21
And he arose in the night, and took his two wives, his two handmaids   32:22
and his eleven children to the ford of Jabbok.
And he helped them ford the river with everything he owned.   32:23

Jacob was left alone. And a man wrestled with him until dawn.   32:24
And when the man saw that he could not defeat Jacob,   32:25
he struck Jacob's hip out of joint as they wrestled.
The man said, "Let me go, for the day breaks."   32:26
Jacob said, "I will not let you go until you bless me."
The man said, "What is your name?" And he said, "Jacob."   32:27
The man said, "Your name shall no more be Jacob. It shall be Israel,   32:28
for you have struggled with God and with man, and you have prevailed."
Jacob said, "What is your name?" He said, "Why do you ask my name?"   32:29
And he blessed Jacob there in that place.
Jacob named that place Peniel, and said,   32:30
"I have seen God face to face, and my life is saved."
Jacob left Peniel as the sun rose upon him. He limped because of his hip.   32:31
Therefore, to this day, the children of Israel do not eat the meat   32:32
of the upper thigh, because that is where Jacob was struck.

Chapter 33

Jacob lifted up his eyes, and behold, Esau came, and with him   33:1
four hundred men. Jacob grouped the children with their mothers:
Leah, and Rachel, and the two handmaids.
He put the handmaids and their children in front, and Leah   33:2
and her children after, and Rachel and Joseph last.
He walked ahead of them, bowing himself to the ground seven times,   33:3
until he came near to his brother.
Esau ran to meet him, and embraced him,   33:4
and fell on his neck and kissed him. And they both wept.
Esau saw the women and children, and said, "Who are these with you?"   33:5
Jacob said, "The children whom God has graciously given your servant."
Then the handmaidens came near, they and their children, and bowed.   33:6
Then Leah with her children came near, and bowed.   33:7
After her came Joseph and Rachel, and they bowed.

Esau said, "What are all these herds that I met?" Jacob said,   33:8
"They are meant to find grace in the sight of my lord."
Esau said, "I have enough, my brother. Keep what you have for yourself."   33:9
Jacob said, "No, I pray you, if I have now found grace in your sight,   33:10
then receive my present from my hand. Seeing your face is like
seeing the face of God, and you are pleased with me.
I pray you, receive my blessing that I have brought to you,   33:11
for God has dealt graciously with me, and I have enough."
And he urged Esau. And Esau accepted.
Esau said, "Let us take our journey and go on. I will lead the way."   33:12
Jacob said, "My lord can see that the children are tender, and the flocks   33:13
and herds are with young. If the men should overdrive them
even for one day, all the flocks will die.
I pray you, my lord, travel ahead of your servant, and I will come   33:14
more slowly, according to the pace of the animals that
go before me and what the children are able to endure.
I will come to my lord in Seir."
Esau said, "I will leave you some of the men with me." Jacob said,   33:15
"What need is there? It is enough to find grace in the sight of my lord."
And so Esau left that day on his journey to Seir.   33:16

Jacob journeyed to Succoth, and built a house, and made shelters   33:17
for his animals. Therefore he named the place Succoth.
Then he went from Padanaram to Shalem, a city in Shechem,   33:18
in the land of Canaan, and pitched his tent outside the city.
He bought a field from the children of Hamor, Shechem's father,   33:19
for a hundred pieces of silver, and there pitched his tent.
And he erected there an altar, and called it Elelohe-Israel.   33:20

Chapter 34

Dinah, the daughter of Leah, who she bore to Jacob,   34:1
went out to see the daughters of the land.
When Shechem, son of Hamor the Hivite, leader of that country,   34:2
saw her, he took her and lay with her, and defiled her.
Then his heart cleaved unto Dinah, daughter of Jacob.   34:3
He fell in love, and he spoke tenderly to her.
Shechem said to his father Hamor, "Get me this girl for my wife."   34:4
Jacob heard that Shechem had defiled his daughter Dinah. His sons were   34:5
with his cattle in the field, so Jacob held his peace until they had come.
Hamor and his son Shechem went out to Jacob to talk with him.   34:6
The sons of Jacob came out of the field when they heard of it.   34:7
They were angry and outraged, because Shechem had disgraced Israel
by raping Jacob's daughter—a thing not to be done!
Hamor said, "The soul of my son Shechem longs for your daughter.   34:8
I pray you, give her to him for his wife.
And let our people be joined. Give your daughters unto us,   34:9
and take our daughters unto you.
Live with us. All the land shall be open to you.   34:10

Live here, trade here, acquire possessions and property here."
Shechem said to Dinah's father and brothers, "Let me find grace   34:11
in your eyes, and whatever you ask of me, I will give.
Ask me for as large a gift as you want, and I will give it.   34:12
Only give me this girl for my wife."

The sons of Jacob answered Shechem and Hamor deceitfully,   34:13
because Shechem had defiled their sister Dinah.
They said to them, "We cannot give our sister to one   34:14
who is uncircumcised, for that would be a disgrace to us.
But we will agree to this marriage if every male among you   34:15
will become like us, and be circumcised.
Then will we give our daughters unto you, and we will take your   34:16
daughters unto us, and we will dwell with you,
and we will become one people.
But if you will not agree to be circumcised,   34:17
then will we take our daughter, and we will be gone."
Their words were agreeable to Hamor and Shechem.   34:18
The young man did not delay in this, because he loved Jacob's daughter,   34:19
and he was the most honorable in his father's house.

So Hamor and Shechem his son went to the gate of their city,   34:20
and communed with the men there, saying,
"These men want peace. Let them live here, and trade here.   34:21
The land is large enough for all of us. Let us take their daughters
unto us for wives, and let us give them our daughters.
These men will consent to live with us, to be one people,   34:22
if every male among us be circumcised, as they are circumcised.
Will not their cattle and their goods and every beast of theirs   34:23
become ours? Let us consent, and they will dwell with us."
All the men agreed with Hamor, and every male was circumcised.   34:24
Then on the third day, when the men were sore from circumcision,   34:25
two of Jacob's sons, Simeon and Levi, Dinah's brothers, took up
their swords and attacked the city by surprise, and killed all the males.
They killed Hamor and Shechem his son with the edge of the sword,   34:26
and took Dinah out of Shechem's house.
When the other sons of Jacob came upon the dead,   34:27
they plundered the city because their sister had been defiled.
They took their sheep, and their oxen, and their asses,   34:28
and all that was in the city and the fields around.
They took all their wealth. They took all their children and all   34:29
their wives captive, and took even all that was in their houses.
Afterwards, Jacob said to Simeon and Levi, "You have caused trouble   34:30
for me, and made me a stench among the inhabitants of the land,
among the Canaanites and the Perizzites. I am few in number.
They shall gather together against me, and kill me.
I and my house shall be destroyed."
His sons said, "Should he treat our sister as a harlot?"   34:31

Chapter 35

God said to Jacob, "Go to Bethel and dwell there. Make there an altar   35:1
to the God who appeared to you when you fled from your brother Esau."
So Jacob said to his household, and to all who were with him, "Put away   35:2
your strange idols, purify yourselves, and put on clean clothes.
Let us arise and go to Bethel. I will make there an altar to the God   35:3
who answered me in the day of my distress,
and who has been with me wherever I have gone."
And they gave to Jacob all the strange idols in their hands, and all the   35:4
earrings in their ears, and Jacob hid them under the oak tree by Shechem.
And they journeyed. The terror of God was upon the cities   35:5
around them, so they did not pursue the sons of Jacob.
Jacob came to Luz, in the land of Canaan, which is Bethel,   35:6
he and all the people who were with him.
There he built an altar and called the place Elbethel,   35:7
because God appeared to him there when he fled from his brother.

Then Rebekah's nurse Deborah died, and she was buried   35:8
in Bethel under an oak. And it was called Allonbachuth.
God again appeared to Jacob, when he came out   35:9
of Padanaram, and blessed him.
God said, "Your name is Jacob, but no longer shall it be your name.   35:10
Israel is your name." And he named him Israel.
God said to him, "I am God Almighty. Be fruitful and multiply.   35:11
A nation, and a nation of nations, shall descend from you,
and kings shall be born of your seed.
The land that I gave to Abraham and Isaac, I now give to you.   35:12
And to your seed after you, I will also give the land."
Then God withdrew from him in the place where he spoke.   35:13

Jacob set up a pillar in the place where God talked with him,   35:14
a pillar of stone. And he poured an offering of wine,
and he poured oil upon the pillar.
Jacob named the place God spoke with him, Bethel.   35:15
Then they journeyed from Bethel. And while they were still   35:16
some distance from Ephrath, Rachel went into hard labor.
While she travailed, the midwife said to her,   35:17
"Fear not. You shall have another son."
As her soul departed her in death, Rachel named her son Benoni.   35:18
But his father called him Benjamin.
Rachel died, and she was buried on the way to Ephrath,   35:19
which is Bethlehem. Jacob set a pillar upon her grave,
which is the marker of Rachel's grave to this day.   35:20

Israel continued his journey, and he pitched his tent   35:21
on the other side of the tower of Edar.
While Israel dwelt in that land, Reuben went unto Bilhah,   35:22
his father's concubine, and lay with her. And Israel heard of it.

The sons of Jacob were twelve:

The sons of Leah were Reuben, Jacob's firstborn,　　35:23
and Simeon, Levi, Judah, Issachar and Zebulun.

The sons of Rachel were Joseph and Benjamin.　　35:24

The sons of Bilhah, Rachel's handmaid, were Dan and Naphtali.　　35:25

The sons of Zilpah, Leah's handmaid, were Gad and Asher.　　35:26
These were the sons of Jacob, born to him in Padanaram.

Jacob came home to Isaac his father, to Mamre, to the city of Arbah,　　35:27
which is Hebron, where Abraham and Isaac sojourned.

The days of Isaac were a hundred and eighty years.　　35:28

Then Isaac gave up the ghost and died.　　35:29
He was gathered unto his ancestors, being old and full of days.
He was buried by his sons Esau and Jacob.

Chapter 36

These were the generations of Esau, who is Edom.　　36:1

Esau chose his wives from the daughters of Canaan:　　36:2
Adah, daughter of Elon the Hittite, and Aholibamah,
daughter of Anah and granddaughter of Zibeon the Hivite,

and Bashemath, daughter of Ishmael and sister of Nebajoth.　　36:3

Adah bore Eliphaz to Esau. Bashemath bore Reuel.　　36:4

Aholibamah bore Jeush, Jaalam and Korah. These were the sons of Esau,　　36:5
who were born to him in the land of Canaan.

Esau took his wives, and his sons and daughters, and all the persons　　36:6
of his house, and his cattle, and all his beasts, and all the goods
he had acquired in the land of Canaan,
and went to another country, away from his brother Jacob.

For their wealth was too great for them to dwell together,　　36:7
and the land where they sojourned could not support all their cattle.

So Esau, who is Edom, went to dwell in Mount Seir.　　36:8

These were the generations of Esau, father of the Edomites, in Mount Seir:　　36:9

The names of Esau's sons were Eliphaz, son of Adah,　　36:10
and Reuel, son of Bashemath.

The sons of Eliphaz were Teman, Omar, Zepho, Gatam and Kenaz.　　36:11

Timna was a concubine to Eliphaz, Esau's son, and she bore Amalek　　36:12
to Eliphaz. These were the sons of Esau's wife Adah.

The sons of Reuel were Nahath, Zerah, Shammah and Mizzah.　　36:13
These were the sons of Esau's wife Bashemath.

The sons of Esau's wife Aholibamah, daughter of Anah　　36:14
and granddaughter of Zibeon, were Jeush, Jaalam and Korah.

The tribal chiefs from Esau's son Eliphaz, his firstborn,　　36:15
were chief Teman, chief Omar, chief Zepho, chief Kenaz,

chief Korah, chief Gatam and chief Amalek. These were the chiefs　　36:16
who came of Eliphaz in the land of Edom.
These were the sons of Esau's wife Adah.

The tribal chiefs from Esau's son Reuel, were chief Nahath,　　36:17

chief Zerah, chief Shammah and chief Mizzah.
These were the chiefs who came of Reuel in the land of Edom.
These were the sons of Esau's wife Bashemath.
These were the chiefs of Esau's wife Aholibamah: Chief Jeush,   36:18
chief Jaalam and chief Korah. These were the chiefs that came
of Aholibamah, the daughter of Esau's wife Anah.
These were the sons of Esau, and these were their chiefs.   36:19

The sons of Seir the Horite, who inhabited the land,   36:20
were Lotan, Shobal, Zibeon, Anah,
Dishon, Ezer and Dishan. These were the chiefs of the Horites,   36:21
the children of Seir in the land of Edom.
The children of Lotan were Hori and Hemam. Lotan's sister was Timna.   36:22
The children of Shobal were Alvan, Manahath, Ebal, Shepho and Onam.   36:23
The children of Zibeon were Ajah and Anah. This was the Anah who found   36:24
the springs in the wilderness as he fed the asses of his father Zibeon.
The children of Anah were Dishon and Aholibamah, the daughter of Anah.   36:25
The children of Dishon were Hemdan, Eshban, Ithran and Cheran.   36:26
The children of Ezer were Bilhan, Zaavan and Akan.   36:27
The children of Dishan were Uz and Aran.   36:28
The chiefs who came of the Horites were chief Lotan,   36:29
chief Shobal, chief Zibeon, chief Anah,
chief Dishon, chief Ezer and chief Dishan. These were the chiefs   36:30
that came of Hori, according to their tribes in the land of Seir.

These were the kings that reigned in the land of Edom,   36:31
before any king reigned over the children of Israel:
Bela the son of Beor reigned in Edom. The name of his city was Dinhabah.   36:32
Bela died, and Jobab son of Zerah of Bozrah, reigned in his stead.   36:33
Jobab died, and Husham of Temani reigned in his stead.   36:34
Husham died, and Hadad son of Bedad, who defeated Midian   36:35
in Moab, reigned in his stead. The name of his city was Avith.
Hadad died, and Samlah of Masrekah reigned in his stead.   36:36
Samlah died, and Saul of Rehoboth by the River reigned in his stead.   36:37
Saul died, and Baalhanan son of Achbor reigned in his stead.   36:38
Baalhanan son of Achbor died, and Hadar reigned in his stead.   36:39
The name of his city was Pau. His wife was Mehetabel,
daughter of Matred and granddaughter of Mezahab.
These were the names of the chiefs that came of Esau,   36:40
according to their families, after their places, by their names:
Chief Timnah, chief Alvah, chief Jetheth,
chief Aholibamah, chief Elah, chief Pinon, chief Kenaz,   36:41
chief Teman, chief Mibzar, chief Magdiel and chief Iram.   36:42
These were the tribal chiefs of Edom, according to their settlements   36:43
in the land they possessed. This was Esau, father of the Edomites.

Chapter 37

Jacob lived in the land where his father sojourned, in the land of Canaan. 37:1
These were the generations of Jacob.
Joseph, a boy of seventeen, took care of the flock with his brothers, 37:2
the sons of Bilhah and Zilpah, his father's wives. And Joseph brought
to his father a bad report about what his brothers were doing.
Israel loved Joseph more than all his children, because he was 37:3
the son of his old age. And he made him a coat of many colors.
His brothers saw that their father loved him more than them, 37:4
and they hated him, and could not speak peaceably to him.
Joseph dreamed a dream, and he told his brothers of it, 37:5
and they hated him even more.
Joseph said, "Hear, I pray you, this dream I have dreamed: 37:6
We were binding sheaves in the field, and my sheaf arose and stood 37:7
upright. Your sheaves stood upright around it, and bowed to my sheaf."
His brothers said, "Shall you reign over us? Shall you have dominion 37:8
over us?" And they hated him even more for his dreams, and his words.

Joseph dreamed another dream, and told it to his brothers. 37:9
He said, "I have dreamed another dream, and behold, the sun
and the moon and the eleven stars made obeisance to me."
He told this to his father and his brothers. And his father rebuked him, 37:10
saying, "What is this dream you have dreamed? Shall I and your mother
and your brothers indeed bow down to the ground to you?"
His brothers envied him, but his father kept his words in mind. 37:11
And his brothers went to feed their father's flock in Shechem. 37:12
Israel said to Joseph, "Do not your brothers feed the flock in Shechem? 37:13
Come, I will send you to them." Joseph said, "I am ready."
Israel said, "Go, I pray you, see if all is well with your brothers 37:14
and with the flocks, and bring me word again."
So he sent him out of the valley of Hebron, and he went to Shechem.
And a man found him wandering in the field, 37:15
and asked him, "What are you looking for?"
Joseph said, "My brothers. I pray you, tell me where they feed their flocks." 37:16
The man said, "They have departed from here. I heard them say, 'Let us go 37:17
to Dothan.'" So Joseph went after his brothers and found them in Dothan.

When they saw Joseph afar off, even before 37:18
he came near to them, they conspired to kill him.
They said one to another, "Behold, this dreamer comes. 37:19
Come, let us kill him and cast him into a dry well. We will say, 'An evil 37:20
beast has devoured him.' Then we shall see what becomes of his dreams."
When Reuben heard this, he delivered Joseph 37:21
from their hands, saying, "Let us not kill him."
Reuben said, "Shed no blood. Cast him into a well in the desert, 37:22
but lay no hand on him." He said this that he might save Joseph
from their hands and deliver him back to his father.
When Joseph came to his brothers, they stripped him 37:23

of his coat, his coat of many colors that he wore,
and they cast him into a well, which was empty. There was no water in it.　37:24
Then they sat down to eat bread. And they looked up and saw　37:25
a band of Ishmaelites coming from Gilead, with camels bearing
spices and balm and myrrh, on their way to Egypt.
Judah said to his brothers, "What profit us　37:26
if we kill our brother and conceal his blood?
Let us sell him to the Ishmaelites, and not lay our hands on him.　37:27
For he is our brother and our flesh." And his brothers agreed.

The Ishmaelites were merchantmen from Midian, and they lifted　37:28
Joseph up out of the well. So Joseph was sold to the Midianites
for twenty pieces of silver. And they took him into Egypt.
When Reuben returned, Joseph was not in the well!　37:29
And Reuben rent his clothes. He went to his brothers and said,
"The boy is not there! What shall we do?"　37:30
So they took Joseph's coat and killed a young goat,　37:31
then they dipped the coat in the blood.
They took the coat of many colors to their father, and said,　37:32
"We found this. Do you know whether it is your son's coat?"
And he knew it. He said, "It is my son's coat. An evil beast　37:33
has devoured him. Without doubt, Joseph has been torn to pieces."
And Jacob rent his clothes, and put sackcloth around his waist,　37:34
and he mourned his son for many days.
All his sons and daughters came to comfort him. But he refused　37:35
to be comforted. He said, "I will go to the underworld
mourning my son." And Joseph's father wept for him.
Meanwhile, the Midianites sold Joseph in Egypt, to Potiphar,　37:36
an officer of Pharaoh and captain of the guard.

Chapter 38

Judah moved away from his brothers and went to stay　38:1
with an Adullamite named Hirah.
There Judah saw the daughter of Shuah, a Canaanite.　38:2
He took her for his wife, and went to her and lay with her.
She conceived, and bore a son, and she named him Er.　38:3
She conceived again, and bore a son, and she named him Onan.　38:4
She conceived yet again, and bore a son, and she named him Shelah.　38:5
She was in Chezib when she bore him.
Judah chose a wife for Er, his firstborn, whose name was Tamar.　38:6
But Er was wicked in the sight of the Lord, and the Lord killed him.　38:7
So Judah said to Onan, "Go to your brother's wife and lay with her.　38:8
Produce a descendent for your brother."
But Onan knew that the child would not be his, so when he lay　38:9
with his brother's wife, he spilled his seed onto the ground,
lest he should give a descendant to his brother.
This so displeased the Lord that he killed Onan also.　38:10
So Judah said to Tamar, "Remain a widow in your father's house until　38:11

my son Shelah is grown, unless he perhaps dies as his brothers did."
And Tamar went to live in her father's house.

Time passed, and Judah's wife, the daughter of Shuah, died.   38:12
After Judah was comforted, he went to his sheepshearers
at Timnath, he and his friend Hirah the Adullamite.
And someone told Tamar, saying, "Behold, your father-in-law   38:13
went to Timnath to shear his sheep."
So she put away her widow's garments, and she decorated herself,   38:14
and covered her face with a veil. Then she went and sat near the gate
of Enaim, which is on the way to Timnath. For she was angry that Shelah
was a grown man, yet Judah had not given her to him as a wife.
When Judah saw her, he thought she was a harlot,   38:15
because she was decorated and her face was veiled.
He turned to her, not knowing she was his daughter-in-law,   38:16
and said, "I pray you, let me come unto you."
Tamar said, "What will you give to lay with me?"
Judah said, "I will send you a young goat from the flock."   38:17
Tamar said, "Will you give me a pledge till you send it?"
Judah said, "What pledge shall I give?" She said, "Your signet ring   38:18
and cord, and the staff you carry." So he gave them to her,
and he lay with her, and she conceived by him.
Then she arose and went away. And she took off her veil,   38:19
and put on the garments of her widowhood.

Judah sent his friend the Adullamite with the young goat, to receive   38:20
his pledge back from the woman's hand, But he found her not.
He asked the men of the place, "Where is the harlot who was   38:21
by the wayside?" They said, "There was no harlot there."
So he returned to Judah, and said, "I cannot find her,   38:22
and the men of the place said there was no harlot there."
Judah said, "Let her keep my things, lest I become a laughingstock.   38:23
I sent the goat but you could not find her."
Three months after, Judah was told, "Your daughter-in-law   38:24
has played the harlot, and she is with child by whoredom."
Judah said, "Bring her forth, and let her be burnt."
When she was brought out, she sent a message to her father-in-law,   38:25
saying, "I am pregnant by the man who owns this signet, cord and staff.
I pray you, acknowledge who owns these."
Judah acknowledged them, and said, "She's been more righteous than me,   38:26
for I did not give her to my son Shelah." Judah did not lay with her again.
And in the time of Tamar's travail, twins were in her womb.   38:27
When she delivered, one put out his hand, and the midwife   38:28
tied a scarlet thread on it, saying, "This one came out first."
But he drew back his hand, and behold, the other came out.   38:29
The midwife said, "How have you broken out first?"
Therefore he was named Pharez.
Afterward his brother came out, with the scarlet thread on his hand.   38:30
He was named Zarah.

Chapter 39

When Joseph was taken to Egypt, Potiphar, an officer of Pharaoh   39:1
and captain of the guard, an Egyptian, bought him
from the Ishmaelites who had brought him there.
And the Lord was with Joseph. He became a prosperous man,   39:2
and he served in the house of his master, the Egyptian.
His master saw that the Lord was with Joseph,   39:3
and that the Lord made all that he did prosper.
So Joseph found grace in Potiphar's sight, and became   39:4
his trusted servant. Potiphar made him overseer of his house,
and put him in charge of all that he owned.
From the time he made Joseph overseer of his house and all that he had,   39:5
the Lord blessed the Egyptian's house for Joseph's sake. And the blessing
of the Lord was upon all that he had in his house, and in his fields.
Potiphar gave all that he had into Joseph's care,   39:6
and did not concern himself with anything except the food he ate.

Now, Joseph was a handsome man, both in form and face.
His master's wife cast her eyes upon Joseph, and she said, "Lie with me."   39:7
But he refused. He said, "My master has me as his servant, and he knows   39:8
not what goes on in his house. He has placed all that he has in my charge.
There is none in this house greater than me.   39:9
He has withheld nothing from me but you, because you are his wife.
How can I do this great wickedness, and sin against God?"
Yet every day she asked him again to lie with her,   39:10
but he did not listen, and did not lie with her or be with her.
Then one day Joseph came into the house to do business,   39:11
and none of the other men of the house were there.
And she grabbed him by his garment, saying, "Lie with me!"   39:12
But he freed himself and fled, leaving his garment in her hand.
And when he left his garment in her hand and fled,   39:13
she called to the men of her house, and spoke to them, saying,   39:14
"See, he has brought in a Hebrew to mock us.
He came unto me to lie with me, and I cried with a loud voice.
When he heard my voice cry out, he fled and left his garment with me."   39:15
And she laid up his garment by her, until his lord came home.   39:16
Then she spoke to him, saying, "The Hebrew servant   39:17
 you brought to us came unto me to mock me.
And I cried out, and he fled, leaving his garment with me."   39:18

When Joseph's master heard the words of his wife, saying,   39:19
"This is what your servant did to me," he became furious.
And he put Joseph in prison, in the place where   39:20
Pharaoh's prisoners were held. So Joseph was a prisoner.
But the Lord was with Joseph, and showed him mercy,   39:21
and gave him favor in the sight of the keeper of the prison.
The keeper of the prison put all the prisoners under Joseph's authority,   39:22
and whatever was done, Joseph was in charge of it.

The keeper of the prison did not concern himself with anything   39:23
in Joseph's charge, because the Lord was with Joseph,
and whatever Joseph did, the Lord made prosper.

Chapter 40

Some time after, both the chief wine steward, and the chief baker   40:1
for Pharaoh offended their lord, the king of Egypt.
And Pharaoh was angry with his two servants,   40:2
the chief wine steward and the chief baker.
He put them in the custody of the captain of the guard,   40:3
in the prison where Joseph was held.
The captain charged Joseph with them, and Joseph   40:4
attended them, and they continued a season in custody.
And they both dreamed a dream the same night, each dream   40:5
having its own meaning for the Pharaoh's wine steward,
and the baker, who were held there in prison.
When Joseph went in to them in the morning, he saw they were troubled.   40:6
He asked the Pharaoh's servants who were in custody with him,   40:7
"Why are your faces downcast today?"
They said, "We each have had a dream, but there is no one   40:8
to interpret them." Joseph said, "Do not interpretations belong to God?
I pray you, tell me your dreams."

So the wine steward told his dream to Joseph: "In my dream a vine   40:9
was before me, and the vine had three branches. The branches budded,   40:10
and blossoms shot forth, and clusters brought forth ripe grapes.
Pharaoh's cup was in my hand, and I took the grapes and pressed them   40:11
into Pharaoh's cup, and I gave the cup into Pharaoh's hand."
Joseph said to him, "This is the interpretation of your dream: 40:12
The three branches are three days.
After three days Pharaoh shall lift up your head and restore you   40:13
to your position, and you will deliver Pharaoh's cup into his hand,
as you did when you were chief wine steward.
But remember me when it is well with you, and show kindness to me,   40:14
I pray you. Make mention of me to Pharaoh, and get me out of this prison.
For I was stolen away out of the land of the Hebrews, and here also   40:15
I have done nothing that they should put me in prison."
When the baker saw that the interpretation was good,   40:16
he said to Joseph, "In my dream I had three white baskets on my head.
In the top basket there were of all manner of baked goods for Pharaoh.   40:17
And birds came and ate them out of the basket."
Joseph said to him, "This is the interpretation of your dream: 40:18
The three baskets are three days.
After three days Pharaoh shall cut off your head and hang you   40:19
from a tree, and birds will come and eat the flesh of your body."

And so it was that the third day was Pharaoh's birthday,   40:20
and he gave a feast for all his servants.

And there he gave audience to the wine steward and the baker.
He restored the chief wine steward to his place,   40:21
and he again gave Pharaoh's cup into his hand.
And he hanged the baker, as Joseph had interpreted.   40:22
But the wine steward remembered not Joseph. He forgot him.   40:23

Chapter 41

Two years later, Pharaoh dreamed that he stood by the Nile.   41:1
And there came up out of the river seven   41:2
healthy fattened cows, and they fed in a meadow.
Then seven other cows, sickly and thin, came up out of the river,   41:3
and stood by the fattened cows at the edge of the river.
The seven sickly thin cows ate up the seven healthy fattened cows.   41:4
And Pharaoh awoke.
Then he slept again and dreamed a second time, and beheld   41:5
seven ears of corn come up on one stalk, full and good.
Then seven more ears, thin, and scorched   41:6
by the east wind, sprung up after them.
And the seven thin ears devoured the seven full ears.   41:7
Then Pharaoh awoke, and beheld it was a dream.

And his spirit was troubled, and he sent for all the magicians   41:8
and all the wise men of Egypt. And Pharaoh told them his dreams.
But no one could interpret them for Pharaoh.
Then the chief wine steward spoke to Pharaoh, saying,   41:9
"I now remember a promise I failed to keep:
When Pharaoh was angry with your servant, you sent me   41:10
and the chief baker to the prison of the captain of the guard.
And we each dreamed a dream the same night, he and I,   41:11
and each dream had its own meaning.
There was a young man with us, a Hebrew, a servant   41:12
to the captain of the guard. And we told him our dreams,
and he interpreted to each of us the meaning of our dreams.
And it came to pass just as he interpreted to us.   41:13
Pharaoh restored me to my position, and hanged the chief baker."

So Pharaoh sent for Joseph, and they quickly brought him from prison.   41:14
He shaved himself, and changed his clothes, and went unto Pharaoh.
Pharaoh said to him, "I have dreamed a dream that none   41:15
can interpret, and I have heard that you can interpret dreams."
Joseph answered Pharaoh, saying, "It is not from me.   41:16
God shall give Pharaoh an answer of peace."
Pharaoh said to Joseph, "In my dream I stood upon the bank of the river.   41:17
And there came up out of the river seven cows,   41:18
healthy and fattened, and they fed in a meadow.
Then seven other cows came up after them, sickly and thin,   41:19
worse than any I have ever seen in Egypt.
The sickly cows ate up the fattened cows,   41:20

and after they had eaten them, I could not tell they had eaten them, 41:21
for they were still as thin as before. Then I awoke.
Then I slept again, and dreamed, and in my dream 41:22
seven ears of corn came up in one stalk, full and good.
Then seven ears more came up, withered, thin, blasted by the east wind. 41:23
And the thin ears devoured the good ears. 41:24
I told this to the magicians, but none could interpret it to me."

Joseph said to Pharaoh, "The two dreams of Pharaoh are one dream. 41:25
God has shown Pharaoh what he is about to do.
The seven good cows and the seven good ears are seven years of plenty. 41:26
The two dreams are one.
The seven sickly cows that came up, and the seven thin ears 41:27
blasted by the east wind, are seven years of famine.
This is just as I have told Pharaoh. 41:28
What God is about to do, he has shown to Pharaoh.
There will come seven years of great plenty throughout all Egypt. 41:29
Then there shall arise after them seven years of famine. All the plenty 41:30
in the land of Egypt shall be forgotten, and famine shall consume the land.
Plenty shall neither be known nor remembered in the land, 41:31
because the famine that follows will be so grievous.
The reason the dream was given to Pharaoh twice is that this is firmly 41:32
established by God, and God will soon bring it to pass.

"Therefore let Pharaoh find a man who is discreet and wise, 41:33
and give him authority over the land of Egypt.
Let Pharaoh also appoint officers to take up a fifth part 41:34
of the harvest of the land of Egypt in the seven years of plenty.
Let them gather food from the good years and store it under 41:35
the hand of Pharaoh. Let them store food for the cities.
That food should be stored for the seven years of famine that will come, 41:36
so that Egypt will not perish from famine."
This plan was good in the eyes of Pharaoh, and in the eyes of his servants. 41:37
Pharaoh said to his servants, "Can we find another man such as this one, 41:38
a man in whom the spirit of God lives?"
Pharaoh said to Joseph, "Since God has shown you all this, 41:39
there is none so discreet and wise as you.
You shall be in charge of my kingdom, and my people shall be ruled 41:40
by your word. Only I, the enthroned king, will be greater than you."
Then Pharaoh said to Joseph, 41:41
"I now give you charge over all the land of Egypt."
Pharaoh took his ring from his hand and put it on Joseph's hand. And he 41:42
arrayed him in clothes of fine linen, and put a gold chain around his neck.
He put Joseph in his second-best chariot, and criers went before him, 41:43
crying, "Bow down." Thus Pharaoh made him governor over all of Egypt.
And Pharaoh said to Joseph, "I am Pharaoh, and without your approval, 41:44
no man shall lift his hand or foot in all of Egypt."
Pharaoh called Joseph Zaphnathpaaneah, and he gave him Asenath, 41:45
the daughter of Potipherah, priest of On, to be his wife.

And Joseph went out over all the land of Egypt.
Joseph was thirty years old when he stood before Pharaoh, king of Egypt.   41:46
Joseph left the presence of Pharaoh, and traveled throughout all of Egypt.

In those seven years of plenty the earth produced by handfuls.   41:47
Joseph gathered up the food of those seven years of plenty in Egypt,   41:48
and stored the food in the cities. In each city he laid up
the food produced from the fields around it.
The grain he stored was like the sands of the sea, so much that   41:49
he stopped counting, for it was beyond numbering.
Before the years of famine came, his wife Asenath, daughter   41:50
of Potipherah, priest of On, bore two sons unto Joseph.
Joseph named the firstborn Manasseh, for he said,   41:51
"God has made me forget my troubles caused by my father's house."
He named the second son Ephraim,   41:52
"For God has caused me to be fruitful in the land of my affliction."

The seven years of plenty in the land of Egypt ended.   41:53
Then the seven years of dearth began, just as Joseph had said.   41:54
The dearth was in all lands, but in Egypt there was bread.
Then the land of Egypt became famished, and the people   41:55
cried to Pharaoh for bread. And Pharaoh said to all Egyptians,
"Go to Joseph, and whatever he says to you, do."
The famine was over all the face of the earth.   41:56
Joseph opened all the storehouses, and sold to the Egyptians,
for the famine waxed great in the land of Egypt.
Then all countries came into Egypt to buy grain from Joseph,   41:57
because the famine was so great in all the lands.

Chapter 42

When Jacob heard that there was grain in Egypt, he said to his sons,   42:1
"Why are you standing around looking at one another?
I have heard there is grain in Egypt.   42:2
Go there and buy grain for us, that we may live, not die."
So ten of Joseph's brothers went to buy grain in Egypt.   42:3
But Jacob did not send Joseph's brother Benjamin,   42:4
for he feared some harm might befall him.
And the sons of Israel came to Egypt with all the others to buy grain,   42:5
for the famine was great in the land of Canaan.

Now, the governor over all of Egypt was Joseph, and it was he   42:6
who sold to all the people who came. And Joseph's brothers came,
and they bowed down before him, their faces on the earth.
Joseph saw they were his brothers, but he acted as a stranger,   42:7
and spoke roughly to them, saying, "Where are you from?"
They said, "From the land of Canaan. We have come to buy food."
Joseph knew his brothers, but they knew him not.   42:8
And Joseph remembered the dreams he dreamed of them, and said,   42:9
"You are spies, come to find the weaknesses of this land."

They said, "No, my lord. Your servants come just to buy food.	42:10
We are all brethren, and we are honest men. We are not spies."	42:11
Joseph said, "No, you come to see the weak spots of the land."	42:12
They said, "We are twelve brothers, sons of one man in the land of Canaan.	42:13
The youngest is this day with our father, and one is no longer living."
Joseph said, "It is as I have said. You are spies.	42:14
But here is how you may prove yourselves: On the Pharaoh's life,	42:15
you shall not leave here until your youngest brother comes.
Send one of you to fetch your brother, and the rest shall be kept in prison.	42:16
We shall see if your words be proved, if there is any truth in you,
else by the Pharaoh's life, you surely are spies."
And he put them all together to prison for three days.	42:17

On the third day Joseph said to them,	42:18
"Do this and you will live, for I am a God-fearing man:
If you are honest men, let one of you be kept in prison	42:19
and the rest of you take grain to the hungry of your houses.
But bring your youngest brother to me, so that your words be verified.	42:20
Do this and you will not die." And they agreed.
They said to each other, "We are guilty concerning our brother,	42:21
in that we saw the anguish of his soul when he begged us,
but we listened not. Therefore this distress is come upon us."
Reuben said, "Did I not tell you, 'Do not sin against this boy'?	42:22
But you listened not. Now is the reckoning for his blood."
They did not know that Joseph understood them,	42:23
for he had spoken to them through an interpreter.
And Joseph went away from them and wept. When he returned again,	42:24
he spoke with them, then took Simeon and bound him before their eyes.
Then Joseph ordered their sacks to be filled with grain,	42:25
and every man's money to be restored into his sack,
and to give them food for their journey. And thus it was done.
They loaded their asses with the grain and departed.	42:26
When they stopped for the night, one of them opened a sack	42:27
to feed his ass and saw the money, for it was at the top of the sack.
He said , "My money is restored. It is in my sack!" And their hearts	42:28
failed them, and they were afraid, saying, "What has God done to us?"

When they came to Jacob their father, in the land of Canaan,	42:29
they told him all that befell them, saying,
"The man who is the lord of the land spoke roughly to us,	42:30
and took us for spies of the country.
We said to him, 'We are honest men. We are not spies.	42:31
We are twelve brothers, sons of our father. One no longer lives,	42:32
and the youngest is with our father in the land of Canaan.'
And the man, the lord of the country, said to us, 'Hereby shall	42:33
I know that you are true men: Leave one of your brothers here with me,
take food for the famine of your households, and go.
Then bring your youngest brother to me. By this I shall know	42:34
you are not spies, but that you are true men.

And I will return your brother, and you may trade in this land.'"
Then they opened their sacks, and behold, every man's money   42:35
was in his sack. And when both they and their father
saw the bundles of money, they were afraid.
Jacob their father said to them, "You have bereaved me of my children.   42:36
Joseph is gone and Simeon is gone, and now you would
take Benjamin away. I am the one who suffers!"
Reuben said to him, "Kill my two sons if I do not bring him back to you.   42:37
Put him in my care and I will return him to you."
But Jacob said, "My son shall not go with you, for his brother is dead   42:38
and he is all I have left. Something might befall him on the way,
and my old age and sorrow would send me to the grave."

Chapter 43

And the famine waxed sore in the land.   43:1
When they had eaten up the grain they had brought out of Egypt,   43:2
their father said to them, "Go again, buy us a little food."
Judah said to him, "The man did solemnly warn us, saying,   43:3
'You shall not see my face unless your brother is with you.'
If you will send our brother with us, we will go and buy food.   43:4
But if you will not send him, we will not go. For the man said,   43:5
'You shall not see my face unless your brother is with you.'"
Israel said, "Why were you so cruel to me,   43:6
to tell the man that you had another brother?"
They said, "The man asked us directly about ourselves and our kindred,   43:7
saying, 'Is your father yet alive? Do you have another brother?'
We just answered his questions. How could we know
he would say, 'Bring your brother here'?"
Judah said to Israel his father, "Send the boy with me and we will go,   43:8
that we may live and not die—ourselves, and you, and our children.
I will be sure of his safety, and you can hold me responsible.   43:9
If I do not bring him back to you, and place him
here before you, then let me bear the blame forever.
If we had not delayed, we would have returned twice by now."   43:10
Israel said, "If it must be so, then do this: Take the best products   43:11
of our land with you. Give the man a present—
a little balm, a little honey, spices, myrrh, nuts, almonds.
Take double the money, and take back the money that was in your sacks.   43:12
Perhaps it was an oversight.
Now take your brother and go again to the man.   43:13
And may God Almighty give you mercy before the man,   43:14
that he may send back Simeon and Benjamin. As for me,
if I must be bereaved of my children, then I shall be bereaved."

So his sons took the gift, and double the money, and Benjamin,   43:15
and went to Egypt. And they received an audience with Joseph.
When Joseph saw Benjamin with them, he said to his chief servant,   43:16
"Take these men to my house. Slaughter an animal and prepare it,

for these men shall dine with me at noon."
The servant did as Joseph ordered. He brought the men to Joseph's house. 43:17
And they were afraid because they were being brought to Joseph's house. 43:18
They said, "Because of the money that was returned in our sacks
the first time, we have been brought here, that he may overpower us,
and capture us, and make slaves of us and steal our asses."
So they went to the steward of Joseph's house, 43:19
and spoke with him at the door of the house, saying,
"O sir, we came here once before and bought food. 43:20
And when we stopped for the night, we opened our sacks 43:21
and every man's money was in the mouth of his sack—
our money in full weight. Now we have brought it back.
And other money have we brought in our hands to buy food. 43:22
We do not know who put our money in our sacks."
The steward said, "Peace be to you, fear not. Your God, 43:23
and the God of your father, must have put treasure in your sacks.
I received your payment." Then he brought Simeon out to them.
And he took them all into Joseph's house. And he gave them water 43:24
To wash their feet. And he gave their asses feed.

Then they made ready their gift before Joseph came at noon, 43:25
for they heard that they would eat bread there.
When Joseph came home, they presented him the gift 43:26
they had brought, and bowed low before him.
Joseph asked them of their welfare, and said, "Is your father well, 43:27
the old man of whom you spoke? Does he yet live?"
They answered, "Your servant our father is in good health." 43:28
And they bowed down their heads, and made obeisance.
Then Joseph saw his brother Benjamin, his own mother's son. 43:29
And he said, "Is this your younger brother of whom you spoke?
God be gracious to you, my son."
Joseph's heart went out to his brother, and he felt he would weep, 43:30
so he hurried to his bed chamber, and there he wept.
Then he washed his face, and came out again. 43:31
He controlled his feelings, and said, "Serve the meal."
Joseph was served by himself, his brothers were served by themselves, 43:32
and the Egyptians who ate with him were served by themselves,
because Egyptians do not eat bread with Hebrews,
for that is an abomination to Egyptians.
They were seated before Joseph according to age, from the firstborn 43:33
to the youngest. And they around looked at each other,
and they marveled at one another.
Joseph sent them food from his table, sending Benjamin five times 43:34
as much as the others. And they drank, and were merry with him.

Chapter 44

Afterwards, Joseph commanded the steward of his house, saying, 44:1
"Fill the men's sacks with food, as much as they can carry,

and put every man's money in the mouth of his sack."

And put my cup, the silver cup, in the mouth of the sack of the youngest,   44:2
along with his food money. And the steward did what Joseph ordered.

At dawn, the men were sent off with their food on their asses.   44:3

When they left the city, but were not far away, Joseph said to his steward,   44:4
"Go, follow after them, and when you overtake them,
say to them, 'Why have you repaid good with evil?

You have taken the cup my master drinks from to divine God's plans.   44:5
What you have done is a serious crime.'"

And the steward overtook them, and he spoke to them these same words.   44:6

They said to him, "Why does my lord speak these words?   44:7
God forbid that your servants should do such a thing.

The money we found in our sacks' we brought back again.   44:8
Why would we steal silver or gold from your lord's house?

If any of your servants is found with it, he will be put to death,   44:9
and the rest of us will be slaves to your master."

The steward said, "Let it be as you say, but only the one   3:10
who has taken the cup shall be my slave. The rest of you shall go free."

Then every man quickly lowered his sack to the ground, and opened it.   44:11

And the steward searched, beginning with the eldest and ending   44:12
with the youngest. And the cup was found in Benjamin's sack.

Then they rent their clothes in grief, and every man   44:13
loaded up his ass and returned to the city.

When Judah and his brothers came to Joseph's house,   44:14
he was still there, and they fell on the ground before him.

Joseph said to them, "What is this you have done?   44:15
Did you not know that a man such as me can divine the truth?"

Judah said, "What can we say to my lord? What words can we speak?   44:16
How shall we clear ourselves? God has revealed your servants guilt,
and now we are my lord's slaves, all of us,
not just he in whose sack the cup was found."

Joseph said, "God forbid that I should do so. But the man   44:17
in whose hand the cup was found, he shall be my slave.
As for the rest of you, arise and go in peace to your father."

Then Judah came near to him and said, "My lord, I pray you,   44:18
let your servant speak a word in my lord's ears, and let not
your anger burn against your servant, for you are like Pharaoh.

My lord asked his servants, 'Have you a father, or a brother?'   44:19

And we said to my lord, 'We have a father, an old man, and a little one,   44:20
a child of his old age. His brother is dead, and he alone
is left of his mother, and his father loves him.'

You said to your servants, 'Bring him to me, that I may see him.'   44:21

And we said to my lord, 'The boy cannot leave his father,   44:22
for if he should leave his father, his father would die.'

And you said to your servants, 'Unless your youngest brother   44:23
comes here with you, you shall see my face no more.'

We went to your servant my father, and told him the words of my lord.   44:24

Then after a time our father said, 'Go again and buy us food.' 44:25
We said, 'We cannot go there. If our youngest brother goes with us, 44:26
then will we go, for we will not see the man's face
unless our youngest brother is with us.'
Your servant my father said, 'You know that my wife bore me two sons. 44:27
One disappeared, and I said, "Surely he is torn in pieces by a wild beast," 44:28
and I have not seen him since.
If you take this one also from me, and some harm comes to him, 44:29
my old age and sorrow will send me to my grave.'
Therefore if I go to your servant my father without the boy— 44:30
because his life is so bound up with the boy's life—
it shall come to pass that when he sees the boy is not with us, 44:31
he will die. Your servants will have sent the gray head
of our father to his grave in grief.
Your servant guaranteed the safety of the boy to my father, saying, 44:32
'If I do not bring him back to you, I shall bear the blame forever.'
Now therefore, I pray you, let your servant abide instead of the boy 44:33
as slave to my lord, and let the boy go with his brothers.
How can I go to my father without the boy? I could not bear 44:34
to see the misery that would come to my father."

Chapter 45

Then Joseph could no longer control his feelings 45:1
in front of his servants, and he cried out, "Everyone leave me!"
So no one attended Joseph as he made himself known to his brothers.
He wept so loudly the Egyptians and all Pharaoh's household heard. 45:2
Joseph said to his brethren, "I am Joseph. Does my father yet live?" 45:3
His brothers could not answer, for they were terrified by his presence.
Joseph said, "Come near to me, I pray you." And they came near. 45:4
He said, "I am Joseph, your brother, whom you sold into Egypt.
Do not be grieved, nor angry with yourselves that you sold me here. 45:5
God sent me before you to preserve life.
For two years famine has been in the land, and for five more years 45:6
there shall be neither planting nor harvest.
God sent me before you to preserve your posterity on earth, 45:7
and to save your lives by a great deliverance.
It was not you who sent me here, but God. He has made me a father 45:8
to Pharaoh, and lord of all his house, and ruler throughout all of Egypt.
Now go quickly to my father, and tell him, 'Your son Joseph says, 45:9
"God has made me lord of all Egypt. Come to me without delay.
You shall dwell in the land of Goshen, and you shall be near me— 45:10
you and your children, and your children's children,
and your flocks, and herds, and all that you have.
And there I will nourish you, so that you and your household, 45:11
and all that you have, do not come to ruin.
For there are five more years of famine to come."'
Now your eyes see, and the eyes of my brother Benjamin see, 45:12

that it is truly the mouth of Joseph that speaks to you.
So tell my father of all my glory in Egypt, and of all that you have seen.   45:13
Make haste, and bring my father here."

And Joseph fell upon his brother Benjamin's neck and wept.   45:14
And Benjamin wept upon his neck.
Then he kissed all his brothers, and wept upon them.   45:15
And his brothers lost their fear, and talked with him.
News of this reached Pharaoh's house: "Joseph's brethren have come."   45:16
And it pleased both Pharaoh and his servants.
Pharaoh said to Joseph, "Tell your brethren this: 45:17
Load up your pack animals and go back to the land of Canaan.
Get your father and your households and come to me. I will give you   45:18
the best things of Egypt, and you shall eat the fat of the land.
Tell them also to take wagons out of Egypt for your children,   45:19
and for your wives. Bring your father and come.
Do not be concerned about your possessions,   45:20
for the best of all the land of Egypt is yours."

The sons of Israel did as they were told. Joseph gave them wagons,   45:21
according to Pharaoh's command, and gave them provisions for the way.
To each of them he gave a change of clothes, but to Benjamin he gave   45:22
three hundred pieces of silver and five changes of clothes.
And to his father he sent ten asses laden with the good things of Egypt,   45:23
and ten she-asses laden with corn and bread and meat,
and rations for his father for the journey.
He sent his brothers away, saying, "See that you do not fall out   45:24
along the way." And they departed. They went out of Egypt,
and came into the land of Canaan, unto Jacob their father.   45:25
They told him, "Joseph is yet alive. He is governor over all of Egypt."   45:26
And Jacob's heart fainted, for he believed them not.
They told him all the words Joseph had spoken, and when he saw   45:27
the wagons Joseph had sent to carry him, his spirit revived.
Israel said, "I am convinced. My son Joseph yet lives.   45:28
I will go and see him before I die."

Chapter 46

So Israel took his journey with all that he had, and came to Beersheba.   46:1
And he offered sacrifices to the God of his father Isaac.
God spoke to Israel in the visions of the night, saying, "Jacob, Jacob."   46:2
And Jacob said, "Here am I."
God said, "I am Almighty God, the God of your father. Fear not   46:3
to go into Egypt, for there I will make of you a great nation.
I will go with you into Egypt, and I will surely bring you out again.   46:4
And when you die, Joseph's hand shall close your eyes."
Then Jacob went on from Beersheba, and the sons of Israel   46:5
carried Jacob their father, and their children and their wives,
in the wagons that Pharaoh had sent to carry them.

They took their cattle, and their goods they had gotten in the land   46:6
of Canaan, and went into Egypt, Jacob and all his children.

His sons, and his sons' sons, and his daughters, and his sons' daughters,   46:7
and all his children, he brought with him into Egypt.

These are the names of the children of Israel who came   46:8
into Egypt with Jacob: Reuben, Jacob's firstborn,
and the sons of Reuben: Hanoch, Phallu, Hezron and Carmi.   46:9
And Simeon, and the sons of Simeon: Jemuel, Jamin, Ohad,   46:10
Jachin, Zohar and Shaul, whose mother was a Canaanite.
And Levi, and the sons of Levi: Gershon, Kohath and Merari.   46:11
And Judah, and the sons of Judah: Shelah, Pharez and Zerah,   46:12
for Judah's sons Er and Onan died in the land of Canaan.
And Pharez, and the sons of Pharez: Hezron and Hamul.
And Issachar, and the sons of Issachar: Tola, Phuvah, Job and Shimron.   46:13
And Zebulun, and the sons of Zebulun: Sered, Elon and Jahleel.   46:14
These were the sons Leah bore to Jacob, along with his daughter Dinah.   46:15
All the souls of his sons and his daughters with Leah were thirty-three.

And Gad, and the sons of Gad: Ziphion, Haggi,   46:16
Shuni, Ezbon, Eri, Arodi and Areli.
And Asher, and the sons of Asher: Jimnah, Ishuah, Isui and Beriah,   46:17
and Serah their sister, and the sons of Beriah: Heber and Malchiel.
These were the sons of Zilpah, who Laban gave to Leah his daughter,   46:18
and she bore unto Jacob sixteen souls.

The sons of Jacob's wife Rachel were Joseph and Benjamin.   46:19
Unto Joseph in the land of Egypt were born Manasseh and Ephraim,   46:20
who Asenath—daughter of Potipherah, priest of On—bore to him.
The sons of Benjamin were Belah, Becher, Ashbel,   46:21
Gera, Naaman, Ehi, Rosh, Muppim, Huppim and Ard.
These were the sons of Rachel, who bore unto Jacob fourteen souls.   46:22

And Dan, and the son of Dan: Hushim.   46:23
And Naphtali, and the sons of Naphtali: Jahzeel, Guni, Jezer and Shillem.   46:24
These were the sons of Bilhah, who Laban gave to Rachel his daughter,   46:25
and she bore unto Jacob seven souls.
All the souls who came to Egypt with Jacob, who came out of his loins,   46:26
besides Jacob's sons' wives, were sixty-six souls.
The sons of Joseph, who were born to him in Egypt, were two souls.   46:27
All the souls of the house of Jacob who came into Egypt, were seventy.

Jacob sent Judah before him to Joseph, to direct the way to Goshen.   46:28
And they came into the land of Goshen.
Joseph made ready his chariot, and went to Goshen to meet Israel,   46:29
his father. And he presented himself to his father,
and he fell on his neck, and wept a long while.
Israel said, "Now let me die, for you are alive, and I have seen your face."   46:30
Joseph said to his brothers, and to all his father's house,   46:31
"I will go tell Pharaoh, 'My brethren and all my father's house,

who were in the land of Canaan, have come to me.
These men are shepherds and keepers of cattle, and they   46:32
have brought their flocks and their herds, and all that they have.'
When Pharaoh summons you and asks, 'What is your occupation?'   46:33
You shall say, 'Your servants have been keepers of cattle   46:34
from our youth until now, both we and our forefathers.'
Thus, you may dwell in the land of Goshen.
For Egyptians think all shepherds are beneath their dignity."

Chapter 47

Joseph went to Pharaoh and said, "My father and my brethren,   47:1
and their flocks and herds, and all that they own, have come out
of the land of Canaan, and are now in the land of Goshen."
And from his brethren he chose five men, and presented them to Pharaoh.   47:2
Pharaoh said to his brethren, "What is your occupation?" They said ,   47:3
"Your servants are shepherds, both we and also our fathers.
We have come to sojourn in your land awhile. Your servants have   47:4
no pasture for their flocks, for the famine is sore in the land of Canaan.
Therefore, we pray you, let your servants dwell in the land of Goshen."
Pharaoh said to Joseph, "Your father and your brethren have come to you.   47:5
The land of Egypt is before you. Settle your father and brethren in the best 47:6
of the land. Let them settle in the land of Goshen. And if you know any
capable men among them, give them charge over my livestock."

Joseph took his father Jacob before Pharaoh. And Jacob blessed Pharaoh.   47:7
Pharaoh said to Jacob, "How old are you?"   47:8
Jacob said, "The days of the years of my wanderings are a hundred and   47:9
thirty years. Few and difficult have been the years of my life, far fewer
than the years of the lives of my fathers in the days of their wanderings."
Jacob blessed Pharaoh again, then went from his presence.   47:10
So Joseph settled his father and his brethren, and gave them property   47:11
in the land of Egypt, in the best location of the land of Rameses,
just as Pharaoh had ordered.
And Joseph provided food for his father and his brethren,   47:12
and all his father's household, according to the needs of their families.

Then there was no food in the land, for the famine was severe.   47:13
And the people of Egypt and Canaan became weak with hunger.
Joseph collected all the money paid to Egypt for grain, and the money   47:14
from Canaan for grain, and deposited it in Pharaoh's house.
And when all the other money in Egypt and Canaan was spent,   47:15
the Egyptians came to Joseph, and said, "Give us bread.
Why should we die before your eyes? Our money is gone."
Joseph said, "Give me your livestock. I will give you grain   47:16
for your livestock if you have no money."
So they brought their cattle to Joseph, and Joseph gave them   47:17
grain in exchange for their horses and flocks and herds and asses.
And he fed them with bread for livestock for all that year.

When that year was ended, they came to him the next year, and said,   47:18
"We will not hide it from my lord, that our money is gone,
and my lord also has our livestock. We have nothing left,
as you can see, my lord, but our bodies and our lands.
Shall we die before your eyes, both we and our land?   47:19
Buy us and our land for bread, and we and our land will be
servants unto Pharaoh. And give us seed, that we may live, not die,
and that the land should not become desolate."
So Joseph bought all of Egypt's farmland for Pharaoh.   47:20
For every Egyptian sold his field as the famine prevailed over him.
And all the land became Pharaoh's.

As for the people, Joseph moved them into cities,   47:21
from one end of Egypt to the other.
The only land he did not buy was the land of the priests, for the priests   47:22
received a subsidy from Pharaoh, and they could subsist on that,
so they did not have to sell their farmland.
Then Joseph said to the people, "I have bought you and your land   47:23
for Pharaoh. Now here is seed for you to sow the land.
When you harvest, you shall give a fifth part to Pharaoh.   47:24
Four parts shall be your own, to seed the field, and for your food,
and for your household, and for your children."
They said, "You have saved our lives. Let us find grace   47:25
in the sight of my lord, and we will be Pharaoh's servants."
Joseph made this a law over the land of Egypt, and to this day Pharaoh   47:26
receives a fifth part, except from the land of the priests.

Israel dwelt in Egypt, in the land of Goshen, and they acquired   47:27
possessions there, and were fruitful and multiplied.
Jacob lived in Egypt seventeen years, so the days   47:28
of his life were a hundred forty-seven years.
As time drew near for Israel to die, he called his son Joseph, and said,   47:29
"If now I have found grace in your sight, I pray you, put your hand
under my thigh, and promise to deal kindly and truly with me.
I pray you, do not bury me in Egypt.
I want to lie with my fathers. Take me out of Egypt, and bury me   47:30
where they are buried." Joseph said, "I will do as you ask."
Israel said, "Swear to me." And Joseph swore to him.   47:31
And Israel bowed in gratitude upon his bed.

Chapter 48

Some time later, Joseph was told that his father had weakened.   48:1
So he went to him with his two sons, Manasseh and Ephraim.
When Jacob was told, "Your son Joseph has come to you,"   48:2
he strengthened himself, and sat up in bed.
And Jacob said to Joseph, "God Almighty appeared to me   48:3
at Luz in the land of Canaan, and he blessed me,
and said to me, 'Behold, I will make you fruitful, and multiply you,   48:4

and I will make of you a multitude. And I will give
this land to your descendants for an everlasting possession.'
Now, your two sons, Ephraim and Manasseh, who were born   48:5
to you in the land of Egypt before I came here, are mine,
just as much as my sons Reuben and Simeon are mine.
The children you beget after them, shall not be considered mine,   48:6
and their inheritance will come through Ephraim and Manasseh.
My reason is that when I came from Padan, Rachel your mother died, 48:7
to my great sorrow, in the land of Canaan on the road,
when there was but a little way to go to Ephrath.
I buried her there, on the way to Ephrath, which is Bethlehem."
Then Israel beheld Joseph's sons, and said, "Who are these?"   48:8
Joseph said, "They are my sons, whom God has given me in this place." 48:9
Israel said, "Bring them to me, I pray you, and I will bless them."
Now, the eyes of Israel were dim with age, so he could not see.   48:10
Joseph brought them near, and he kissed them, and embraced them.
Israel said to Joseph, "I did not think I would ever see your face again, 48:11
and now God has also shown me your children."
Joseph took them from his father's knees, and bowed his face to the earth. 48:12

Then Joseph took them both, Ephraim in his right hand,   48:13
toward Israel's left hand, and Manasseh in his left hand,
toward Israel's right hand, and brought them near to him.
Israel stretched out his right hand, and laid it upon Ephraim's head, 48:14
who was the younger, and his left hand upon Manasseh's head,
crossing his hands, though Manasseh was the firstborn.
And he blessed them, saying, "May the God, before whom my fathers 48:15
Abraham and Isaac walked, the God who fed me all my life to this day,
the angel who protected me from evil, bless these boys.   48:16
Through them let my name be kept alive, and the names of my fathers,
Abraham and Isaac. May they grow into a multitude on earth."
When Joseph saw that his father laid his right hand upon the head 48:17
of Ephraim, it displeased him. And he lifted his father's hand,
to move it from Ephraim's head to Manasseh's head.
And Joseph said to his father, "Not that way, my father.   48:18
This is the firstborn. Put your right hand on his head."
But his father refused, saying, "I know, my son, I know.   48:19
He also shall become a people, and he too shall be great.
But his younger brother shall be greater than he.
His descendants shall become a multitude of nations."
And he blessed them, saying, "Israelites shall name you when they 48:20
give blessings, saying, "May God make you as Ephraim and Manasseh."
Thus he set Ephraim before Manasseh.
Israel said to Joseph, "Behold, I die. But God will be with you,   48:21
and will bring you again to the land of your fathers.
I have given to you one portion more than your brethren—   48:22
the land I took from the Amorite with my sword and my bow."

Chapter 49

Jacob sent for his sons, and said, "Gather yourselves together,	49:1
that I may tell you what will befall you in the last days.	
Come and listen, sons of Jacob, and hear Israel your father.	49:2
Reuben, you are my firstborn, the first fruit of my strength and virility.	49:3
Yours is the excellence of dignity, and of power.	
But you are as unstable as water, and you will not excel,	49:4
because you went to your father's bed—to my couch—and defiled it.	

Jacob sent for his sons, and said, "Gather yourselves together, that I may tell you what will befall you in the last days. 49:1
Come and listen, sons of Jacob, and hear Israel your father. 49:2
Reuben, you are my firstborn, the first fruit of my strength and virility. 49:3
Yours is the excellence of dignity, and of power.
But you are as unstable as water, and you will not excel, 49:4
because you went to your father's bed—to my couch—and defiled it.

"Simeon and Levi are brothers. 49:5
Cruelty, and instruments of violence are their way.
O my soul, come not into their council. May my honor not be united 49:6
with their assembly. For in their anger they murdered men,
and in their self-will they hamstrung oxen for sport.
Cursed be their anger, for it is fierce, and their rage, for it is cruel. 49:7
I will disperse them in Jacob, and scatter them in Israel.

"Judah, you are he whom your brethren shall praise. 49:8
Your hand shall be on the neck of your enemies.
Your father's children shall bow down before you.
Judah is a young lion. From your prey, my son, you return and lie down. 49:9
And when a lion is stretched out, who shall disturb him?
The scepter shall not depart from Judah until Shiloh comes, nor the 49:10
ruler's staff from between his feet. Unto him shall the people gather.
He tethers his foal to the vine, and his ass's colt to the choice vine. 49:11
He washes his robes in wine, and his clothes in the blood of grapes.
His eyes shall be red with wine, and his teeth white with milk. 49:12

"Zebulun shall live by the sea, and he shall be a haven 49:13
for ships, and his territory shall reach unto Zidon.
Issachar is a strong ass, kneeling down between two burdens. 49:14
He saw that his resting place was good, and that the land was pleasant. 49:15
He bowed his shoulder to the load, and became a servant in forced labor.
Dan shall judge his people, as one of the tribes of Israel. 49:16
Dan shall be a serpent by the way, an adder in the path that bites 49:17
the horse's heel, so that his rider falls off backward.
I have waited for your salvation, O Lord. 49:18
Gad shall be attacked by raiders, but he shall overcome at last. 49:19
Asher's food shall be rich, and he shall provide royal delicacies. 49:20
Naphtali is a deer let loose. He produces beautiful words. 49:21

"Joseph is a fruitful bough by a well, whose branches run over the wall. 49:22
The archers have attacked him, and shot at him, and hated him. 49:23
But his bow remained steady, and his arms were made strong 49:24
by the mighty God of Jacob, the shepherd, the stone of Israel,
and by the God of your father, who shall help you, and by the Almighty, 49:25
who shall bless you with the blessings of heaven above,
with the blessings of the deep that lies under,
with the blessings of the breasts, and of the womb.

The blessings of your father surpass the blessings of my ancestors,   49:26
unto the utmost bounties of the everlasting hills.
May these blessings rest on the head of Joseph,
on the crown of him who was separated from his brethren.
Benjamin is a ravenous wolf. In the morning he devours his prey,   49:27
and at night he divides the spoils."

These are the twelve tribes of Israel, and this is what   49:28
their father said of them. And he blessed them, every one.
According to his individual blessing for each, he blessed them.
And he charged them, and said to them, "Gather me unto my ancestors.   49:29
Bury me with my fathers in the cave of the field of Ephron the Hittite,
in the cave in the field of Machpelah, which is near Mamre,   49:30
in the land of Canaan, which Abraham bought with the field
of Ephron the Hittite, for a burying place.
There they buried Abraham, and Sarah his wife.   49:31
There they buried Isaac, and Rebekah his wife. And there I buried Leah.
The purchase of the field and of the cave was from the children of Heth."   49:32
When Jacob finished commanding his sons, he pulled his feet up into   49:33
the bed and gave up the ghost. And he was gathered unto his ancestors.

Chapter 50

Joseph fell upon his father's face, and wept upon him, and kissed him.   50:1
Joseph commanded his servants the physicians to embalm his father.   50:2
And the physicians embalmed Israel.
Forty days were fulfilled for him. That is the time it takes for embalming.   50:3
The Egyptians mourned him for seventy days.
And when the days of his mourning were past, Joseph spoke   50:4
to the house of Pharaoh, saying, "If now I have found grace in your eyes,
I pray you, speak these words for me to Pharaoh:
'My father made me swear, saying, "When I die put me to rest in the place   50:5
I have made ready for myself in the land of Canaan, and there shall you
bury me." Now therefore let me go, I pray you, to bury my father,
and I will come again.'"
Pharaoh said, "Go and bury your father, as he made you swear."   50:6

So Joseph left to bury his father. And with him went all the servants   50:7
of Pharaoh, and all the elders of his house, and all the elders of Egypt,
and all the house of Joseph, and his brethren, and his father's house.   50:8
Only their children, and their flocks and their herds,
did they leave in the land of Goshen.
There went with him chariots and horsemen. It was a very great company.   50:9
When they came to the threshing floor of Atad, which is on the other side   50:10
of the Jordan river, they observed a solemn and sorrowful period of
lamentation. And Joseph performed mourning ceremonies for seven days.
When the inhabitants of the land, the Canaanites, saw them mourning   50:11
on the floor of Atad, they said, "This is a solemn mourning by the
Egyptians." So it was called Abelmizraim, which is beyond Jordan.

Jacob's sons did for him as he had commanded them. 50:12

They carried him into the land of Canaan and buried him in the cave 50:13
of the field of Machpelah, near Mamre, that Abraham
bought from Ephron the Hittite for a burying place.
After he buried his father, Joseph returned to Egypt, 50:14
he and his brethren, and all who went with him to bury his father.

Now, when Joseph's brothers realized their father's death 50:15
freed Joseph, they said, "Perhaps now Joseph will hate us,
and will avenge all the evil we did to him."
They went to Joseph, and said, "Your father commanded us before he died. 50:16
He said, 'Tell Joseph, "I pray you, forgive the trespass of your brothers 50:17
and their sin. For they did evil unto you."' And now, we pray you,
forgive the trespass of the servants of the God of your father."
Joseph wept when they spoke to him.
His brothers bowed down before him and said, "We are your servants." 50:18
Joseph said to them, "Fear not. Am I in the place of God? 50:19
As for you, you did evil against me, but God meant it for good— 50:20
to bring to it pass as it is this day, that I save the lives of many people.
Fear not. I will nourish you and your children." 50:21
And he comforted them, and spoke kindly to them.
Joseph dwelt in Egypt, he and his father's house. 50:22

Joseph lived a hundred and ten years.
Joseph saw Ephraim's children of the third generation, and the children 50:23
of Machir, son of Manasseh, were brought up on Joseph's knees.
Joseph said to his brethren, "I die. And God will surely visit you, and bring 50:24
you out of this land, to the land he swore to Abraham, Isaac and Jacob."
And Joseph took an oath from the children of Israel, saying, "When God 50:25
brings you out of this land, you shall carry my bones with you."
Joseph died, being a hundred and ten years old. 50:26
They embalmed him, and he was put in a coffin in Egypt.

The Second Book of Moses Called
Exodus

Chapter 1

These are the names of the Israelites who came into Egypt. **1:1**
Every man and his household came with Jacob:
Reuben, Simeon, Levi, Judah, **1:2**
Issachar, Zebulun, Benjamin, **1:3**
Dan, Naphtali, Gad and Asher. **1:4**
All the souls that came out of the loins of Jacob were seventy souls, **1:5**
for Joseph was already in Egypt.
Joseph died, and all his brethren, and all that generation. **1:6**
The Israelites were fruitful and multiplied. They became numerous **1:7**
and exceedingly strong. The land was filled with them.

Now there arose a new king over Egypt, who knew nothing of Joseph. **1:8**
He said, "The Israelites are stronger and more numerous than we. **1:9**
Let us deal shrewdly with them, lest they multiply more, and if war should **1:10**
occur, they fight with our enemies against us and escape out of the land."
So his officers set taskmasters over the Israelites to afflict them **1:11**
with hard labor. And they built the cities of Pithom
and Ramses to store Pharaoh's treasure and supplies.
But the more they afflicted them, the more they multiplied. **1:12**
And the Egyptians came to despise the Israelites.
They made them slaves and worked them without pity. **1:13**
They made their lives miserable with hard bondage, **1:14**
making mortar and bricks, and doing all manner of work in the fields.
And in all their work they were driven with harsh cruelty.

The king of Egypt spoke to the Hebrew midwives, **1:15**
one of whom was named Shiphrah, and the other, Puah.
He said, "When you attend as midwife to the Hebrew women **1:16**
and see a child born, if it is a son, kill him. If it is a daughter, let her live."
But the midwives feared God, and did not do as the king **1:17**
of Egypt commanded them, but saved the men children alive.
The king of Egypt called for the midwives, and said to them, **1:18**
"Why have you saved the men children alive?"
The midwives said to Pharaoh, "Because Hebrew women are not **1:19**
like Egyptian women. They are more vigorous, and the children
are already delivered before the midwives come to them."
So the Lord dealt well with the midwives. And the Israelites multiplied, **1:20**
and became even more numerous and strong.
And because the midwives revered God, **1:21**
the Lord gave them families and households of their own.

But Pharaoh gave orders to all Egyptians, saying,   1:22
"Every Hebrew son who is born, you shall cast into the river,
but every daughter you shall save alive."

Chapter 2

Now, a man of the house of Levi took as a wife a Levite woman.   2:1
The woman conceived, and bore a son. When she saw   2:2
that he was a goodly child, she hid him for three months.
Then when she could no longer hide him, she wove a basket of reeds   2:3
and sealed it with pitch and resin. She put the child in the basket,
and set it among the bulrushes by the river bank.
The child's sister stood afar off, to see what would happen to him.   2:4

The daughter of Pharaoh came down to bathe,   2:5
while her maidservants walked by the river's edge. She saw
the basket among the bulrushes, and she sent a maid to fetch it.
When she opened it she saw the child, and the child was weeping.   2:6
She had compassion for him, and said,
"This is one of the Hebrews' children."
Then the child's sister said to Pharaoh's daughter,   2:7
"Shall I go get a nurse from the Hebrew women,
that she may nurse the child for you?"
Pharaoh's daughter said to her, "Go."   2:8
So the girl went to the child's own mother and brought her.
And Pharaoh's daughter said to her, "Take this child   2:9
away and nurse it for me, and I will pay you."
So the child's mother took the child back, and nursed it.
The child grew, and she brought him to Pharaoh's daughter,   2:10
and he became her son. And she named him Moses,
"Because I drew him out of the water."

One day after Moses was grown, he went out to his brethren   2:11
and saw their forced labor. There he saw an Egyptian
beating a Hebrew, one of his brethren.
He looked around and saw that no one was watching,   2:12
so he killed the Egyptian, and buried him in the sand.
The next day he went back out and saw two Hebrew   2:13
men fighting, and he said to the one who started it,
"Why are you abusing your fellow Hebrew?"
The man said, "Who made you ruler and judge over us?   2:14
Are you going to kill me like you killed the Egyptian?"
Moses became afraid, thinking, "My deed is known."
When Pharaoh heard about it, he ordered Moses killed.   2:15
But Moses fled from Pharaoh, and went to live in the land of Midian.
One day he sat down by a well.

Now, the priest of Midian had seven daughters, and they came   2:16
and drew water, and filled the troughs to water their father's flock.
Some shepherds came and tried to drive them away,   2:17

but Moses stood up and helped them, and watered their flock.
When they came home to Reuel, their father, he said, 2:18
"How is it that you have come home so soon today?"
They said, "An Egyptian delivered us from some shepherds, 2:19
and also drew water enough for us, and watered the flock."
He said to his daughters, "So where is he? Why did you 2:20
leave him behind? Invite him to come eat bread with us."
Moses stayed and dwelt with Reuel, and was content. 2:21
Reuel gave Moses his daughter Zipporah for his wife,
and she bore him a son. Moses named him Gershom, 2:22
for he said, "I have been a stranger in a strange land."
Time passed, and the king of Egypt died. The Israelites were crying out 2:23
in anguish at their bondage, and their cry came to the ears of the Lord.
The Lord heard their moaning, and he remembered 2:24
his covenant with Abraham, and with Isaac, and with Jacob.
And the Lord looked upon the Israelites, and had respect for them. 2:25

Chapter 3

Moses kept the flock of his father-in-law, the Jethro, priest of Midian. 3:1
One day he led the flock to the edge of the wilderness
and came to Horeb, the mountain of God.
There the Lord appeared to him in a flame of fire out of the midst 3:2
of a bush. The bush burned with fire, but the bush was not consumed.
Moses said to himself, "I must go over and see this great sight, 3:3
why the bush is not burning up."
When the Lord saw that Moses had turned to come see, 3:4
he called to him out of the midst of the bush, and said,
"Moses, Moses." And Moses said, "Here I am."
The Lord said, "Do not come any closer. Take off your shoes. 3:5
Where you stand is holy ground."
Then the Lord said, "I am the God of your father, the God of Abraham, 3:6
the God of Isaac, and the God of Jacob."
And Moses hid his face, for he was afraid to look upon the Lord.

The Lord said, "I have seen the affliction of the Israelites in Egypt. 3:7
I have heard their cry under their masters, and I know their sorrows.
I have come to deliver them from the Egyptians, and to bring them out 3:8
of that land into a good land, a large land flowing with milk and honey,
a place where the Canaanites, and the Hittites, and the Amorites,
and the Perizzites, and the Hivites, and the Jebusites all dwell.
The cries of the Israelites have come to me, and I have seen 3:9
how greatly the Egyptians oppress them.
Come, and I will send you to Pharaoh, 3:10
that you may bring the Israelites out of Egypt."
Moses said, "Who am I to go to Pharaoh 3:11
and bring the Israelites out of Egypt?"
The Lord said, "I will be with you. And when you have brought 3:12
the Israelites out of Egypt, you shall serve God on this mountain.

This shall be the sign that I am the one who sent you."
Moses said, "When I go to the Israelites and say to them,   3:13
'The God of your fathers has sent me to you,' they will ask me,
'What is his name?' And what shall I tell them?"
The Lord said to Moses, "I Am That I Am.   3:14
Tell the Israelites, 'I AM has sent me to you.'"

The Lord said, "Tell the Israelites, 'The Lord God of your fathers,   3:15
the God of Abraham, Isaac and Jacob, has sent me to you.'
This is my name forever. This is my memorial to all your generations.
Go. Gather the elders of Israel together and tell them, 'The Lord God   3:16
of your fathers, the God of Abraham, Isaac and Jacob, appeared to me,
saying, "I have looked upon you and seen what is done to you in Egypt,
and I will bring you out of the bondage of Egypt, into the land of the   3:17
Canaanites, and the Hittites, and the Amorites, and the Perizzites, and the
Hivites and the Jebusites, into a land flowing with milk and honey."'

"They shall listen to your voice, and you shall go—you and the elders   3:18
of Israel—to the king of Egypt, and you shall say to him, 'The Lord God
of the Hebrews has met with us. We beseech you, let us go on a three-day
journey into the wilderness, so that we can make offerings to the Lord.'
I am sure that the king of Egypt will not let you go   3:19
unless forced by a mighty hand.
So I will reach out my hand, and strike Egypt in their midst   3:20
with all my wonders. Then he will let you go.
I will give your people favor in the sight of the Egyptians,   3:21
so that when you go, you shall not go empty-handed.
But that every Hebrew woman shall ask of her Egyptian neighbors,   3:22
and of any Egyptian who visits her house, jewels of silver, and jewels
of gold, and fine clothes, and you shall put them on your sons,
and on your daughters, and thus you shall plunder the Egyptians."

Chapter 4

Moses said, "But they will not believe me, nor heed my voice,   4:1
for they will say, 'The Lord has not appeared to you.'"
The Lord said, "What is that in your hand?" Moses said, "A rod."   4:2
The Lord said, "Cast it on the ground." So Moses cast it on the ground.   4:3
And it became a serpent, and he fled from it.
The Lord said, "Reach out and take it by the tail."   4:4
Moses reached out and caught it. And it became again his rod.
"Do this so that they may believe that the Lord God of their fathers,   4:5
the God of Abraham, Isaac and Jacob, has appeared to you."
Then the Lord said, "Put your hand into your coat." So Moses put his hand   4:6
inside his coat. When he took out, it was like that of a leper, white as snow.
The Lord said, "Put your hand inside your coat again." Moses put his hand   4:7
into his coat, and when he took it out it was back like his other flesh.
"If they do not believe you or heed the voice of the first sign,   4:8
they will believe the voice of the second sign.

And if they will not believe these two signs, nor heed your voice,   4:9
take water from the river Nile and pour it on dry land.
The water you take out of the river, shall become blood on dry land."

Moses said, "O my Lord, I am not eloquent. I have never been so,   4:10
nor am I now after you have spoken to your servant.
I am slow of speech and have a thick tongue."
The Lord said, "Who has made man's mouth? Who takes away his voice   4:11
or hearing? Who makes him see or be blind? Is it not the Lord?
Therefore go. I will help you speak. I will teach you what to say."   4:12
Moses said, "O my Lord, I pray you, send someone else."   4:13
The Lord became angry with Moses. But then he said, "What about Aaron   4:14
the Levite, your brother? I know he can speak well. He is on his way
to meet you, and when he sees you, he will be glad in his heart.
Speak to him and tell him what to say. I will be your mouth,   4:15
and his mouth, and I will teach you what to do.
He shall be your spokesman to the people. He shall be   4:16
your spokesman, and you shall be like God to him.
Take your rod with you so that you can do signs."   4:17

So Moses returned to the Jethro, his father-in-law, and said to him,   4:18
"I pray you, let me return to my brethren in Egypt, to see if they
are yet alive. Jethro said to Moses, "Go in peace."
The Lord said to Moses in Midian, "Return to Egypt.   4:19
All who sought to kill you are now dead."
So Moses took his wife and his sons, set them upon asses, and returned   4:20
to Egypt. Moses carried the rod of the Lord in his hand.
The Lord said to Moses, "Do all the wonders I have given you before   4:21
Pharaoh. But I will harden his heart, and he will not let the people go.
Then say to Pharaoh, 'The Lord says, "Israel is my firstborn son,   4:22
and I say to you, 'Let my son go, that he may serve me.   4:23
If you refuse to let him go, I will kill your firstborn son.'"'

Now, as Moses and his family lodged for the night along the way,   4:24
the Lord confronted Moses and tried to kill him.
Zipporah took a sharpened flint, cut off the foreskin of her son,   4:25
and touched Moses' feet with it, saying, "You are a husband of blood."
So the Lord left Moses alone. Then Zipporah said,   4:26
"You are a husband of blood because of circumcision."

The Lord said to Aaron, "Go into the wilderness to meet Moses."   4:27
So he went and met him on the mount of God, and kissed him.
Moses told Aaron all the words the Lord had sent him to say,   4:28
and all the signs he had commanded him to give.
So Moses and Aaron gathered together all the elders of Israel.   4:29
Aaron spoke all the words the Lord had spoken to Moses,   4:30
and in the sight of the people Moses showed the signs given him.
And the people believed. And when they heard the Lord had looked   4:31
upon them and seen their affliction, they bowed their heads in worship.

Chapter 5

Moses and Aaron went to Pharaoh and said, "The Lord God of Israel says,   5:1
'Let my people go, that they may hold a feast to me in the wilderness.'"
Pharaoh said, "Who is the Lord, that I should obey his order   5:2
to let Israel go? I know not the Lord, neither will I let Israel go."
And they said, "The God of the Hebrews has met with us. Let us go on   5:3
a three days' journey into the desert, and sacrifice to the Lord our God,
lest he fall upon us with pestilence or the sword."
Pharaoh said to them, "Why do you, Moses and Aaron,   5:4
take your people from their work? Get back to your burdens.
Your people are numerous, and you let them rest from their labors."   5:5
That same day Pharaoh commanded the taskmasters of the Hebrews: 5:6
"You shall not give straw to the people to make bricks as before.   5:7
Let them go and gather straw for themselves.
But see that they make the same number of bricks. Do not reduce the   5:8
number. For they are idle, and crying, 'Let us go and sacrifice to our God.'
Let there more work be laid upon the men, that they may labor hard,   5:9
and have no time to listen to words of deception."

So the taskmasters and their officers went out and spoke to the people,   5:10
saying, "Thus spoke Pharaoh: 'I will not give you straw.
Get straw where you can. Yet none of your work shall be diminished.'"   5:11
So the people scattered throughout all Egypt to gather stubble.   5:12
And the taskmasters hurried them, saying,   5:13
"Fulfill your daily quotas as when there was straw!"
And the officers of the Israelites, who Pharaoh's taskmasters had set   5:14
over them, were beaten and questioned, "Why have you not fulfilled
your number of bricks as before, both yesterday and today?"
Then the officers of the Israelites cried unto Pharaoh, saying,   5:15
"Why do you treat your servants like this?
There is no straw given to your servants, yet they say to us, 'Make bricks,'   5:16
and they beat your servants. But the fault is with your own people!"

Pharaoh said, "You are lazy. You are idle. That is why you say,   5:17
'Let us go and make sacrifices to the Lord.'
Get back to work. There shall be no straw given you,   5:18
yet you shall deliver the same number of bricks."
The officers of the Israelites saw how impossible their situation was   5:19
when they were told, "You shall not diminish your daily quota of bricks."
They left Pharaoh and met Moses and Aaron, who were waiting for them.   5:20
And they said to them, "May the Lord look upon you and judge. For you   5:21
have made our stench abhorrent to Pharaoh and his servants.
You have put a sword in their hand to kill us with."
Moses returned to the Lord, and said, "Lord, why have you   5:22
so abused these people? Why have you sent me?
Since I came to Pharaoh to speak in your name, he has done   5:23
more evil to my people, and you have done nothing to deliver them!"

Chapter 6

The Lord said to Moses, "Now you shall see what I do to Pharaoh.   6:1
By a strong hand he shall be forced to let them go,
and with a strong hand he shall drive them out of his land."
Then the Lord said to Moses, "I am Yahweh.   6:2
I appeared to Abraham, Isaac and Jacob by the name Almighty God,   6:3
but I was not known to them by my true name, Yahweh.
I established my covenant with them, to give them the land of Canaan,   6:4
the land of their pilgrimage, wherein they sojourned.
I have heard the cries of the Israelites, who are kept as slaves   6:5
by the Egyptians, and I have remembered my covenant.
Tell the Israelites that I say, 'I am Yahweh. I will deliver you   6:6
from the burdens of the Egyptians, and I will rid you of their bondage.
I will free you with great power, and with great acts of judgment.
I will take your people to me, and I will be to you a God, and you shall   6:7
know that I am the Lord who frees you from the yoke of the Egyptians.
I will guide you to the land I swore to Abraham, Isaac and Jacob.   6:8
I will give it you for a heritage. I am Yahweh.'"

Moses told this to the Israelites, but they did not listen,   6:9
because of their broken spirit and exhaustion from hard labor.
Then Yahweh spoke to Moses, saying,   6:10
"Go to Pharaoh. Tell him to let the Israelites go out of his land."   6:11
Moses said to Yahweh, "The Israelites have not listened to me.   6:12
How then shall Pharaoh hear me—I who have uncircumcised lips?"
Then Yahweh spoke to Moses and Aaron about the Israelites   6:13
and Pharaoh, and he commanded them to bring the Israelites out of Egypt.
These were the heads of their fathers' houses: The sons of Reuben,   6:14
firstborn of Israel, were Hanoch, Pallu, Hezron and Carmi.
These were the families of Reuben.
The sons of Simeon were Jemuel, Jamin, Ohad, Jachin, Zohar and Shaul,   6:15
born to a Canaanite. These were the families of Simeon.
The sons of Levi were Gershon, Kohas and Merari.   6:16
The years of the life of Levi were a hundred thirty-seven years.
The sons of Gershon were Libni and Shimi.   6:17
The sons of Kohas were Amram, Izhar, Hebron and Uzziel.   6:18
The years of the life of Kohas were a hundred thirty-three years.
The sons of Merari were Mahali and Mushi.   6:19
These were the families of Levi according to their generations.
Amram took Jochebed, his father's sister, as a wife,   6:20
and she bore him Aaron and Moses.
The years of the life of Amram were a hundred and thirty-seven years.

The sons of Izhar were Korah, Nepheg and Zichri.   6:21
The sons of Uzziel were Mishael, Elzaphan and Zithri.   6:22
Aaron took Elisheba, daughter of Amminadab, sister of Naashon,   6:23
as a wife, and she bore him Nadab, Abihu, Eleazar and Ithamar.
The sons of Korah were Assir, Elkanah and Abiasaph.   6:24

These were the families of the Korhites.
Eleazar, Aaron's son, took one of the daughters of Putiel as a wife, 6:25
and she bore him Phinehas. These were the heads
of the Levite families, according to their generations.
These are the people Yahweh meant when he said to Aaron and Moses, 6:26
"Bring the Israelites out of Egypt, according to their tribes and families."
It was the same Moses and Aaron of these families 6:27
who told Pharaoh to let the Israelites go out from Egypt.
On the day Yahweh spoke to Moses in the land of Egypt, 6:28
Yahweh said, "I am Yahweh. Tell Pharaoh everything I have said to you." 6:29
And Moses said to Yahweh, "But I have uncircumcised lips. 6:30
Why should Pharaoh listen to me?"

Chapter 7

Yahweh said to Moses, "I shall make you as a god to Pharaoh, 7:1
and Aaron your brother shall be your prophet.
You shall speak all that I command you, and Aaron shall 7:2
tell it to Pharaoh, so that he sends the Israelites out of his land.
But I will harden Pharaoh's heart, so that I can multiply 7:3
my signs and wonders in the land of Egypt.
Pharaoh will not listen to you, so that I may lay my hand upon Egypt 7:4
with great judgments, and bring the Israelites out of Egypt as an army.
When I lay my hand upon Egypt, and bring out the Israelites, 7:5
the Egyptians shall know that I am Yahweh."
Moses and Aaron did as Yahweh commanded them. 7:6
Moses was eighty years old, and Aaron eighty-three years old, 7:7
when they spoke to Pharaoh.

Yahweh spoke to Moses and Aaron, saying, 7:8
"When Pharaoh says to you, 'Show me a wonder,' Moses shall say to 7:9
Aaron, 'Cast your rod before Pharaoh, and it shall become a serpent.'"
So Moses and Aaron went to Pharaoh and did as Yahweh commanded. 7:10
Aaron cast down his rod before Pharaoh and it became a serpent.
Then Pharaoh called the wise men and sorcerers— 7:11
the magicians of Egypt—and they did likewise with their spells.
Every man cast down his rod, and they all became serpents. 7:12
Then Aaron's rod swallowed up all their rods.
But Pharaoh's heart was hardened, 7:13
and he did not heed them, as Yahweh had said.

Yahweh said to Moses, "Pharaoh's heart is hardened. 7:14
He refuses to let the people go.
Get to Pharaoh in the morning, when he goes to the river. 7:15
Stand at the water's edge when he comes, and confront him.
Take with you the rod that turned into a serpent.
Say to him, 'The Lord God of the Hebrews has sent me to you, saying, 7:16
'Let my people go, that they may serve me in the wilderness.'
But you have not listened.

Therefore, thus saith the Lord, 'By this you shall know that I am the Lord: 7:17
With the rod I hold in my hand, I shall touch the waters of the river,
and the waters shall be turned to blood.
The fish in the river shall die, and the river shall stink,   7:18
and the Egyptians shall loathe to drink the water of the river.'"
Then Yahweh said to Moses, "Say to Aaron, 'Take up your rod and stretch   7:19
out your hand upon the waters of Egypt, upon their streams, upon their
rivers, upon their ponds, and upon all their pools of water, that they may
become blood. And there will be blood throughout all the land
of Egypt, both in vessels of wood, and in vessels of stone.'"

So Moses and Aaron did as Yahweh commanded. Aaron lifted the rod,   7:20
and in the sight of Pharaoh and his servants, struck the waters of the river.
And the waters of the river turned to blood.
The fish in the river died, and the river stank, and the Egyptians could not   7:21
drink the water, and there was blood throughout all the land of Egypt.
But the magicians of Egypt did likewise with their spells, and Pharaoh's   7:22
heart was hardened. He would not listen to them, as Yahweh had said.
Pharaoh turned and went into his house, and took none of this to heart.   7:23
All the Egyptians dug wells near the river for water to drink,   7:24
for they could not drink the water of the river itself.
Seven days past after Yahweh struck the Nile.   7:25

Chapter 8

Then Yahweh said to Moses, "Go to Pharaoh, and say to him,   8:1
'The Lord says, "Let my people go, that they may serve me.
If you refuse, I will send a plague of frogs across all your land.   8:2
The river shall bring forth frogs abundantly, and they will come into your   8:3
house, and your bedchamber, and your bed, and into the houses of your
servants and your people, and into your ovens and your baking bowls.
Frogs will crawl up on you, and on your people and your servants.'"   8:4
Then Yahweh told Moses, "Say to Aaron, 'Stretch forth your rod over the   8:5
streams and rivers and ponds, and cause frogs to come upon the land.'"
And Aaron stretched out his rod over the waters of Egypt,   8:6
and frogs came up, and covered the land of Egypt.
Then the magicians did likewise with their spells,   8:7
and brought forth frogs upon the land of Egypt.

Pharaoh called for Moses and Aaron, and said, "Entreat the Lord,   8:8
to take away the frogs from me and my people, and I will
let your people go, that they may sacrifice to the Lord."
So Moses said to Pharaoh, "I give you the honor of choosing when   8:9
I should entreat the Lord for you, and for your servants and your people,
to take the frogs from your houses, that they remain in the river only."
Pharaoh said, "Tomorrow." And Moses said, "Let it be as you say,   8:10
so that you will know there is none like the Lord our God.
The frogs will depart from you, and from your houses, and from   8:11
your servants and people. They shall remain in the river only."

Then Moses and Aaron left Pharaoh, and Moses pleaded with Yahweh 8:12
concerning the frogs he had brought against Pharaoh.
Yahweh did as Moses asked. And all the frogs in the houses, 8:13
and the villages, and the fields, died.
They were gathered into heaps, and the land stank. 8:14
But when Pharaoh saw there was respite, he hardened his heart 8:15
and did not listen to them, as Yahweh had said.

Yahweh said to Moses, "Tell Aaron, 'Stretch out your rod, and strike 8:16
the dust of the land, that it may become lice throughout all of Egypt.'"
And they did so. Aaron stretched out his rod and struck 8:17
the dust of the earth, and it became lice in man and beast.
All the dust of the land became lice throughout all of Egypt.
The magicians tried to bring forth lice with their spells, 8:18
but they could not. So there were lice upon man and beast.
The magicians said to Pharaoh, "This is the work of God." 8:19
But Pharaoh's heart was hardened,
and he did not listen to them, as Yahweh had said.

Yahweh said to Moses, "Rise up early in the morning 8:20
and go to Pharaoh as he comes forth to the water, and say to him,
'The Lord says, "Let my people go, that they may serve me.
If you do not let my people go, I will send swarms of flies upon you, 8:21
and your servants and people, and into your houses. Swarms of flies shall
fill the houses of Egyptians, and cover the ground on which they stand.
And on that day I will set apart the land of Goshen, in which my people 8:22
dwell, so that no swarms of flies will be there. This is so you
may know that I am the Lord in the midst of the earth.
I will put a barrier between my people and your people. 8:23
This sign will happen tomorrow.'"

And Yahweh did so. Great clouds of flies came into Pharaoh's house, 8:24
and into the houses of his servants, and houses over all of Egypt.
The land was ruined by the swarms of flies.
Pharaoh called for Moses and Aaron, and said, 8:25
"Go and sacrifice to your God here in the land."
Moses said, "It would not be right to do so, because the sacrifices 8:26
we offer will offend Egyptians. If we openly offer sacrifices
that offend them, will they not stone us?
We will go three days' journey into the wilderness, 8:27
and sacrifice to the Lord our God, as he has commanded us."
And Pharaoh said, "I will let you go, that you may sacrifice to the Lord 8:28
your God in the wilderness, provided that you do not go
very far away. Now make an appeal for me!"
Moses said, "I will appeal to the Lord that tomorrow the swarms of flies 8:29
depart from Pharaoh, and his servants and his people. But let Pharaoh
not deal deceitfully by not letting the people go to sacrifice to their Lord."
So Moses went out from Pharaoh, and appealed to Yahweh. 8:30
And Yahweh did as Moses asked. He removed the swarms of flies 8:31

from Pharaoh, and his servants and his people. There remained not one.
But Pharaoh again hardened his heart, and he would not let the people go. 8:32

Chapter 9

Then Yahweh said to Moses, "Go to Pharaoh and tell him, 'The Lord God 9:1
of the Hebrews says, "Let my people go, that they may serve me.
For if you refuse to let them go, and hold them here, 9:2
the hand of the Lord will strike your livestock in the field. 9:3
Upon the cattle, the horses, the asses, the camels,
the oxen and the sheep, there shall come a deadly disease.
And the Lord shall distinguish between the cattle of Israel 9:4
and the cattle of Egypt. Nothing of Israel's shall die.'"
The Lord appointed a set time, saying, 9:5
"Tomorrow the Lord shall do this in the land."
The next day Yahweh did as he had said. All the cattle 9:6
of Egypt died, but none of the cattle of Israel died. Not one.
Pharaoh asked, and was told, that not one of the cattle 9:7
of the Israelites had died. And the heart of Pharaoh
was hardened, and he did not let the people go.

Yahweh said to Moses and Aaron, "Take handfuls of ashes from a kiln, 9:8
and let Moses throw the ash toward heaven in the sight of Pharaoh.
It shall become soot over all the land of Egypt. And the soot 9:9
will cause boils and blains to break out on the skin of man
and the hide of beasts, throughout all the land of Egypt."
So they took ashes from a kiln, and stood before Pharaoh. 9:10
Moses threw the ash toward heaven. And it became soot.
And boils and blains broke forth upon man and beast over all of Egypt.
The magicians could not even stand before Moses because 9:11
the boils were upon them, as they were upon all Egyptians.
But Yahweh hardened the heart of Pharaoh, 9:12
and he did not listen to them, as Yahweh had said.

Yahweh said to Moses, "Rise up early in the morning and stand 9:13
before Pharaoh. Say to him, 'The Lord God of the Hebrews says,
"Let my people go, that they may serve me.
For this time I will send all my plagues upon your heart, 9:14
and upon your servants, and upon your people,
that you may know there is none like me in all the earth.
I will stretch out my hand and strike you and your people 9:15
with pestilence, and you shall be cut off from the earth.
This is the reason I have kept you alive, to show you my power, 9:16
and so that my name may be revered throughout all the earth.
Are you still so proud as to not let my people go? 9:17
Tomorrow about this time I will cause it to rain a grievous hail, such as 9:18
has not been seen in Egypt from the foundation of the land until now.
Therefore gather your livestock, and all that you have in the fields. 9:19
For upon every man and beast that is in the field, and not brought home,

the hail shall come down heavy on them, and they shall die.'"
Those among the officials of Pharaoh who feared the word   9:20
of the Lord, rushed their servants and livestock into shelters.
Those who regarded not the word of the Lord,   9:21
left their servants and cattle in the field.

Yahweh said to Moses, "Stretch forth your hand toward heaven,   9:22
that there may be hail on all the land of Egypt—
upon man, and beast, and every herb of the field."
Moses stretched forth his rod toward heaven, and Yahweh   9:23
sent thunder and lightning, and fire ran along the ground,
and Yahweh rained hail upon all the land of Egypt.
There was hail and fire, and it was so severe that none like it   9:24
had occurred in all the land of Egypt since it became a nation.
The hail rained on all of Egypt—all that was in the field, both man   9:25
and beast—and it struck every herb of the field, and broke every tree.
But in the land of Goshen, where the Israelites dwelt, there was no hail.   9:26

Pharaoh called for Moses and Aaron, and said to them, "I have sinned   9:27
this time. The Lord is righteous. I and my people are wicked.
It is enough. Entreat the Lord that there be no more   9:28
thunderings and hail, and I will let you go."
Moses said to him, "As soon as I am gone from the city, I will spread my   9:29
hands unto the Lord, and the thunder shall cease, and neither shall there
be any more hail, that you may know that the earth is the Lord's.
But even now I know that you and your servants do not yet fear the Lord.   9:30
The flax and the barley were destroyed, for the barley   9:31
was in the ear, and the flax was budding.
The wheat and the rye were not destroyed, for they had not yet come up."   9:32
Moses went out of the city and spread his hands unto Yahweh.   9:33
And the thunder stopped, and the hail ceased to rain upon the earth.
When Pharaoh saw that the hail and thunder had ceased,   9:34
he sinned yet again. He hardened his heart, he and his servants.
The heart of Pharaoh was hardened, and he would not   9:35
let the Israelites go, just as Yahweh had spoken to Moses.

Chapter 10

Yahweh said to Moses, "Go to Pharaoh. I have hardened his heart and   10:1
the hearts of his servants, so that I might show these signs before them.
And so that you can tell your children and your grandchildren   10:2
what I have done in Egypt, and the signs I have done among them,
that all may know that I am Lord."
Moses and Aaron went to Pharaoh, and said to him, "The Lord God   10:3
of the Hebrews says, 'How long will you refuse to humble yourself
before me? Let my people go, that they may serve me.
If you refuse, tomorrow I will bring locusts into your land.   10:4
They shall cover the face of the earth so that you will not be able   10:5
to see the ground, and they shall eat all that remains from the hail.

They shall eat every herb and tree that grows in the field.
They shall fill your houses, and the houses of your servants and of all 10:6
Egyptians. Your fathers and grandfathers have never seen anything
like this in their lifetimes.'" Then Moses turned away and left Pharaoh.

Pharaoh's servants said to him, "How long shall this man 10:7
be a snare to us? Let them go, that they may serve their Lord.
Can you not see that Egypt is being destroyed?"
So Moses and Aaron were brought to Pharaoh, and he said, 10:8
"Go, serve the Lord your God. But who are they that shall go?"
Moses said, "We will go with our young and our old, 10:9
with our sons and our daughters, with our flocks and our herds.
For we must hold a feast to the Lord."
Pharaoh said, "The Lord would indeed need to be with you 10:10
if I ever let you go with your children. You are up to no good.
It shall not be so. Go with the men only, for that is what you have 10:11
been asking." Then they were driven out from Pharaoh's presence.

So Yahweh said to Moses, "Stretch out your hand over Egypt, 10:12
so that locusts swarm over the land and eat
every herb of the field that the hail has left."
Moses stretched forth his rod over the land of Egypt, and Yahweh 10:13
brought an east wind upon the land all that day and all that night.
When it was morning, the east wind brought the locusts.
The locusts swarmed over all of Egypt, and invaded the whole land. 10:14
Such an army of locusts had never happened before, and never will again.
They covered the face of the earth, so that the land was darkened. 10:15
They ate every herb of the field, and all the fruit the hail had left.
There remained nothing green of the trees, or of the herbs, in all of Egypt.
Pharaoh quickly called for Moses and Aaron, and said, 10:16
"I have sinned against the Lord your God, and against you.
Therefore, I pray you, forgive my sin only this once, and entreat 10:17
the Lord your God, that he may take away this deadly disaster."
So Moses went out from Pharaoh, and entreated Yahweh. 10:18
And Yahweh changed the wind to a west wind that carried off the locusts 10:19
and cast them into the Red Sea. Not one locust remained in all of Egypt.
But Yahweh hardened Pharaoh's heart. He would not let the Israelites go. 10:20

Yahweh said to Moses, "Stretch your hand toward heaven, that there may 10:21
be a great darkness over all of Egypt, a darkness so dark it can be felt."
So Moses stretched his hand toward heaven, 10:22
and a thick darkness pervaded all of Egypt for three days.
Egyptians could not see one another, and no one arose 10:23
from his place for three days. But the Israelites had light.
Pharaoh called Moses and said, "Go, serve the Lord. 10:24
Let your flocks and herds stay here, but your children can go with you."
Moses said, "You must give us sacrifices and burnt offerings, 10:25
that we may sacrifice unto the Lord our God.
Our cattle must also go with us. There shall not be a hoof left behind. 10:26

We must take them to serve the Lord our God, for we know not
what sacrifice we must offer until we get there."
But Yahweh again hardened Pharaoh's heart. He would not let them go.   10:27
Pharaoh said, "Get out of here! And do not come before me again.   10:28
The next time you see my face, you will die!"
Moses said, "Let it be as you say. I will see your face no more."   10:29

Chapter 11

Yahweh said to Moses, "I will bring one more plague upon Pharaoh,   11:1
and upon Egypt. Afterwards he will let you go. And when
he does let you go, he shall eagerly thrust you out by force.
So speak now in the ears of the people, and let every man borrow from his   11:2
neighbor, and every woman from her neighbor, jewels of silver and gold."
Yahweh gave the Hebrews favor in the sight of the Egyptians.   11:3
Moreover, Moses was honored in the land of Egypt—in the sight
of Pharaoh's servants, and in the sight of the Egyptian people.

Moses said to Pharaoh, "Thus saith the Lord: 11:4
'About midnight I will go out into the midst of Egypt,
and all the firstborn in the land of Egypt shall die, from the firstborn   11:5
of Pharaoh who sits on his throne, to the firstborn of the maidservant
behind the mill, to the firstborn of every beast.
And there shall be a great cry throughout all of Egypt,   11:6
such as there never has been, nor shall anymore ever be like it.
But as for the children Israel, not even a dog shall growl against them,   11:7
that all may know the Lord distinguishes between Egypt and Israel.
And all your officials shall come to me, and bow down to me, saying,   11:8
"Get out, you and all the people who follow you." After that I will get out.'"
Then Moses, burning with anger, left Pharaoh.
Yahweh said to Moses, "Pharaoh will not listen to you,   11:9
so that my wonders may be multiplied in the land of Egypt."
Moses and Aaron did all these wonders before Pharaoh, but Yahweh   11:10
hardened Pharaoh's heart, so that he would not let the Israelites go.

Chapter 12

Yahweh said to Moses and Aaron in the land of Egypt,   12:1
"This month shall be to you the beginning of months.   12:2
It shall be the first month of the year to you.
Tell the congregation of Israel: 'On the tenth day of this month, every man   12:3
shall take a lamb, according to his father's house, one lamb for a house.
If the household is too small for the lamb, let him and his   12:4
nearest neighbor share it, according to the number of souls.
Everyone shall have an equal portion of the lamb.
Your lamb shall be without blemish, a male of the first year.   12:5
You shall take it from the sheep or from the goats.
You shall keep it until the fourteenth day of that month, and the   12:6
whole assembly of the congregation of Israel shall kill it that evening.

And they shall take the blood, and paint it on the two door posts and   12:7
the upper door beam of the houses, wherein they shall eat the lamb.
They shall eat the flesh in that night, roasted with fire.   12:8
They shall eat it with unleavened bread and bitter herbs.
Do not eat it raw nor boiled in water, but roasted with fire,   12:9
with its head and legs and inner organs.
And do not let any of it remain past morning.   12:10
That which remains of it in the morning, you shall burn with fire.
You shall eat it with your loins girded, your shoes on your feet   12:11
and your staff in your hand. And you shall eat it in haste.
It is the Passover of Yahweh.

"For I will pass through the land this night, and I will kill   12:12
all the firstborn of Egypt, both man and beast.
Against all the gods of Egypt I will execute judgment. I am Yahweh.
The blood will be a sign upon the houses where you are.   12:13
When I see the blood, I will pass over you. No evil shall come
for your destruction when I punish the land of Egypt.
This day shall be to you a memorial. You shall keep it   12:14
as a feast day to Yahweh throughout all your generations.
You shall keep it as a feast day by law forever.
For seven days you shall eat unleavened bread. On the first day   12:15
take all leaven from your houses. For whoever eats leavened bread
from the first day until the seventh, shall be cut off from Israel.
The first day shall be a holy occasion, and the seventh day   12:16
shall be a holy occasion. No manner of work shall be done these days,
save that which every man must do to eat. That only may you do.
Observe these seven days as the Feast of Unleavened Bread.   12:17
For on this day I brought you out of the land of Egypt as an army.
Observe this day by law in your generations forever.
In the first month, you shall eat unleavened bread from the evening   12:18
of the fourteenth day until the evening of the twenty-first day.
For seven days there shall be no leaven in your houses. For whoever   12:19
eats leavened bread shall be cut off from the congregation of Israel,
whether he is a stranger or born in the land.
You shall eat nothing leavened.   12:20
In all your houses you shall eat only unleavened bread."

Then Moses called together the elders of Israel, and said to them,   12:21
"Take a lamb from your family's flocks and slaughter it for the Passover.
Then take a bunch of hyssop, dip it in the lamb's blood in the bowl,   12:22
and brush the lintel and the door posts with the lamb's blood.
None of you shall go out the door of his house until morning.
For Yahweh will pass through to punish the Egyptians. And when he sees   12:23
the blood on the lintel and the door posts, he will pass over that door,
and will not let the destroyer come into your houses to strike you.
You shall observe this as a law to you and your descendants forever.   12:24
When you come into the land Yahweh will give you,   12:25
as he has promised, you shall observe this service.

When your children say to you, 'What do you mean by this service?'   12:26
You shall say, 'It is the remembrance of the Passover of Yahweh,   12:27
who passed over the houses of Israel when he struck the Egyptians,
yet delivered our houses.'" And the people bowed their heads in worship.
The Israelites did as Yahweh commanded Moses and Aaron they do.   12:28

Then, at midnight, Yahweh killed all the firstborn in the land of Egypt—   12:29
from the firstborn of Pharaoh on his throne, to the firstborn of the
prisoner in the dungeon. And the firstborn of all livestock also.
Pharaoh rose up in the night, he and his servants and all Egyptians, and a   12:30
great cry went up over all of Egypt. For in every house someone had died.
Pharaoh called for Moses and Aaron that night and said,   12:31
"Get up! Go out from my people, you and all the Israelites.
Go worship the Lord, as you have said.
Take your flocks and your herds as you have said,   12:32
and be gone. Also, give me your blessing."
And so it was that all the Egyptians pushed the Israelites   12:33
to leave the country in haste, lest, "We all be dead men."
So the people took their unleavened dough before it was risen, and their   12:34
kneading bowls, and wrapped them in their clothes upon their shoulders.
And the Israelites did as Moses had told them. They borrowed   12:35
from the Egyptians fine clothing, and jewelry of silver and gold.
Yahweh gave the Israelites favor in the sight of the Egyptians, so that they   12:36
gave them the things that they asked. Thus the Israelites plundered Egypt.

And so the Israelites journeyed from Rameses to Succoth—   12:37
six hundred thousand men on foot, and their women and children.
A mixed multitude of beasts went with them: 12:38
herds and flocks, and all manner of livestock.
They baked unleavened cakes from the dough they brought out of Egypt.   12:39
It was unleavened because they were driven out of Egypt
in such haste they had no time to prepare food for themselves.
The time the Israelites dwelt in Egypt was four hundred and thirty years.   12:40
And at the end of four hundred and thirty years, exactly to the day,   12:41
all the hosts of Yahweh went out from the land of Egypt.
It was a night of vigil for Yahweh as he brought them out of Egypt,   12:42
and so it is now a night of vigil unto Yahweh, to be observed
by the Israelites in all their generations.

Yahweh said to Moses and Aaron,   12:43
"This is the law of the Passover: No foreigner shall partake of it.
Every man's servant who is bought for money,   12:44
once he has been circumcised, may partake of it.
But a foreigner or a hired servant shall not partake of it.   12:45
It shall be eaten all in one house, and you shall not take any of the meat   12:46
from that house, and neither shall you break any of the bones.
And all the congregation of Israel shall keep it.   12:47
When a stranger sojourns with you, and he would keep   12:48
the Passover of Yahweh, first let all his males be circumcised,

then let him come near and keep it. He shall then be as one
born in the land, for no uncircumcised person shall eat of it.
One law shall apply to both those who are homeborn,   12:49
and to the strangers who sojourn among you."
All the Israelites did as Yahweh commanded Moses and Aaron.   12:50
On that very day, Yahweh brought the Israelites out of Egypt as an army. 12:51

Chapter 13

Yahweh spoke to Moses, saying,   13:1
"Sacrifice unto me all your firstborn. Whatever opens the matrix   13:2
among the Israelites, both of man and of beast, it is mine."
Moses said to the people, "Remember this day, in which you came out   13:3
from Egypt, out of the house of bondage. For by the strength of his hand
Yahweh brought you out from this place. Let no leavened bread be eaten.
This day, in the month Abib, you came out.   13:4
When Yahweh brings you into the land of the Canaanites,   13:5
and the Hittites, and the Amorites, and the Hivites, and the Jebusites—
which he swore to your fathers to give you, a land flowing with
milk and honey—you shall keep this service in this month.
For seven days you shall eat unleavened bread,   13:6
and on the seventh day, there shall be a feast to Yahweh.
Unleavened bread shall be eaten for seven days, and no leavened bread   13:7
shall be seen with you, nor shall there be leaven with you in all your land.
You shall tell your son in that day, 'We do this   13:8
because of what Yahweh did for me when I came out of Egypt.'
It shall be a sign to you on your hand, and a remembrance   13:9
between your eyebrows, that Yahweh's law shall be in your words.
For with a strong hand Yahweh brought you out of Egypt.
You shall keep this law in this season from year to year.   13:10

"When Yahweh brings you into the land of the Canaanites,   13:11
as he swore to you and your fathers, and gives it to you,
you shall sacrifice to Yahweh all that opens the matrix. Every firstling 13:12
that comes of one of your beasts, the males shall be Yahweh's.
The firstling of an ass you can buy back with a lamb. If you will not buy 13:13
back the ass, you must break his neck. Like this, all the firstborn males
among your own children you must buy back.
When your son asks you in a time to come, 'What is this?'   13:14
you shall say to him, 'By strength of hand Yahweh
brought us out of Egypt, out of the house of bondage.
When Pharaoh would not let us go, Yahweh killed all the   13:15
firstborn in Egypt, both the firstborn of man and the firstborn of beast.
Therefore I sacrifice to Yahweh all males who open the matrix,
and the firstborn among my children I buy back.
It shall be a sign upon your hand, and a mark between your eyebrows,   13:16
for by strength of hand Yahweh brought us out of Egypt.'"

When Pharaoh let the people go Yahweh did not lead them through   13:17
the land of the Philistines, although that was near. For Yahweh thought,
"When they see war, they may have regrets and return to Egypt."
Rather, Yahweh led the people by way of the wilderness   13:18
near the Red Sea, and the Israelites left Egypt as an army.
Moses took the bones of Joseph with him. For Joseph had made   13:19
the Israelites swear an oath, saying, "God will surely remember you,
and when he does, you shall carry my bones away with you."
They journeyed from Succoth and camped in Etham, near the wilderness.   13:20
By day Yahweh went before them in a column of clouds to lead the way,   13:21
and by night in a pillar of fire to give light. So they traveled day and night.
Every day the column of clouds, and every night the pillar of fire,   13:22
was ever before the people.

Chapter 14

Yahweh spoke to Moses, saying,   14:1
"Tell the Israelites to turn back and camp near Pihahiroth,   14:2
between Migdol and the sea, over by Baalzephon. Camp there by the sea.
Pharaoh will think, 'The Israelites are lost and confused.   14:3
The wilderness has trapped them.'
I will harden Pharaoh's heart, and he shall follow after them,   14:4
and I shall gain honor and glory at the expense of Pharaoh and his army,
that the Egyptians may know I am the Lord." And Israel did so.
It was told to the king of Egypt that the people fled. And the hearts of   14:5
Pharaoh and his servants were turned against the people, and they said,
"Why have we done this? Why have we let Israel go from serving us?"
So Pharaoh made ready his chariot, and took his people with him.   14:6
He took six hundred elite chariots, and all the other   14:7
chariots of Egypt, with captains over every one of them.
Yahweh hardened the heart of Pharaoh, and he pursued after   14:8
the Israelites, who had gone out from Egypt with a high hand.
The Egyptians pursued after them, all the horses and chariots   14:9
of Pharaoh, and all his horsemen, and all his army. And they overtook
Israel encamped by the sea, beside Pihahiroth, before Baalzephon.

When Pharaoh drew nigh, the Israelites beheld that the Egyptians   14:10
had marched after them, and they were sore afraid.
They said to Moses, "Weren't there enough graves in Egypt that you   14:11
had to take us into the wilderness to die? What have you done to us?
Why have you brought us out of Egypt?
Did we not tell you this same thing in Egypt? Did we not say,   14:12
'Let us alone, that we may serve the Egyptians? Better for us
to serve the Egyptians, than to die in the wilderness.'"
Moses said to the people, "Fear not. Stand still and see the salvation   14:13
of Yahweh, which he will show you today. For the Egyptians
you see here today, you shall see no more forever.
Yahweh shall fight for you, and you shall hold your peace."   14:14

Yahweh said to Moses, "Why do you cry out to me? 14:15
Tell the Israelites to go forward.
Lift up your rod, stretch your hand out over the sea, and divide it. 14:16
The Israelites shall go on dry ground through the midst of the sea.
I will harden the hearts of the Egyptians, and they shall follow you. 14:17
And I will gain honor at the expense of Pharaoh, and all his army,
and all his chariots, and all his horsemen.
The Egyptians shall know that I am the Lord, when I have gotten my 14:18
honor upon Pharaoh, upon his chariots, and upon his horsemen."
The agent of Yahweh, who went before the camp of Israel, 14:19
moved to a place behind them, so that the pillar of fire and cloud
that had gone before them, now stood behind them.
It stood between the camp of the Egyptians and the camp of Israel. 14:20
It was a cloud and darkness to the Egyptians, but gave light by night
to Israel, so that neither camp came near the other all night.

Then Moses stretched out his hand over the sea. And Yahweh caused 14:21
the sea to go back by a strong east wind all that night, and the sea
was divided, and between the waters was dry land.
The Israelites passed through the sea upon dry ground, 14:22
with a wall of water on their right, and a wall of water on their left.
Then the Egyptians pursued them into the midst of the parted sea, 14:23
all Pharaoh's horses, and his chariots, and his horsemen.
Yahweh looked upon the army of the Egyptians that morning from the 14:24
pillar of fire and cloud, and visited them with trouble and confusion.
He struck their chariot wheels, so that they drove with difficulty. 14:25
And the Egyptians said, "Let us flee from the face of Israel.
The Lord fights for them against us."
Yahweh said to Moses, "Stretch out your hand over the sea, that the 14:26
waters may come upon the Egyptians, their chariots and their horsemen."
So Moses stretched forth his hand over the sea. And as dawn appeared, 14:27
the sea flowed back together while the Egyptians fled in retreat.
And Yahweh destroyed the Egyptians with the sea.
For the waters returned, covering the chariots, and the horsemen 14:28
and the whole army of Pharaoh. There remained not one of them.

Thus the Israelites walked on dry land in the midst of the sea, 14:29
with a wall of water on their right, and a wall of water on their left.
Yahweh saved Israel that day from the hands of the Egyptians, 14:30
and Israel saw the Egyptian dead bodies on the seashore.
When Israel saw the great power of Yahweh against the Egyptians, 14:31
they feared Yahweh, and they believed Yahweh and his servant Moses.

Chapter 15

Then Moses and the sons of Israel sang this song unto Yahweh: 15:1
"I will sing unto Yahweh, for he has triumphed gloriously.
The horse and his rider he has thrown into the sea.
Yahweh is my strength and song, and he has become my salvation. 15:2

He is my God, and I praise him. He is my father's God, and I exalt him.

Yahweh is a man of war. Yahweh is his name. 15:3

Pharaoh's chariots and his army he cast into the sea. 15:4
His chosen captains are drowned in the Red Sea.

The depths have covered them. They sank to the bottom like stone. 15:5

Your right hand, O Lord, is glorious in power. 15:6
Your right hand, O Lord, dashed the enemy to pieces.

Your greatness has overthrown those who rose up against you. 15:7
Your burning wrath consumed them like straw.

With the breath of your nostrils the waters were moved, 15:8
the floods stood upright as a wall, and the depths became dry ground.

"The enemy said, 'I will pursue, I will overtake, I will divide 15:9
the spoils of war and my lust shall be satisfied upon them.
I will draw my sword and my hand shall destroy them.'

You blew your wind and the sea covered over them. 15:10
They sank like lead in the mighty waters.

Who is like you, O Lord, among the gods? Who is like you, 15:11
glorious in holiness, fearful in praises, doing wonders?

You stretched out your right hand and the earth swallowed them. 15:12

In your mercy you led forth the people you have redeemed. 15:13
You have guided them by your strength unto your holy abode.

The people shall hear, and be afraid. 15:14
Sorrow shall take hold of the people of Palestina.

The chiefs of Edom shall be amazed. The mighty men of Moab 15:15
shall tremble, and all the inhabitants of Canaan shall melt away.

Fear and dread shall fall upon them. By the greatness of your arm 15:16
they shall be as still as a stone until your people pass through, O Lord,
until the people you have redeemed pass through.

"You shall bring your people in, and plant them in the mountain 15:17
of your heritage, in the place, O Lord, that you have made your home,
in the sanctuary, O Lord, that your hands have created.

Yahweh shall reign forever and ever. 15:18

For the chariots and horses of Pharaoh, and all his horsemen, 15:19
went into the sea, and Yahweh brought the waters of the sea upon them.
But the Israelites walked on dry land in the midst of the sea."

Then Miriam the prophetess, sister of Aaron, took a timbrel in her hand, 15:20
and all the women went out after her with timbrels, dancing.

And Miriam answered them: "Sing to Yahweh, for he has triumphed 15:21
gloriously. The horse and his rider he has thrown into the sea."

So Moses brought Israel from the Red Sea, and they went out into the 15:22
wilderness of Shur. After three days they still had found no water.

And when they came to Marah, they could not drink the waters, 15:23
for they were bitter. Therefore they named it Marah.

The people murmured against Moses, saying, "What shall we drink?" 15:24

Moses pleaded to Yahweh, and Yahweh showed him a tree, 15:25
which when a branch is cast into water, the waters were made sweet.

There at Marah, Yahweh gave them a law and a covenant,
saying, "If you will diligently listen to the voice of Yahweh your God,   15:26
and will do what is right in his sight, and will heed his commandments
and keep all his laws, I will bring none of the plagues upon you that
I brought upon Egypt. For I am the Lord who heals you."
Then they came to Elim, where there were twelve wells of water   15:27
and seventy palm trees. They encamped there by the waters.

Chapter 16

Then all the congregation of the Israelites journeyed from Elim.   16:1
On the fifteenth day of the second month after departing out of Egypt,
they came to the wilderness of Sin, which is between Elim and Sinai.
The whole congregation of Israel murmured   16:2
against Moses and Aaron in the wilderness.
The people said to them, "Would to God we had died by the hand   16:3
of Yahweh in the land of Egypt, when we sat by the meat pots,
and ate our fill of bread. For you have brought us into this
wilderness to kill our whole assembly with hunger!"
Then Yahweh said to Moses, "I will rain bread from heaven.   16:4
The people shall go out and gather only a certain amount every day,
that I may test them, whether they will walk in my law, or not.
On the sixth day when they count what they have brought in,   16:5
it shall be twice as much as they gathered on the other days."

So Moses and Aaron said to the Israelites, "At evening,   16:6
you shall know that Yahweh has brought you out of Egypt.
In the morning, you shall see the glory of Yahweh. Your murmurings have   16:7
been heard by Yahweh. Who are we, that you murmur against us?"
Moses said, "Yahweh shall give you meat in the evening, and in the   16:8
morning your fill of bread. Yahweh hears your murmurings against him.
For who are we? Your murmurings are against Yahweh, not us."
Moses said to Aaron, "Say to all the congregation of Israel,   16:9
'Come near before Yahweh, for he has heard your murmurings.'"
As Aaron spoke to the whole congregation of Israel, they looked toward   16:10
the wilderness, and the glory of Yahweh appeared in the clouds.
Yahweh spoke to Moses, saying ,   16:11
"I have heard the murmurings of the Israelites. Tell them,   16:12
'At evening you shall eat meat, and in the morning you shall be
filled with bread. And you will know that I am the Lord your God.'"

That evening flocks of quail flew down and covered the camp.   16:13
And in the morning, dew covered the ground.
When the dew dried, small white flakes, thin as frost, lay on the ground.   16:14
When the Israelites saw it, they said one to another, "What is this?"   16:15
For they knew not what it was. Moses said to them,
"This is the bread the Lord has given you to eat.
And this is what the Lord has commanded: 'Let every man gather   16:16
according to the needs of his family, at the rate of one omer per person.

Let every man gather what is needed for his household.'"
The Israelites did so. Some gathered more, some less.   16:17
And when it was measured with an omer, he that gathered much   16:18
had nothing over, and he that gathered little had no lack.
Everyone had gathered according to his needs.
Moses said, "Let no man leave any of it until morning."   16:19
But some did not listen to Moses, and left it out until morning.   16:20
It bred worms, and it stank. And Moses was angry with them.
So they gathered it every morning, every man according to his needs,   16:21
and when the sun waxed hot, it melted.

On the sixth day they gathered twice as much, two omers per man.   16:22
And all the leaders of the congregation came and told Moses.
Moses told them, "Yahweh has said, 'Tomorrow is the rest of the holy   16:23
sabbath unto Yahweh. Bake what you will bake today, and boil what
you will boil. But that which remains may be kept over until morning."
They laid some up until morning, as Moses said.   16:24
And it did not stink, nor did it have worms.
Moses said, "Eat that today, for today is a sabbath unto Yahweh.   16:25
Today you shall not find it in the field.
For six days you shall gather it, but on the seventh day,   16:26
which is the sabbath, there shall be none."
Yet some of the people went out on the seventh day   16:27
to gather, but they found none.
Yahweh said to Moses, "How long shall you refuse   16:28
to keep my commandments and my laws?
Look, Yahweh has given you the sabbath, so therefore he gives you   16:29
two days' food on the sixth day. Every man shall stay in his place
on the sabbath. Let no man go out on the seventh day."
So the people rested on the seventh day.   16:30

The Israelites called what they gathered *manna*. It was like   16:31
coriander seed, white, and it tasted like wafers made with honey.
Moses said, "This is what Yahweh has commanded: 'Fill an omer with   16:32
manna to be kept throughout your generations, that they may see the
bread I fed you in the wilderness when I brought you forth from Egypt.'"
Moses said to Aaron, "Take a pot, put an omer full of manna in it,   16:33
and lay it up before Yahweh, to be kept for your generations."
As Yahweh had commanded Moses, so Aaron did lay it up   16:34
with the covenant document for safekeeping.
The Israelites ate manna for forty years, until they came to an inhabited 16:35
land. They ate manna until they came to the border of Canaan.
An omer is a tenth part of an ephah.   16:36

Chapter 17

The Israelites journeyed from the wilderness of Sin, according   17:1
to the commandment of Yahweh, and encamped in Rephidim.
There was no water for the people to drink,

and the people chided Moses, saying, "Give us water that we may drink." 17:2
Moses said, "Why do you chide me? Why do you tempt the Lord?"
The people sorely thirsted for water. And they murmured 17:3
against Moses, saying, "Why have you brought us out of Egypt?
To kill us and our children and our cattle with thirst?"
Moses pleaded to Yahweh, saying, "What shall I do 17:4
with this people? They are almost ready to stone me."
Yahweh said to Moses, "Go ahead of the people, and bring with you 17:5
some of the elders. Take the rod that you struck the Nile with, and go.
I will stand before you on the rock in Horeb. You shall strike the rock 17:6
with your rod, and water shall come out of it, that the people may drink."
Moses did so in the sight of the elders of Israel.
And he named it Massah, and Meribah, because of the chiding of Israel, 17:7
and because they tempted Yahweh, saying, "Is Yahweh with us or not?"

Then Amalek came to fight with Israel in Rephidim. 17:8
Moses said to Joshua, "Choose a band of men and go fight with Amalek. 17:9
Tomorrow I will stand on the top of the hill with the rod of Yahweh."
So Joshua did as Moses said, and fought with Amalek. 17:10
Moses, Aaron and Hur went up to the top of the hill.
And so it was that when Moses held up his rod, Israel prevailed. 17:11
And when he let down his arms, Amalek prevailed.
But Moses' arms grew heavy. So they put a stone under him, 17:12
and he sat down. Aaron and Hur held up his arms, one on one side,
one on the other, and he held the rod up until the sun went down.
Joshua defeated Amalek and his people with the edge of the sword. 17:13
Yahweh said to Moses, "Write of this victory in a book to be remembered, 17:14
and recite it to Joshua. For I will utterly wipe out
all remembrance of Amalek from under heaven."
Moses built an altar there, and he named it Jehovahnissi, 17:15
"Because Yahweh has sworn that he will have war 17:16
with Amalek from generation to generation."

Chapter 18

Jethro, priest of Midian, Moses' father-in-law, heard what Yahweh did for 18:1
Moses and his people, and that Yahweh had brought Israel out of Egypt.
He had taken in Moses' wife Zipporah after Moses sent her home, 18:2
along with her two sons—one of whom Moses had named Gershom, 18:3
for he said, "I have been a stranger in a strange land."
The name of the other was Eliezer, for he said, "The God of my father 18:4
was my helper, and delivered me from the sword of Pharaoh."
Jethro came with Moses' sons and his wife to Moses in the wilderness, 18:5
where he was encamped at the mount of God.
He said to Moses, "I, your father-in-law Jethro, 18:6
have come to you, with your wife and your two sons."
Moses went out to meet Jethro, and did obeisance, and kissed him. 18:7
They asked each other of their welfare, and they went into the tent.
Moses told his father-in-law all that Yahweh had done to Pharaoh 18:8

and to the Egyptians for Israel's sake, and all the travail that had come
upon them along the way, and how Yahweh delivered them.
Jethro rejoiced for all the goodness Yahweh had done for Israel,   18:9
whom he delivered out of the hand of the Egyptians.
Jethro said, "Blessed be Yahweh, who has delivered you   18:10
out of the hand of the Egyptians, and from the hand of Pharaoh.
He has delivered the people from the yoke of the Egyptians.
Now I know that Yahweh is greater than all other gods.   18:11
For in that which they were proud, he was yet above them."

Then Jethro brought a burnt offering and sacrifices for Yahweh.   18:12
And Aaron came, and all the elders of Israel came
to eat bread with Moses' father-in-law before Yahweh.
The next day, Moses sat as judge for the people,   18:13
and the people stood around Moses from morning till evening.
When Moses' father-in-law saw all that he did for the people, he said,   18:14
"What is this you are doing for the people? Why do you sit alone
while all the people stand around you from morning till evening?"
Moses said, "Because the people come to me to inquire of Yahweh.   18:15
When they have a dispute, they come to me and I judge between one   18:16
or the other, and I make them know the laws and statutes of Yahweh."
Jethro said to him, "What you are doing is not good.   18:17
You will surely wear yourself out, and the people also.   18:18
This thing is too heavy for you. You cannot do it alone.
Listen to me and I will counsel you, and may God be with you.   18:19
Represent the people before Yahweh, and bring their cases to him.
Teach them the laws and statutes. Show them the way   18:20
they must walk, and the work they must do.

"Look for able men among the people, men of truth who fear God   18:21
and hate covetousness. Place them over the people, to be rulers of
thousands, rulers of hundreds, rulers of fifties, and rulers of tens.
Let them judge the people in all seasons. And if it be a great matter   18:22
they shall bring it to you, but every small matter they shall judge.
This will be easier for you, and they shall share your burden.
If you do this, and Yahweh directs you, you will be able to endure.   18:23
And all these people shall go home in peace with their disputes settled."
Moses heeded the voice of his father-in-law, and did all he said.   18:24
Moses chose able men, and made them rulers of the people—   18:25
rulers of thousands, rulers of hundreds, rulers of fifties, and rulers of tens.
And they judged the people in all seasons. The hard cases they brought   18:26
to Moses, but every small matter they judged themselves.
Then Moses let his father-in-law depart, and Jethro went to his own land.   18:27

Chapter 19

In the third month—on the same day of the month that they   19:1
went out of Egypt—the Israelites came into the wilderness of Sinai.
They departed from Rephidim, and came to the desert of Sinai and pitched   19:2

their tents in the wilderness. There Israel camped before the mount.
Moses went up the mountain to Yahweh, and Yahweh   19:3
spoke to him, saying, "Tell the house of Jacob, and tell the Israelites,
'You have seen what I did to the Egyptians,   19:4
and how I lifted you up on eagles' wings and brought you to me.
Now therefore, if you will obey my voice and keep my covenant, you shall   19:5
be a special treasure to me above all people. For all the earth is mine.
You shall be to me a kingdom of priests and a holy nation.'   19:6
These are the words you shall speak to the Israelites."

So Moses called together the elders of the people and put   19:7
before them all the words Yahweh had commanded him to speak.
And the people answered together, saying, "All that Yahweh   19:8
has spoken we will do." And Moses returned their words to Yahweh.
Yahweh said, "Look, I come to you in a thick cloud, so that the people   19:9
may hear when I speak with you, and thus believe you forever."
Moses told the words of the people to Yahweh.
Yahweh said to Moses, "Go to the people and sanctify them   19:10
today and tomorrow, and let them wash their clothes.
By the third day let them be ready. For on the third day   19:11
Yahweh will come down on Mount Sinai in sight of all the people.
Set boundaries around the mountain, and tell them, 'Take heed   19:12
that you do not go into the mount, or even go near the base.
For whoever touches the mount shall be put to death.'
And he must be stoned or shot with arrows, for no hand shall touch him   19:13
who touches the mount. Whether it be man or beast, he shall not live.
Only when the trumpet sounds long, shall they come up the mount."
Moses went down from the mount and sanctified the people.   19:14
And they washed their clothes. He said to the men,
"Be ready by the third day, and do not lay with your wives."   19:15

On the morning of the third day there was thunder and lightning,   19:16
and a thick cloud upon the mount, and the sound of a trumpet
broke forth so exceedingly loud that all the people in the camp trembled.
Moses brought the people out of the camp to meet with Yahweh,   19:17
and they stood at the foot of the mountain.
Mount Sinai was enveloped in smoke, because Yahweh descended   19:18
upon it in fire. The smoke rose up like the smoke of a furnace,
and the whole mountain violently quaked.
When the trumpet sounded long, and waxed louder and louder,   19:19
Moses spoke, and Yahweh answered him in a voice like thunder.
Yahweh came down on Mount Sinai, and he called Moses   19:20
to the top of the mountain. And Moses went up.
Yahweh said to Moses, "Go down and order the people,   19:21
lest they break through to see Yahweh, and many of them perish.
Let the priests who come near to Yahweh sanctify themselves,   19:22
lest Yahweh break forth upon them."
Moses said to Yahweh, "The people cannot come up to Mount Sinai,   19:23
for you charged us, saying, 'Set bounds around the mount and sanctify it.'"

Yahweh said to him, "Away. Get you down. You and Aaron can come up,   19:24
but let not the priests and the people push through
to come up to Yahweh, lest Yahweh break forth upon them."
So Moses went down to the people and spoke to them.   19:25

Chapter 20

Yahweh spoke all these words, saying,   20:1
"I am Yahweh your God, who brought you out of Egypt,   20:2
and out of the house of bondage.
You shall have no other gods before me.   20:3
You shall not make for yourself any graven image, nor any likeness   20:4
of anything that is in the heavens above, or that is on the earth below,
or that is in the waters beneath the earth.
You shall not bow down to them, nor serve them. For I, Yahweh your God,   20:5
am a jealous God, and to those who hate me I punish their children
for their fathers' sins down to the third and fourth generation.

"But I show mercy to the thousandth generation   20:6
of those who love me and keep my commandments:
You shall not take the name of the Lord your God in vain.   20:7
Yahweh will not hold him guiltless who takes his name in vain.
Remember the sabbath day, and keep it holy.   20:8
For six days you shall labor and do all your work.   20:9
But the seventh day is the sabbath of Yahweh your God. On that day you   20:10
shall do no work—not you, nor your son, nor your daughter, nor your
servants, nor your cattle, nor a stranger who lives among you.
For in six days God made heaven and earth, and the seas   20:11
and all that is in them. And on the seventh day he rested.
And God blessed the sabbath day, and made it holy.
Honor your father and mother, that your days may be long   20:12
upon the land that Yahweh your God gives you.
You shall not kill.   20:13
You shall not commit adultery.   20:14
You shall not steal.   20:15
You shall not bear false witness against your neighbor.   20:16
You shall not covet your neighbor's house. You shall not covet   20:17
your neighbor's wife, nor his manservant, nor his maidservant,
nor his ox, nor his ass, nor anything that is your neighbor's."

All the people heard the thunder and saw the lightning,   20:18
and they heard the voice of the trumpet and saw the mountain smoking.
And when they saw and heard, they moved away.
They said to Moses, "Speak to us and we will hear you,   20:19
but let not Yahweh speak with us, lest we die."
Moses said to the people, "Fear not. Yahweh has come   20:20
only to test you, so that you fear him and do not sin."
But the people moved away and stood far off.   20:21
Moses drew near unto the thick darkness where Yahweh was.

Yahweh said to Moses, "Say this to the Israelites: 20:22
'You have seen that I spoke to you from heaven.
Do not make of me gods of silver. Do not make for yourselves gods of gold.   20:23
An altar of earth you shall make for me. And on it you shall sacrifice   20:24
your burnt offerings, and your peace offerings of sheep and oxen.
In every place I record my name I will come to you, and I will bless you.
If you make me an altar of stone, do not build it of hewn stone.   20:25
For if you use your tools upon it, you have polluted it.
And do not build an alter to me with steps leading up to it,   20:26
lest your nakedness be seen under your robe.'

Chapter 21

"These are the laws that you shall set before them: 21:1
If you buy a Hebrew servant, he shall serve six years,   21:2
and in the seventh year he shall go free for nothing.
If he came in by himself, he shall go out by himself.   21:3
If he was married, then his wife shall go out with him.
If his master has given him a wife, and she has born him sons   21:4
or daughters, the wife and her children shall be her master's,
and he shall go out by himself.
If the servant plainly says, "I love my master,   21:5
and my wife and my children. I will not go out free."
Then his master shall bring him to the judges. He shall also bring him   21:6
to the door, or to the door post, and his master shall bore his ear
through with an awl, and he shall serve him forever.
If a man sells his daughter to be a maidservant,   21:7
she shall not go out as the manservants do.
If she does not please her master, who has taken her to himself,   21:8
then he shall let her be redeemed by her family. He has no power
to sell her into a strange land, for he has dealt deceitfully with her.
If he has betrothed her to his son, he shall   21:9
deal with her after the manner of daughters.
If he takes another wife, he shall not diminish her food,   21:10
her clothing, or her marital rights.
If he does not do these three things for her,   21:11
then shall she go out free without payment.

"He that strikes a man and kills him, shall surely be put to death.   21:12
But if he had no evil purpose, and God delivered him into his hand,   21:13
then I will give you a place where the killer may flee.
But if a man attacks his neighbor with guile, and kills him,   21:14
you shall take him from my altar to be put to death.
He that attacks his father or his mother, shall surely be put to death.   21:15
He that steals a man and sells him, or if he is found   21:16
in his possession, shall surely be put to death.
He that curses his father or his mother, shall surely be put to death.   21:17
If men fight, and one hits another with a stone, or with his fist,   21:18
and he does not die but must stay in bed,

if he recovers and is able to walk about with his staff, then he that hit him shall not be punished. But he shall pay for the loss of the injured man's time, and shall provide for his care until he is thoroughly healed.   21:19

"If a man strikes his male or female slave with a rod,   21:20
causing immediate death, he shall surely be punished.
But if the slave continues to live for a day or two,   21:21
he shall not be punished, for the slave is his property.
If while men fight, they hurt a pregnant woman, causing her   21:22
to lose the child, but no other injury occurs, then the guilty
must pay what the husband demands, according to the judges decision.
But if any injury occurs, then you shall give life for life,   21:23
eye for eye, tooth for tooth, hand for hand, foot for foot,   21:24
burning for burning, wound for wound, stripe for stripe.   21:25
If a man strikes the eye of his male or female slave,   21:26
and blinds him or her, he shall let him go free for his eye's sake.
If he knocks out the tooth of his male or female slave,   21:27
he shall let him or her go free for his tooth's sake.

"If an ox gores a man or woman and they die, then the ox shall be stoned,   21:28
and his flesh shall not be eaten. But the owner of the ox shall be blameless.
But if the ox has gored in the past, and his owner knew of it yet   21:29
did not keep it under control, then if it kills a man or woman
the ox shall be stoned, and his owner also shall be put to death.
If compensation is imposed on him instead, the owner   21:30
must pay whatever is demanded of him to save his life.
If the ox gores a young boy or girl, the same judgment shall apply.   21:31
If the ox gores someone's male or female slave, the owner shall give   21:32
their master thirty shekels of silver, and the ox shall be stoned.
If a man uncovers a pit, or if he digs a pit and does not cover it,   21:33
then if an ox or an ass falls into it and dies,
the owner of the pit shall make it good, and give money   21:34
to the owner of the beast, but he may keep the dead animal.
If one man's ox gores another's, and kills it, then they shall sell   21:35
the live ox and divide the money. The dead ox they shall also divide.
But if the ox has gored in the past, and his owner has not kept him   21:36
controlled, he shall pay ox for ox, and the dead ox shall be his."

Chapter 22

"If a man steals an ox or a sheep, and kills or sells it,   22:1
he shall restore five oxen for an ox, and four sheep for a sheep.
If a thief is found stealing at night, and is beaten to death,   22:2
there shall be no blood shed for him.
But if it happens in daylight, the one who kills him is guilty of bloodshed. A   22:3
thief who is caught shall make full restitution.
If he has nothing, he shall be sold to pay for his theft.
If an animal he has stolen is still alive, whether it be an ox,   22:4
an ass, or a sheep, the thief shall restore double.

If one man's animal eats in another man's field or vineyard, the owner   22:5
must make restitution with the best of his own field and vineyard.
If someone's fire gets loose and burns the weeds, and it spreads to   22:6
stacks of corn, or standing corn, or to a whole field, and consumes it,
he who kindled the fire shall surely make restitution.
If someone entrusts his neighbor with money or goods to keep safe, and it   22:7
is stolen out of the man's house, if the thief be found, let him pay double.
If the thief is not found, then the master of the house shall be brought   22:8
to the judges to determine if he has stolen his neighbor's goods.

"For all disputes of ownership, whether it be for an ox, an ass, or sheep,   22:9
or clothing, or any property one challenges another to be his,
both parties shall come before the judges, and whomever
the judges condemn shall pay double to his neighbor.
If someone gives his neighbor an ass, or an ox, or a sheep, or any beast   22:10
to keep safe, and it dies, or is hurt or driven away, with no man seeing it,
then the neighbor shall swear an oath of the Lord to the owner   22:11
that he has not put his hand into his goods, and the owner
shall accept that, and no payment shall be made.
But if the animal is stolen from him, he shall make payment to the owner.   22:12
If it is torn in pieces by a beast, then let him bring the body for evidence,   22:13
and he shall not have to make good for that which was torn.
If a man borrows an animal from his neighbor, and it gets hurt or dies   22:14
when the owner is not with it, he shall surely make it good.
But if the owner of the animal is with it, he shall not make it good.   22:15
If the animal was hired, only the hiring fee is due.

"If a man seduces a young woman who is not betrothed,   22:16
and lies with her, he shall pay the bridal price for her and marry her.
If her father utterly refuses to give her to him, he shall   22:17
still pay her father according to the dowry of virgins.
You shall not suffer a witch to live.   22:18
Whoever has intercourse with a beast shall surely be put to death.   22:19
He who sacrifices to any god except Yahweh, shall be utterly destroyed.   22:20
Do not mistreat a stranger, nor oppress him,   22:21
for you were strangers in the land of Egypt.
Do not mistreat any widow or fatherless child.   22:22
If you mistreat them in any way, and they cry out, I will hear their cry.   22:23
My wrath shall burn, and I will kill you with the sword,   22:24
and your wives shall be widows, and your children shall be fatherless.

"If you lend money to any of the poor among my people,   22:25
do not act like a creditor to him, and do not charge him interest.
If you take a piece of your neighbor's clothing as a pledge for a loan,   22:26
you shall return it to him before the sun goes down.
For that is his only covering for his skin. What shall he sleep in?   22:27
When he cries out to me, I will hear him, for I am merciful.
You shall not revile the gods, nor curse the ruler of your people.   22:28
You shall not delay the offerings of your first ripe fruits and your wine.   22:29

The firstborn of your sons you shall give to me.

Do likewise with your oxen and your sheep. For seven days it shall   22:30
stay with its mother, and on the eighth day you shall give it to me.

You shall be holy men to me. Do not eat flesh that is torn   22:31
by beasts in the field. Throw it to the dogs."

Chapter 23

"Do not spread a false report. Do not join hands   23:1
with the wicked and bear false witness.

Do not follow a crowd in wrongdoing, and do not let prominent   23:2
people sway you into giving testimony that perverts justice.

But neither shall you favor a man's case just because he is poor.   23:3

If you happen upon your enemy's ox or ass gone astray,   23:4
you shall surely bring it back to him.

If you see the ass of him who hates you lying down under his burden,   23:5
and you do not want to help with him, you shall surely help with him.

Do not deny justice to your poor in their causes.   23:6

Do not tell lies or make false accusations, and do not put   23:7
an innocent man to death, for I will not pardon such evil.

Do not take a bribe, for a bribe blinds the wise   23:8
and perverts the words of the righteous.

Do not oppress a stranger, for you know the heart of a stranger,   23:9
seeing that you were strangers in the land of Egypt.

"For six years you shall sow your land and gather its fruits.   23:10

But the seventh year you shall let it rest and lie still, that the poor among   23:11
your people may eat. And what they leave, the beasts of the field shall eat.
In a like manner you shall deal with your vineyard and olive orchard.

For six days you shall do your work, and on the seventh day   23:12
you shall rest, that your oxen and asses may rest, and that the son
of your handmaid, and the stranger, may be refreshed.

In all things I have said to you be circumspect. Make no mention   23:13
of the name of other gods. That shall not be heard from your mouth!

"Three times a year you shall keep a feast to me: 23:14

Observe the Feast of Unleavened Bread. For seven days eat unleavened   23:15
bread during the time appointed in the month Abib. For in Abib,
you came out of Egypt. No one shall appear before me empty-handed.

Observe the Feast of Harvest, when you harvest the first fruits   23:16
of your labors you have sown in the field. Observe the Feast of
Ingathering, when you gather all your labors out of the field at year's end.

Three times a year all your male children must appear before Yahweh.   23:17

You shall not offer the blood of my sacrifice with leavened bread.   23:18
Neither shall the fat of my sacrifice remain until morning.

The best first fruits of your land you shall bring to Yahweh your God.   23:19
You shall not boil a kid in his mother's milk.

"Behold, I send an agent before you, to keep you in the way,   23:20
and to bring you into the place I have prepared.

Beware of him and obey his voice. Provoke him not, 23:21
for he will not pardon your transgressions. My name is in him.
But if you shall indeed obey his voice, and do all that I say, then I will 23:22
be an enemy to your enemies, and an adversary to your adversaries.
My agent shall go before you, and bring you to the Amorites, 23:23
and the Hittites, and the Perizzites, and the Canaanites,
and the Hivites, and the Jebusites. And I will wipe them out.

"You shall not bow to their gods, nor serve them, nor do what they do. 23:24
You shall utterly overthrow them, and break down their images.
You shall serve Yahweh your God, and I shall bless your bread 23:25
and your water, and I will take sickness from your midst.
None shall miscarry their young, nor be barren in your land, 23:26
and I will give you the full measure of your days.
I will send fear of me before you, and I will destroy all the people 23:27
to whom you come. I will make your enemies turn their backs to you.
I will send hornets before you, which shall drive out the Hivite, 23:28
the Canaanite and the Hittite, from before you.
I will not drive them out in one year, lest the land become desolate 23:29
and the beasts of the field multiply against you.
Little by little I will drive them out from before you, 23:30
until your numbers increase, and you inherit the land.
I will set your boundaries from the Red Sea to the sea of the Philistines, 23:31
and from the desert to the river. And I will deliver the inhabitants
of the land into your hand, and you shall drive them out.
You shall make no covenant with them, nor with their gods. 23:32
They must not dwell in your land, lest they make you sin against me. 23:33
For if you serve their gods, they will surely ensnare you."

Chapter 24

Yahweh said to Moses, "Come up to Yahweh, you and Aaron, Nadab 24:1
and Abihu, and seventy elders of Israel, and worship me from a distance.
Moses alone shall come near Yahweh, but the others 24:2
shall not come nigh. Neither shall the people go up with him."
Moses told the people all the words of Yahweh, and all the rules. 24:3
And the people answered with one voice, saying,
"All the words Yahweh has spoken we will do."
Moses put all the words of Yahweh in writing. 24:4
And he rose up early and built an altar at the foot of the mount,
with twelve pillars—for the twelve tribes of Israel.
He brought young men to make burnt offerings, 24:5
and to sacrifice an ox as a peace offering to Yahweh.
Moses took half the blood of the ox and put it in bowls. 24:6
The other half he sprinkled on the altar.
He took the covenant scroll and read it out loud to the people. 24:7
They said, "All that Yahweh has said, will we do and be obedient to."
Moses took the blood, and sprinkled it on the people, 24:8
and said, "This is the blood of the covenant

Yahweh has made with you concerning these words."
Then Moses and Aaron, Nadab and Abihu,   24:9
and seventy elders of Israel went up the mountain.
And they saw the Lord of Israel. Under his feet was a floor   24:10
of sapphire stone, dazzling and clear as the heavens.
He did not lay a hand on the nobles of the Israelites.   24:11
They saw Yahweh, and they ate and drank.

Yahweh said to Moses, "Come up to me on the mount,   24:12
and take your place there. I will give you tablets of stone
with commandments I have written, that you may teach them.
So Moses and his minister Joshua rose up,   24:13
and Moses went up into the mount of God.
He said to the elders, "Wait here until we come back to you.   24:14
Aaron and Hur are with you. If any man has a dispute, go to them."
So Moses went up into the mount, and a cloud covered the mount,   24:15
and the glory of Yahweh was upon Mount Sinai.   24:16
The cloud covered the mount for six days, and on the seventh day
Yahweh called to Moses out of the midst of the cloud.
The glory of Yahweh on top of the mountain   24:17
was like devouring fire in the eyes of the Israelites.
Moses went into the midst of the cloud, and ascended the mount.   24:18
Moses was on the mountain forty days and forty nights.

Chapter 25

Yahweh spoke to Moses, saying,   25:1
"Speak to the Israelites, that they bring me an offering. From every man 25:2
who gives it willingly with his heart, you shall receive my offering.
These are the offerings you shall take of them: Gold, and silver, and brass, 25:3
and blue, and purple, and scarlet, and fine linen, and goat skins,   25:4
and ram skins dyed red, and badger skins, and shittim wood,   25:5
and oil for the light, and spices for anointing oil and for sweet incense, 25:6
and onyx stones, and stones to be set in the ephod, and in the breastplate. 25:7
Let them make me a sanctuary, that I may dwell among them.   25:8
Make it according to all that I tell you. Make it after the pattern   25:9
I now give you for the tabernacle and the furnishings:

"Make an ark of shittim wood. It shall be two cubits and a half   25:10
in length, a cubit and a half in breadth, and a cubit and a half in height.
Overlay it with pure gold. Within and without you shall overlay it,   25:11
and put gold molding all around the top.
Cast four rings of gold for it, and put them in the four corners—   25:12
two rings on one side, and two rings on the other.
Make staves of shittim wood, and overlay them with gold.   25:13
Put the staves into the rings on the sides of the ark,   25:14
that the ark may be borne with them.
The staves shall stay in the rings of the ark, and shall not be taken from it. 25:15
Put the covenant I shall give you into the ark.   25:16

Make a mercy seat of pure gold, two cubits and a half   25:17
in length, and a cubit and a half in breadth.
Make two cherubim of hammered gold for the two ends of the mercy seat.   25:18
Put one cherub on one end, and the other cherub on the other end.   25:19
Make the cherubim the two ends of the mercy seat.
The cherubim shall stretch forth their wings on high,   25:20
covering the mercy seat with their wings,
and they shall look toward one another, facing the mercy seat.
Put the mercy seat on top of the ark.   25:21
Inside the ark, put the covenant I shall give you.
And there I will meet with you. From the mercy seat,   25:22
from between the two cherubim on the ark of the covenant,
I will deliver to you the commandments I give to the Israelites.

"You shall also make a table of shittim wood, two cubits in length,   25:23
one cubit in breadth, and a cubit and a half in height.
Overlay it with pure gold, and put gold molding all around the edges.   25:24
Make a frame for it the width of a hand.   25:25
Put gold molding around the frame.
Make four rings of gold for it, and put the rings   25:26
at the four corners near the table legs.
The rings shall be against the frame, to hold the staves that bear the table.   25:27
Make the staves of shittim wood and overlay them with gold,   25:28
that the table may be borne with them.
Make the dishes, spoons, bowls, covers and pitchers of pure gold,   25:29
and always set showbread on the table before me.   25:30

"Make a lampstand of pure hammered gold. The base, branches,   25:31
bowls, knops and flowers, shall all be of the same hammered gold.
Six branches shall come out of the sides of it—three branches   25:32
on one side, and three branches on the other side.
Each branch shall have three cups shaped like almonds,   25:33
each with a knop and a flower. So it shall be for all six branches.
On the lampstand shall be four bowls shaped like almonds,   25:34
each with their knops and their flowers,
and there shall be a knop under each pair of branches.   25:35
So it shall be for all six branches.
All the knops and branches shall be of the same hammered gold,   25:36
and all the lampstand shall be one work of pure hammered gold.
Make its seven lamps, and set them so that they light the space before it.   25:37
The tongs and the snuffers shall be of pure gold.   25:38
Use a talent of pure gold to make all these vessels.   25:39
Make them after the pattern I showed you on the mount."   25:40

Chapter 26

"Make a tabernacle for me, with ten curtains of fine woven linen—   26:1
blue and purple and scarlet, with cherubim skillfully woven into them.
The length of each curtain shall be twenty-eight cubits, and the breadth   26:2

of each curtain four cubits. Every curtain shall be the same measure.
Five curtains shall be coupled together one to another, 26:3
and the other five curtains shall be coupled one to another.
Make loops of blue on the edge of each set of curtains 26:4
in the selvedge of the coupling, and make both sets the same.
Make fifty loops for each set of curtains, and set them opposite, 26:5
so that the loops may take hold to one another.
Make fifty clasps of gold, and couple the curtains together 26:6
with the claps so that the tabernacle is enclosed as one.

"Make eleven sheets of woven goat hair for a tent over the tabernacle. 26:7
The length of each sheet shall be thirty cubits, and the breadth of each 26:8
sheet four cubits. The eleven sheets shall all be of one measure.
Couple five sheets together, and the other six sheets together. 26:9
Fold the sixth sheet double at the front of the tabernacle.
Make fifty loops on the edge of the outer sheet in one set, 26:10
and fifty loops on the edge of the outer sheet in the second set.
Make fifty clasps of brass, and put the clasps into the loops, 26:11
and couple the tent together, that it may be one.
The half sheet that is left shall hang over the back side of the tabernacle. 26:12
That which remains in the length of the sheets shall drape over 26:13
the sides of the tabernacle, one cubit on each side, to cover it.

"Make a covering for the tent of ram skins dyed red, 26:14
and a covering above that of badger skins.
Make boards for the tabernacle of shittim wood. 26:15
The length of each board shall be ten cubits, 26:16
and the breadth shall be a cubit and a half.
Each board shall have two tenons, set evenly apart, 26:17
and the boards of the tabernacle shall be joined together by these.
Make twenty boards for the south side of the tabernacle, 26:18
and make forty sockets of silver to go in the twenty boards— 26:19
two sockets in each board to receive two tenons.
On the north side of the tabernacle there shall be twenty boards, 26:20
with forty sockets of silver, two sockets in each board. 26:21
For the west and east sides of the tabernacle, make six boards each. 26:22
Make two boards for each of the corners of the tabernacle. 26:23
These shall be coupled below, and above they shall be coupled 26:24
onto one ring. All the corners shall be like this.
So for the corners there shall be eight boards 26:25
and sixteen sockets of silver, two sockets in each board.
Make bars of shittim wood— five bars 26:26
for the boards of the south side of the tabernacle,
five bars for the boards of the north side of the tabernacle, 26:27
and five bars each for the boards on the west and east sides.
The middle bar of the boards shall reach from end to end. 26:28
Overlay the boards with gold, and make rings of gold 26:29
for places for the bars, and overlay the bars with gold.

Then erect the tabernacle according to the pattern 26:30
I showed you on the mountain.

"Make a veil of blue and purple and scarlet. 26:31
Make it of fine linen of cunning work with cherubim woven into it.
Hang it upon the four pillars of shittim wood overlaid with gold, 26:32
on hooks made of gold, set in four sockets of silver.
Hang the veil on the hooks, and place the ark of the covenant 26:33
behind the veil, so that it divides the holy place from the most holy.
Put the mercy seat upon the ark of the covenant in the most holy place. 26:34
Set the table outside the veil, and place the lampstand near the table 26:35
on the south side of the tabernacle, with the table on the north side.
Make a hanging for the door of the tent. Make it blue and purple 26:36
and scarlet, of woven linen wrought with fine needlework.
Make for the hanging five pillars of shittim wood overlaid with gold, 26:37
with hooks of gold, in five sockets cast of brass.

Chapter 27

"Make an altar of shittim wood, five cubits long, and five cubits broad. 27:1
The altar shall be foursquare, and three cubits in height.
Make horns for the four corners, each the same, and overlay it with brass. 27:2
Make pans to receive the ashes, and shovels, and bowls, and fleshhooks, 27:3
and firepans. All these vessels shall be made of brass.
Make a grate for it, a mesh of brass, and upon the grate 27:4
make four bronze rings for the four corners.
Put the grate under the altar, halfway up. 27:5
Make staves of shittim wood for the altar. Overlay them with brass. 27:6
Put the staves into the rings on both sides of the alter, to bear it. 27:7
Make the alter with boards so that it is hollow inside, 27:8
as I showed you on the mountain.

"Make a courtyard for the tabernacle. On the south side there 27:9
shall be hangings of fine woven linen a hundred cubits long.
There shall be twenty pillars, and their twenty sockets shall be of brass. 27:10
The hooks of the pillars and their fillets shall be of silver.
Likewise for the north side: There shall be hangings a hundred 27:11
cubits long, and twenty pillars with twenty sockets of brass,
and the hooks of the pillars and their fillets shall be of silver.
For the breadth of the court on the west side there shall be 27:12
hangings fifty cubits long, with ten pillars and ten sockets.
The breadth of the court on the east side shall also be fifty cubits. 27:13
The hangings on one side of the gate shall be fifteen cubits, 27:14
with three pillars and three sockets.
The hangings on the other side shall be fifteen cubits, 27:15
with three pillars and three sockets.
For the gate of the court there shall be a hanging of twenty cubits, 27:16
of blue and purple and scarlet, of woven linen wrought with fine
needlework. And there shall be four pillars and four sockets.

All the pillars around the court shall be filleted with silver,   27:17
and their hooks shall be of silver, and their sockets shall be of brass.
The length of the court shall be a hundred cubits, and the breadth fifty   27:18
everywhere; the height, five cubits of fine linen with sockets of brass.
All the vessels of the tabernacle, and all the pegs used,   27:19
and all the pegs used for the court, shall be of brass.

"Command the Israelites to bring you pure oil olive,   27:20
beaten for the light, to cause the lamp to burn always
in the tabernacle, outside the veil that is before the covenant.   27:21
Aaron and his sons shall tend the lamp from evening to morning before
Yahweh. This shall be a law throughout the generations of Israel forever."

Chapter 28

"Call Aaron your brother from among the Israelites,   28:1
and his sons with him, that they may serve me as priests—
Aaron and his sons, Nadab, Abihu, Eleazar and Ithamar.
Make holy garments for Aaron for glory and for beauty.   28:2
Speak to those who are wise-hearted, whom I have filled   28:3
with the spirit of wisdom, that they may make Aaron's garments
to consecrate him, that he may minister to me as a priest.
These are the garments they shall make: A breastplate, an ephod, a robe,   28:4
an embroidered coat, a mitre and a girdle. They shall make holy garments
for Aaron and his sons, that he may serve me as a priest.
They shall take gold, and blue, and purple, and scarlet, and fine linen,   28:5
and they shall make the ephod of gold and blue and purple   28:6
and scarlet, of fine woven linen with cunning work.
It shall have two shoulder pieces, joined at the edges.   28:7
The curious girdle of the ephod shall be of the same fine work—   28:8
gold and blue and purple and scarlet, of fine woven linen.

"Take two onyx stones and carve on them the names of the tribes of Israel.   28:9
Six names on one stone, and six names   28:10
on the other stone, in the order of their birth.
With the work of an engraver, like the engravings of a signet,   28:11
you shall engrave the two stones with the names of the tribes of Israel,
then mount them in settings of gold.
Put the two stones on the shoulders of the ephod, as a reminder   28:12
of the Israelites. Aaron shall bear their names upon
his shoulders before Yahweh for a reminder.
Make the settings of gold,   28:13
with two chains of pure gold at the ends,   28:14
braided like ropes, and fastened to the settings.
Make a breastplate for judgment, with cunning work, like for the ephod.   28:15
Make it of gold and blue and purple and scarlet, of fine woven linen.
Foursquare it shall be, and folded in two,   28:16
a handspan in length and a handspan in breadth.
Set in it four rows of gemstones. The first row shall be a sardius,   28:17

a topaz and a carbuncle. This shall be the first row.

The second row shall be an emerald, a sapphire and a diamond. 28:18

The third row shall be a ligure, an agate and an ameyourst. 28:19

The fourth row shall be a beryl, an onyx and a jasper. 28:20
They all shall be mounted in gold settings.

These stones shall be engraved with the names of the twelve tribes 28:21
of Israel, engraved like a signet, each one with a name of a tribe.

"On the breastplate, make two chains of pure gold braided like rope. 28:22

Also on the breastplate make two rings of gold, 28:23
and put the two rings on the ends of the breastplate.

Put the braided chains of gold in the rings on the ends of the breastplate. 28:24

Fasten the other two ends of the chains to the two settings, 28:25
and put them on the shoulder pieces of the ephod.

Make two rings of gold and put them at the border of the 28:26
two ends of the breastplate, on the inside edge of the ephod.

Make two other rings of gold. Put them underneath the sides of the ephod, 28:27
toward the front, near the coupling above the curious girdle.

Bind the breastplate rings to the rings of the ephod with a blue lace, 28:28
so that it is above the curious girdle of the ephod,
and so the breastplate will not come loose from the ephod.

Thus Aaron shall bear the names of the Israelites over his heart, 28:29
in the breastplate of judgment, as a constant reminder
when he goes into the holy place.

Put into the breastplate of judgment the Urim and the Thummim, 28:30
so that they shall be on Aaron's heart when he goes before Yahweh—
so that Aaron shall continually carry the means of judgment
for the Israelites on his heart when he goes before Yahweh.

"Make the robe of the ephod all of blue. 28:31

The opening for the head shall be in the middle of it, with a woven 28:32
hem that will not tear. Make it as if it were a habergeon.

Beneath the hem make pomegranates of blue and purple and scarlet 28:33
around the hem, and bells of gold between them.

A golden bell and a pomegranate, a golden bell and a pomegranate, 28:34
alternating around the hem.

Aaron shall wear this when he serves as priest, so that its sound 28:35
shall be heard when he goes into the holy place before Yahweh,
and when he comes out, so that he does not die.

Make a plate of pure gold for the holy crown, and engrave upon it, 28:36
like the engraving of a signet, 'HOLINESS TO THE LORD.'

Put it on a blue lace, that it may be on the mitre. 28:37
It shall be in the forefront of the mitre.

It shall be on Aaron's head, so that Aaron may bear any sin attached 28:38
to the things the Israelites hallow in their offerings.
It shall always be on his head, so that Israel is accepted before Yahweh.

"Weave the coat of fine linen, and make the mitre of fine linen, 28:39
and make the girdle of fine needlework.

Make coats for Aaron's sons, and girdles and hats, for glory and for beauty. 28:40
Put them on Aaron and his sons, and anoint them, and consecrate them, 28:41
and sanctify them, that they may serve me as priests.
And make them linen under garments that reach from 28:42
their waist to their thighs, to cover their nakedness.
Aaron and his sons shall wear these when they come into the tabernacle, 28:43
or come near the altar in the holy place, so that they do not sin and die.
This shall be a law for Aaron and his descendants forever."

Chapter 29

"This is what you shall do to hallow them so they can serve me as priests: 29:1
Take one young bull, and two rams without blemish,
and take unleavened bread, and unleavened cakes tempered with oil, 29:2
and unleavened wafers anointed with oil. Make these of wheat flour.
Put them into one basket and bring them with the bull and the two rams. 29:3
Then bring Aaron and his sons to the door 29:4
of the tabernacle and wash them with water.
Take the garments and put the coat on Aaron, and the robe of the ephod, 29:5
and the ephod, and the breastplate, and gird him with the curious girdle.
Put the mitre on his head, and put the holy crown on the mitre. 29:6
Then take the anointing oil and pour it on his head, and anoint him. 29:7
Bring his sons and put tunics on them. 29:8
Gird them with girdles, Aaron and his sons, and put the hats on them. 29:9
The priest's office shall be theirs for a perpetual law,
and you shall consecrate Aaron and his sons.

"Have the bull brought before the tabernacle of the congregation, 29:10
and Aaron and his sons shall put their hands on the head of the bull.
Kill the bull before Yahweh, by the door of the tabernacle. 29:11
Take the blood of the bull, and put some on the horns of the altar 29:12
with your finger, then pour the rest of the blood at the bottom of the altar.
Take the fat that covers the inner organs, and the lobe of the liver, 29:13
and the kidneys with the fat that is on them, and burn them on the altar.
The flesh of the bull, and his hide, and his dung, 29:14
you shall burn outside the camp. It is a sin offering.
Then present one ram. Aaron and his sons 29:15
shall put their hands on the head of the ram.
Kill the ram and sprinkle his blood around about the altar. 29:16
Cut the ram into pieces. Wash the inner organs and legs, 29:17
and put them with its pieces and head.
Burn the whole ram on the altar. It is a burnt offering to Yahweh, 29:18
a sweet savor, an offering made unto Yahweh by fire.

"Present the other ram. Aaron and his sons 29:19
shall put their hands on the head of the ram.
Kill the ram and put his blood on the tip of the right ear of Aaron, 29:20
and on the tip of the right ear of his sons, and on the thumb
of their right hand, and on the great toe of their right foot,

and sprinkle the blood around about the alter.

Take of the blood that is on the altar, and the anointing oil, and sprinkle   29:21
it on Aaron, and on his garments, and on his sons, and on the garments
of his sons. And he shall be hallowed. And his garments, and his sons,
and his sons' garments with him, shall be hallowed.

Take of the ram the fat and the rump, and the fat that covers the inner   29:22
organs, and the lobe of the liver, and the two kidneys with the fat
that is on them, and the right shoulder—for it is a ram of consecration—

and one loaf of bread, and one cake of oiled bread, and one wafer   29:23
out of the basket of the unleavened bread that is before Yahweh,

and put it all in the hands of Aaron, and in the hands of his sons.   29:24
They shall wave them as a wave offering before Yahweh.

Then you shall receive them from their hands, and burn them   29:25
on the altar for a burnt offering, for a sweet savor before Yahweh.
It is an offering made by fire unto Yahweh.

"Take the breast of the ram Aaron consecrated, and wave it   29:26
for a wave offering before Yahweh. It shall be your portion.

Sanctify the breast of the wave offering, and the shoulder of the gift   29:27
offering, which is waved and given, whether from the ram of the
consecration, or from anything else meant for Aaron and his sons.

It shall be Aaron's and his sons' part by a law forever,   29:28
for it is a gift offering from the Israelites,
made from the sacrifices of their peace offerings to Yahweh.

Aaron's holy garments shall be his sons' after him.   29:29
They shall be anointed in them, and consecrated in them.

The son who becomes priest in his stead shall wear them for seven days   29:30
when he comes into the tabernacle to minister in the holy place.

Take the ram of the consecration and boil his flesh in the holy place.   29:31

Aaron and his sons shall eat the flesh of the ram, and the bread   29:32
that is in the basket by the door of the tabernacle.

Only they shall eat the food used to consecrate and sanctify them.   29:33
No one else shall eat it, because it is holy.

If any of the meat or bread of the consecrations is left over until morning,   29:34
burn the remainder with fire. It shall not be eaten, because it is holy.

"Do all these things unto Aaron and his sons as I have commanded you.   29:35
For seven days you shall consecrate them.

Offer a bull every day as a sin offering for atonement. Cleanse the altar   29:36
when you make an atonement for it, and anoint it to sanctify it.

For seven days you shall make an atonement for the altar, and sanctify it.   29:37
It shall be an altar most holy, and whatever touches the altar shall be holy.

This is what you shall offer upon the altar: 29:38
Two lambs in their first year, every day, continually.

One lamb you shall offer in the morning, the other lamb in the evening.   29:39

With the first lamb, offer a tenth deal of flour mixed with a fourth of a hin   29:40
of beaten oil, and a fourth of a hin of wine for a drink offering.

With the lamb you sacrifice at evening, do the same for the meat offering   29:41

and the drink offering as in the morning, for a sweet savor—
an offering made by fire unto Yahweh.

"This shall be a continual burnt offering throughout your generations, 29:42
at the door of the tabernacle of the congregation before Yahweh.
There I will meet you, and I will speak to you.
And there I will meet with the Israelites, 29:43
and the tabernacle shall be sanctified by my glory.
I will sanctify the tabernacle of the congregation, and the altar. 29:44
I will also sanctify both Aaron and his sons, to minister to me as priests.
I will dwell among the Israelites, and I will be their God. 29:45
And they shall know that I am Yahweh their God, who brought them forth 29:46
out of Egypt so I could dwell among them. For I am Yahweh, their God.

Chapter 30

"Make an altar to burn incense upon. Make it of shittim wood. 30:1
It shall be foursquare—a cubit in length, a cubit in breadth, and two cubits 30:2
in height. The horns of it shall be the same as the other altar.
Overlay it with pure gold, on the top and the sides all around, 30:3
and put gold molding all around the edges.
Make two gold rings under the molding on two sides of it. 30:4
These shall be for the staves to bear it.
Make the staves of shittim wood and overlay them with gold. 30:5
Put the altar in front of the veil by the ark of the covenant—in front 30:6
of the mercy seat over the covenant, where I will meet with you.
Aaron shall burn sweet incense upon it every morning. 30:7
When he tends the lamps, he shall burn incense upon it,
and when he lights the lamps at evening, he shall burn incense upon it— 30:8
a perpetual incense burning before Yahweh throughout your generations.
Offer no strange incense upon this alter, nor burnt sacrifice, 30:9
nor meat offering, nor drink offering.
Aaron shall make an atonement upon the horns of it once a year 30:10
with the blood of the sin offerings. Once a year he shall make atonement
upon it throughout your generations. It is most holy to Yahweh."

Yahweh spoke to Moses, saying, 30:11
"Take a census of the Israelites to number them. When they are 30:12
numbered, every man shall pay a ransom for his soul to Yahweh.
When they are numbered, no plagues shall be brought upon them.
Everyone who is numbered must pay a half-shekel to the sanctuary— 30:13
a shekel is twenty gerahs—as an offering to Yahweh.
Everyone who is numbered, from twenty years old and above, 30:14
must give this offering to Yahweh.
The rich shall not give more, and the poor shall not give less 30:15
when they make an offering to Yahweh to save their souls.
Take this atonement money of the Israelites and use it 30:16
to support the tabernacle, that it may remind the Israelites
to atone for their souls before Yahweh."

Yahweh spoke to Moses, saying,   30:17
"Make a laver of brass, with a stand of brass, for washing.   30:18
Put it between the tabernacle and the altar. Put water in it.
Aaron and his sons shall wash their hands and feet here.   30:19
When they go into the tabernacle, they shall wash or they shall die.   30:20
When they come near the altar to burn offerings by fire to Yahweh,
they shall wash their hands and feet with water, or they shall die.   30:21
This shall be a law to them forever, throughout all their generations."

Yahweh spoke to Moses, saying ,   30:22
"Take for yourself fine spices: Five hundred shekels of pure myrrh,   30:23
and half as much of sweet cinnamon, two hundred and fifty shekels worth,
and two hundred and fifty shekels worth of sweet calamus,
and five hundred shekels worth of cassia—all based on the value   30:24
of the shekel of the sanctuary—and also a hin of olive oil,
and make of it an oil of holy ointment, an oil after the art   30:25
of the apothecary. It shall be a holy anointing oil.
Anoint the tabernacle with it, and the ark of the covenant,   30:26
and the table and all its vessels, and the lampstand   30:27
and its vessels, and the altar of incense,
and the altar of burnt offering with all its vessels, and the laver,   30:28
and you shall sanctify them, that they may be most holy.   30:29
Whatever touches them shall be holy .
You shall anoint Aaron and his sons, and consecrate them,   30:30
that they may minister to me in the priest's office.
You shall speak to the Israelites, saying,   30:31
'This shall be a holy anointing oil to me throughout your generations.
It shall not be poured upon man's flesh, neither shall you make   30:32
any other like it. The composition of it is holy, and it shall be holy to you.
Whoever compounds anything like it, or whoever   30:33
puts any of it on a stranger, shall be cut off from his people.'"

Yahweh said to Moses, "Take to you sweet spices of stacte, and onycha,   30:34
and galbanum, and pure frankincense—each in equal weight—
and make an incense, a confection after the art   30:35
of the apothecary, tempered together, pure and holy.
Crush it fine, and put it before the covenant in the tabernacle,   30:36
where I will meet with you. It shall be to you most holy.
The incense you make shall not be taken unto yourselves.   30:37
It shall be to you, holy unto Yahweh.
Whoever makes incense like it, shall be cut off from his people."   30:38

Chapter 31

Yahweh spoke to Moses, saying,   31:1
"I have chosen Bezaleel, son of Uri, grandson of Hur of the tribe of Judah,   31:2
and I have filled him with the spirit of God, in wisdom and   31:3
understanding, and in knowledge and all manner of workmanship,
so that he may devise cunning works of gold, and silver and brass,   31:4

and cut stones to set in them, and carve wood,   31:5
and perform all manner of craftsmanship.
And I have given him Aholiab, son of Ahisamach of the tribe of Dan.   31:6
And in the hearts of all who are wise-hearted, I have put wisdom,
that they may make all that I have commanded you:
The tabernacle of the congregation, the ark of the covenant,   31:7
the mercy seat upon it, all the furniture of the tabernacle,
the table and its furniture, the pure lampstand   31:8
with all its furniture, and the altar of incense,
and the altar of burnt offering with all its furniture, and the laver,   31:9
and the cloths of service, and the holy garments for Aaron the priest,   31:10
and the garments for his sons to minister in the priest's office,
and the anointing oil, and the sweet incense for the holy place—   31:11
all that I have commanded you, they shall do."

Yahweh spoke to Moses, saying,   31:12
"Tell the Israelites, 'Keep my sabbath, for it is a sign throughout your   31:13
generations, that you may know I am the Lord who sanctifies you.
Keep my sabbath because it is holy to you. Everyone who violates   31:14
the Sabbath shall be put to death. Whoever does any work
on the sabbath, shall be cut off from his people.
For six days work may be done. The seventh is the sabbath of rest, holy to   31:15
the Lord. Whoever does any work on the sabbath shall be put to death.
The Israelites shall keep the sabbath. They shall observe the sabbath   31:16
throughout their generations as a perpetual covenant.
It is a sign between me and the Israelites forever.   31:17
For in six days God made heaven and earth,
and on the seventh day he rested. And he was refreshed.'"
When he was done speaking with him on Mount Sinai, Yahweh gave   31:18
Moses two tablets of testimony, written in stone with the finger of God.

Chapter 32

When the people saw that Moses had not come down from the mount   32:1
for a long while, they gathered around Aaron and said, "Make us gods
who can lead us! As for this Moses, the man who brought us
out of Egypt, we have no idea what has become of him."
Aaron said to them, "Take the gold earrings from the ears   32:2
of your wives, your sons and your daughters, and bring them to me."
So all the people took the gold earrings from their ears,   32:3
and brought them to Aaron.
Aaron took the gold from them and fashioned it with a graving tool   32:4
into the image of a bull calf. And the people declared,
"These are your gods, O Israel, that brought you out of Egypt."
When Aaron saw their reaction, he built an altar for it.   32:5
And he proclaimed, "Tomorrow is a feast to Yahweh."
The people rose up early on the morrow, and offered burnt offerings,   32:6
and peace offerings. And the people ate, and drank, and played.
Yahweh said to Moses, "Go. Get down there. The people   32:7

you brought out of Egypt have corrupted themselves.
They have turned quickly aside from the way I commanded them.   32:8
They have made a molten calf, and have worshipped it, and have
sacrificed to it, and have said, 'These are your gods, O Israel,
that brought you out of the land of Egypt.'"

Yahweh said to Moses,   32:9
"I have watched this people, and it is a stubborn people.
Now leave me alone! Let my wrath burn hot against them,   32:10
that I may consume them. Then I will make of you a great nation."
Moses beseeched Yahweh his God, and said, "Lord, why does   32:11
your wrath burn hot against your people, who you have brought forth
out of the land of Egypt with great power, and with a mighty hand?
Why let the Egyptians say, 'With an evil plan he brought them out,   32:12
to kill them in the mountains, and wipe them from the face of the earth'?
Turn from your fierce wrath, and repent of this evil against your people.
Remember Abraham, Isaac and Israel, your servants, to whom you   32:13
swore by your own self, and said to them, 'I will multiply your seed
as the stars of heaven, and all this land that I have spoken of
I will give to your seed, and they shall inherit it forever.'"
And Yahweh repented of the evil that he thought to do to his people.   32:14
And Moses went down from the mount with the two tablets of the   32:15
testimony in his hand. The tablets were written on both sides.
On one side and the other were they written .
The tablets were the work of Yahweh, and the writing   32:16
was the writing of Yahweh, graven upon the tablets.

When Joshua heard the noise of the people as they shouted,   32:17
he said to Moses, "It sounds like war in the camp."
He said, "It is not the voice of them who shout for victory. Neither is it the   32:18
voice of them who cry for surrender. It is the sound of singing that I hear."
As soon as Moses came near the camp, he saw the calf and the dancing,   32:19
and his anger burned hot, and he threw the tablets down,
and broke them at the foot of the mountain.
He took the calf they had made and burnt it in the fire, then ground   32:20
it to powder, cast it into water, and made the Israelites drink it.
Moses said to Aaron, "What did these people do to you,   32:21
that you brought so great a sin upon them?"
Aaron said, "Let not your anger burn hot, my lord.   32:22
You know these people are set on mischief.
They said to me, 'Make us gods that can lead us.   32:23
And as for this Moses, the man who brought us out of Egypt,
we do not know what has become of him.'
So I said to them, 'Whoever has any gold, let them take it off.'   32:24
And they gave it me. Then I cast it into the fire, and out came this calf.'"

Moses saw that the people were running wild— for Aaron   32:25
had let them run wild and become a laughingstock to their enemies.
So Moses stood in the gate of the camp, and said, "Who is on the Lord's   32:26

side? Let him come to me." And all the sons of Levi gathered to him.
He said to them, "Thus saith the Lord God of Israel: 'Let every man   32:27
take up his sword. Go from gate to gate throughout the camp,
and each of you shall kill his brother, and his friend, and his neighbor.'"
The Levites did according to the word of Moses,   32:28
and about three thousand men were killed that day.
For Moses had said to them, "Consecrate yourselves to Yahweh today.   32:29
Every man shall kill his son and his brother, that Yahweh
may bestow upon you a blessing this day."

The next day Moses said to the people, "You have sinned a great sin.   32:30
I will go to Yahweh, and perhaps I can make an atonement for your sin."
Moses returned to Yahweh, and said,   32:31
"These people have sinned a great sin, and have made gods of gold.
Yet now, if you will, forgive their sin. If you cannot,   32:32
then I pray you, blot me out of the book you have written."
Yahweh said to Moses, "Whoever has sinned against me,   32:33
him will I blot out of my book.
But for now, lead the people to the place I described to you.   32:34
My agent will go before you. I will punish them
for their sin when the day of reckoning comes."
And so it was that Yahweh sent plagues among the people,   32:35
because they had caused Aaron to make the calf.

Chapter 33

Yahweh said to Moses, "Depart, you and the people you brought out   33:1
of Egypt. Go to the land I swore to Abraham, Isaac and Jacob,
saying, 'I will give it to your descendants.'
I will send an agent before you, and I will drive out the Canaanite,   33:2
the Amorite, the Hittite, the Perizzite, the Hivite and the Jebusite.
Go to a land flowing with milk and honey. But I will not go among you,   33:3
for you are a stubborn people, and I may destroy you along the way."
When the people heard these bad tidings,   33:4
they mourned, and no man put on his jewelry.
For Yahweh had said to Moses, "Tell the Israelites, 'You are a stubborn   33:5
people. If I were to come among you even for a moment, I would
destroy you. Now take off your jewelry while I decide what to do to you.'"
So the Israelites stripped themselves of their jewelry by Mount Horeb.   33:6

Moses took the tabernacle, and pitched it far off from the camp,   33:7
and he called it the Tabernacle of the Congregation. Everyone who
sought Yahweh went to the tabernacle, far away from camp.
When Moses went out to the tabernacle, every man stood at his   33:8
tent door and watched Moses until he was inside the tabernacle.
As Moses entered the tabernacle, the pillar of cloud descended   33:9
and stood at the door of the tabernacle. And Yahweh spoke with Moses.
All the people saw the pillar of cloud stand at the tabernacle door,   33:10
and all the people rose up and worshipped, every man at his tent door.

Yahweh spoke to Moses face-to-face, as a man speaks to his friend, 33:11
then Moses turned to go back to the camp. But his servant Joshua,
a young man, the son of Nun, would not leave the tabernacle.
Moses said to Yahweh, "See, you tell me, 'Raise up this people,' 33:12
but you have not let me know who you will send with me. Yet you say,
'I know you by name, and you have found grace in my sight.'
Therefore, I pray you, if I have found grace in your sight, show me 33:13
now your way, that I may know you and find grace in your sight.
Remember, this nation is your people."

Yahweh said, "My presence shall go with you, and I will give you rest." 33:14
Moses said, "If your presence will not go with me, do not make us leave. 33:15
For how shall anyone know that I and your people have found grace 33:16
in your sight unless you are with us? That is the only difference between
me and my people, and all the other people on the face of the earth."
Yahweh said, "I will do as you have spoken. 33:17
For you have found grace in my sight, and I know you by name."
Moses said, "I beseech you, show me your glory." 33:18
Yahweh said, "I will make all my goodness pass before you, 33:19
and I will proclaim Yahweh, the name of the Lord, before you.
I will be gracious to whom I will be gracious,
and I will show mercy to whom I will show mercy."
Yahweh said, "You cannot see my face, for no man can see me and live." 33:20
Yahweh said, "Behold, there is a place by me. Stand upon the rock. 33:21
When my glory passes by, I will put you in a cleft of the rock, 33:22
and cover you with my hand while I pass by.
I will take my hand away, and you shall see my back. 33:23
But you shall not see my face."

Chapter 34

Yahweh said to Moses, "Hew two tablets of stone like the first. I will 34:1
write upon these tablets the words that were on the tablets you broke.
Be ready in the morning. Come up Mount Sinai in the morning 34:2
and present yourself to me at the top of the mountain.
No man shall come up with you, and let no man be seen anywhere on 34:3
the mount. And do not let the flocks and herds feed near the mountain."
So Moses hewed two tablets of stone, like the first. And he rose up early 34:4
in the morning, and went up Mount Sinai as Yahweh had commanded.
And he took in his hand the two tablets of stone.

Then Yahweh descended in the cloud, and stood there with him. 34:5
And he proclaimed Yahweh, the name of the Lord.
Yahweh paraded before Moses, proclaiming, "Yahweh, Yahweh, 34:6
the all merciful, gracious and patient one, rich in goodness and truth,
keeping mercy for thousands, forgiving iniquity and transgression and sin, 34:7
but by no means leaving the guilty unpunished, who visits
the consequences of the sins of the fathers upon their children,
and their children's children, unto the third and fourth generations."

Moses bowed his head to earth, and worshipped. 34:8

Moses said, "If now I have found grace in your sight, O Lord, 34:9
I pray you, let my Lord go among us. For it is a stubborn people.
Pardon our iniquity and our sin, and take us for your inheritance."

Yahweh said, "Behold, I shall now make a covenant: Before all your people 34:10
I will do marvels, such as have not been done in all the earth,
nor in any nation. All the people you live among shall see the work
of Yahweh, for it is a shocking thing that I will do with you.

Observe that which I command you today. Behold, I drive out 34:11
before you the Amorite, and the Canaanite, and the Hittite,
and the Perizzite, and the Hivite, and the Jebusite.

Take heed that you do not make a covenant with the inhabitants 34:12
of the land where you are going, lest it become a snare in your midst.

Destroy their altars, break their images, and cut down their sacred poles. 34:13

"You shall worship no other god but me. 34:14
For the Lord, whose name is Jealous, is a jealous god.

Make no covenant with the inhabitants of the land. For when they 34:15
go whoring after their gods, and do sacrifices unto their gods,
they may invite you, and you might eat of his sacrifice.

And you might take their daughters unto your sons, 34:16
and when their daughters go whoring after their gods,
your sons might go whoring after their gods with them.

You shall make no images of gods. 34:17

Keep the Feast of Unleavened Bread. For seven days 34:18
eat unleavened bread in the time of the month Abib.
For in the month Abib you came out from Egypt.

Everything that opens the matrix is mine—every firstborn male 34:19
among you, and among your livestock, whether ox or goat or sheep.

The firstborn of an ass you may redeem with a lamb, 34:20
but if you do not pay the ransom, you must break his neck.
For the firstborn of your sons, you should pay the ransom.
No one shall appear before me empty-handed.

For six days you shall work, but on the seventh day you shall rest. 34:21
Even in the times of planting and harvest, you shall rest.

You shall observe the Feast of Harvest of the first fruits 34:22
of the wheat harvest, and the Feast of Ingathering at year's end.

Three times a year all your males must 34:23
appear before Yahweh, God of Israel.

I will drive out nations before you, and extend your borders. 34:24
No one will try to take your land when you appear
before Yahweh your God three times a year.

You shall not offer the blood of my sacrifice with leaven. Nor shall 34:25
any of the sacrifice of the Feast of the Passover be left until morning.

You shall bring the best of the first fruits of your land 34:26
into the house of Yahweh your God.
You shall not boil a kid in his mother's milk."

Then Yahweh said to Moses, "Write down these words. 34:27

For by these words I make a covenant with you, and with Israel."
Moses was with Yahweh forty days and forty nights.   34:28
He did not eat bread, nor drink water. And he wrote upon the tablets
the words of the covenant, the Ten Commandments.

When Moses came down from Mount Sinai with the two tablets   34:29
of testimony in his hand, when he came down from the mountain,
Moses did not know that his face shone because he spoke with Yahweh.
When Aaron and all the Israelites saw Moses, and beheld   34:30
the skin of his face shining, they were afraid to come near him.
But Moses called them closer, and Aaron and all the rulers   34:31
of the congregation came near, and Moses talked with them.
Afterward, all the Israelites came near, and Moses told them   34:32
the commandments Yahweh had given him on Mount Sinai.
When Moses had done speaking with them, he put a veil over his face.   34:33
Whenever Moses went into the tabernacle to speak with Yahweh,   34:34
he removed the veil. And when he came out,
he told the Israelites that which he was commanded.
But the Israelites would see the face of Moses, that his face shone.   34:35
So Moses put the veil back on his face until next he spoke with Yahweh.

Chapter 35

Moses gathered all the Israelites together and said to them,   35:1
"These are the things Yahweh has commanded you to do:
For six days work shall be done, but the seventh day shall be a holy day,   35:2
a sabbath to Yahweh. Whoever does work this day shall be put to death.
You shall kindle no fire in your homes on the sabbath day."   35:3
Moses spoke to all the Israelites, saying,   35:4
"These are the things Yahweh has commanded you to do:
Take up among you an offering to Yahweh. Whoever has a willing heart,   35:5
let him bring an offering of gold, and silver, and brass,
and blue, and purple, and scarlet, and fine linen, and goats' hair,   35:6
and ram skins dyed red, and badger skins, and shittim wood,   35:7
and oil for the light, and spices for anointing oil and for sweet incense,   35:8
and onyx stones, and stones to be set in the ephod the breastplate.   35:9

Every wise-hearted man shall come and make   35:10
all that Yahweh has commanded:
His tabernacle, and his tent, and his covering, and his clasps,   35:11
and his boards, and his bars, and his pillars, and his sockets,
and the ark, and its staves, and the mercy seat,   35:12
and the veil of the covering,
and the table, and its staves, and all its vessels, and the showbread,   35:13
and the lampstand, and the furniture,   35:14
and the lamps, and the oil for the lamps,
and the incense altar, and its staves, and the anointing oil, and the sweet   35:15
incense, and the hanging for the door at the entrance of the tabernacle,
and the altar of burnt offering, with its brass grate, and its staves,   35:16

and all its vessels, and the laver and its stand,
and the hangings of the court, and the pillars and their sockets, 35:17
and the hanging for the door of the courtyard,
and the pegs of the tabernacle, and the pegs of the court, and their ropes, 35:18
and the cloths of service to do service in the holy place, 35:19
and the holy garments for Aaron the priest,
and the garments for his sons to minister in the priest's office."
All the congregation of the Israelites departed from the presence of Moses. 35:20

Then they came, everyone whose heart stirred him, everyone 35:21
whose spirit had made him willing, and they brought their offerings
to the tabernacle for all its works, and for the holy garments.
They came, both men and women, as many whose hearts were willing, 35:22
and they brought bracelets, and earrings, and rings, and tablets—
all jewels of gold. Everyone presented an offering of gold to Yahweh.
Everyone who had blue, and purple, and scarlet, and fine linen, 35:23
and goats' hair, and red skins of rams, and badger skins, brought them.
Everyone who had an offering of silver and brass brought it to Yahweh. 35:24
Everyone who had shittim wood that could be used, brought it.
All the women who were wise-hearted, and spun cloth with their hands, 35:25
brought what they had spun—blue and purple and scarlet, of fine linen.
All the women whose heart stirred them in wisdom spun goats' hair. 35:26
The rulers of the people brought onyx stones, 35:27
and stones to be set in the ephod and the breastplate,
and spices, and oil for the light, and for the anointing oil, 35:28
and for the sweet incense.
The Israelites brought a willing offering to Yahweh, every man and 35:29
woman whose heart made them willing to bring it for all manner of work
that Yahweh had commanded to be made by Moses.

Moses said to the Israelites, "Behold, Yahweh has called by name 35:30
Bezaleel, son of Uri, grandson of Hur, of the tribe of Judah.
And he has filled him with the spirit of God—in wisdom, 35:31
in understanding, in knowledge, and in all manner of workmanship—
to devise curious work, to work in gold, and in silver, and in brass, 35:32
and in the cutting of stones, and the setting of stones, 35:33
and the carving of wood, to make all manner of cunning works.
And he has given him the ability to teach, 35:34
both he and Aholiab, son of Ahisamach, of the tribe of Dan.
He has given their hearts the wisdom to create all manner of works— 35:35
of the engraver, the artisan, the embroiderer, the weaver of fine linen
in blue and purple and scarlet. They can do any kind of skillful work."

Chapter 36

"Bezaleel and Aholiab, and every wise-hearted man whom Yahweh has 36:1
given the wisdom and understanding to work for the service of the
sanctuary, shall work according to all that Yahweh has commanded."
Moses called Bezaleel and Aholiab, and every wise-hearted man 36:2

in whose heart Yahweh had put wisdom, and everyone whose
heart stirred him to come into the work, to do it.
And they received from Moses all the offerings the Israelites   36:3
had brought for the work to make the sanctuary.
And the Israelites brought yet more offerings every morning.
All the wise-hearted men who did the work of the sanctuary,   36:4
left the work they were doing, one by one,
and came to Moses, saying, "The people bring much more   36:5
than needed for the work Yahweh commanded to make."
So Moses gave orders that it be proclaimed throughout the camp,   36:6
"Let neither man nor woman make any more offerings for the work
of the sanctuary." And the people were restrained from bringing more.
For what they had was sufficient for all the work, and even too much.   36:7

Bezaleel, and the wise-hearted men who helped him with the work of the   36:8
tabernacle, made ten curtains of fine woven linen, of blue and purple
and scarlet, with cherubim of artful workmanship woven into them.
The length of one curtain was twenty-eight cubits, and the breadth   36:9
four cubits. And the curtains were all of one size.
He coupled five curtains one to another,   36:10
and the other five curtains he coupled one to another.
He made loops of blue on the edge of one curtain from the selvedge   36:11
in the coupling. He did likewise on the outermost edge
of the coupling of the second set.
He made fifty loops in one curtain, and fifty loops on the edge   36:12
of the coupling of the second. The loops held one curtain to the other.
He made fifty clasps of gold, and coupled the curtains one to the other   36:13
with the clasps, so that it became one tabernacle.
He made eleven sheets of goat hair for the tent over the tabernacle.   36:14
The length of one sheet was thirty cubits, and the breadth four cubits.   36:15
The eleven sheets were of one size.
He coupled five sheets together, and the other six sheets together.   36:16
He made fifty loops in the coupling on the outermost edge of the sheets,   36:17
and fifty loops on the edge of the sheet that couples to the second.
He made fifty clasps of brass to couple the tent together, so it was one.   36:18
He made a covering for the tent of ram skins dyed red,   36:19
and a covering of badger skins above that.

He made boards for the tabernacle of shittim wood, standing up.   36:20
The length of a board was ten cubits, and the breadth a cubit and a half.   36:21
Each board had two tenons, equally distant one from the other.   36:22
He made all the boards of the tabernacle like this.
He made twenty boards for the south side of the tabernacle,   36:23
and made forty sockets of silver for the boards— two sockets in one board   36:24
for two tenons, and two sockets in the other boards for two tenons.
For the north side of the tabernacle he made twenty boards   36:25
and forty sockets of silver, two sockets in each board.   36:26
For the east and west sides of the tabernacle he made six boards each,   36:27
and for the corners he made two boards each.   36:28

These were coupled at the bottom, and coupled 36:29
at the top to one ring. He did this for each corner.
So for the corners there were eight boards 36:30
and sixteen sockets of silver, for each board had two sockets.

He made bars of shittim wood— 36:31
five bars for the south side of the tabernacle,
five bars for the north side of the tabernacle, 36:32
and five bars each for the east and west sides.
He made the middle bar to shoot through 36:33
the boards from one end to the other.
He overlaid the boards with gold, and made rings of gold 36:34
to hold the bars, and overlaid the bars with gold.
He made a veil of blue and purple and scarlet, 36:35
of fine linen, with cherubims of cunning work woven into it.
He made four pillars of shittim wood and overlaid them with gold, 36:36
with hooks of gold, and he cast for them four sockets of silver.
He made a hanging for the tabernacle door, of blue and purple 36:37
and scarlet, of fine woven linen and cunning needlework.
He made five pillars for the door hanging, with hooks, and he overlaid 36:38
their chapiters and fillets with gold. Their five sockets were of brass.

Chapter 37

Bezaleel made the ark of shittim wood—two and a half cubits in length, 37:1
a cubit and a half in breadth, and a cubit and a half in height.
He overlaid it with pure gold within and without, 37:2
and made a molding of gold to go around it.
He cast for it four rings of gold to be set by the four corners, 37:3
two rings on one side, and two rings on the other.
He made staves of shittim wood, and overlaid them with gold. 37:4
He put the staves into the rings on the sides of the ark, to bear it. 37:5
He made the mercy seat of pure gold. Two and a half cubits 37:6
was the length, and a cubit and a half the breadth.
He made two cherubim of gold, each hammered out of one piece, 37:7
for the two ends of the mercy seat—
one cherub on the end of one side, the other on the end 37:8
of the other side. He placed the cherubim on the two ends.
And the cherubim spread their wings on high, and their wings covered 37:9
the mercy seat, and they faced each other over the mercy seat.

He made the table of shittim wood, two cubits in length, 37:10
a cubit in breadth, and a cubit and a half in height,
and he overlaid it with pure gold, with a molding of gold all around it. 37:11
He made a frame a handwidth wide all around it, 37:12
with a crown of gold for the border.
And he cast for it four rings of gold, and he put the rings 37:13
at the four corners, near the table legs,
against the frame, as places for the staves to bear the table. 37:14

He made the staves of shittim wood, and overlaid them with gold.	37:15
And he made the vessels for the table—its dishes, and spoons,	37:16
and bowls, and covers—of pure gold.	

He made the lampstand of pure hammered gold. Its shaft and branches, 37:17
and bowls and knops and flowers, were all of the same piece.
Six branches came out of the sides, three branches on one side, 37:18
and three branches on the other side.
Each branch had three bowls made after the fashion of almonds, 37:19
and each bowl had a knop and a flower. All six branches were like this.
On the lampstand itself were four bowls, 37:20
made like almonds, with knops and flowers.
There was a knop under each pair of branches, 37:21
according to the six branches going out of it.
All the knops and flowers and branches 37:22
were of one piece of pure hammered gold.
He made for it seven lamps, with snuffers and snuff dishes of pure gold. 37:23
He used a talent of pure gold to make all the vessels. 37:24

He made the incense altar of shittim wood. The length of it was a cubit, 37:25
and the breadth was a cubit. It was foursquare. Two cubits was the height.
The horns were the same as the other alter.
And he overlaid it all with pure gold—the top of it, the sides all around, 37:26
and the horns. And he made a gold molding all around its crown.
And he made two rings of gold for it, under the crown, on the sides 37:27
by the two corners, to be places for the staves to bear it.
He made the staves of shittim wood, and overlaid them with gold. 37:28
He made the holy anointing oil, and the pure incense of sweet spices, 37:29
according to the work of an apothecary.

Chapter 38

He made the altar for burnt offerings of shittim wood. It was foursquare, 38:1
five cubits in length, five cubits in breadth. It was three cubits in height.
He made horns for it, one for each of the four corners, 38:2
each the same, and overlaid them with brass.
He made all the vessels for the altar of brass—the pots, 38:3
the shovels, the basins, the flesh hooks and the fire pans.
He made for the altar a brass grate, a mesh network 38:4
under the compass of it, about halfway up.
And he cast four rings for the corners of the brass grate, 38:5
to be places for the staves.
He made the staves of shittim wood, and overlaid them with brass. 38:6
He put the staves into the rings on the sides of the altar, to bear it. 38:7
He made the altar of boards, hollow inside.
He made the laver of brass, and its base of brass—from the brass mirrors 38:8
of the women who assembled at the door of the tabernacle.

And he made the courtyard. On the south side the hangings 38:9
of the court were a hundred cubits of fine woven linen.

There were twenty pillars, and their twenty sockets were brass. 38:10
The hooks of the pillars and their fillets were silver.
On the north side the hangings were a hundred cubits. There were twenty 38:11
pillars and brass sockets. The hooks and their fillets were silver.
The hangings on the west side were fifty cubits, with ten pillars 38:12
and brass sockets, and hooks and fillets of silver.
And for the east side, fifty cubits. 38:13
The hangings on one side of the court gate were fifteen cubits, 38:14
their pillars three, and their sockets three.
On the other side of the court gate, on this hand and that hand, 38:15
were hangings of fifteen cubits, their pillars three, and their sockets three.
All the hangings of the court were of fine woven linen. 38:16
The sockets for the pillars were brass, the hooks of the pillars and their 38:17
fillets were silver, and the overlaying of their chapiters were silver.
All the pillars of the court were filleted with silver.
The hanging for the gate of the court was needlework of blue 38:18
and purple and scarlet, of fine woven linen, twenty cubits in length,
and five cubits in the height, just like the hangings of the court.
It had four pillars and four brass sockets, with hooks of silver, 38:19
and chapiters and fillets overlayed with silver.
All the pegs of the tabernacle, and of the courtyard, were brass. 38:20

This is the account of the tabernacle, the tabernacle of the covenant, 38:21
that was recorded by the Levites, under the direction of Ithamar,
son of Aaron the priest, according to the instructions of Moses.
Bezaleel son of Uri, grandson of Hur, of the tribe of Judah, 38:22
made all that Yahweh commanded Moses.
With him was Aholiab, son of Ahisamach, of the tribe of Dan, 38:23
an engraver, a skillful artisan, and an embroiderer in blue
and purple and scarlet, of fine woven linen.
All the gold that was used for the work in the building of the sanctuary, 38:24
the gold from the offerings, was twenty-nine talents, and seven hundred
thirty shekels, based on the value of the shekel of the sanctuary.
The silver from the congregation totaled one hundred talents, 38:25
and one thousand seven hundred and seventy-five shekels.
This amounts to a bekah for every man—that is, half a shekel, 38:26
based on the shekel of the sanctuary—for everyone
twenty years old and upward numbered in the census,
which was six hundred three thousand, five hundred and fifty men.

From the hundred talents of silver were cast the sockets of the sanctuary, 38:27
and the sockets of the veil. A hundred sockets were made from
a hundred talents—one talent per socket.
From the one thousand seven hundred seventy-five shekels, he made 38:28
hooks for the pillars, and overlaid their chapiters, and filleted them.
The brass offering was seventy talents, 38:29
and two thousand four hundred shekels.
From this he made the sockets for the door of the tabernacle, and the 38:30
brass altar, and the brass grate for it, and all the vessels of the altar,

and the sockets of the court, and the sockets of the court gate,   38:31
and all the pegs of the tabernacle, and all the pegs of the courtyard.

Chapter 39

Of the blue and purple and scarlet, they made garments of service,   39:1
to minister in the holy place, and the holy garments for Aaron,
as Yahweh commanded Moses.
They made the ephod of fine woven linen of gold, blue, purple and scarlet.   39:2
They beat gold into thin plates, and cut it into wires, and wove it in with   39:3
the blue and purple and scarlet, in the fine linen, with cunning work.
They made shoulder pieces, and coupled them together by the two edges.   39:4
The curious girdle of the ephod was of the same fine woven linen   39:5
of gold, blue, purple and scarlet, as Yahweh commanded Moses.
They wrought onyx stones, engraved, as signets are engraved,   39:6
with the names of the tribes of Israel, and set the stones in gold.
And they put them on the shoulders of the ephod, as stones for   39:7
a memorial to the Israelites, as Yahweh commanded Moses.

They made the breastplate of cunning work, like the work of the ephod,   39:8
of gold, blue, purple and scarlet, of fine woven linen.
They made it foursquare, and doubled—a hand span in length,   39:9
and a hand span in breadth when doubled.
And they set in it four rows of stones.   39:10
The first row was a sardius, a topaz and a carbuncle.
The second row was an emerald, a sapphire and a diamond.   39:11
The third row was a ligure, an agate and an ameyourst.   39:12
The fourth row was a beryl, an onyx and a jasper.   39:13
All the stones were set in gold.
And the stones were engraved, like the engravings of a signet, with the   39:14
names of the twelve tribes of Israel, each stone with the name of a tribe.

They made chains of pure gold, braided like ropes, for the breastplate.   39:15
They made two gold settings and two gold rings,   39:16
and they put the two rings in the two ends of the breastplate.
They put the two braided chains of gold in the two rings   39:17
on the ends of the breastplate.
And they fastened the two braided chains in the two settings,   39:18
and put them on the shoulder pieces of the ephod, in front.
They made two gold rings, and attached them to the two ends   39:19
of the breastplate, on the border of it, on the inside edge.
They made two other gold rings, and attached them to the two sides   39:20
of the ephod, the lower part, toward the front, near the coupling,
just above the curious girdle of the ephod.
They tied the breastplate by its rings to the rings of the ephod with a   39:21
blue lace, so that it rested above the curious girdle, and so the breastplate
did not come loose from the ephod, as Yahweh commanded Moses.

They made the robe of the ephod of woven work, all of blue.   39:22
There was an opening for the head in the middle of the robe, like the hole   39:23

of a habergeon, with a woven hem around the opening so it did not tear.
On the hems of the robe they made pomegranates of blue   39:24
and purple and scarlet, of fine woven linen.
They made bells of pure gold, and put them between   39:25
the pomegranates on the hem of the robe—
a bell and a pomegranate, a bell and a pomegranate, all around   39:26
the hem of the minister's robe, as Yahweh commanded Moses.
They made coats of fine woven linen for Aaron and his sons,   39:27
and a mitre of fine linen, and hats and undergarments of fine linen,   39:28
and a girdle of fine linen, with blue and purple and scarlet needlework,   39:29
as Yahweh commanded Moses.
They made a plate of pure gold for the holy crown, and engraved   39:30
upon it, like the engraving of a signet, "HOLINESS TO THE LORD. "
And they tied to it a blue lace, and fastened it   39:31
high on the mitre, as Yahweh commanded Moses.

Thus was all the work of the tabernacle finished. The Israelites   39:32
did everything exactly as Yahweh commanded Moses.
And they brought the tabernacle to Moses—the tent,   39:33
and all its furniture, and its clasps, boards, bars, pillars and sockets,
and the covering of ram skins dyed red, and the covering   39:34
of badger skins, and the veil of the covering,
and the ark of the covenant, and its staves, and the mercy seat,   39:35
and the table, and all its vessels, and the showbread,   39:36
and the lampstand with its lamps set in order,   39:37
and all its vessels, and oil for light,
and the golden altar, and the anointing oil, and the sweet incense,   39:38
and the hanging for the tabernacle door,
and the brass altar, and its grate of brass, and its staves,   39:39
and all its vessels, and the laver with its stand,
and the hangings of the court, and its pillars and sockets,   39:40
and the hanging for the court gate, and its ropes and pegs,
and all the vessels for the service of the tabernacle,
and the cloths to do service in the holy place, and the holy garments for   39:41
Aaron the priest, and his sons' garments, to minister in the priest's office.
Thus did the Israelites do all the work as Yahweh commanded Moses,   39:42
And Moses looked upon all the work, and beheld that they had done   39:43
the work as Yahweh commanded. And Moses blessed them.

Chapter 40

Yahweh spoke to Moses, saying,   40:1
"On the first day of the first month you shall set up the tabernacle.   40:2
Put the ark of the covenant in it, and cover the ark with the veil.   40:3
Bring in the table, and set in order the things that are to be upon it.   40:4
Bring in the lampstand and light the lamps.
Place the gold altar for incense in front of the ark of the covenant,   40:5
and put up the hanging of the door to the tabernacle.
Place the altar of the burnt offering in front of the door of the tabernacle.   40:6

Place the laver between the tent and the altar, and put water in it.	40:7
Set up the court all around, and hang the hanging at the courtyard gate.	40:8
Take the anointing oil and anoint the tabernacle and all that is in it,	40:9

Place the laver between the tent and the altar, and put water in it. — 40:7

Set up the court all around, and hang the hanging at the courtyard gate. — 40:8

Take the anointing oil and anoint the tabernacle and all that is in it, — 40:9
to hallow it, and all its vessels. And it shall be holy.

Anoint the altar of the burnt offering and all its vessels, — 40:10
to sanctify the altar. It shall be an altar most holy.

Anoint the laver and its stand, to sanctify it. — 40:11

Bring Aaron and his sons to the door of the tabernacle — 40:12
and wash them with water.

Put the holy garments on Aaron, and anoint him, and sanctify him, — 40:13
that he may minister to me in the priest's office.

Bring his sons, and clothe them with coats. — 40:14

Anoint them, as you anointed their father, that they may minister — 40:15
to me in the priest's office. Their anointing shall establish an
everlasting priesthood throughout their generations."

And Moses did all that Yahweh commanded. — 40:16

So in the first month of the second year, on the first day — 40:17
of the month, the tabernacle was raised up.

Moses raised up the tabernacle, and fastened its sockets, — 40:18
and set up the boards, and put in the bars, and raised up its pillars.

And he spread the tent over the tabernacle, and put the covering — 40:19
of the tent above it, as Yahweh had commanded him.

He put the covenant into the ark, and set the staves on the ark, — 40:20
and set the mercy seat above the ark.

He brought the ark into the tabernacle, and set up the veil of the covering, — 40:21
and covered the ark of the covenant, as Yahweh had commanded him.

He put the table in the tent, on the north side, outside the veil. — 40:22

And he set the bread in order upon it before Yahweh, — 40:23
as Yahweh had commanded him.

He put the lampstand in the tent, near the table, on the south side. — 40:24

And he lit the lamps before Yahweh, as Yahweh had commanded him. — 40:25

He put the golden altar in the tent of the congregation in front of the veil. — 40:26

And he burnt sweet incense on it, as Yahweh had commanded him. — 40:27

He set up the hanging of the door of the tabernacle. — 40:28

He put the altar of burnt offering by the door of the tabernacle. — 40:29
And he offered upon it the burnt offering and the meat offering,
as Yahweh had commanded him.

He set the laver between the tent and the altar, and put water in it. — 40:30

And Moses and Aaron and his sons washed their hands and their feet. — 40:31

When they went into the tent, and when they came near the altar, — 40:32
they washed, as Yahweh commanded Moses.

He raised up the court around the tabernacle and the altar, — 40:33
and set up the hanging of the court gate. Thus Moses finished the work.

Then a cloud came over the tent of the congregation, — 40:34
and the glory of Yahweh filled the tabernacle.

Moses was not able to enter the tent because the cloud — 40:35

was upon it, and the glory of Yahweh filled the tabernacle.
From then on, whenever the cloud arose from over the tabernacle,   40:36
the Israelites would journey to their next encampment.
If the cloud was upon the tabernacle, they did not journey until it arose.   40:37
The cloud of Yahweh was upon the tabernacle by day, and fire was   40:38
upon it by night, in the sight of all Israel, throughout all their journeys.

The Third Book of Moses Called
Leviticus

Chapter 1

Yahweh called to Moses out of the tabernacle, and told him   1:1
to speak to the children of Israel, saying, "When any of you   1:2
brings an offering of livestock to me, your offering may be
from the ox herds, or from the flocks of sheep or goats.
If your offering is a burnt sacrifice of the herd,   1:3
let it be a male without blemish. You shall offer it of your own
voluntary will at the door of the tabernacle before me.
You shall put your hand upon the head of the burnt offering,   1:4
and it shall be accepted as an atonement for you.
You shall kill the bull before me, and the priests, Aaron's sons,   1:5
shall sprinkle the blood around the altar by the door of the tabernacle.
Then you shall skin the burnt offering and cut it into pieces.   1:6
The sons of Aaron the priest shall put fire upon the altar,   1:7
and lay the wood in order upon the fire.
The priests, Aaron's sons, shall arrange the pieces, and the head,   1:8
and the fat in order on the wood of the alter fire.
The animal's insides and his legs you shall wash in water.   1:9
And the priest shall burn all of it on the altar, to be a burnt sacrifice,
an offering made by fire for a sweet savor unto Yahweh.

"If your offering of a burnt sacrifice is from the flocks   1:10
of sheep or goats, you shall bring a male without blemish.
You shall kill it on the north side of the altar before me.   1:11
The priests, Aaron's sons, shall sprinkle his blood around the altar.
And you shall cut it into pieces, with its head and its fat, and the priest   1:12
shall lay them in order on the wood of the alter fire.
The animal's insides and his legs you shall wash in water.   1:13
And the priest shall burn all of it on the altar, to be a burnt sacrifice,
an offering made by fire for a sweet savor unto Yahweh.

"If the burnt sacrifice for your offering to me is fowls,   1:14
you shall bring turtledoves or pigeons.
The priest shall bring it to the altar, and wring off his head, and burn it   1:15
on the altar. And the blood of it shall be wrung out at the side of the altar.
You shall pluck away its crop and its feathers,   1:16
and cast them on the east side of the altar, with the ashes.
You shall cleave it between the wings, but not tear it apart.   1:17
And the priest shall burn it upon the wood fire of the altar, to be a burnt
sacrifice, an offering made by fire for sweet savor unto Yahweh.

Chapter 2

"When anyone offers a grain offering to Yahweh, his offering must   2:1
be of fine flour. He shall pour oil on it, and put frankincense on it.
And he shall bring it to Aaron's sons the priests. A priest shall take   2:2
a handful of the flour and oil, with the frankincense on it, and burn it
upon the altar, as an offering made by fire, of sweet savor unto Yahweh.
The remainder of the offering shall be given to Aaron and his sons.   2:3
It is a most holy offering to Yahweh made by fire.
If you bring a grain offering baked in the oven, it shall be unleavened   2:4
cakes of fine flour mixed with oil, or unleavened wafers anointed with oil.
If your offering is a grain offering baked in a pan,   2:5
it shall be of fine flour, unleavened, mixed with oil.
Break it into pieces and pour oil on it. It is a grain offering.   2:6
If your offering is a grain offering cooked in the frying pan,   2:7
it shall be made of fine flour with oil.
Bring the grain offering that is made of these things to Yahweh.   2:8

"'When it is presented to the priest, he shall bring it to the altar.
The priest shall take from the grain offering a memorial portion,   2:9
and burn it upon the altar. It is an offering made by fire,
of a sweet savor unto Yahweh.
That which is left of the grain offering shall be given to Aaron   2:10
and his sons. It is a most holy offering to me made by fire.
No grain offering brought to me shall be made with leaven. You shall   2:11
burn no leaven, nor any honey, in any offering to me made by fire.
As for the offering of the first fruits, you shall offer them to me,   2:12
but they shall not be burnt on the altar for a sweet savor.
Every offering of grain shall be seasoned with salt. Do not omit   2:13
the salt of the covenant of your God from your grain offering.
All your offerings shall be offered with salt.
If you offer a grain offering of your first fruits to me, offer your   2:14
first green ears of grain dried by the fire—grain beaten out of full ears.
Put oil on it, and put frankincense on it. It is a grain offering.   2:15
The priest shall burn a memorial portion—a part of the grain and oil,   2:16
with the frankincense on it. It is an offering made by fire unto Yahweh.

Chapter 3

"If his offering is a sacrifice for a peace offering, chosen from the herd,   3:1
whether male or female, he shall offer it without blemish before Yahweh.
He shall lay his hand upon the head of his offering, and kill it at the door   3:2
of the tabernacle of the congregation. Aaron's sons the priests
shall sprinkle the blood on the altar and around it.
And he shall offer the sacrifice of the peace offering as an offering   3:3
made by fire unto me—the fat that covers the entrails,
and all the fat that is upon the inner organs, and the two kidneys,
and the fat that is on them near the flanks, and the prime lobe   3:4
of the liver, which shall be removed with the kidneys.

Then Aaron's sons shall burn it on the altar, upon the burnt sacrifice   3:5
that is on top of the wood on the fire. It is an offering made by fire,
of a sweet savor unto Yahweh.
If his offering for a sacrifice of peace offering unto Yahweh   3:6
be of the flock, whether male or female, it shall be without blemish.
If he offers a lamb for his offering, then he shall offer it before Yahweh.   3:7
He shall lay his hand upon the head of his offering,   3:8
and kill it before the tabernacle of the congregation.
And Aaron's sons shall throw its blood all around the altar.
He shall offer the sacrifice of the peace offering, an offering made by fire   3:9
unto Yahweh, all the fat and the whole rump—cut close to the backbone—
and the fat that covers the organs, and the fat that covers the entrails,
and the two kidneys, and the fat that is upon them, which is by the flanks,   3:10
and the prime lobe of the liver along with the kidneys, he shall offer.
And the priest shall burn it upon the altar.   3:11
It is the food of the offering made by fire unto Yahweh.
If his offering be a goat, he shall offer it before Yahweh.   3:12
He shall lay his hand upon its head and kill it before the tabernacle,   3:13
then the sons of Aaron shall sprinkle its blood around the altar.
He shall then make his offering—an offering made by fire unto Yahweh—   3:14
of the fat that covers the innards, and the fat that is upon the innards,
and the two kidneys, and the fat that is upon them by the flanks,   3:15
and the caul above the liver, which he shall take away with the kidneys.
And the priest shall burn them upon the altar. It is the food of the offering   3:16
made by fire for a sweet savor—all the fat is Yahweh's.
Let it be a perpetual statute for all your generations throughout   3:17
all your houses, that you eat neither fat nor blood."

Chapter 4

Yahweh spoke to Moses, saying to   4:1
tell the children of Israel, "If a soul sins against any of Yahweh's   4:2
commandments through ignorance of the things
that ought not be done, and does any of them,
or if the anointed priest sins and brings guilt upon the people,   4:3
let him bring a young bull without blemish for a sin offering to Yahweh.
He shall bring the bull to the door of the tabernacle and lay his hand   4:4
upon the bull's head, and kill the bull before Yahweh.
The anointed priest shall take the bull's blood,   4:5
and bring it to the tabernacle of the congregation.
And the priest shall dip his finger in the blood, and sprinkle the blood   4:6
seven times before Yahweh in front of the veil of the sanctuary.
The priest shall put some of the blood on the horns of the altar   4:7
of sweet incense before Yahweh, which is in the tabernacle,
then pour all the blood of the bull at the bottom of the altar
of the burnt offering, which is at the door of the tabernacle.
And he shall take from the bull all the fat for the sin offering—   4:8
the fat that covers the innards, and all the fat that is upon the innards,

and the two kidneys, and the fat that is upon them by the flanks, 4:9
and the caul above the liver, which he shall take away with the kidneys,
just as it was taken from the bull of the sacrifice of peace offerings— 4:10
and the priest shall burn them upon the altar of the burnt offering.
The skin of the bull, and all his flesh, and his head, 4:11
and his legs, and his innards and his dung—
the whole bull he shall carry outside the camp to a clean place 4:12
where the ashes are poured out, and burn him on a wood fire.
Where the ashes are poured out, he shall be burnt.

"If the whole congregation of Israel sins through ignorance, 4:13
and the sin be hidden from the eyes of the assembly,
and they have done things that should not be done,
and are guilty of breaking any of the commandments of Yahweh,
then when that sin becomes known the congregation shall offer a young 4:14
bull for the sin, and bring him before the tabernacle of the congregation.
The elders of the congregation shall lay their hands upon 4:15
the head of the bull and the bull shall be killed before Yahweh.
The anointed priest shall bring the bull's blood to the tabernacle. 4:16
And the priest shall dip his finger in the blood, and in front of 4:17
the veil of the tabernacle, sprinkle it seven times before Yahweh.
He shall put some of the blood upon the horns of the altar that is before 4:18
Yahweh in the tabernacle, and shall pour out all the blood at the bottom
of the altar of the burnt offering, which is at the door of the tabernacle.
He shall take all his fat from him, and burn it upon the altar. 4:19
He shall do with the bull as he did with the bull for a sin offering, and the 4:20
priest shall make an atonement for them, and it shall be forgiven them.
And he shall carry the bull outside the camp, and burn him 4:21
as he burned the first bull. It is a sin offering for the congregation.

"If a ruler has sinned through ignorance against any of Yahweh's 4:22
commandments and is guilty concerning things that should not be done,
when his sin comes to his knowledge, he shall bring as his offering 4:23
a kid of the goats, a male without blemish.
He shall lay his hand upon the head of the goat, and kill it in the place 4:24
where they kill the burnt offering before Yahweh. It is a sin offering.
The priest shall take of the blood of the sin offering with his finger, 4:25
and put it upon the horns of the altar of the burnt offering, and shall
pour out its blood at the bottom of the altar of the burnt offering.
And he shall burn all his fat upon the altar, as with the fat of the 4:26
sacrifice of peace offerings. And the priest shall make an atonement
for him concerning his sin, and it shall be forgiven him.

"If one of the common people sins through ignorance, 4:27
and is guilty of doing things that ought not be done
concerning any of Yahweh's commandments,
when his sin comes to his knowledge he shall bring his offering, 4:28
a kid of the goats, a female without blemish, for his sin.
He shall lay his hand upon the head of the sin offering, 4:29

and kill the sin offering in the place of the burnt offering.
The priest shall take of its blood with his finger and put it   4:30
upon the horns of the altar of the burnt offering,
and shall pour out all the blood at the bottom of the altar.
And he shall take away all the fat, just as the fat is taken off the sacrifice   4:31
of peace offerings, and the priest shall burn it upon the altar for a sweet
savor unto Yahweh. The priest shall make an atonement for him,
and it shall be forgiven him.
If he bring a lamb for a sin offering, it shall be a female without blemish.   4:32
He shall lay his hand upon the head of the sin offering   4:33
and kill it in the place where they kill the burnt offering.
The priest shall take of the blood of the sin offering with his finger   4:34
and put it upon the horns of the altar of the burnt offering,
and he shall pour out all the blood at the bottom of the altar.
And he shall take away all the fat, just as the fat of the lamb is taken away   4:35
from the sacrifice of the peace offerings, and the priest shall burn it upon
the altar, according to the offerings made by fire unto Yahweh. And the
priest shall make an atonement for his sin, and it shall be forgiven him.

Chapter 5

"Anyone who does not give sworn testimony to a sin   5:1
he has witnessed or known of, shall bear the consequences.
Anyone who touches any unclean thing, whether it be a carcass of an   5:2
unclean beast, or a carcass of unclean cattle, or the carcass of unclean
creeping things—even if unknowingly—he becomes unclean and is guilty.
Anyone who unknowingly touches the uncleanness of man—whatever   5:3
that uncleanness might be—when he becomes aware of it, shall be guilty.
Anyone who carelessly swears an oath with his lips, whether it be   5:4
to do good or evil, becomes guilty when he realizes what he has done.
And so shall it be, that when anyone is guilty   5:5
of one of these things, he shall confess that he has sinned.
And he shall bring as his sin offering unto Yahweh a female   5:6
from the flock, a lamb or a kid of the goats. And the priest shall
make an atonement for him concerning his sin.
If he is not able to bring a lamb, he shall bring for his trespass   5:7
two turtledoves or two young pigeons unto Yahweh—
one for a sin offering, and the other for a burnt offering.
He shall bring them to the priest, who shall offer that which is for the sin   5:8
offering first, and wring off his head from his neck, but shall not divide it.
The priest shall sprinkle some of the blood on the side of the altar.   5:9
The rest of the blood shall be wrung out at the bottom of the altar.
It is a sin offering.
Then he shall offer the second for a burnt offering, in the proper manner.   5:10
The priest shall make an atonement for his sin, and it shall be forgiven.
If he be not able to bring two turtledoves or two young pigeons, then   5:11
he that sinned shall bring the tenth part of an ephah of fine flour for a sin
offering. He shall put no oil or frankincense upon it, for it is a sin offering.

He shall bring it to the priest, and the priest shall take a handful of it 5:12
as a memorial, and burn it on the altar, according to the offerings
made by fire unto Yahweh. It is a sin offering.
The priest shall make an atonement for him as to 5:13
the sin he has committed, and it shall be forgiven him.
The rest of the flour shall be the priest's, as a grain offering."

Yahweh spoke to Moses, saying, 5:14
"If anyone commits a trespass, and sins through ignorance against 5:15
the holy things of Yahweh, he shall bring unto Yahweh a ram without
blemish out of the flocks—of a proper value in shekels of silver,
as determined by the sanctuary—for a trespass offering.
He shall make amends for the harm he has done in the holy thing, 5:16
and shall give another fifth part of the ram's value to the priest.
The priest shall make an atonement for him with the ram
of the trespass offering, and it shall be forgiven him.
If anyone commits any sin that is forbidden by the 5:17
commandments of Yahweh, even though he is not aware of it,
he is guilty and shall bear the consequences.
He shall bring a ram without blemish out of the flock, 5:18
of proper value, for a trespass offering unto the priest.
The priest shall make an atonement for him concerning his ignorance
of the sin he committed, and it shall be forgiven him.
It is a trespass offering. He has certainly trespassed against Yahweh." 5:19

Chapter 6

 Yahweh spoke to Moses, saying, 6:1
"If anyone sins and commits a trespass against Yahweh, who lies to his 6:2
neighbor about that which was delivered into his care, or pledged in
fellowship, or takes something away by force, or deceives his neighbor,
or finds something that was lost and lies concerning it, or swears falsely— 6:3
in any and all these trespasses that a man does, thereby sinning,
it shall be, because he is guilty of sin, that he shall restore that which 6:4
he took violently away, or the thing he has deceitfully gotten,
or that which was delivered him to keep, or the lost thing he found,
or that about which he has sworn falsely. He shall restore it 6:5
to the principal, and shall add the fifth part more, and give it
to him to whom it appertains in the day of his trespass offering.
He shall bring as his trespass offering to Yahweh a ram without blemish 6:6
out of the flock, with proper estimation of value,
for a trespass offering, and give it to the priest.
The priest shall make an atonement for him before Yahweh, 6:7
and his trespasses shall be forgiven him for anything he has done."

Yahweh spoke to Moses, saying to 6:8
tell Aaron and his sons, "This is the law of the burnt offering: 6:9
The burnt offering shall be kept upon the altar all night
into the morning, and the fire upon the altar shall be kept burning.

The priest shall put on his linen garment and his linen breeches,   6:10
and he shall take up the ashes of the burnt offering on the altar,
and he shall put them beside the altar.
Then he shall take off his garments and put on other garments,   6:11
and carry the ashes outside the camp to a clean place.
The fire upon the altar shall be kept burning. It shall not be put out.   6:12
The priest shall burn wood on it every morning and lay the burnt offering
in order upon it. And he shall burn thereon the fat of the peace offerings.
The fire shall ever be burning upon the altar. It shall never go out.   6:13

"This is the law of the grain offering: The sons of Aaron   6:14
shall offer it before Yahweh in front of the altar.
The priest shall take a handful of the flour of the grain offering, and of the   6:15
oil and frankincense that is upon the grain offering, and shall burn it upon
the altar, even the memorial portion, for a sweet savor unto Yahweh.
The remainder of it Aaron and his sons shall eat.   6:16
With unleavened bread shall it be eaten in the holy place.
In the court of the tabernacle of the congregation they shall eat it.
It shall not be baked with leaven. I have given it unto them   6:17
for their portion of my offerings made by fire. It is most holy,
as is the sin offering, and the trespass offering.
All the males among the children of Aaron shall eat of it.   6:18
It shall be a statute forever in your generations concerning the offerings
to Yahweh made by fire. Everyone who touches them shall be holy."

Yahweh said to Moses,   6:19
"This is the offering of Aaron and of his sons, which they shall offer unto   6:20
Yahweh in the day he is anointed: The tenth part of an ephah of fine flour
for a perpetual grain offering, half of it in the morning, and half at night.
In a pan it shall be made with oil, and when it is baked, you shall   6:21
bring it in, and the pieces of the baked grain offering
you shall offer for a sweet savor unto Yahweh.
The priest from among Aaron's sons who is anointed to succeed him   6:22
shall offer it. It is a statute forever unto Yahweh. It shall be wholly burnt.
Every grain offering for the priest shall be wholly burnt.   6:23
It shall not be eaten."

Yahweh spoke to Moses, instructing him   6:24
to tell Aaron and his sons, "This is the law of the sin offering: 6:25
In the place where the burnt offering is killed,
the sin offering shall be killed before Yahweh. It is most holy.
The priest who offers it for sin shall eat it. In the holy place   6:26
shall it be eaten, in the court of the tabernacle of the congregation.
Whatever touches the flesh thereof shall be holy. And where there is   6:27
blood on any garment, you shall wash that garment in the holy place.
If the meat is boiled in a clay pot, the pot shall be broken. If it is boiled   6:28
in a metal pot, the pot shall be scoured and rinsed in water.
All the males among the priests shall eat thereof. It is most holy.   6:29

No sin offering from which blood is brought into the tabernacle to make   6:30
atonement in the holy place shall be eaten. It shall be burnt in the fire.

Chapter 7

"Likewise this is the law of the trespass offering. It is most holy.   7:1
In the place where they kill the burnt offering they shall kill the trespass   7:2
offering, and the blood thereof shall be sprinkled round about the altar.
He shall offer of it all the fat, the rump, the fat that covers the innards,   7:3
and the two kidneys, and the fat that is on them by the flanks, and the caul   7:4
that is above the liver, which he shall take away with the kidneys.
The priest shall burn them upon the altar for an offering   7:5
made by fire unto Yahweh. It is a trespass offering.
Every male among the priests shall eat of it.   7:6
It shall be eaten in the holy place. It is most holy.
As the sin offering is, so is the trespass offering. There is one law for both.   7:7
The priest who makes atonement with it shall have the offering.
The priest who offers any man's burnt offering shall have for himself   7:8
the skin of the burnt offering that he offered.
And all the grain offering that is baked in the oven, and all that is dressed   7:9
in the frying pan, and in the pan, belongs to the priest who offered it.
Every grain offering, whether mixed with oil or dry,   7:10
shall belong to all the sons of Aaron equally.

"This is the law of the peace offerings you shall offer unto Yahweh: 7:11
If he offers it for a thanksgiving, then he shall offer with the sacrifice   7:12
of thanksgiving unleavened cakes mingled with oil, and unleavened
wafers anointed with oil, and cakes mingled with oil, of fine flour, fried.
Besides the cakes, he shall offer leavened bread   7:13
with the sacrifice of thanksgiving of his peace offerings.
And of it he shall offer one loaf out of the oblation   7:14
for a special offering to Yahweh, and it shall belong to
the priest who sprinkles the blood of the peace offerings.
The flesh of the sacrifice of his peace offerings for thanksgiving   7:15
shall be eaten the same day it is offered.
He shall not leave any of it until the morning.
If the sacrifice of his offering is a vow, or a voluntary offering,   7:16
it shall be eaten the same day he offers his sacrifice,
and on the morrow also the remainder of it shall be eaten.
But the remainder of the flesh of the sacrifice   7:17
shall be burnt with fire on the third day.
If any of the flesh of the sacrifice of his peace offerings is eaten   7:18
on the third day, it shall not be accepted, neither shall it be
imputed unto him who offers it. It shall be an abomination,
and the one who eats of it shall bear his iniquity.
Flesh that touches any unclean thing shall not be eaten,   7:19
but shall be burnt with fire. Only clean flesh shall be eaten.
Anyone who is unclean and eats of the flesh of the sacrifice of peace   7:20
offerings that pertain to Yahweh, shall be cut off from his people.

Moreover, anyone who touches any unclean thing, such as an unclean	7:21
man, or an unclean beast, or any abominable unclean thing,	
and eats of the flesh of the sacrifice of peace offerings	
that pertain to Yahweh, shall be cut off from his people."	

Yahweh spoke to Moses, — 7:22
telling him to speak to the children of Israel, saying, — 7:23
"You shall eat no fat of an ox, or a sheep or a goat.
The fat of any animal that dies of itself, or is killed by other beasts, — 7:24
may be used in other ways, but in no wise shall you eat of it.
For whosoever eats the fat of the beast that men offer by fire — 7:25
unto Yahweh, shall be cut off from his people.
Moreover, you shall eat no manner of blood, — 7:26
whether it be of fowl or of beast, in any of your dwellings.
Whoever eats any manner of blood shall be cut off from his people." — 7:27

Yahweh spoke unto Moses, — 7:28
telling him to speak to the children of Israel, saying, — 7:29
"He who would offer the sacrifice of his peace offerings unto Yahweh
shall himself bring to Yahweh the sacrifice of his peace offerings.
By his own hands he shall bring the offerings made by fire unto Yahweh. — 7:30
He shall bring the fat with the breast, that the breast
may be waved as a wave offering before Yahweh.
The priest shall burn the fat upon the altar, — 7:31
but the breast shall belong to Aaron and his sons.
The right shoulder you shall give to the priest for a heave offering — 7:32
from the sacrifices of your peace offerings.
Whoever among the sons of Aaron that offers the blood of the — 7:33
peace offerings, and the fat, shall have the right shoulder for his part.
For I have taken the wave-breast and the heave-shoulder of the — 7:34
sacrifices of the peace offerings of the children of Israel, and have
given them to Aaron the priest, and to his sons, by statute, forever.
This is the portion given to Aaron and his sons out of the offerings — 7:35
to Yahweh made by fire, on the day he anointed them
to minister to Yahweh as priests.
Yahweh commanded these be given from the children of Israel, in the day — 7:36
that he anointed them, by a statute forever throughout their generations.
This is the law of the burnt offering, of the grain offering, — 7:37
of the sin offering, of the trespass offering, of the consecrations,
and of the sacrifice of the peace offerings,
which Yahweh commanded Moses on Mount Sinai, on the day — 7:38
he commanded the children of Israel to offer their oblations
to Yahweh, in the wilderness of Sinai."

Chapter 8

Yahweh spoke to Moses, saying, — 8:1
"Take Aaron and his sons, and the garments, and the anointing oil, and a — 8:2
bull for the sin offering, and two rams, and a basket of unleavened bread,

and gather all the congregation together unto the door of the tabernacle." 8:3
Moses did as Yahweh commanded him, and the assembly was gathered 8:4
together unto the door of the tabernacle of the congregation.
Moses said to the congregation, "This is what Yahweh has commanded." 8:5
Then Moses brought Aaron and his sons, and washed them with water. 8:6
He put the coat upon Aaron, and girded him with the girdle, and clothed 8:7
him with the robe, and put the ephod upon him, and girded him
with the curious girdle of the ephod, and bound it to him.
He put the breastplate upon him, 8:8
and put the Urim and the Thummim in the breastplate.
He put the mitre upon his head, and upon the mitre, in the forefront, 8:9
he put the golden plate, the holy crown, as Yahweh commanded him.
Then Moses took the anointing oil and anointed 8:10
the tabernacle and all therein, sanctifying them.
He sprinkled the oil upon the altar seven times, anointing the altar 8:11
and all its vessels, both the laver and its foot, to sanctify them.
Then he poured some of the anointing oil upon Aaron's head, 8:12
and anointed him, and sanctified him.
Moses brought Aaron's sons and put coats upon them, and girded them 8:13
with girdles, and put hats upon them, as Yahweh commanded him.
He brought the bull for the sin offering, and Aaron and his sons 8:14
laid their hands upon the head of the bull for the sin offering.
Then Moses killed it, and took some of the blood and put it upon the horns 8:15
of the altar round about with his finger, and purified the altar,
and poured the blood at the bottom of the altar,
and sanctified it, to make reconciliation upon it.
Then he took the fat that was upon the innards, and caul above the liver, 8:16
and the two kidneys and their fat, and burned it upon the altar.
But the bull, and his hide, and his flesh, and his dung he burnt 8:17
with fire outside the camp, as Yahweh commanded Moses.

He brought the ram for the burnt offering, and Aaron 8:18
and his sons laid their hands upon the head of the ram.
Moses killed it, and sprinkled the blood upon the altar round about. 8:19
He cut the ram into pieces and burned the head, and the pieces and the fat. 8:20
Moses washed the innards and the legs in water, and burned the whole 8:21
ram upon the altar. It was a burnt sacrifice for a sweet savor,
an offering made by fire unto Yahweh, as Yahweh had commanded him.
He brought the other ram, the ram of consecration, and Aaron 8:22
and his sons laid their hands upon the head of the ram.
Moses killed it, and put some of the blood on the tip of Aaron's right ear, 8:23
and on the thumb of his right hand, and on the great toe of his right foot.
Then he brought Aaron's sons and put of the blood upon the tip of their 8:24
right ears, and upon the thumbs of their right hands, and upon the great
toes of their right feet, and sprinkled blood upon the altar round about.
He took the fat and the rump, and the fat upon the innards, and the caul 8:25
above the liver, and the two kidneys and their fat, and the right shoulder,
and out of the basket of unleavened bread that was before Yahweh, 8:26

he took one unleavened cake, and a cake of oiled bread, and one wafer,
and put them on the fat, and upon the right shoulder.
And he gave it all into Aaron's hands, and into his sons' hands,   8:27
and waved them as a wave offering before Yahweh.
Then Moses took these out of their hands, and burned them   8:28
on the altar, along with the burnt offering. They were consecrations
for a sweet savor, an offering made by fire unto Yahweh.
Moses took the breast and waved it for a wave offering, for this was   8:29
Moses' part of the ram of consecration, as Yahweh had commanded him.
Moses took of the anointing oil, and of the blood that was upon the altar,   8:30
and sprinkled it upon Aaron and his garments, and upon his sons and
his sons' garments, sanctifying Aaron and his sons, and their garments.

Moses said to Aaron and his sons: "Boil the flesh at the door   8:31
of the tabernacle, and there eat it, along with the bread in the basket
of consecrations, as I commanded, saying, 'Aaron and his sons shall eat it.'
That which remains of the flesh and the bread you shall burn with fire.   8:32
You shall not go out of the door of the tabernacle for seven days, until the   8:33
days of your consecration end. For seven days he shall consecrate you.
What was done this day, was as Yahweh commanded,   8:34
to make an atonement for you.
Therefore you shall abide at the door of the tabernacle day and night   8:35
for seven days, and keep the charge of Yahweh so that you do not die.
For so I am commanded."
Aaron and his sons did all the things Yahweh had commanded Moses.   8:36

Chapter 9

It came to pass on the eighth day, that Moses   9:1
called Aaron and his sons and the elders of Israel.
He said to Aaron: "Take a young calf for a sin offering, and a ram   9:2
without blemish for a burnt offering, and offer them before Yahweh.
And unto the children of Israel say: 'Take a kid of the goats   9:3
for a sin offering, and a calf and a lamb, both of the first year,
without blemish, for a burnt offering.
Also take a bull and a ram for peace offerings to sacrifice before Yahweh,   9:4
and a grain offering mixed with oil. For today Yahweh will appear to you.'"

So they brought that which Moses commanded before the tabernacle.   9:5
All the congregation drew near and stood before Yahweh.
Moses said: "This is what Yahweh commanded that you do,   9:6
and the glory of Yahweh shall appear unto you."
Moses said to Aaron: "Go to the altar and offer your sin offering   9:7
and burnt offering, and make an atonement for yourself,
and for the people. Offer the offering of the people,
and make an atonement for them, as Yahweh commanded."
So Aaron went to the altar and killed the calf   9:8
of the sin offering, which was for himself.
The sons of Aaron brought the blood to him, and he dipped   9:9

his finger in the blood and put it upon the horns of the altar,
and poured out the blood at the bottom of the altar.
The fat and the kidneys, and the caul above the liver of the sin offering,   9:10
he burnt upon the altar, as Yahweh commanded Moses.
The flesh and the hide he burnt with fire outside the camp.   9:11

He killed the burnt offering, and Aaron's sons presented unto him   9:12
the blood, which he sprinkled round about upon the altar.
They presented the burnt offering to him with the pieces thereof,   9:13
and the head, and he burned them upon the altar.
He washed the innards and the legs, and burned them   9:14
along with the burnt offering on the altar.
He brought the people's offering, and took the goat, which was the   9:15
sin offering, and killed it, and offered it for sin, as the first offering.
He brought the burnt offering, and offered it according to the command.   9:16
He brought the grain offering and took a handful thereof,   9:17
and burnt it upon the altar, beside the burnt sacrifice of the morning.
He killed the bull and the ram for a sacrifice of peace offerings,   9:18
which was for the people. Aaron's sons presented the blood to him,
which he sprinkled upon the altar round about,
and the fat of the bull and of the ram, and the rump, and that which   9:19
covers the innards, and the kidneys, and the caul above the liver.
They put the fat upon the breasts, and Aaron burned the fat on the altar.   9:20
The breasts and the right shoulder Aaron waved   9:21
for a wave offering before Yahweh, as Moses commanded.
Aaron lifted up his hand toward the people and blessed them,   9:22
and came down from the offering of the sin offering,
and the burnt offering, and the peace offerings.
Moses and Aaron went into the tabernacle, then came out and blessed   9:23
the people, and the glory of Yahweh appeared unto all the people.
And there came a fire out from before Yahweh   9:24
that consumed upon the altar the burnt offering and the fat.
When the people saw this, they all shouted and fell on their faces.

Chapter 10

Nadab and Abihu, the sons of Aaron, each took their censer,   10:1
and put hot coals in them and laid incense thereon,
and offered strange fire before Yahweh, which he had not commanded.
And fire came out from Yahweh, which devoured them.   10:2
And they died before Yahweh.
Moses said to Aaron: "This is what Yahweh meant when he said,   10:3
'I will be sanctified in them that come nigh unto me, and before
all the people I will be glorified.'" And Aaron held his peace.
Moses called Mishael and Elzaphan, the sons of Uzziel,   10:4
the uncle of Aaron, and said to them: "Come near.
Carry your brethren from before the sanctuary out of the camp."
So they went near, and carried them in their coats   10:5
out of the camp, as Moses had said.

Moses said to Aaron, and to Eleazar and Ithamar, his sons who still lived: 10:6
"Do not uncover your heads nor rend your clothes, lest you die,
and lest wrath come upon all the people. Let your brethren,
and the whole house of Israel, bewail the burning Yahweh has kindled.
Do not go out from the door of the tabernacle, lest you die. 10:7
For the anointing oil of Yahweh is upon you."
And they did according to the word of Moses.

Yahweh spoke to Aaron, saying, 10:8
"Do not drink wine nor strong drink when you go into 10:9
the tabernacle, neither you nor your sons, lest you die.
This shall be a statute forever throughout your generations,
so that you may know the difference between holy and unholy, 10:10
and between unclean and clean,
and that you may teach the children of Israel all the statutes 10:11
Yahweh has spoken unto them through Moses."

Moses said to Aaron, and to Eleazar and Ithamar, his sons who were left: 10:12
"Take the grain that remains of the offerings to Yahweh made by fire,
and eat it without leaven beside the altar, for it is most holy.
Eat it in the holy place, because it is your due, and your sons' due, 10:13
from the sacrifices of Yahweh made by fire, for so I am commanded.
And the wave breast and heave shoulder you shall eat in a clean place— 10:14
you and your sons, and your daughters with you—
for they are your due, and your sons' due, which are given
out of the sacrifices of peace offerings of the children of Israel.
The heave shoulder and the wave breast they shall bring 10:15
with the offerings made by fire of the fat, to wave it for a wave offering
before Yahweh, and it shall be yours, and your sons' with you,
by a statute forever, as Yahweh has commanded."

Moses diligently sought the goat of the sin offering and found 10:16
it was burned, and he was angry with Eleazar and Ithamar,
the sons of Aaron who were left alive, saying,
"Why have you not eaten the sin offering in the holy place, 10:17
knowing it is most holy, and that Yahweh has given it you to bear the
iniquity of the congregation, to make atonement for them before Yahweh?
The blood of it was not brought into the holy place. 10:18
You should have eaten it in the holy place, as I commanded."
Aaron said to Moses: "Behold, this day my sons have offered their 10:19
sin offering and their burnt offering before Yahweh. And such grave
things have befallen me this day. If I had eaten the sin offering today,
would it have been accepted in the sight of Yahweh?"
When Moses heard this, he was content. 10:20

Chapter 11

Yahweh spoke to Moses and Aaron, telling them 11:1
to speak to the children of Israel, saying: "These are the beasts 11:2
you shall eat from among all the beasts on the earth.

You shall eat beasts that have divided hooves and also chew the cud. 11:3
But you shall not eat beasts like the camel, that chew the cud, 11:4
yet do not have divided hooves. He is unclean to you.
Likewise, you shall not eat the coney, that chews the cud, 11:5
yet does not have divided hooves. He is unclean unto you.
Also you shall not eat the hare. He chews the cud, 11:6
yet does not have divided hooves and is unclean to you.
And you shall not eat the swine. Though he has divided hooves, 11:7
he does not chew the cud. He is unclean to you.
You shall not eat his flesh, nor touch his carcass. He is unclean to you. 11:8
From the waters of the rivers and seas, 11:9
you shall eat whatever has fins and scales.
Anything in the seas and rivers that does not have fins and scales— 11:10
of all that moves in the waters, and of any living thing in the waters—
shall be an abomination to you.
You shall not eat of their flesh, 11:11
and their carcasses shall be an abomination to you.
Whatsoever in the waters that has no fins nor scales 11:12
shall be an abomination to you.

"Among the fowls, these are they which you shall not eat and which 11:13
shall be an abomination to you: the eagle, the ossifrage, the osprey,
the vulture, and the kite after his kind, 11:14
and every raven after his kind, 11:15
and the owl, the night hawk, the cuckow, and the hawk after his kind, 11:16
and the little owl, the cormorant, and the great owl, 11:17
and the swan, the pelican, and the gier eagle, 11:18
and the stork, the heron after her kind, and the lapwing, and the bat. 11:19
Any flying insect that creeps on all fours shall be an abomination to you. 11:20
Except you may eat flying insects that creep on all fours 11:21
if they have jointed legs with which to leap upon the ground.
You may eat the locust after his kind, and the bald locust after his kind, 11:22
and the beetle after his kind, and the grasshopper after his kind.
But all other flying creeping things that have four feet 11:23
shall be an abomination unto you.
Whoever touches the carcass of these shall be unclean until evening. 11:24
And whoever carries any part of the carcass of these 11:25
shall wash his clothes, and will be unclean until evening.
The carcass of every beast with divided hooves, yet is not completely 11:26
cloven-footed, and that also does not chew the cud, is unclean to you.
Everyone who touches these is unclean.

"Whatever goes upon his paws, among all manner of beasts 11:27
that go on all fours, is unclean to you.
Whoever touches their carcasses shall be unclean until evening.
He that carries their carcass shall wash his clothes, 11:28
and be unclean until evening. They are unclean to you.
These also shall be unclean to you among the things that creep 11:29
upon the earth: The weasel, the mouse, the tortoise after his kind,

and the ferret, the chameleon, the lizard, the snail, and the mole.   11:30
These are unclean to you among all that creep.   11:31
Whoever touches their dead bodies shall be unclean until evening.
And any vessel upon which one of these falls when dead shall be unclean.   11:32
Whether the vessel be of wood, or cloth, or skin, or sackcloth—
whatever vessel wherein any work is done—it must be put into water,
and it shall be unclean until evening. In this way it shall be cleansed.
Every earthen vessel into which any of these dead things fall   11:33
shall be unclean, and you shall break it.
Any food touched by water from these unclean vessels is unclean,   11:34
and any drink that has been in such vessels is unclean.
Everything on which any part of their carcass falls is unclean,   11:35
whether it be oven, or ranges for pots. They shall be broken down,
for they are unclean, and shall be unclean to you.
Nevertheless a spring or pit, wherein there is plenty of water,   11:36
is clean, but that which touches a carcass in it is unclean.
If any part of a carcass falls upon seed that is to be sown, it is clean.   11:37
But if water has been put upon the seed, and any part of a carcass   11:38
falls upon it, the seed shall be unclean to you.

"If any beast of which you may eat dies naturally,   11:39
whoever touches its carcass shall be unclean until evening.
Whoever eats of the carcass shall wash his clothes,   11:40
and be unclean until evening. Also, whoever carries the carcass
shall wash his clothes, and be unclean until evening.
Every creeping thing that creeps upon the earth   11:41
shall be an abomination to you. It shall not be eaten.
Whatever moves on its belly, or upon all fours, or has many feet,   11:42
you shall not eat, for they are an abomination.
Do not make yourselves abominable with any creeping thing.   11:43
Do not make yourselves unclean with them, or defile yourself with them.
For I am Yahweh, your God. You shall therefore sanctify yourselves   11:44
and be holy, for I am holy. You shall not defile yourselves
with any manner of creeping thing that creeps upon the earth.
I am Yahweh, who brought you out of Egypt so that I could be your God.   11:45
You shall therefore be holy, for I am holy.
This is the law of the beasts, and the fowl, and of every living creature that   11:46
moves in the waters, and of every creature that creeps upon the earth:
Know the difference between the unclean and the clean,   11:47
and between beasts that may be eaten and beasts that may not be eaten.

Chapter 12

Yahweh spoke to Moses, telling him to   12:1
speak to the children of Israel, saying, "If a woman conceives and   12:2
bears a male child, she shall be unclean for seven days after the birth.
On the eighth day the flesh of his foreskin shall be circumcised.   12:3
She shall then continue in the blood of her purifying for thirty-three days.   12:4
She shall touch no hallowed thing, nor come into the sanctuary,

until the days of her purifying are fulfilled.
If she bears a female child, she shall be unclean for two weeks after the 12:5
birth, and shall continue in the blood of her purifying for sixty-six days.
When the days of her purifying are fulfilled, for a son or for a daughter, 12:6
she shall bring a lamb of the first year for a burnt offering, and a young
pigeon or a turtledove for a sin offering, to the door of the
tabernacle of the congregation and give them to the priest,
who shall offer it before Yahweh, and make an atonement for her, 12:7
and she shall be cleansed from the issue of her blood.
This is the law for her that has born a male or a female.
If she is not able to bring a lamb, she shall bring two turtledoves or two 12:8
young pigeons—one for a burnt offering, the other for a sin offering—
and the priest shall make an atonement for her, and she shall be clean.

Chapter 13

Yahweh spoke to Moses and Aaron, saying, 13:1
"When a man has a rising, a scab, or a bright spot 13:2
in the skin of his flesh, like the plague of leprosy, he shall be
brought to Aaron the priest, or to one of his sons the priests.
The priest shall look at the sore in the skin, and if the hair in the sore 13:3
has turned white, and the sore is deeper than the skin of his flesh,
it is a plague of leprosy, and the priest shall pronounce him unclean.
If the bright spot is white and not deeper than the skin, and the hair 13:4
in it has not turned white, then the priest shall isolate him for seven days.
On the seventh day the priest shall look, and if the sore is the same, 13:5
and not spread on the skin, the priest shall isolate him seven days more.
After seven days the priest shall look on him again, and if the sore is 13:6
somewhat dark and not spread on the skin, it is but a scab and the priest
shall pronounce him clean. He shall wash his clothes and be clean.
But if the sore has spread much abroad on the skin after he has been 13:7
seen by the priest for his cleansing, he shall see the priest again.
And if the priest sees that the sore has spread on the skin, 13:8
then the priest shall pronounce him unclean. It is a leprosy.

"When the plague of leprosy is in a man he shall be brought to the priest. 13:9
The priest shall see him, and if the rising is white in the skin, and it has 13:10
turned the hair white, and there is quick raw flesh in the rising,
it is an old leprosy. The priest shall pronounce him unclean, 13:11
and shall not shut him up, for he is unclean.
If a leprosy breaks out abroad on the skin, and covers all the skin, 13:12
from his head to his feet, wherever the priest looks,
the priest shall consider the leprosy to have covered all his flesh, 13:13
and shall pronounce him clean. It is all turned white. He is clean.
But if raw flesh appears on him, he is unclean. 13:14
And when the priest sees the raw flesh, he shall pronounce him 13:15
to be unclean, for raw flesh is unclean. It is a leprosy.
But if the raw flesh turns and is changed to white, 13:16
he shall come again to the priest,

and the priest shall see him, and if the plague has turned white,   13:17
the priest shall pronounce him clean. He is clean.

"When the skin of the flesh has a boil that is healed,   13:18
and in the place of the boil there is a white rising, or a bright spot   13:19
that is white and somewhat reddish, and it is shown to the priest,
if the priest sees it is slightly lower than the skin, and the hair   13:20
of it has turned white, the priest shall pronounce him unclean.
It is a plague of leprosy broken out of the boil.
If the priest looks upon it and there are no white hairs therein,   13:21
and if it is not lower than the skin, but is somewhat dark,
then the priest shall shut him up for seven days.
But if it has spread much abroad on the skin,   13:22
the priest shall pronounce him unclean. It is a plague.
If the bright spot stays in one place, and does not spread,   13:23
it is a burning boil, and the priest shall pronounce him clean.
If there is a burn on the flesh, and the burn   13:24
has a bright white spot, somewhat reddish, or all white,
the priest shall look upon it, and if the hair in the bright spot has turned   13:25
white, and it is deeper than the skin, it is a leprosy broken out of the
burning. The priest shall pronounce him unclean. It is a plague of leprosy.
But if there is no white hair in the bright spot, and it is not lower than   13:26
the skin, but is somewhat dark, the priest shall shut him up for seven days.
On the seventh day the priest shall look upon him,   13:27
and if it has spread much abroad on the skin,
the priest shall pronounce him unclean. It is the plague of leprosy.
But if the bright spot stays in place, and does not spread on the skin,   13:28
and is somewhat dark, it is a rising of the burning, and the priest
shall pronounce him clean. It is an inflammation of the burning.

"If a man or woman has a plague upon the head or the beard,   13:29
the priest shall look and if it is deeper than the skin, and there   13:30
is yellow thin hair in it, the priest shall pronounce him unclean.
It is a dry scall, a leprosy upon the head or beard.
If the priest looks upon the scall and it is not deeper than the skin,   13:31
and there is no black hair in it, the priest shall shut up him for seven days.
On the seventh day the priest shall look upon the plague,   13:32
and if the scall has not spread, and there is no yellow hair in it,
and the scall is not deeper than the skin,
he shall be shaven—but the scall shall not be shaved—   13:33
and the priest shall shut him up seven days more.
On the seventh day the priest shall look upon the scall, and if the scall   13:34
has not spread on the skin, nor is it deeper than the skin, the priest
shall pronounce him clean. He shall wash his clothes and be clean.
If the scall has spread on the skin after his cleansing,   13:35
the priest shall look on him, and if he sees the scall spread out   13:36
on the skin, the priest need not seek for yellow hair. He is unclean.
But if the priest sees the sore is unchanged, and that there is   13:37
black hair grown up therein, the scall is healed, and he is clean.

The priest shall pronounce him clean.
If a man or a woman has bright white spots on their skin,   13:38
the priest shall look, and if the bright spots be darkish white,   13:39
it is a freckled spot that grows on the skin. He is clean.

"A man whose hair has fallen off his head is bald, yet is he clean.   13:40
He whose hair has fallen off from the front of his head   13:41
is forehead bald, yet is he clean.
If there be on the bald head or bald forehead a reddish-white sore,   13:42
it is a leprosy sprung up on his bald head or bald forehead.
The priest shall look upon it, and if the rising of the sore   13:43
is reddish-white, as leprosy appears on the skin of the flesh,
he is a leprous man. He is unclean. The priest shall   13:44
pronounce him utterly unclean. His plague is on his head.
The leper whom the plague is upon shall wear torn clothes, and unbind   13:45
his hair, and cover his upper lip, and shall cry out, 'Unclean, unclean.'
All the days wherein the plague is upon him he shall be defiled.   13:46
He is unclean. He shall live alone and dwell outside the camp.

"His garment is also contaminated by the plague of leprosy,   13:47
whether it be a woolen garment, or a linen garment,
whether it be in the warp or woof of linen or of wool,   13:48
whether it be in a skin, or in anything made of skin.
If the plague is greenish or reddish in the garment or in the skins,   13:49
either in the warp or the woof, or in anything made of skins,
it is a plague of leprosy and shall be shown to the priest.
The priest shall see the plague, and shut up the garment for seven days.   13:50
On the seventh day he shall look at the garment. If the plague has spread   13:51
in the garment, either in the warp or in the woof, or in a skin, or in any
work that is made of skin, the plague is a fretting leprosy. It is unclean.
He shall therefore burn that garment wherein be the plague,   13:52
whether warp or woof, in wool or in linen, or anything of skin,
for it is a fretting leprosy. It shall be burnt in the fire.
If the priest looks and the plague has not spread in the garment,   13:53
either in the warp or the woof, or in anything of skin,
the priest shall command that they wash the garment   13:54
the plague is upon, and he shall shut it up seven days more.
Then the priest shall look again on the garment after it is washed,   13:55
and if the plague has not changed color—even though it has not spread—
it is unclean. You shall burn it in the fire. It is infected,
whether the infection be within or without.
If the priest sees the plague is somewhat dark after washing, he shall   13:56
tear it out of the garment or skin, out of the warp or out of the woof,
and if it still appears in the garment, either in the warp or the woof or   13:57
skin, it is a spreading plague. You shall burn the infected piece with fire.
If the garment, either warp or woof or anything of skin, is free of plague   13:58
when you wash it, then wash it a second time and it shall be clean.
This is the law of the plague of leprosy in a garment of wool or linen,   13:59
either in the warp or woof, or of skins, to pronounce it clean or unclean."

Chapter 14

Yahweh spoke to Moses, saying, 14:1
"This shall be the law of the leper in the day of his cleansing: 14:2
The priest shall go forth out of the camp and look at the leper, 14:3
and if the plague of leprosy is healed,
the priest shall command that two birds, alive and clean, and cedar wood, 14:4
and scarlet, and hyssop be brought for him who is to be cleansed.
The priest shall command that one of the birds be killed 14:5
over an earthen vessel filled with spring water.
As for the living bird, he shall take it, and the cedar wood, 14:6
and the scarlet, and the hyssop, and shall dip them all
in the blood of the bird that was killed over the running water.
And he shall sprinkle that blood seven times upon him 14:7
who is to be cleansed from the leprosy, and shall pronounce him clean.
Then he shall let the living bird loose into the open field.
He who is to be cleansed shall wash his clothes, shave off all his hair 14:8
and wash himself in water, that he may be clean. After that he shall
come into the camp, and tarry abroad out of his tent seven days.
On the seventh day, he shall shave off all his hair again—off his head, 14:9
his beard, his eyebrows—all his hair he shall shave off. He shall
wash his clothes, and also his flesh in water, and he shall be clean.

"On the eighth day he shall take two male lambs without blemish, one ewe 14:10
lamb of the first year without blemish, and three-tenths of an ephah
of fine flour mixed with oil, for a grain offering, and one measure of oil.
The priest who makes him clean shall present the man who is to be made 14:11
clean, and those offerings, before Yahweh at the door of the tabernacle.
The priest shall take one male lamb for a trespass offering, and the 14:12
measure of oil, and wave them for a wave offering before Yahweh.
He shall slay the lamb in the place where he kills sin offerings 14:13
and burnt offerings, in the holy place. For just as the sin offering
is the priest's, so is the trespass offering. It is most holy.
The priest shall take some of the blood of the trespass offering 14:14
and put it on the tip of the right ear of him who is to be cleansed,
and on the thumb of his right hand, and on the great toe of his right foot.
The priest shall take some of the measure of oil 14:15
and pour it into the palm of his own left hand.
The priest shall dip his right finger in the oil in his left hand, 14:16
and sprinkle the oil with his finger seven times before Yahweh.
And the priest shall put oil on the tip of the right ear of him who 14:17
is to be cleansed, and on the thumb of his right hand, and on
the great toe of his right foot—all upon the blood of the trespass offering.
The remnant of oil in his hand the priest shall pour on the head of him 14:18
who is to be cleansed, and make an atonement for him before Yahweh.
The priest shall offer the sin offering and make an atonement 14:19
for him who is to be cleansed. Afterward he shall kill the burnt offering.

The priest shall offer the burnt offering and the grain offering | 14:20
upon the altar, and make an atonement for him, and he shall be clean.

"If he is poor and has not much, he shall take one lamb for a trespass | 14:21
offering, to make an atonement for him, and one-tenth of an ephah
of fine flour mixed with oil for a grain offering, and a measure of oil,
and two turtledoves or two young pigeons, such as he is able to get. | 14:22
One shall be a sin offering and the other a burnt offering.
He shall bring them to the priest on the eighth day for his cleansing, | 14:23
to the door of the tabernacle of the congregation, before Yahweh.
The priest shall take the lamb of the trespass offering, and the | 14:24
measure of oil, and wave them for a wave offering before Yahweh.
The priest shall kill the lamb of the trespass offering, and take some of | 14:25
the blood and put it on the tip of the right ear of him who is to be cleansed,
and on the thumb of his right hand, and on the great toe of his right foot.
The priest shall pour some of the oil into the palm of his own left hand, | 14:26
and sprinkle with his right finger some of the oil | 14:27
from his left hand seven times before Yahweh.
The priest shall put oil from his hand on the tip of the right ear of him who | 14:28
is to be cleansed, and on the thumb of his right hand, and on the great toe
of his right foot—upon the places of the blood of the trespass offering.
The rest of the oil in the priest's hand he shall put upon the head of him | 14:29
who is to be cleansed, to make an atonement for him before Yahweh.
He shall offer the one of the turtledoves | 14:30
or the young pigeons, such as he can get—
one for a sin offering, and the other for a burnt offering— | 14:31
along with the grain offering, and the priest shall make
an atonement for him who is to be cleansed before Yahweh.
This is the law for him whom the plague of leprosy is upon, | 14:32
and who cannot afford the normal offerings for his cleansing."

Yahweh spoke to Moses and to Aaron, saying, | 14:33
"When you come into the land of Canaan, which I give to you | 14:34
for a possession, and I put the plague of leprosy in a house of that land,
and he who owns the house comes and tells the priest, | 14:35
'It seems to me there is a plague in the house,'
the priest shall command that they empty the house before | 14:36
he goes into it, so that nothing else in the house becomes unclean.
Afterward the priest shall go in to see the house.
And if he sees the plague is in the walls of the house, in greenish | 14:37
or reddish hollows that are deeper than the surface of the wall,
the priest shall leave the house, and shut up the house for seven days. | 14:38
On the seventh day the priest shall come again, and shall look, | 14:39
and if the plague has spread into the walls of the house,
the priest shall command that any stones contaminated | 14:40
with the plague be cast into an unclean place outside the city.
And he shall have the inside of the house completely scraped, and the dust | 14:41
that is scraped off shall be poured out in an unclean place outside the city.
New stones shall be put in place of the unclean stones, | 14:42

146

and new mortar shall be used to plaster the inside of the house.

If the plague comes again, and breaks out in the house after the stones   14:43
have been taken away and the house has been scraped and plastered,
the priest shall come and look, and if the plague has spread in the house,   14:44
it is a fretting leprosy in the house. It is unclean.
And they shall tear down the house—the stones and the timber, and all   14:45
the mortar of the house—and carry it out of the city to an unclean place.
Whoever goes into the house while it is shut up is unclean until evening.   14:46
Whoever lies down or eats in the house shall wash his clothes.   14:47
If the priest comes in and looks, and the plague has not spread   14:48
in the house after the house was plastered, then the priest shall
pronounce the house clean, because the plague is healed.
He shall take to cleanse the house two birds,   14:49
and cedar wood, and scarlet, and hyssop.
He shall kill one of the birds in an earthen vessel over running water,   14:50
and he shall take the cedar wood, and the hyssop, and the scarlet,   14:51
and the living bird, and dip them in the blood of the slain bird,
and in the running water, then sprinkle the house seven times.
He shall cleanse the house with the blood of the bird, and with   14:52
the running water, and with the living bird, and with the cedar wood,
and with the hyssop, and with the scarlet.
He shall then let the living bird go in the open fields outside the city,   14:53
and make an atonement for the house, and it shall be clean.
This is the law for all manner of the plague of leprosy, and scall,   14:54
and for the leprosy of a garment, and of a house,   14:55
and for a rising, and for a scab, and for a bright spot—   14:56
to teach when it is unclean and when it is clean. This is the law of leprosy."   14:57

Chapter 15

Yahweh spoke to Moses and Aaron, telling them   15:1
to speak to the children of Israel, and say unto them,   15:2
"When a man has a fluid discharge from his genitals, he is unclean.
This is his uncleanness, whether his genitals flow with the discharge,   15:3
or the discharge has stopped, it is his uncleanness.
Every bed whereon he lies that has the discharge is unclean,   15:4
and everything whereon he sits is unclean.
Whoever touches his bed shall wash his clothes,   15:5
and bathe himself in water, and be unclean until evening.
Whoever sits on anything whereon he who has the issue has sat shall   15:6
wash his clothes, and bathe himself in water, and be unclean until evening.
He that touches the flesh of him who has the issue shall wash his clothes,   15:7
and bathe himself in water, and be unclean until evening.
If he who has the discharge spits upon he who is clean, the clean one shall   15:8
wash his clothes, and bathe himself in water, and be unclean until evening.
Whatever saddle he who has the discharge rides upon is unclean.   15:9
Whoever touches anything that was under him is unclean   15:10
until evening, and he that carries any of those things shall wash

his clothes, and bathe himself in water, and be unclean until evening.

If he who has a discharge touches someone without first
washing his hands in water, that person shall wash his clothes,
and bathe himself in water, and be unclean until evening.   15:11

If he who has a discharge touches an earthen vessel, that vessel   15:12
shall be broken, or if it be a vessel of wood, it shall be rinsed in water.

When he who has a discharge is cleansed of his issue, he shall number   15:13
to himself seven days for his purification. He shall wash his clothes,
and bathe his flesh in running water, and he shall be clean.

On the eighth day he shall bring two turtledoves or two young pigeons   15:14
to the door of the tabernacle before Yahweh, and give them to the priest.

The priest shall offer one of them for a sin offering, and the other   15:15
for a burnt offering, and make an atonement for him before Yahweh.

"If a man has a seminal emission, he shall wash   15:16
all his flesh in water, and be unclean until evening.

Every garment and every skin that has the semen upon it   15:17
shall be washed with water, and be unclean until evening.

If the seminal emission is from copulation with a woman,   15:18
they both shall bathe in water, and be unclean until evening.

When a woman has a discharge of blood due to menstruation, she shall be   15:19
put apart seven days. Whoever touches her shall be unclean until evening.

Everything she lies upon in her separation shall be unclean.   15:20
Everything she sits upon is also unclean.

Whoever touches her bed shall wash his clothes,   15:21
and bathe himself in water, and be unclean until evening.

Whoever touches anything she sat upon shall wash his clothes,   15:22
and bathe himself in water, and be unclean until evening.

Whether it be on her bed or on something she sat upon,   15:23
whoever touches it shall be unclean until evening.

If a man lies with her and her menstrual blood is upon him,   15:24
he shall be unclean seven days, and the bed he laid upon is unclean.

If a woman has an issue of blood outside her time of menstruation,   15:25
or if her menstruation goes beyond seven days, her uncleanness
shall continue for as long as the issue flows. She is unclean.

Every bed she lies upon during her issue shall be as the bed of her   15:26
menstruation, and whatever she sits upon shall also be unclean.

Whoever touches those things shall be unclean, and shall wash his clothes,   15:27
and bathe himself in water, and be unclean until evening.

When her issue of blood ceases to flow, she shall   15:28
number to herself seven days, and after that she is clean.

On the eighth day she shall bring two turtledoves or two young pigeons   15:29
to the priest, to the door of the tabernacle of the congregation.

The priest shall offer one for a sin offering and the other for a burnt   15:30
offering, and he shall make an atonement for her before Yahweh.

Thus shall you separate the children of Israel from their uncleanness,   15:31
so that they do not defile my tabernacle, which is among them,
and therefore be killed for their uncleanness.

This is the law for him who has a genital discharge,   15:32
and him who has a seminal emission, and is defiled therewith,
and for a woman during menstruation, and for men and women who   15:33
have any discharge, and for men who lie with a woman who is unclean."

Chapter 16

Yahweh spoke to Moses after the death of the two sons of Aaron,   16:1
who offered before Yahweh and were killed.
Yahweh said to Moses, "Tell Aaron your brother that he may come   16:2
only at the proper times into the holy place—within the veil before
the mercy seat that is upon the ark—otherwise he will be killed.
For that is where I will appear, in the cloud above the mercy seat.
Aaron shall only come into the holy place with a young bull   16:3
for a sin offering, and a ram for a burnt offering.
He shall put on the holy linen coat, and the linen breeches, and be girded   16:4
with a linen girdle, and attired with the linen mitre. These are holy
garments. Therefore shall he wash his flesh in water, and put them on.
He shall take from the congregation of the children of Israel two kids   16:5
of the goats for a sin offering, and one ram for a burnt offering.
Aaron shall offer his bull of the sin offering, which is for himself,   16:6
and make an atonement for himself, and for his house.

"He shall then present the two goats before Yahweh   16:7
at the door of the tabernacle of the congregation.
Aaron shall cast lots upon the two goats—   16:8
one lot for Yahweh, and the other lot for the scapegoat.
Aaron shall bring the goat upon which Yahweh's lot fell,   16:9
and offer him for a sin offering.
The goat on which the lot fell to be the scapegoat, shall be   16:10
presented alive before Yahweh, to make an atonement with him,
and to let him go for a scapegoat into the wilderness.

"Aaron shall bring the bull of the sin offering, which is for himself,   16:11
and make an atonement for himself, and for his house,
and shall kill the bull of the sin offering, which is for himself.
He shall take a censer full of burning coals from the altar before Yahweh,   16:12
and two handfuls of sweet incense beaten small, and bring it into the veil.
He shall put the incense on the fire before Yahweh, so that the cloud of the   16:13
incense covers the mercy seat on the ark of the covenant, lest he be killed.
He shall take of the blood of the bull, and sprinkle it with his finger   16:14
upon the mercy seat eastward, and before the mercy seat
he shall sprinkle the blood with his finger seven times.

"Then he shall kill the goat of the sin offering, which is for the people,   16:15
and bring his blood within the veil, and do with that blood as he did
with the blood of the bull—sprinkle it before the mercy seat, and upon it.
He shall make an atonement for the holy place, because of   16:16
the uncleanness of the children of Israel, and because of their
transgressions in all their sins. And so shall he do also for the tabernacle

of the congregation, which they enter with their uncleanness.
There shall be no one in the tabernacle while he makes an atonement   16:17
in the holy place, until he comes out, having made an atonement for
himself, and for his household, and for all the congregation of Israel.
He shall then go to the altar before Yahweh, and make an atonement for it,   16:18
and he shall take of the blood of the bull, and of the blood of the goat,
and put it upon the horns of the altar round about.
He shall sprinkle of the blood upon it with his finger seven times,   16:19
and cleanse it, and hallow it from the uncleanness of the children of Israel.

"When he has made an end of reconciling the holy place, and the   16:20
tabernacle of the congregation, and the altar, he shall bring the live goat.
Aaron shall lay both his hands upon the head of the live goat, and confess   16:21
over him all the iniquities of the children of Israel, and all their sins
and transgressions, putting them all upon the head of the goat,
and shall send the goat away by the hand of a fit man into the wilderness.
And so the goat shall bear all their iniquities into a land not inhabited.   16:22
It shall be let go in the wilderness.

"Aaron shall come into the tabernacle and take off the linen garments   16:23
he put on when he went into the holy place, and shall leave them there.
He shall wash his flesh with water in the holy place, and put on other   16:24
garments, and come forth and offer his burnt offering, and the burnt
offering of the people, and make an atonement for himself and the people.
The fat of the sin offering he shall he burn upon the altar.   16:25
He that let the goat go for the scapegoat shall wash his clothes,   16:26
and bathe his flesh in water, and afterward come into the camp.
The bull for the sin offering, and the goat for the sin offering, whose blood   16:27
was brought in to make atonement in the holy place, shall be carried
outside the camp, and their skin, flesh and dung shall be burned with fire.
He that burns them shall wash his clothes, and bathe his flesh in water,   16:28
and afterward he shall come into the camp.

"This shall be a statute unto you forever: In the seventh month, on the   16:29
tenth day of the month, you shall deny yourself, and do no work at all,
whether you are of Israel, or a stranger who sojourns here among you.
For on that day the shall priest make an atonement for you,   16:30
to cleanse you, that you may be clean from all your sins before Yahweh.
It is a sabbath of rest for you. You shall deny yourself, by a statute, forever.   16:31
The priest who is anointed and consecrated to minister as priest   16:32
in his father's stead, shall make the atonement,
and shall put on the linen clothes—the holy garments.
He shall make an atonement for the holy sanctuary. And he shall make   16:33
an atonement for the tabernacle of the congregation, and for the altar,
and for the priests, and for all the people of the congregation.
This shall be an everlasting statute unto you, to make an atonement   16:34
for the children of Israel for all their sins once a year."
Moses did as Yahweh commanded.

Chapter 17

Yahweh spoke to Moses, telling him to   17:1
speak to Aaron, and to his sons, and to all the children of Israel,   17:2
saying that Yahweh has commanded thus:
"Any man of the house of Israel who kills an ox, or lamb   17:3
or goat in the camp, or who kills it outside of the camp,
and does not bring it to the door of the tabernacle as an offering   17:4
to Yahweh, shall be guilty of bloodshed. He has spilled blood,
and shall be cut off from among his people.
This is so the children of Israel will bring the sacrifices they offer   17:5
in the open field to the door of the tabernacle, to the priest,
and offer them for peace offerings unto Yahweh.
The priest shall sprinkle the blood upon the altar of Yahweh at the door   17:6
of the tabernacle, and burn the fat for a sweet savor unto Yahweh.
They shall no more offer their sacrifices to devils,   17:7
after whom they have gone a-whoring.
This shall be a statute forever unto them throughout their generations.

"Whatever man of the house of Israel, or of the strangers   17:8
who sojourn among you, who offers a burnt offering of sacrifice,
and does not bring it to the door of the tabernacle to offer it   17:9
to Yahweh, that man shall be cut off from among his people.
Whatever man of Israel, or of the strangers who sojourn among you,   17:10
who eats any manner of blood, I will set my face against that soul
who eats blood, and will cut him off from among his people.
The life of the flesh is in the blood. I have given it to you   17:11
upon the altar to make an atonement for your souls.
It is the blood that makes an atonement for the soul.
Therefore I said unto the children of Israel, 'No soul of you shall eat blood,   17:12
neither shall any stranger that sojourns among you eat blood.'
Whatever man there be of the children of Israel, or of the strangers   17:13
who sojourn among you, who hunts and catches any beast or fowl
that may be eaten, he shall pour out its blood and cover it with dust,
for it is the life of all flesh. The blood of it is the life thereof. Therefore I say   17:14
to the children of Israel, 'You shall eat the blood of no manner of flesh, for
the life of all flesh is the blood thereof. Whosoever eats it shall be cut off.'
Every soul—whether it be one of your own country, or a stranger—   17:15
who eats that which died of itself, or that which was torn apart by beasts,
shall wash his clothes, and bathe himself in water,
and be unclean until evening. Then he shall be clean.
If he does not wash them, nor bathe his flesh, he shall bear his iniquity."   17:16

Chapter 18

Yahweh spoke to Moses, telling him to   18:1
speak to the children of Israel, and say to them, "I am Yahweh, your God.   18:2
Do not follow the practices of Egypt, wherein you dwelt, nor those   18:3
of Canaan, whither I bring you. You shall not live by their laws.

You shall follow my judgments, and keep my laws. I am Yahweh, your God. 18:4

You shall therefore keep my statutes, and my judgments, 18:5
which if a man does, he shall live in them. I am Yahweh.

None of you shall approach anyone who is kin to you 18:6
for sexual intercourse. I am Yahweh.

The nakedness of your father, or the nakedness of your mother, you shall 18:7
not uncover. She is your mother. You shall not uncover her nakedness.

The nakedness of your father's wife you shall not not uncover. 18:8
Her nakedness belongs to your father.

The nakedness of your sister, the daughter of your father, or of your 18:9
mother, whether she be born at home or abroad, you shall not uncover.

The nakedness of your son's daughter, or your daughter's daughter, 18:10
you shall not uncover, for they are your own flesh.

The nakedness of your father's wife's daughter, begotten of your father, 18:11
is your sister. You shall not uncover her nakedness.

You shall not uncover the nakedness of your father's sister. 18:12
She is your father's near kinswoman.

You shall not uncover the nakedness of your mother's sister. 18:13
She is your mother's near kinswoman.

You shall not uncover the nakedness of the wife 18:14
of your father's brother. She is your aunt.

You shall not uncover the nakedness of your daughter-in-law. 18:15
She is your son's wife. You shall not uncover her nakedness.

You shall not uncover the nakedness of your brother's wife. 18:16
Her nakedness belongs to him.

You shall not uncover the nakedness of a woman and her daughter. 18:17
Neither shall you uncover the nakedness her son's daughter, or her
daughter's daughter, for they are her near kinswomen. It is wickedness.

You shall not take a sister of your wife as a wife to rival her, 18:18
and to uncover her nakedness, so long as your wife is alive.

You shall not approach a woman to uncover her nakedness 18:19
while she is put apart for her uncleanness.

Moreover, you shall not lie carnally with your neighbor's wife, 18:20
to defile yourself with her.

You shall not let any of your seed pass through the fire to Molech, 18:21
neither shall you profane the name of your God. I am Yahweh.

You shall not lie with a man as you would with a woman. 18:22
It is an abomination.

You shall not lie with any beast to defile yourself with it. 18:23
Neither shall any woman mate with a beast. It is perversion.

Do not defile yourselves in any of these things. For the nations 18:24
I cast out before you defiled themselves in these things,

and the land itself was defiled. Therefore I visited great iniquity 18:25
upon it, and the land vomited out her inhabitants.

Therefore keep my statutes and my judgments, and do not commit 18:26
any of these abominations, whether you be of this nation,

or a stranger who sojourns here.

For all these abominations were done by the men   18:27
of this land before you, and the land was defiled.
If you defile the land it will spew you out,   18:28
as it spewed out the nations that were before you.
Whoever commits any of these abominations   18:29
shall be cut off from their people.
Therefore keep my laws. Do not commit not any of these abominable acts,   18:30
which were committed before you, so that you do not defile yourselves.
I am Yahweh, your God."

Chapter 19

Yahweh spoke to Moses, telling him to   19:1
speak to the whole congregation of the children of Israel, and say to them, 19:2
"You shall be holy, for I, Yahweh your God, am holy.
Every man shall respect his mother and his father,   19:3
and keep my sabbaths. I am Yahweh, your God.
Do not turn to idols, nor make for yourselves molten gods.   19:4
I am Yahweh, your God.
If you offer a sacrifice of peace offerings   19:5
unto Yahweh, you shall offer it of your own will.
It shall be eaten the same day you offer it, and on the morrow.   19:6
If any remains until the third day, it shall be burnt in the fire.
If any is eaten on the third day, it is abominable. It shall not be accepted. 19:7
Anyone who eats it shall bear his iniquity, because he has profaned the   19:8
hallowed thing of Yahweh, and he shall be cut off from among his people.
When you reap the harvest of your land, you shall not wholly reap the   19:9
corners of your field, nor shall you gather the gleanings of your harvest.
And you shall not glean your vineyard, neither shall you gather every   19:10
grape of your vineyard. You shall leave some for strangers and the poor.
I am Yahweh, your God.

"You shall not steal, nor deal falsely, nor lie one to another.   19:11
You shall not swear by my name falsely. Neither shall you   19:12
profane the name of your God. I am Yahweh.
You shall not defraud your neighbor, nor rob him. The wages   19:13
of him you hire shall not abide with you overnight until morning.
You shall not curse the deaf, nor put a stumbling block before the blind, 19:14
but shall fear your God. I am Yahweh.
You shall not be unrighteousness in judgment. You shall not favor   19:15
the person of the poor, nor honor the person of the mighty,
but with righteousness you shall judge your neighbor.
You shall not go up and down as a talebearer among your people.   19:16
Neither shall you stand against the blood of your neighbor. I am Yahweh.
You shall not hate your brother in your heart, but you shall rebuke   19:17
your neighbor's sins, lest you suffer his sins upon yourself.
You shall not avenge, nor bear any grudge against the children   19:18
of your people. You shall love your neighbor as yourself. I am Yahweh.

You shall keep my statutes. You shall not breed your livestock   19:19
with a diverse kind. You shall not sow your field with mixed seed,
and neither shall you wear a garment woven of both linen and wool.
If a man lies carnally with a female slave who is betrothed to another man, 19:20
but has not been released or given her freedom, the woman shall be
scourged, but they shall not be put to death, because she was not free.
The man shall bring a ram to the door of the tabernacle   19:21
of the congregation, for his trespass offering unto Yahweh.
The priest shall make an atonement for him before Yahweh   19:22
with the ram of the trespass offering, for his sin which he has done,
and the sin which he has done shall be forgiven him.
When you come into the land and have planted all manner of trees   19:23
for food, you shall count the fruit thereof as uncircumcised. For three
years it shall be as uncircumcised to you. You shall not eat of it.
In the fourth year all the fruit shall be holy, a praise offering unto Yahweh. 19:24
In the fifth year you may eat the fruit, that it may increase its yield to you. 19:25
I am Yahweh, your God.

"Do not eat meat with blood in it. Do not practice sorcery or divination. 19:26
Do not shape the hair of your head, nor trim the ends of your beard.   19:27
Do not make cuttings in your flesh for the dead,   19:28
nor tattoo marks upon your skin. I am Yahweh.
Do not prostitute your daughter and cause her to be a whore,   19:29
lest the land fall into whoredom, and become full of wickedness.
You shall keep my sabbaths, and reverence my sanctuary. I am Yahweh. 19:30
Do not consult spirit mediums, nor seek after wizards and be defiled. 19:31
I am Yahweh, your God.
You shall stand in the presence of the hoary head, and honor   19:32
the face of the old man. Fear your God. I am Yahweh.
If a stranger sojourns with you in your land, you shall not vex him.   19:33
A stranger who dwells with you shall be to you as one born among you. 19:34
You shall love him as yourself, for you were strangers in the land of Egypt.
I am Yahweh, your God.
Do not act unjustly in judgments of length, weight, or measure.   19:35
You shall have just scales, just weights, a just ephah, and a just hin.   19:36
I am Yahweh, your God, who brought you out of the land of Egypt.
You shall observe all my statutes and all my judgments, and do them. 19:37
I am Yahweh."

Chapter 20

Yahweh spoke to Moses, telling him to   20:1
say to the children of Israel, "Any of the people of Israel, or any stranger 20:2
who sojourns in Israel, who gives one of his children in sacrifice
to Molech, shall be put to death. The people of the land shall stone him.
I will set my face against him and cut him off from his people, for he gave 20:3
his seed to Molech, defiled my sanctuary, and profaned my holy name.
If the people of the land look away when he   20:4
gives of his seed unto Molech, and do not kill him,

I will set my face against that man, and against his family—and against 20:5
all who go whoring after him, prostituting themselves with Molech—
and I will cut them off from among the people.
I will set my face against anyone who turns to familiar spirits and wizards, 20:6
and goes whoring after them. I will cut him off from the people.
Therefore sanctify yourselves and be holy, for I am Yahweh, your God. 20:7
You shall keep my statutes and do them. I am Yahweh, who sanctifies you. 20:8

"Everyone who curses his father or his mother shall be put to death, for he 20:9
has cursed his father or mother. His own blood shall be upon his hands.
If a man commits adultery with another man's wife—with his neighbor's 20:10
wife—both the adulterer and the adulteress shall be put to death.
If man lies with his father's wife, he has uncovered his father's nakedness. 20:11
Both of them shall be put to death. Their blood is upon their own heads.
If a man lies with his daughter-in-law, both of them shall be put to death. 20:12
They have wrought confusion. Their blood shall be upon them.
If a man lies with a man as with a woman, it is an abomination. 20:13
They shall both be put to death. Their blood shall be upon them.
If a man takes a wife and also her mother, it is wickedness. They shall 20:14
all be burnt with fire so that there be no wickedness among you.
If a man lies with a beast, he shall be put to death. The beast shall be slain. 20:15
If a woman approaches any beast, and mates with it, you shall kill 20:16
both the woman and the beast. Their blood shall be upon them.

"If a man takes his sister, his father's daughter, or his mother's daughter, 20:17
and sees her nakedness, and she sees his nakedness, it is a wicked thing.
They shall be cut off in the sight of their people. He has uncovered
his sister's nakedness, and he shall bear his iniquity.
If a man lies with a woman having her period and uncovers her 20:18
nakedness, she has uncovered the fountain of her blood, and he has
discovered her fountain. Both of them shall be cut off from their people.
You shall not uncover the nakedness of your mother's sister, nor of your 20:19
father's sister, for they are near kin, and all shall bear their iniquity.
If a man lies with his uncle's wife, he has uncovered his uncle's nakedness. 20:20
Both shall bear their sin, and they shall die childless.
If a man takes his brother's wife, it is an unclean thing. He has 20:21
uncovered his brother's nakedness, and they shall be childless.
Therefore keep all my statutes and all my judgments, and do them, 20:22
so that the land I bring you to dwell in does not spew you out.
Do not follow the statutes of the nations I drove out before you. 20:23
They committed all these offenses, and therefore I abhorred them.
But to you I have said, 'You shall inherit their land. I will give it 20:24
to you to possess, a land that flows with milk and honey.
I am Yahweh, your God, who has separated you from other people.'
Therefore differentiate between clean beasts and unclean, and between 20:25
clean and unclean fowls. Do not make yourselves abominable by beasts
or fowls, or by any living thing that I have separated from you as unclean.
And you shall be holy unto me. For I, Yahweh, am holy, 20:26
and I have severed you from other people, that you should be mine.

Any man or woman who has a familiar spirit, or who is a wizard, shall be put to death. You shall stone them. Their blood shall be upon them." 20:27

Chapter 21

Yahweh spoke to Moses, saying to tell the priests, the sons of Aaron, "A priest shall not be defiled for the dead among the people, 21:1

but only for his kin who is near to him, that is, for his mother, his father, his son, his daughter, and his brother, 21:2

and for his virgin sister who is close to him because she has no husband. For her he may be defiled. 21:3

Being a chief among his people, he shall not otherwise defile himself. 21:4

Priests shall not shave their heads bald, nor trim off the ends of their beards, nor make any cuttings in their flesh. 21:5

They shall be holy unto their God, and not profane the name of their God. For they make offerings by fire to Yahweh. The bread of their God they do offer. Therefore they shall be holy. 21:6

They shall not take a wife who is a whore, or is profane. Nor shall they take a woman who is divorced. A priest must be holy unto his God. 21:7

"Therefore you shall sanctify him, for he offers the bread of your God. He shall be holy to you, for I, Yahweh, who sanctifies you, am holy. 21:8

If the daughter of a priest profanes herself by playing the whore, she profanes her father. She shall be burnt with fire. 21:9

He who is the high priest among his brethren, upon whose head the anointing oil was poured, and who is consecrated to put on the garments, shall not uncover his head, nor rend his clothes. 21:10

Neither shall he go near any dead body and thus defile himself, even for his father or for his mother. 21:11

He shall not go out of the sanctuary nor profane the sanctuary of his God, for the crown of the anointing oil of his God is upon him. I am Yahweh. 21:12

He shall take a wife in her virginity. 21:13

He shall not take a widow, or a divorced woman, or a profane woman, or a harlot. He shall take a virgin of his own people as his wife. 21:14

He shall not in any way profane his seed, for I, Yahweh, do sanctify him." 21:15

Yahweh spoke to Moses, telling him to speak to Aaron, saying, 21:16

"Whoever of your descendants has any defect, 21:17

shall not approach to offer the bread of his God.

Any man who has an imperfection shall not approach, whether a blind man, or a lame man, or he who has a flat nose or anything superfluous, 21:18

or who has a broken foot or broken hand, 21:19

or a hunchback, or a dwarf, or he who has a blemish in his eye, 21:20

or scurvy, or scabs, or damaged testicles.

No seed of Aaron the priest who has a blemish shall come nigh to offer the offerings of Yahweh made by fire. He has a defect. 21:21

He shall not come nigh to offer the bread of his God.

He shall eat the bread of his God, both of the holy, and of the most holy. 21:22

But he shall not go in unto the veil, nor come nigh to the altar. Because of 21:23

his defect, he would profane my sanctuary, and I, Yahweh, do sanctify it."
Moses told this to Aaron and his sons, and to all the children of Israel. 21:24

Chapter 22

Yahweh spoke to Moses, telling him to 22:1
speak to Aaron and his sons, saying, "Separate yourselves from the holy 22:2
things of the children of Israel. Respect that which they hallow unto me,
lest you profane my holy name. I am Yahweh.
Any of your descendants who goes unto the holy things 22:3
that the children of Israel hallow unto Yahweh, having uncleanness
upon him, shall be cut off from my presence. I am Yahweh.
Any of your descendants who is a leper, or who has a running discharge, 22:4
shall not eat of the holy things until he is clean. Any man who touches
anything made unclean by the dead, or who has an emission of semen,
or who touches any creeping thing, whereby being made unclean, or who 22:5
touches a person who is unclean—whatever the uncleanness may be—
the person who touches any such things shall be unclean until evening, 22:6
and shall not eat of the holy things unless he washes his flesh with water.
When the sun is down he shall be clean, and shall afterward 22:7
eat of the holy things, because it is his food.

"He shall not eat that which dies of itself, or is torn apart by beasts, 22:8
lest he defile himself therewith. I am Yahweh.
The priests shall keep my ordinance, lest they bear sin for it, 22:9
and die for having profaned it. I, Yahweh, do sanctify them.
No stranger, or guest of a priest, or hired hand shall eat of the holy things. 22:10
But if a priest buys servants, they shall eat of it, and children 22:11
born to the servants of his house, shall also eat of it.
If the priest's daughter is married to a stranger, 22:12
she may not eat of the offerings of holy things.
If the priest's daughter is a widow or divorced, and has no child, 22:13
and is returned to her father's house as in her youth,
she shall eat her father's food. But no stranger shall eat of it.
If a man eats of the holy things unwittingly, he shall 22:14
give an equal amount, plus one-fifth, back to the priest.
The priests shall not profane the holy things 22:15
offered unto Yahweh by the children of Israel,
or allow those who are not priests to eat holy things, thereby suffering 22:16
them to bear the iniquity of trespass. For I, Yahweh, do sanctify them."

Yahweh spoke to Moses, telling him to 22:17
speak to Aaron and his sons, and to all the children of Israel, saying, 22:18
"Whenever anyone of the house of Israel, or of the strangers in Israel,
offers an oblation unto Yahweh for a burnt offering—
whether to fulfill a vow, or of his free will—
he shall offer of his own will a male without blemish 22:19
from the herds of cattle, sheep or goats.
Do not offer what has a blemish. It shall not be accepted on your behalf. 22:20

Whenever you offer a peace offering of cattle or sheep unto Yahweh,   22:21
whether to fulfill a vow, or as a free will offering,
it must be perfect to be accepted. It shall have no blemish.
You shall not offer unto Yahweh those that are blind, or broken,   22:22
or maimed, or that have a wen, or scurvy, or scabs. Do not make
an offering of them by fire upon the altar unto Yahweh.
You may offer a bull or a lamb that is deformed or stunted   22:23
for a freewill offering, but it shall not be accepted to fulfill a vow.
You shall not offer unto Yahweh that which is bruised, or crushed,   22:24
or broken or cut. Neither shall you make any such offerings on your land.
You shall not offer any of these for the bread of your God   22:25
even if they come from a sojourner's hand. Corruption and blemishes
are upon them. They shall not be accepted on your behalf."

Yahweh spoke to Moses, saying,   22:26
"When a bull or sheep or goat is born, it shall remain with its mother   22:27
for seven days. From the eighth day forward it shall be accepted
as an offering made by fire unto Yahweh.
Whether it be a cow or ewe, you shall not kill   22:28
a mother and her young on the same day.
When you offer a sacrifice of thanksgiving   22:29
unto Yahweh, offer it of your own will.
It shall be eaten that same day. Leave none   22:30
of it until the morrow. I am Yahweh.
Therefore you shall keep my commandments, and do them. I am Yahweh.   22:31
You shall not profane my holy name. I will be hallowed   22:32
among the children of Israel. I am the Lord who hallows you,
who brought you out of the land of Egypt to be your God. I am Yahweh.   22:33

Chapter 23

Yahweh spoke to Moses, telling him to   23:1
speak to the children of Israel, and say unto them, "The feasts that you   23:2
shall proclaim to be holy convocations, these are the feasts of Yahweh.
For six days you shall work, but the seventh day is the sabbath of rest,   23:3
a holy convocation. You shall do no work that day.
It is the sabbath of Yahweh in all your dwellings.
These are the feasts of Yahweh, the holy convocations,   23:4
that you shall proclaim in their seasons:
On the fourteenth day of the first month at evening is Yahweh's Passover.   23:5
On the fifteenth day of the same month is the Feast of Unleavened   23:6
Bread unto Yahweh. For seven days you must eat unleavened bread.
On the first day you shall have a holy convocation.   23:7
You shall do no servile work this day.
You shall offer an offering made by fire unto Yahweh for seven days.   23:8
The seventh day is a holy convocation. You shall do no servile work."

Yahweh spoke to Moses, telling him to   23:9
speak to the children of Israel, and say to them, "When you come into   23:10

the land I give unto you, and reap the harvest thereof, you shall
bring a sheaf of the first fruits of your harvest to the priest.
And he shall wave the sheaf before Yahweh, to be accepted for you.   23:11
On the morrow after the sabbath the priest shall wave it.
And you shall offer that day when you wave the sheaf, a male lamb   23:12
without blemish of the first year for a burnt offering unto Yahweh.
The grain offering shall be two-tenth deals of fine flour mixed with oil,   23:13
an offering made by fire for a sweet savor unto Yahweh.
The drink offering shall be of wine, the fourth part of a hin.
You shall eat neither bread, nor roasted corn, nor fresh grain until   23:14
the very day you bring an offering to your God. This shall be a statute
forever throughout your generations, in all your dwellings.
You shall count seven sabbaths from the day after the sabbath   23:15
that you brought the sheaf of the wave offering.
On the day after the seventh sabbath shall be fifty days,   23:16
and you shall offer a new grain offering unto Yahweh.
You shall bring out of your houses two wave loaves of two-tenth deals.   23:17
They shall be of fine flour, and shall be baked with leaven.
They are the first fruits, given unto Yahweh.
You shall offer with the bread seven lambs of the first year, without   23:18
blemish, and one young bull, and two rams. They shall be for a burnt
offering unto Yahweh—with the grain offerings and drink offerings—
an offering made by fire, of sweet savor unto Yahweh.
You shall sacrifice one kid of the goats for a sin offering,   23:19
and two lambs of the first year for a peace offering.
The priest shall wave them with the bread of the first fruits   23:20
for a wave offering before Yahweh, along with the two lambs.
They are holy to Yahweh, and shall be given to the priest.
You shall make a proclamation on the same day, that it may be a holy   23:21
convocation unto you. You shall do no servile work this day. This shall be
a statute forever in all your dwellings, throughout your generations.
When you reap the harvest of your land, you shall not harvest the corners   23:22
of your field, neither shall you gather any gleanings of your harvest.
You shall leave them for strangers and the poor. I am Yahweh, your God."

Yahweh spoke to Moses, telling him to   23:23
speak to the children of Israel, saying, "In the seventh month,   23:24
on the first day of the month, you shall you have a sabbath—
a memorial of blowing of trumpets, a holy convocation.
You shall do no servile work this day, but you shall offer   23:25
a sacrifice made by fire unto Yahweh."
Yahweh spoke to Moses, saying,   23:26
"Also, on the tenth day of this seventh month there shall be a day   23:27
of atonement. It shall be a holy convocation unto you, and you shall
deny yourselves, and offer a sacrifice made by fire unto Yahweh.
You shall do no work on this day, for it is a day of atonement,   23:28
to make an atonement for you before Yahweh, your God.
Whoever does not deny himself on this day,   23:29

shall be cut off from among his people.
Whoever does any work on this day among his people, I will destroy. 23:30
You shall do no manner of work. It shall be a statute forever 23:31
throughout your generations, in all your dwellings.
It shall be unto you a sabbath of rest, and you shall deny yourself. 23:32
On the ninth day of the month, from evening to the next evening,
you shall you celebrate this sabbath."

Yahweh spoke to Moses, telling him to 23:33
speak to the children of Israel, saying, "On the fifteenth day of the seventh 23:34
month shall begin the Feast of Tabernacles, for seven days unto Yahweh.
On the first day shall be a holy convocation. You shall do no servile work. 23:35
For seven days you shall offer a sacrifice made by fire unto Yahweh. 23:36
The eighth day shall be a holy convocation unto you,
and you shall offer a sacrifice made by fire unto Yahweh.
It is a solemn assembly, and you shall do no servile work this day.
These are the feasts of Yahweh, which you shall proclaim as holy 23:37
convocations, to offer sacrifices made by fire unto Yahweh—a burnt
offering, a grain offering, a communal sacrifice, and drink offerings."

"This is in addition to the sabbaths of Yahweh, and all your gifts, and all 23:38
your vows, and all your free will offerings that you give unto Yahweh.
On the fifteenth day of the seventh month, when you have gathered in 23:39
the fruit of the land, you shall keep a feast unto Yahweh for seven days.
The first day shall be a sabbath, and the eighth day shall be a sabbath.
On the first day you shall take the boughs of goodly trees, and branches 23:40
of palm trees, and the boughs of thick trees, and willows of the brook,
and you shall rejoice before Yahweh, your God, for seven days.
You shall keep this feast unto Yahweh seven days each year. It is a statute 23:41
forever in your generations, that you celebrate it in the seventh month.
You shall dwell in huts for seven days. All Israelites shall dwell in huts, 23:42
so that your generations may know that I made the children of Israel 23:43
dwell in huts when I brought them out of Egypt. I am Yahweh, your God."
And Moses declared unto the children of Israel the feasts of Yahweh. 23:44

Chapter 24

Yahweh spoke to Moses, telling him to 24:1
command the children of Israel to bring pure olive oil, 24:2
pressed for the lamps, so the lamps will burn continually.
"Outside the veil of the testimony, in the tabernacle of the congregation, 24:3
let Aaron see that lamps burn continually before Yahweh from evening
until morning. This shall be a statute forever in your generations.
He shall arrange the lamps upon the pure candlestick before Yahweh. 24:4
He shall take fine flour, and bake twelve cakes, 24:5
with two-tenths of a deal in each cake.
He shall set them in two rows, six in a row, on the table before Yahweh. 24:6
He shall put pure frankincense upon each row, that it may be on the bread 24:7
for a memorial—an offering made by fire unto Yahweh.

Every sabbath he shall set it in order before Yahweh,   24:8
on behalf of the children of Israel, by an everlasting covenant.
It shall be Aaron's and his sons'. They shall eat it in the holy place, for it is   24:9
a most holy him offering made by fire to Yahweh. This is a rule forever."

The son of an Israelite woman, whose father was an Egyptian,   24:10
went out among the children of Israel and a fight broke out
in the camp between him and an Israelite man.
And the son of the Israelite woman (whose name was Shelomith,   24:11
daughter of Dibri, of the tribe of Dan) cursed and blasphemed
the name of Yahweh. They brought him to Moses,
and put him under guard until they might hear the verdict of Yahweh.   24:12
Yahweh spoke to Moses, saying,   24:13
"Bring forth him that has cursed outside the camp, and let all who heard   24:14
him lay their hands upon his head, and let all the congregation stone him.
And you shall speak to the children of Israel, saying,   24:15
'Whoever curses his God shall bear his sin.
Whoever blasphemes the name of Yahweh, shall be put to death. All the   24:16
congregation shall stone him. The stranger, as well as he who was born in
the land, shall be put to death when he blasphemes the name of Yahweh.
He that kills any man shall surely be put to death.   24:17
He that kills a beast shall make it good, beast for beast.   24:18
If a man injures his neighbor, as he has done, so shall it be done to him.   24:19
Breach for breach, eye for eye, tooth for tooth.   24:20
As he has caused injury to a man, so shall it be done to him again.
He that kills a beast, shall restore it.   24:21
He that kills a man, shall be put to death.
You shall have one manner of law—for the stranger, as well as   24:22
for one of your own country. For I am Yahweh, your God.'"
Moses spoke to the children of Israel, that they should bring forth   24:23
him who had cursed outside the camp, and stone him with stones.
And the children of Israel did as Yahweh commanded Moses.

Chapter 25

Yahweh spoke to Moses on Mount Sinai, telling him to   25:1
speak to the children of Israel, and say unto them, "When you come   25:2
into the land that I give you, the land shall keep a sabbath unto Yahweh.
For six years you shall sow your field, and for six years   25:3
you shall prune your vineyard and gather the fruit thereof.
But the seventh year shall be a sabbath of rest for the land, a sabbath   25:4
for Yahweh. You shall neither sow your field, nor prune your vineyard.
That which grows of its own accord, you shall not reap for your harvest,   25:5
nor shall you gather grapes of your vines. It is a year of rest for the land.
Whatever the sabbath of the land produces of itself, shall be food for you,   25:6
and for your servant, and your maid, and your hired hand,
and the stranger who sojourns with you,
and for your cattle, and the beasts on your land.   25:7
All that the land produces of itself is your food.

And you shall count off seven sabbath years—   25:8
seven times seven years, which is forty-nine years.
Then on the tenth day of the seventh month, on the day of atonement,   25:9
you shall cause the trumpet of the Jubilee to sound throughout the land.
You shall hallow the fiftieth year, and proclaim liberty throughout   25:10
all the land for all the inhabitants. It shall be a Jubilee for you.
Every man shall return to his property, and to his family.
The fiftieth year shall be a Jubilee for you. You shall not sow, nor reap   25:11
grain that grows of itself, nor gather the grapes of your undressed vines.
For it is the Jubilee. It shall be holy unto you.   25:12
You shall eat only what the land produces of itself.

"In the year of this Jubilee every man shall return to his family property.   25:13
And if you sell something to your neighbor, or buy something   25:14
from your neighbor's hand, you shall not cheat one another.
When you buy land from your neighbor, count the number of years since   25:15
the Jubilee, and he will sell to you based on the years left for harvests.
If the number of years left for harvest is great, the price shall increase.   25:16
If the years left are few, the price will diminish,
because it is the number of harvests that is being bought and sold.
You shall not cheat one another. You shall fear your God.   25:17
I am Yahweh, your God.
Obey my laws, accept my judgments, and live by them,   25:18
so that you may dwell in the land in safety.
The land shall yield her fruit, and you shall eat your fill,   25:19
and you shall dwell in the land in safety.
If you ask, 'What shall we eat in the seventh year,   25:20
when we do not sow, nor gather our crops?'
I tell you, I shall command my blessing upon you   25:21
in the sixth year, and it shall bring forth fruit for three years.
You shall sow the eighth year and eat of old fruits until the ninth year.   25:22
Until those fruits come in, you shall eat of the old store.

"The land shall not be owned forever, for the land is mine.   25:23
You are strangers and sojourners with me.
In all the land of your possession you shall grant   25:24
the right of redemption by him who sold it to you.
If your neighbor becomes poor and must sell some of his land,   25:25
any of his kin may buy back that which his relation has sold.
If the man has no kin to redeem it, but he is later able to redeem it himself,   25:26
let him count the years since the sale and restore the overplus   25:27
to the man who bought it, so that it may return to his possession.
If he is not able to redeem it himself, the land shall remain in the hand   25:28
of the buyer until the Jubilee year. In that year it shall be returned
to the original owner and he shall have his land back.
If a man sells a dwelling house in a walled city, he may redeem it   25:29
within a year after it is sold. He has a full year to redeem it.
If it is not redeemed within a full year, the house in the walled city   25:30
shall be established forever to him who bought it,

162

throughout his generations. It shall not go out in the Jubilee.

Houses in villages with no wall around them shall be counted as the fields 25:31
of the country. They may be redeemed, and they shall go out in the Jubilee.

"The cities of the Levites, and the houses of the cities 25:32
in their possession, may be redeemed by the Levites at any time.
If a man buys from a Levite a house in a Levite city, that house shall 25:33
go out in the year of Jubilee, for the houses of the cities of the Levites
are their permanent possession among the children of Israel.
The fields of the suburbs of their cities may not be sold, 25:34
for they are their perpetual possession.

"If your neighbor becomes poor and cannot support himself, you shall 25:35
provide for him as if he were a stranger, a sojourner living among you.
Take no usury or profit from him, but fear your God, 25:36
that your brother may live among you.
Do not charge interest on money, nor profit from food you lend him. 25:37
I am Yahweh, your God, who brought you forth out of the land of Egypt, 25:38
to give you the land of Canaan, and to be your God.
If your neighbor becomes poor and sells himself to you, 25:39
do not make him work like a slave.
But as a hired servant, as a sojourner, he shall be with you, 25:40
and shall serve you until the year of Jubilee.
Then he shall depart from you, both him and his children with him, 25:41
and shall return to his own family, and to the land of his fathers.
For they are my servants, whom I brought forth out of the land of Egypt. 25:42
They shall not be sold as slaves.
You shall not rule over them harshly, but shall fear your God. 25:43

"Regarding male and female slaves, you shall buy 25:44
your slaves from the heathen nations around you.
You can also buy slaves from the families of sojourners among you, 25:45
and of the children they begat in your land. These may be your property.
And you may give them as an inheritance to your children after you, 25:46
to inherit for a possession. They shall be your slaves forever.
But you shall not rule harshly over your brethren, the children of Israel.
If a sojourner among you becomes rich, and an Israelite who is poor 25:47
sells himself to the stranger, or to one of the stranger's family,
the Israelite may be redeemed again by one of his brethren. 25:48
His uncle, or his uncle's son, or any close relation may redeem him. 25:49
Or, if he is able, he may redeem himself.

"He shall count with the man who bought him from the year he was sold 25:50
until the year of Jubilee. The price of his redemption shall be according
to that number of years, at the price of wages for a hired servant.
If there are many years until Jubilee, the redemption price 25:51
shall be in fair proportion to the original purchase price.
If there remain but a few years until the year of the Jubilee, 25:52
he shall pay for his redemption according to his years of servitude.
The stranger who buys the Israelite shall treat him like a hired servant, 25:53

and shall not rule harshly over him in your eyes.

If he is not redeemed in these years, he shall go out 25:54
in the year of Jubilee, both he, and his children with him.

For the children of Israel are servants to me. They are my servants 25:55
whom I brought forth out of the land of Egypt. I am Yahweh, your God."

Chapter 26

"You shall make no idols nor graven images, nor build statues. 26:1
Neither shall you set up any image cut of stone in your land,
to bow down to it. For I am Yahweh, your God.

You shall keep my sabbaths and reverence my sanctuary. I am Yahweh. 26:2

If you walk in my statutes and keep my commandments, and do them, 26:3

I will give you rain in due season, and the land shall yield 26:4
her increase, and the trees of the field shall yield their fruit.

Your threshing season shall last until the grape harvest, 26:5
and the grape harvest shall last until sowing time.
You shall eat your bread to the full, and dwell in your land safely.

I will give you peace in the land, and you shall lie down, 26:6
and none shall make you afraid. I will rid the land of evil beasts,
and the sword shall not go through your land.

You shall chase your enemies, and they shall fall before you by the sword. 26:7

Five of you shall chase a hundred, and a hundred of you shall put 26:8
ten thousand to flight. Your enemies shall fall before you by the sword.

I will have respect for you, and make you fruitful, 26:9
and multiply you, and establish my covenant with you.

You shall eat the old store, and bring forth the old because of the new. 26:10

I will set my tabernacle among you, and my soul shall not abhor you. 26:11

I will walk among you. I will be your God, and you shall be my people. 26:12

I am Yahweh, your God, who brought you forth out of the land of Egypt, 26:13
that you should not be their slaves. I have broken
the bonds of your yoke, and made you walk upright.

"But if you do not hearken unto me, and do not do all my commandments, 26:14
or if you despise my statutes and abhor my judgments, and thus 26:15
do not do my commandments, or if you break my covenant,

I will terrorize you with incurable diseases and burning fevers 26:16
that melt your eyes, and I will cause you sorrow of heart.
You shall sow your seed in vain, for your enemies shall eat it.

I will set my face against you, and you shall be slain 26:17
by your enemies. Those who hate you shall reign over you,
and you shall flee even when no one pursues you.

And if you still for all this will not hearken unto me, 26:18
I will punish you seven times more harshly for your sins.

I will break the pride of your power. 26:19
I will make your heaven as iron, and your earth as brass.

Your strength shall be spent in vain, for your land shall not yield 26:20
her increase, nor shall the trees of the land yield their fruits.

If you walk contrary unto me, and will not hearken unto me, 26:21

I will bring seven times more plagues upon you according to your sins.

I will set wild beasts upon you to rob you of your children, destroy your 26:22
cattle and make you few in number. Your highways shall be desolate.

If you will not be reformed by these things, but walk contrary unto me, 26:23
then I will also walk contrary to you, and I will punish you 26:24
seven times more harshly for your sins.

I will bring a sword upon you to avenge the quarrel of my covenant, 26:25
and when you are gathered together in your cities, I will send a pestilence
among you, and you shall be delivered into the hand of the enemy.

And when I have broken the staff of your bread, ten women shall bake 26:26
your bread in one oven, and they shall deliver you your bread by weight.
You will eat, but you will not be satisfied.

"If you do not for all this hearken unto me, but still walk contrary unto me, 26:27
then I will also walk contrary unto you, in fury, 26:28
and I, even I, will chastise you seven times for your sins.

You shall eat the flesh of your sons, and the flesh of your daughters. 26:29

I will destroy your high places, and cut down your images, and cast 26:30
your carcasses upon the carcasses of your idols, and I shall abhor you.

I will make waste of your cities, and bring your sanctuaries unto 26:31
desolation, and I will not smell the savor of your sweet odors.

I will bring the land to desolation. 26:32
Your enemies who dwell there shall be astonished.

I will scatter you among the heathen, and will draw out a sword after you. 26:33
Your land shall be desolate, and your cities laid waste.

Then shall the land enjoy her sabbaths, as it lies desolate and you are 26:34
in your enemies' land. Then shall the land rest and enjoy her sabbaths.

As long as it lies desolate it shall rest, because it did not rest 26:35
in your sabbaths, when you dwelt upon it.

Upon those who are left alive, I will send faintness of heart in the lands 26:36
of their enemies. The sound of a shaken leaf shall chase them, and they
shall flee as if from a sword, and they shall fall when no one pursues them.

They shall fall one upon another, as if before a sword, when none 26:37
pursue them. You shall have no power to stand before your enemies.

You shall perish among the heathen, 26:38
and the land of your enemies shall eat you up.

Those who are left shall pine away in their iniquity in your enemies' lands, 26:39
and also in the iniquities of their fathers shall they pine away.

"But if they confess their iniquity, and the iniquity of their fathers, 26:40
and that they trespassed against me, and walked contrary unto me,
and that I also have walked contrary unto them, and have brought them 26:41
into the land of their enemies—if then their uncircumcised hearts be
humbled, and they accept the punishment of their iniquity—
then will I remember my covenant with Jacob, and my covenant with 26:42
Isaac, and my covenant with Abraham. And I will remember the land.

The land shall be without them, and shall enjoy her sabbaths while she 26:43
lies desolate. And they shall accept the punishment of their iniquity,
because they despised my judgments and abhorred my statutes.

Yet for all that, when they are in the land of their enemies I will not   26:44
cast them away, neither will I abhor them, nor destroy them utterly,
nor break my covenant with them. For I am Yahweh, their God.
I will for their sakes remember the covenant of their ancestors,   26:45
whom I brought forth out of Egypt in the sight of the heathen,
that I might be their God. I am Yahweh."
These are the statutes and judgments and laws Yahweh made between   26:46
him and the children of Israel on Mount Sinai by the hand of Moses.

Chapter 27

Yahweh spoke to Moses, telling him to   27:1
speak to the children of Israel, and say unto them, "When a man   27:2
makes a solemn promise to Yahweh concerning the value of a person,
the value shall be fifty shekels of silver for a male between twenty   27:3
and sixty years old, based on the shekel of the sanctuary.
If it is for a female, the value shall be thirty shekels.   27:4
If it is for someone between five years old and twenty years old,   27:5
the value shall be twenty shekels for a male, and ten shekels for a female.
If it is for a child from one month old to five years old, the value shall   27:6
be five shekels of silver for a male, and three shekels for a female.
If it is for someone sixty years old and above, the value shall   27:7
be fifteen shekels for a male, and ten shekels for a female.
If he who promises cannot afford to pay full value, he shall present himself   27:8
to the priest, and the priest shall set a value according to his ability to pay.
If the solemn promise concerns a beast to offer unto Yahweh,   27:9
any such animal given to Yahweh shall be holy.
He shall not alter the promise—to exchange a good for a bad, or a bad   27:10
for a good. If he exchanges one beast for another, both shall be holy.
If it is an unclean beast that cannot be offered unto Yahweh,   27:11
he shall present the beast before the priest.
The priest shall value it, and whether it be high or low,   27:12
as the priest says, so shall it be.
If the promise maker instead wishes to buy it back,   27:13
he shall pay the set value plus one-fifth more.

"When a man sanctifies his house to be holy unto Yahweh,   27:14
the priest shall estimate its value, and whether it is high or low,
as the priest estimates, so shall it stand.
If he who sanctified his house wishes to redeem it, he shall pay   27:15
one-fifth more than the estimate and it shall be his.
If a man would sanctify unto Yahweh some part of a field in his   27:16
possession, the value shall be set according to the seed needed
to plant it, at the rate of fifty shekels of silver per homer of barley seed.
If he sanctifies his field in the year of Jubilee, its value shall remain fixed.   27:17
If he sanctifies his field after the Jubilee, the priest shall   27:18
calculate the value based on the years that remain until
the next Jubilee, and the value will be reduced accordingly.
If he who sanctified the field wishes to redeem it, he shall pay   27:19

one-fifth more than the estimated value and it shall be returned to him.
If he does not wish to redeem the field, or if he has sold it to another man, 27:20
it can no longer be redeemed by anyone.
Then, when the field goes out in the Jubilee, it shall become 27:21
a holy field devoted unto Yahweh, and it shall belong to the priest.
If a man sanctifies unto Yahweh a field he has bought 27:22
that is not part of his family property,
the priest shall calculate its value based on the years remaining until the 27:23
Jubilee, and that man shall pay it in full that day as a holy gift to Yahweh.
In the year of the Jubilee the field shall return to the original owner, 27:24
to him to whom it is family property.
All your estimations shall be according to the shekel 27:25
of the sanctuary, which is twenty gerahs to a shekel.

No one shall dedicate a firstling of his animals, whether it be an ox or goat 27:26
or sheep, for they already belong to Yahweh. No man can sanctify them.
If it is an unclean animal, he can redeem it for the priest's estimation 27:27
plus one-fifth. If it is not redeemed, it shall be sold for its set value.
However, nothing that a man has unconditionally consecrated 27:28
unto Yahweh—whether a human, an animal or a field—can be sold
or redeemed. Every consecrated thing is most holy to Yahweh.
Humans who are consecrated in this way cannot be ransomed. 27:29
They must be put to death.
All the tithes of the land, whether of seed, 27:30
or of fruit, is Yahweh's. It is holy unto Yahweh.
If a man would redeem any of his tithes, he shall add a fifth part more. 27:31
Concerning the tithe of the herds, or of the flocks—of whatever passes 27:32
under the shepherd's staff—one-tenth shall be holy and given to Yahweh.
He shall not determine good or bad for his tithe, and neither shall he 27:33
exchange one for the other. If he exchanges one for another, both shall
be holy and given to Yahweh, and they cannot be redeemed."
These are the commandments Yahweh gave to Moses 27:34
on Mount Sinai for the children of Israel.

Moses and Aaron Appear Before Pharaoh, Gustave Dore

The Fourth Book of Moses Called
Numbers

Chapter 1

Yahweh spoke to Moses in the wilderness of Sinai, in the tabernacle | 1:1
of the congregation, on the first day of the second month,
in the second year after they came out of Egypt, saying,
"Take a census of all the children of Israel, after their families, | 1:2
after the house of their fathers, with the names of every male.
From twenty years old and upward, all males in Israel who are able to go | 1:3
to war shall be counted by you and Aaron, and registered for their armies.
Take with you one man of every tribe, the head of his father's house. | 1:4
These are the names of the men who shall go with you: | 1:5
Of the tribe of Reuben, Elizur the son of Shedeur.
Of Simeon, Shelumiel the son of Zurishaddai. | 1:6
Of Judah, Nahshon the son of Amminadab. | 1:7
Of Issachar, Nethaneel the son of Zuar. | 1:8
Of Zebulun, Eliab the son of Helon. | 1:9
Of the children of Joseph: Of Ephraim, Elishama the son of Ammihud; | 1:10
of Manasseh, Gamaliel the son of Pedahzur.
Of Benjamin, Abidan the son of Gideoni. | 1:11
Of Dan, Ahiezer the son of Ammishaddai. | 1:12
Of Asher, Pagiel the son of Ocran. | 1:13
Of Gad, Eliasaph the son of Deuel. | 1:14
Of Naphtali, Ahira the son of Enan. | 1:15
These are the renowned of the congregation, chiefs of the tribes | 1:16
of their fathers, heads of the thousands of Israel."
So Moses and Aaron took these men who were mentioned by name, | 1:17
and assembled all the congregation together on the first day of the second | 1:18
month, and they recorded people's ancestry, by the house of their fathers,
and registered all the males, twenty years old and upward, by name.
As Yahweh commanded, so they counted them in the wilderness of Sinai. | 1:19

The children of Reuben, Israel's eldest son, were recorded by clan, | 1:20
by family, by the house of their fathers. Every male from twenty years old
upward, all who were able to go to war, were registered by name.
The numbers of the tribe of Reuben were 46,500. | 1:21
The children of Simeon were recorded by clan, by family, by the house | 1:22
of their fathers. Every male from twenty years old upward,
all who were able to go to war, were registered by name.
The numbers of the tribe of Simeon were 59,300. | 1:23

The children of Gad were recorded by clan, by family, by the house | 1:24
of their fathers. Every male from twenty years old upward,

all who were able to go to war, were registered by name

The numbers of the tribe of Gad were 45,650.   1:25

The children of Judah were recorded by clan, by family, by the house   1:26
of their fathers. Every male from twenty years old upward,
all who were able to go to war, were registered by name.
The numbers of the tribe of Judah were 14,600.   1:27

The children of Issachar were recorded by clan, by family, by the house   1:28
of their fathers. Every male from twenty years old upward,
all who were able to go to war, were registered by name.
The numbers of the tribe of Issachar were 54,400.   1:29
The children of Zebulun were recorded by clan, by family, by the house   1:30
of their fathers. Every male from twenty years old upward,
all who were able to go to war, were registered by name.
The numbers of the tribe of Zebulun were 57,400.   1:31

The children of Joseph's son Ephraim were recorded by clan, by family,   1:32
by the house of their fathers. Every male from twenty years old upward,
all who were able to go to war, were registered by name.
The numbers of the tribe of Ephraim were 40,500.   1:33
The children of Joseph's son Manasseh were recorded by clan, by family,   1:34
by the house of their fathers. Every male from twenty years old upward,
all who were able to go to war, were registered by name.
The numbers of the tribe of Manasseh were 32,200.   1:35

The children of Benjamin were recorded by clan, by family, by the house   1:36
of their fathers. Every male from twenty years old upward,
all who were able to go to war, were registered by name.
The numbers of the tribe of Benjamin were 35,400.   1:37
The children of Dan were recorded by clan, by family, by the house   1:38
of their fathers. Every male from twenty years old upward,
all who were able to go to war, were registered by name.
The numbers of the tribe of Dan were 62,700.   1:39

The children of Asher were recorded by clan, by family, by the house   1:40
of their fathers. Every male from twenty years old upward,
all who were able to go to war, were registered by name.
The numbers of the tribe of Asher were 41,500.   1:41
The children of Naphtali were recorded by clan, by family, by the house   1:42
of their fathers. Every male from twenty years old upward,
all who were able to go to war, were registered by name.
The numbers of the tribe of Naphtali were 53,400.   1:43

These are those who were numbered by Moses and Aaron,   1:44
and the twelve chiefs of Israel, one from each tribe.
And so, all males twenty years old and upward who were   1:45
able to go to war were registered for the armies of Israel.
The total who were numbered were 603,550.   1:46
The Levites, belonging to their own ancestral tribe,   1:47
were not numbered among them.

For Yahweh had spoken to Moses, saying,   1:48
"You shall not number the tribe of Levi,   1:49
nor take their census with the children of Israel.
You shall appoint the Levites over the tabernacle of testimony   1:50
and all the vessels and things that belong to it. They shall care for it
and minister unto it, and they shall encamp around the tabernacle.
When it is time to break camp, the Levites shall take down the tabernacle,   1:51
and when the tabernacle is to be erected, the Levites shall set it up.
Any stranger who comes near it shall be put to death.
The children of Israel shall pitch their tents, every man by his own camp,   1:52
and by his own standard, throughout their hosts.
But the Levites shall pitch round about the tabernacle of testimony,   1:53
that there be no wrath upon the congregation of the children of Israel.
The Levites shall keep guard over the tabernacle of testimony."
The children of Israel did according to all that Yahweh commanded Moses.   1:54

Chapter 2

Yahweh spoke to Moses and Aaron, saying,   2:1
"The Israelites shall pitch their tents, each by his own standard,   2:2
with the ensign of his father's house, far off from the tabernacle.
Those of the standard of Judah shall pitch their tents, according to   2:3
their armies, on the east side toward the rising of the sun.
Nahshon, son of Amminadab, shall be captain of the children of Judah.
The total forces of his host number 74,600.   2:4
The tribe of Issachar shall pitch next to him.   2:5
Nethaneel, son of Zuar shall be captain of the children of Issachar.
The total forces of his host number 54,400.   2:6
Then the tribe of Zebulun. Eliab, son of Helon,   2:7
shall be captain of the children of Zebulun.
The total forces of his host number 57,400.   2:8
The total forces in the hosts of Judah number 186,400.   2:9
These shall set forth first.

"Those of the standard of Reuben shall pitch their tents   2:10
on the south side, according to their armies.
Elizur, son of Shedeur, shall be captain of the children of Reuben.
The total forces of his host number 46,500.   2:11
The tribe of Simeon shall pitch by them. Shelumiel, son of Zurishaddai,   2:12
shall be captain of the children of Simeon.
The total forces of his host number 59,300.   2:13
Then the tribe of Gad. Eliasaph, son of Reuel,   2:14
shall be captain of the sons of Gad.
The total forces of his host number 45,650.   2:15
The total forces in the hosts of Reuben number 151,450.   2:16
They shall set forth in the second rank.

"Next the tabernacle of the congregation shall move forward,   2:17
with the tribe of the Levites in the middle of the armies,

in the same order as they camp, each by his own standard.

Those of the standard of Ephraim shall camp on the west side,   2:18
according to their armies. Elishama, son of Ammihud,
shall be captain of the sons of Ephraim.
The total forces of his host number 40,500.   2:19
The tribe of Manasseh shall be by him. Gamaliel, son of Pedahzur,   2:20
shall be captain of the children of Manasseh.
The total forces of his host number 32,200.   2:21
Then the tribe of Benjamin. Abidan, son of Gideoni,   2:22
shall be captain of the sons of Benjamin.
The total forces of his host number 35,400.   2:23
The total forces in the hosts of Ephraim number 108,100.   2:24
They shall go forward in the third rank.

"Those of the standard of Dan shall be on the north side, by their armies.   2:25
Ahiezer, son of Ammishaddai, shall be captain of the children of Dan.
The total forces of his host number 62,700.   2:26
The tribe of Asher shall camp by them. Pagiel, son of Ocran,   2:27
shall be captain of the children of Asher.
The total forces of his host number 41,500.   2:28
Then the tribe of Naphtali. Ahira, son of Enan,   2:29
shall be captain of the children of Naphtali.
The total forces of his host number 53,400.   2:30
The total forces in the hosts of Dan number 157,600.   2:31
They shall go last with their standards."

These are the children of Israel who were counted, according to the house   2:32
of their fathers. The total forces of the hosts of Israel numbered 603,550.
The Levites were not numbered among the children of Israel,   2:33
as Yahweh commanded Moses.
The children of Israel did according to all that Yahweh commanded Moses.   2:34
They pitched by their standards, and so set forward,
each after their families, according to the house of their fathers.

Chapter 3

These are the generations of Aaron and Moses,   3:1
in the day Yahweh spoke with Moses on Mount Sinai.
These are the names of the sons of Aaron: 3:2
Nadab, the firstborn, and Abihu, Eleazar and Ithamar.
These are the names of the sons of Aaron, the priests who were anointed,   3:3
whom he consecrated to minister in the priest's office.
Nadab and Abihu were killed by Yahweh when they offered strange fire   3:4
before Yahweh in the wilderness of Sinai. They had no children. Eleazar
and Ithamar ministered as priests in the sight of Aaron, their father.

Yahweh spoke to Moses, saying,   3:5
"Bring the tribe of Levi near, and present them   3:6
before Aaron the priest, that they may minister unto him.
They shall keep his charge, and the charge of the whole   3:7

congregation of the tabernacle, to do the service of the tabernacle.
They shall keep all the instruments of the tabernacle of the congregation, 3:8
and the charge of the children of Israel, to do the service of the tabernacle.
You shall give the Levites to Aaron and to his sons. 3:9
They are wholly given to him out of the children of Israel.
You shall appoint Aaron and his sons to attend to the priest's office. 3:10
Any stranger who comes near shall be put to death."
Yahweh spoke to Moses, saying, 3:11
"I have taken the Levites instead of all the firstborns of the children 3:12
of Israel, who open the matrix. The Levites are mine
because all the firstborns are mine. On the day I killed all the firstborn 3:13
sons of Egypt I hallowed unto myself all the firstborn males of Israel,
both man and beast. They are mine. I am Yahweh."

Yahweh spoke to Moses in the wilderness of Sinai, saying, 3:14
"Number the children of Levi after the house of their fathers, by their 3:15
families. Every male from a month old and upward shall be counted."
So Moses numbered them, as Yahweh commanded. 3:16
These were the names of the sons of Levi: Gershon, Kohath and Merari. 3:17
These were the names of the sons of Gershon: Libni and Shimei. 3:18
The sons of Kohath: Amram, Izehar, Hebron and Uzziel. 3:19
The sons of Merari: Mahli and Mushi. These are the families 3:20
of the Levites, according to the house of their fathers.
Of Gershon was the family of the Libnites, and the family of the Shimites. 3:21
These are the families of the Gershonites.
Their numbers, all the males from a month old upward, were 7,500. 3:22

"Families of the Gershonites shall pitch behind the tabernacle westward. 3:23
Eliasaph, son of Lael, shall be chief of the house of the Gershonites. 3:24
The charge of the sons of Gershon in the tabernacle of the congregation 3:25
shall be the tabernacle, the tent and the covering thereof,
the hanging for the door of the tabernacle,
the hangings of the court, the curtain for the door of the court, 3:26
the altar round about, the tent ropes, and all the service thereof."

Of Kohath were the families of the Amramites, Izeharites, Hebronites, 3:27
and Uzzielites. These are the families of the Kohathites.
Their numbers, all the males from a month old upward, 3:28
were 8,600, keeping the charge of the sanctuary.
"The families of Kohath shall pitch on the side of the tabernacle south. 3:29
Elizaphan, son of Uzziel, shall be chief of the families of the Kohathites. 3:30
Their charge shall be the ark, the table, the candlesticks, the altars, 3:31
the vessels of the sanctuary, the hangings, and all the service thereof.
Eleazar, son of Aaron the priest, shall be head of the chiefs of the Levites, 3:32
and have oversight of them who keep the charge of the sanctuary."

Of Merari were the families of the Mahlites, 3:33
and the Mushites. These are the families of Merari.
Their numbers, all the males from a month old upward, were 6,200. 3:34
"Zuriel, son of Abihail, shall be chief of the families of Merari. 3:35

They shall pitch on the side of the tabernacle northward.
The charge of the sons of Merari shall be the boards of the tabernacle, 3:36
its bars, its pillars, its sockets, all the vessels and the service thereof,
and the pillars of the court, including their sockets, pins and ropes. 3:37
Those who encamp before the tabernacle toward the east, shall be 3:38
Moses and Aaron and his sons, keeping charge of the sanctuary for
the children of Israel. Any stranger who comes near shall be put to death."
The numbers of the Levites, all the males from a month old upward, which 3:39
Moses and Aaron counted at the commandment of Yahweh, were 22,000.

Yahweh said to Moses, "Number all the firstborn males of the children 3:40
of Israel from a month old and upward, and record their names.
Take the Levites for me—I am Yahweh—instead of all the firstborn 3:41
of the children of Israel. And take the cattle of the Levites
instead of all the firstlings of the cattle of the Israelites."
Moses numbered, as Yahweh commanded him, 3:42
all the firstborn males among the children of Israel.
All the firstborn males, from a month old and upward, were 22,273. 3:43

Yahweh spoke to Moses, saying, 3:44
"Take the Levites instead of the firstborn of the children of Israel, and the 3:45
Levites' cattle instead of their cattle. The Levites are mine. I am Yahweh.
Since there are 273 more firstborns of Israel 3:46
than the number of Levites, these must be redeemed.
Collect five shekels apiece for them, after the shekel of the sanctuary, 3:47
which is twenty gerahs to a shekel,
and give this money—the price of redemption for those 3:48
over the number of Levites—to Aaron and his sons."
So Moses took the redemption money for those who were 3:49
over and above those redeemed by the Levites.
From the firstborn of the children of Israel he took the money, 3:50
1,365 shekels, after the shekel of the sanctuary.
Moses gave the money to Aaron and his sons, as Yahweh commanded. 3:51

Chapter 4

Yahweh spoke to Moses and to Aaron, saying, 4:1
"Take a census of the sons of Kohath from among the Levites, 4:2
after their families, after the house of their fathers—
all those between thirty and fifty years old who enter the host— 4:3
to work in the tabernacle of the congregation.
This shall be the service of the sons of Kohath in the tabernacle, 4:4
concerning the most holy things:
When its time to break camp, Aaron and his sons shall take down 4:5
the covering veil and cover the ark of the covenant with it.
They shall put the covering of badger skins upon it, and shall 4:6
spread over it a cloth wholly of blue, and shall put the staves in the ark.
On the table of showbread they shall spread a cloth of blue, and put upon 4:7
it the dishes, spoons, bowls and goblets. The continual bread shall be on it.

"They shall spread upon these things a cloth of scarlet, and cover   4:8
them with badger skins, and they shall put in the staves thereof.
With a cloth of blue they shall cover the candlestick of the light, and its   4:9
lamps and tongs and snuff dishes, and all the oil vessels for its service.
They shall wrap all this with badger skins, and put it on a bar.   4:10
Upon the golden altar they shall spread a cloth of blue and cover it   4:11
with a blanket of badger skins, and they shall put in the staves thereof.
They shall take all the instruments of ministry for the sanctuary, put them   4:12
in a cloth of blue, cover them with badger skins, and put them on a bar.
They shall take the ashes from the altar and spread a purple cloth upon it.   4:13
Then they shall put upon it all the vessels of the altar with which they   4:14
minister—the censers, flesh hooks, shovels and basins—and they shall
cover it with a blanket of badger skins and put the staves in it.

"When Aaron and his sons have finished preparing the sanctuary   4:15
and all the vessels of the sanctuary, as the camp is set to move forward,
the sons of Kohath shall come to bear it all. But they shall not
touch any holy thing, lest they die. These things are the burden
of the sons of Kohath in the tabernacle of the congregation.
To the office of Eleazar, son of Aaron the priest, pertains the oil   4:16
for the light, the sweet incense, the grain offering, the anointing oil,
and the oversight of all the sanctuary and the vessels thereof."
Yahweh spoke to Moses and to Aaron, saying,   4:17
"Do not cut off the tribe of the families of the Kohathites from the Levites.   4:18
But so that they may live and not die when they approach holy things,   4:19
Aaron and his sons shall appoint each of them his service and his burden.
They shall not go in when the holy things are being covered, lest they die."   4:20

Yahweh spoke to Moses, saying,   4:21
"Take also the sum of the sons of Gershon,   4:22
throughout the houses of their fathers, by their families.
Number all those from thirty to fifty years old, all who are   4:23
eligible to perform service in the tabernacle of the congregation.
These are the duties of the Gershonites, their service and their burdens: 4:24
They shall bear the curtains of the tabernacle, their covering,   4:25
and the covering of badger skins upon them, and the hanging
for the door of the tabernacle of the congregation.
Also the hangings of the court—which is all round the tabernacle and   4:26
altar—and the hanging for the gate of the court, and its ropes, and all the
instruments of their service. Whatever is necessary for these they shall do.
Aaron and his sons shall be in charge of all the work of the sons   4:27
of the Gershonites, in all their burdens, and in all their service.
They shall assign to each their service and their burdens.
This is the service of the sons of Gershon in the tabernacle.   4:28
They shall serve under the direction of Ithamar, son of Aaron the priest.

"As for the sons of Merari, you shall number them   4:29
after their families, by the house of their fathers.
You shall number all those from thirty to fifty years old, all who are   4:30

eligible for service, to do the work of the tabernacle of the congregation.

This is their charge in the tabernacle: The boards of the tabernacle, 4:31
and the bars, and pillars, and sockets thereof.

Also the pillars of the court, and their sockets, pins and cords, 4:32
and all the instruments of their service.
You will list by name the instruments in their charge.

This is the service of the sons of Merari in the tabernacle of the 4:33
congregation, under the hand of Ithamar, son of Aaron the priest."

Moses and Aaron and the chief of Israel numbered the sons 4:34
of the Kohathites, after their families, and after the house of their fathers.

They numbered all those from thirty to fifty years old, all who were 4:35
eligible to enter the service, for the work in the tabernacle.

Those who were counted numbered 2,750. 4:36

These were they who were numbered of the families of the Kohathites, 4:37
all that might do service in the tabernacle of the congregation, who Moses
and Aaron did number according to the commandment of Yahweh.

And they numbered the sons of Gershon, 4:38
throughout their families, and by the house of their fathers,

from thirty to fifty years old, all who were eligible to enter the service, 4:39
for the work in the tabernacle of the congregation.

Those who were numbered, throughout their families, 4:40
by the house of their fathers, were 2,630.

These are they who were numbered of the families of the sons of Gershon, 4:41
of all who might do service in the tabernacle of the congregation, whom
Moses and Aaron did number according to the commandment of Yahweh.

And they numbered the sons of Merari, 4:42
throughout their families, by the house of their fathers,

from thirty to fifty years old, all who were eligible to enter the service, 4:43
for the work in the tabernacle of the congregation.

Those who were counted numbered 3,200. 4:44

These are those who were numbered of the families of the sons of Merari, 4:45
whom Moses and Aaron numbered according to the word of Yahweh.

All who were numbered of the Levites, whom Moses, Aaron and the chief 4:46
of Israel numbered, after their families and the house of their fathers,

from thirty to fifty years old, everyone who came to do the service 4:47
of the ministry, and the service of the burden in the tabernacle,

were a total of 8,580. 4:48

According to the commandment of Yahweh they were numbered by the 4:49
hand of Moses, everyone according to his service, and according to his
burden. Thus were they numbered, as Yahweh commanded Moses.

Chapter 5

Yahweh spoke to Moses, saying, 5:1
"Command the children of Israel to put out of the camp every leper, 5:2
everyone who has an issue, and whoever is defiled by the dead.

Put both male and female outside the camp, so that they   5:3
do not defile the camps in the midst of which I dwell."
And the children of Israel did so, and put them outside the camp.   5:4
As Yahweh spoke unto Moses, so the children of Israel did.
Yahweh spoke to Moses, telling him to   5:5
speak to the children of Israel, saying, "When a man or woman commits   5:6
any sin that men commit, and so trespasses against Yahweh, and is guilty,
they shall confess their sin, and recompense for their trespass a specified   5:7
amount, plus one-fifth, and give it to him whom was trespassed against.
If the man has no kinsman to receive payment, let the trespass   5:8
be recompensed unto Yahweh and given to the priest. This is in addition
to the ram of atonement, whereby an atonement shall be made for him.
Every offering of the holy things of the children of Israel   5:9
that they bring to the priest, shall be his.
Every man's hallowed things shall be his own,   5:10
but whatever anyone gives to a priest, shall be the priest's."

Yahweh spoke to Moses, telling him to   5:11
speak to the children of Israel, and say to them, "If a man's wife   5:12
goes astray, and commits a trespass against him,
and is defiled by having intercourse with another man,   5:13
and it is kept secret from her husband, and there are no
witnesses against her, nor was she caught in the act,
but the spirit of jealousy comes upon him, and he becomes jealous of his   5:14
wife who was defiled, or even if he is jealous and she was not defiled,
then the man shall bring his wife to the priest, and he shall bring an   5:15
offering for her—the tenth part of an ephah of barley meal. He shall pour
no oil upon it, nor put frankincense thereon, for it is an offering of
jealousy, an offering of memorial, bringing iniquity to remembrance.
And the priest shall bring her near, and set her before Yahweh.   5:16
And the priest shall pour holy water into an earthen vessel, and shall take   5:17
dust from the floor of the tabernacle and put it into the water.

"The priest shall set the woman before Yahweh, and uncover the woman's   5:18
head, and put the offering of memorial in her hands, the jealousy offering,
and the priest shall have in his hand the bitter water that causes the curse.
The priest shall charge her by an oath, and say, 'If no man has lain with   5:19
you, and if you have not gone aside to uncleanness with another instead
of your husband, you are free from this bitter water that causes the curse.
But if you have gone aside to another instead of your husband,   5:20
and if you are defiled, and a man beside your husband has lain with you,
Yahweh shall make your name a curse among your people,   5:21
and cause your womb to rot, and your belly to swell.
This water that causes the curse shall go into your bowels, to make your   5:22
belly swell and your womb rot.' And the woman shall say, 'Amen, amen.'
And the priest shall write these curses in a book,   5:23
and he shall blot them out with the bitter water.

"And he shall make the woman drink the bitter water that causes   5:24
the curse, and the water shall enter into her, and become bitter.
The priest shall take the jealousy offering out of the woman's hand,   5:25
wave the offering before Yahweh, and offer it upon the altar.
The priest shall take a handful of the offering, a memorial portion,   5:26
and burn it upon the altar. Afterward he shall make her drink the water.
When she drinks the water, it shall come to pass that if she has been   5:27
defiled, and has trespassed against her husband, the water that causes
the curse shall enter into her and become bitter. Her belly will swell,
her womb will rot, and she will be a curse among her people.
But if the woman was not defiled, but is clean,   5:28
she shall be free, and she shall conceive children.
This is the law of jealousies, when a wife goes aside   5:29
to another instead of her husband and is defiled,
or when the spirit of jealousy comes upon a man, and he is jealous   5:30
over his wife. He shall set the woman before Yahweh,
and the priest shall execute upon her all this law.
Then shall the man be guiltless from iniquity,   5:31
and the woman shall bear her iniquity."

Chapter 6

Yahweh spoke to Moses, telling him to   6:1
speak to the children of Israel, and say, "When a man or woman   6:2
shall isolate themselves, to vow the vow of a Nazarite—
to consecrate themselves unto Yahweh—
he shall separate himself from wine and strong drink, and shall drink   6:3
no vinegar of wine, nor vinegar of strong drink. Neither shall he drink
any liquor of grapes, nor eat moist grapes, nor dried grapes.
For all the days of his vow of separation he shall eat nothing   6:4
produced by the grapevine, not even its seeds or skin.
For all the days of his vow of isolation there shall no razor come upon   6:5
his head, until the days be fulfilled in which he separates himself
unto Yahweh. He shall be holy, and let the locks of the hair grow long.
For all the days he separates himself he shall not go near a corpse.   6:6
He shall not make himself unclean for his father, mother, brother or sister   6:7
when they die, because the consecration of his God is upon his head.
For all the days of his separation he is holy unto Yahweh.   6:8

"If a man dies suddenly nearby him, defiling the head of the Nazarite,   6:9
he shall shave his head on the seventh day—on the day of his cleansing.
On the eighth day he shall bring two turtledoves or two young pigeons   6:10
to the priest, to the door of the tabernacle of the congregation.
The priest shall offer one for a sin offering, the other for a burnt offering,   6:11
and shall make an atonement for him, for the sin he acquired
from the dead. And he shall hallow his head that same day.
He shall consecrate unto Yahweh the days of his separation, and shall   6:12
bring a lamb of the first year for a trespass offering. But the days
that went before shall be lost, because his separation was defiled.

This is the law of the Nazarite, when the days of his isolation are fulfilled: 6:13
He shall be brought to the door of the tabernacle of the congregation,
and he shall offer unto Yahweh one male lamb of the first year without 6:14
blemish for a burnt offering, one ewe lamb of the first year without
blemish for a sin offering, one ram without blemish for peace offerings,
a basket of unleavened bread of fine flour mixed with oil, 6:15
and wafers of unleavened bread anointed with oil,
along with his grain offering, and his drink offering.

"The priest shall bring them before Yahweh, 6:16
and shall offer his sin offering, and his burnt offering.
And he shall offer the ram for a sacrifice of peace offerings 6:17
unto Yahweh with the basket of unleavened breads.
The priest shall also offer his grain offering, and his drink offering.
The Nazarite shall shave the head of his separation at the door 6:18
of the tabernacle, and shall take the hair of the head of his separation,
and put it in the fire that is under the sacrifice of the peace offerings.
The priest shall take the sodden shoulder of the ram, and one unleavened 6:19
loaf out of the basket, and one unleavened wafer, and shall put them upon
the hands of the Nazarite, after the hair of his separation is shaven.
And the priest shall wave them for a wave offering before Yahweh. 6:20
This is holy for the priest, with the wave breast and heave shoulder.
After that the Nazarite may drink wine.
This is the law of the Nazarite who has vowed, and of his offerings unto 6:21
Yahweh for his separation, along with whatever else he can afford to offer.
According to the vow he vows, so he must do."

Yahweh spoke to Moses, telling him to 6:22
speak to Aaron and his sons, saying, "In this way you shall 6:23
bless the children of Israel, by saying unto them:
'The Lord bless you, and keep you. 6:24
The Lord make his face to shine upon you, and be gracious unto you. 6:25
The Lord lift up his countenance upon you, and give you peace.' 6:26
They shall put my name upon the children of Israel, and I will bless them." 6:27

Chapter 7

It came to pass that on the day Moses had fully set up the tabernacle, 7:1
and had anointed and sanctified it, and had anointed and sanctified
all the instruments, and the altar, and all its vessels,
that the princes of Israel, heads of the houses of their fathers, who were 7:2
chiefs of the tribes and were over them who were numbered, offered.
They brought their offerings before Yahweh: Six covered wagons and 7:3
twelve oxen—one wagon for two princes, and one ox for each prince.
They brought them before the tabernacle.
Yahweh spoke to Moses, saying, 7:4
"Take it of them that it may be used for the service of the tabernacle. 7:5
Give it to the Levites, to every man according to his service."
So Moses took the wagons and the oxen, and gave them to the Levites. 7:6

He gave two wagons and four oxen   7:7
to the sons of Gershon, according to their service.
Four wagons and eight oxen he gave to the sons of Merari, according   7:8
to their service, under the hand of Ithamar, son of Aaron the priest.
But unto the sons of Kohath he gave none, because the service of the   7:9
sanctuary belonging to them was to be borne upon their shoulders.

The chiefs' offerings were for the dedication of the altar, on the days 7:10
of its anointing. They presented their offerings before the altar.
Yahweh said to Moses, "They shall offer their offerings,   7:11
each prince on his day, for the dedication of the altar.
He that offered his offering the first day was Nahshon,   7:12
son of Amminadab, of the tribe of Judah.
His offering was one silver charger weighing a hundred and thirty shekels, 7:13
and one silver bowl of seventy shekels—
both full of fine flour mixed with oil for a grain offering—
one spoon of ten shekels of gold, full of incense,   7:14
one young bull, one ram, one lamb of the first year for a burnt offering, 7:15
one kid of the goats for a sin offering,   7:16
and for a sacrifice of peace offerings, two oxen, five rams,   7:17
five male goats, and five lambs of the first year.
This was the offering of Nahshon, son of Amminadab.

On the second day Nethaneel, son of Zuar, prince of Issachar, did offer. 7:18
His offering was one silver charger weighing a hundred and thirty shekels, 7:19
and one silver bowl of seventy shekels—
both full of fine flour mixed with oil for a grain offering—
one spoon of gold of ten shekels, full of incense,   7:20
one young bull, one ram, one lamb of the first year for a burnt offering, 7:21
one kid of the goats for a sin offering,   7:22
and for a sacrifice of peace offerings, two oxen, five rams,   7:23
five male goats, and five lambs of the first year.
This was the offering of Nethaneel, son of Zuar.

On the third day Eliab, son of Helon,   7:24
prince of the children of Zebulun, did offer.
His offering was one silver charger weighing a hundred and thirty shekels, 7:25
and one silver bowl of seventy shekels—
both full of fine flour mixed with oil for a grain offering—
one golden spoon of ten shekels, full of incense,   7:26
one young bull, one ram, one lamb of the first year for a burnt offering, 7:27
one kid of the goats for a sin offering,   7:28
and for a sacrifice of peace offerings, two oxen, five rams,   7:29
five male goats, and five lambs of the first year.
This was the offering of Eliab, son of Helon.

On the fourth day Elizur, son of Shedeur,   7:30
prince of the children of Reuben, did offer.
His offering was one silver charger weighing a hundred and thirty shekels, 7:31
and one silver bowl of seventy shekels—

both full of fine flour mixed with oil for a grain offering—

one golden spoon of ten shekels, full of incense,   7:32

one young bull, one ram, one lamb of the first year for a burnt offering,   7:33

one kid of the goats for a sin offering,   7:34

and for a sacrifice of peace offerings, two oxen, five rams,   7:35

five male goats, and five lambs of the first year.

This was the offering of Elizur, son of Shedeur.

On the fifth day Shelumiel, son of Zurishaddai,   7:36

prince of the children of Simeon, did offer.

His offering was one silver charger weighing a hundred and thirty shekels,   7:37

and one silver bowl of seventy shekels—

both full of fine flour mixed with oil for a grain offering—

one golden spoon of ten shekels, full of incense,   7:38

one young bull, one ram, one lamb of the first year for a burnt offering,   7:39

one kid of the goats for a sin offering,   7:40

and for a sacrifice of peace offerings, two oxen, five rams,   7:41

five male goats, and five lambs of the first year.

This was the offering of Shelumiel, son of Zurishaddai.

On the sixth day Eliasaph, son of Deuel,   7:42

prince of the children of Gad, did offer.

His offering was one silver charger weighing a hundred and thirty shekels,   7:43

and one silver bowl of seventy shekels—

both full of fine flour mixed with oil for a grain offering—

one golden spoon of ten shekels, full of incense,   7:44

one young bull, one ram, one lamb of the first year for a burnt offering,   7:45

one kid of the goats for a sin offering,   7:46

and for a sacrifice of peace offerings, two oxen, five rams,   7:47

five male goats, and five lambs of the first year.

This was the offering of Eliasaph, son of Deuel.

On the seventh day Elishama, son of Ammihud,   7:48

prince of the children of Ephraim, did offer.

His offering was one silver charger weighing a hundred and thirty shekels,   7:49

and one silver bowl of seventy shekels—

both full of fine flour mixed with oil for a grain offering—

one golden spoon of ten shekels, full of incense,   7:50

one young bull, one ram, one lamb of the first year for a burnt offering,   7:51

one kid of the goats for a sin offering,   7:52

and for a sacrifice of peace offerings, two oxen, five rams,   7:53

five male goats, and five lambs of the first year.

This was the offering of Elishama, son of Ammihud.

On the eighth day Gamaliel, son of Pedahzur,   7:54

prince of the children of Manasseh, did offer.

His offering was one silver charger weighing a hundred and thirty shekels,   7:55

and one silver bowl of seventy shekels—

both full of fine flour mixed with oil for a grain offering—

one golden spoon of ten shekels, full of incense,   7:56

one young bull, one ram, one lamb of the first year for a burnt offering, 7:57
one kid of the goats for a sin offering, 7:58
and for a sacrifice of peace offerings, two oxen, five rams, 7:59
five male goats, and five lambs of the first year.
This was the offering of Gamaliel, son of Pedahzur.

On the ninth day Abidan, son of Gideoni, 7:60
prince of the children of Benjamin, did offer.
His offering was one silver charger weighing a hundred and thirty shekels, 7:61
and one silver bowl of seventy shekels—
both full of fine flour mixed with oil for a grain offering—
one golden spoon of ten shekels, full of incense, 7:62
one young bull, one ram, one lamb of the first year for a burnt offering, 7:63
one kid of the goats for a sin offering, 7:64
and for a sacrifice of peace offerings, two oxen, five rams, 7:65
five male goats, and five lambs of the first year.
This was the offering of Abidan, son of Gideoni.

On the tenth day Ahiezer, son of Ammishaddai, 7:66
prince of the children of Dan, did offer.
His offering was one silver charger weighing a hundred and thirty shekels, 7:67
and one silver bowl of seventy shekels—
both full of fine flour mixed with oil for a grain offering—
one golden spoon of ten shekels, full of incense, 7:68
one young bull, one ram, one lamb of the first year for a burnt offering, 7:69
one kid of the goats for a sin offering, 7:70
and for a sacrifice of peace offerings, two oxen, five rams, 7:71
five male goats, and five lambs of the first year.
This was the offering of Ahiezer, son of Ammishaddai.

On the eleventh day Pagiel, son of Ocran, 7:72
prince of the children of Asher, did offer.
His offering was one silver charger weighing a hundred and thirty shekels, 7:73
and one silver bowl of seventy shekels—
both full of fine flour mixed with oil for a grain offering—
one golden spoon of ten shekels, full of incense, 7:74
one young bull, one ram, one lamb of the first year for a burnt offering, 7:75
one kid of the goats for a sin offering, 7:76
and for a sacrifice of peace offerings, two oxen, five rams, 7:77
five male goats, and five lambs of the first year.
This was the offering of Pagiel, son of Ocran.

On the twelfth day Ahira, son of Enan, 7:78
prince of the children of Naphtali, did offer.
His offering was one silver charger weighing a hundred and thirty shekels, 7:79
and one silver bowl of seventy shekels—
both full of fine flour mixed with oil for a grain offering—
one golden spoon of ten shekels, full of incense, 7:80
one young bull, one ram, one lamb of the first year for a burnt offering, 7:81
one kid of the goats for a sin offering, 7:82

and for a sacrifice of peace offerings, two oxen, five rams, 7:83
five male goats, and five lambs of the first year.
This was the offering of Ahira, son of Enan.

Thus were the offerings by the princes of Israel on the day the altar was 7:84
anointed: Twelve silver chargers, twelve silver bowls, twelve gold spoons.
Each charger of silver weighed a hundred and thirty shekels, each bowl 7:85
weighed seventy. All the silver vessels together weighed 2,400 shekels.
The golden spoons were twelve, full of incense, weighing ten shekels 7:86
apiece. All the golden spoons together weighed 120 shekels.
The bulls for the burnt offering were twelve, the rams twelve, the lambs 7:87
of the first year twelve. The kids of the goats for the sin offering, twelve.
All the livestock for the sacrifice of the peace offerings were twenty-four 7:88
bulls, sixty rams, sixty male goats, and sixty lambs of the first year.
This was the dedication of the altar after it was anointed.

When Moses went into the tabernacle to speak with Yahweh, he heard 7:89
the voice of Yahweh speaking to him from the mercy seat upon the ark
of the covenant. From between the two cherubim, Yahweh spoke to him.

Chapter 8

Yahweh spoke to Moses, telling him to 8:1
speak to Aaron, and say to him, "Set up the seven lamps 8:2
so that they give light in front of the lampstand."
And Aaron did so. He set up the lamps to give light 8:3
in front of the lampstand, as Yahweh commanded Moses.
The lampstand was of hammered gold, from its base to its flowers, 8:4
worked according to the pattern Yahweh had shown Moses.

Yahweh spoke to Moses, saying, 8:5
"Take the Levites from among the children of Israel and cleanse them. 8:6
Sprinkle purifying water upon them, and let them shave all their flesh, 8:7
and wash all their clothes, and so make themselves clean.
Then let them take a young bull, with his grain offering of fine flour 8:8
mixed with oil, and take another young bull for a sin offering.
Bring the Levites before the tabernacle of the congregation 8:9
and gather together the whole assembly of the children of Israel.
Bring the Levites before Yahweh, and let the children of Israel 8:10
put their hands upon the Levites.
And let Aaron offer the Levites before Yahweh, for an offering 8:11
of the children of Israel, that they may execute the service of Yahweh.
The Levites shall lay their hands upon the heads of the bulls, 8:12
and you shall offer one for a sin offering, and the other
for a burnt offering unto Yahweh, to make an atonement for the Levites.
And you shall set the Levites before Aaron, and before his sons, 8:13
and offer them for an offering unto Yahweh.
Thus shall you separate the Levites from among the children of Israel, 8:14
and the Levites shall be mine.

"After that the Levites shall go in to do the service of the tabernacle of the   8:15
congregation, and you shall cleanse them, and offer them for an offering.
For they are wholly given unto me from among the children of Israel,   8:16
instead of the firstborn of the children of Israel, who open the matrix.
Instead of your firstborn sons, I take the Levites unto me.
For all the firstborn of the children of Israel are mine, both man and beast.   8:17
On the day I killed every firstborn of Egypt, I sanctified them for myself.
I have taken the Levites instead of the firstborn of the children of Israel.   8:18
And I have given the Levites to Aaron and his sons, to do the service   8:19
of the tabernacle, and to make an atonement for the children of Israel,
that there be no plague among them when they come into the sanctuary."

Moses, and Aaron, and all the congregation of the children of Israel,   8:20
did to the Levites according to all that Yahweh commanded Moses.
And the Levites were purified, and they washed their clothes.   8:21
And Aaron offered them as an offering before Yahweh,
and made an atonement for them, to cleanse them.
After that the Levites went in to do their service in the tabernacle   8:22
of the congregation, before Aaron and his sons. As Yahweh had
commanded Moses concerning the Levites, so they did unto them.
Yahweh spoke to Moses, saying,   8:23
"This is the rule for the Levites: From twenty-five years old and upward   8:24
they shall do the service of the tabernacle of the congregation.
At the age of fifty years they shall cease doing the service   8:25
of the tabernacle and shall serve no more.
They shall assist their brethren in small tasks, but shall do no service.   8:26
Thus shall you assign to the Levites their work."

Chapter 9

Yahweh spoke to Moses in the wilderness of Sinai, in the first month   9:1
of the second year after they came out of the land of Egypt, saying,
"Let the children of Israel keep the Passover in its appointed season.   9:2
On the fourteenth day of this month, at evening, you shall keep it   9:3
in its appointed season. According to all the rites of it,
and according to all its ceremonies, you shall keep it."
Moses spoke to the children of Israel, that they should keep the Passover.   9:4
And they kept the Passover, on the fourteenth day of the first month,   9:5
at evening, in the wilderness of Sinai. According to all that Yahweh
commanded Moses, so did the children of Israel do.

There were certain men who were defiled by a dead body, and so could   9:6
not keep the Passover. They came before Moses and Aaron on that day
and said to them, "We were defiled by the dead body of a man.   9:7
Can we not then make an offering to Yahweh in his appointed season?"
Moses said to them, "Do nothing until I hear what Yahweh commands."   9:8
Yahweh told Moses to   9:9
tell the children of Israel, "If any of you or of your posterity   9:10
is unclean by reason of a dead body, or are on a journey afar off,

184

you shall still keep the Passover unto Yahweh.
On the fourteenth day of the second month at evening 9:11
you shall keep it, and eat unleavened bread and bitter herbs.
Leave none of it until morning, nor break any bone of it. 9:12
According to all the ordinances of the Passover you shall keep it.
But anyone who is clean, and is not on a journey, yet does keep the 9:13
Passover, shall be cut off from among his people, because he did not bring
the offering of Yahweh in his appointed season. That man bears his sin.
If a stranger sojourns among you, and will keep the Passover unto 9:14
Yahweh, according to the rules and manner of the Passover, so shall he do.
There is one rule for both strangers and he who is born in the land."

On the day the tabernacle was set up, a cloud covered the tabernacle. 9:15
At evening it took on the appearance of fire, which lasted until morning.
So it was from then on, that the cloud covered it by day, 9:16
and took on the appearance of fire by night.
When the cloud moved from the tabernacle, the children of Israel 9:17
journeyed, and where the cloud abided, the children of Israel made camp.
At the commandment of Yahweh the children of Israel journeyed, 9:18
and at his command they pitched their tents. And there they stayed
for as long as the cloud abided upon the tabernacle.
When the cloud tarried long upon the tabernacle many days, 9:19
the children of Israel kept the charge of Yahweh, and did not journey.
When the cloud was only a few days upon the tabernacle, 9:20
they waited in their tents and journeyed when Yahweh commanded.
When the cloud abided only from evening to morning, they journeyed that 9:21
morning. Whether the cloud was taken up by day or night, they journeyed.
Whether it was two days, or a month, or a year that the cloud tarried 9:22
upon the tabernacle, the children of Israel abode in their tents
and journeyed not. But when it was taken up, they journeyed.
At the commandment of Yahweh they rested in the tents, and at the 9:23
commandment of Yahweh they journeyed. They kept the charge
of Yahweh, at the commandment of Yahweh, by the hand of Moses.

Chapter 10

Yahweh spoke to Moses, saying, 10:1
"Make two trumpets of hammered silver, and use them 10:2
for calling the assembly, and for the journeying of the camps.
When they are sounded, all the assembly shall assemble themselves 10:3
to you at the door of the tabernacle of the congregation.
If only one trumpet is sounded, the princes—the heads 10:4
of the thousands of Israel—shall gather themselves unto you.
When you sound an alarm, the camps that lie to the east shall go forward. 10:5
When you sound a second alarm, the camps that lie to the south 10:6
shall take their journey. An alarm shall signal their journeys.
When the congregation is to be gathered together, 10:7
the trumpets shall be blown, but not sound an alarm.
The sons of Aaron, the priests, shall blow the trumpets. 10:8

This shall be an ordinance forever, throughout your generations.

If you go to war in your land against an enemy that oppresses you,   10:9
blow an alarm with the trumpets, and you shall be remembered before
Yahweh your God, and you shall be saved from your enemies.

In the days of your gladness, and on your solemn days, and at the   10:10
beginnings of your months, you shall blow the trumpets over your
burnt offerings, and over the sacrifices of your peace offerings, that they
may be to you a memorial before your God. I am Yahweh, your God.”

It came to pass on the twentieth day of the second month, in the second   10:11
year, that the cloud was taken up from the tabernacle of the testimony.

So the children of Israel took their journeys out of the wilderness of Sinai,   10:12
until the cloud rested in the wilderness of Paran.

They took their first journey according to   10:13
the commandment of Yahweh by the hand of Moses.

The standard of the camp of the children of Judah went first.   10:14
Nahshon, son of Amminadab commanded their host.

Commanding the host of the tribe of the children of Issachar   10:15
was Nethaneel, son of Zuar.

Commanding the host of the tribe of the children of Zebulun   10:16
was Eliab, son of Helon.

The tabernacle was taken down, and the sons of Gershon   10:17
and the sons of Merari set forward, bearing the tabernacle.

Then the standard of the camp of Reuben set forward.   10:18
Commanding their host was Elizur, son of Shedeur.

Commanding the host of the tribe of the children of Simeon   10:19
was Shelumiel, son of Zurishaddai.

Commanding the host of the tribe of the children of Gad   10:20
was Eliasaph, son of Deuel.

Then the Kohathites set forward, bearing the holy things of the sanctuary.   10:21
The tabernacle would be set up before their arrival.

Then the standard of the camp of the children of Ephraim set forward.   10:22
Commanding their host was Elishama, son of Ammihud.

Commanding the host of the tribe of the children of Manasseh   10:23
was Gamaliel, son of Pedahzur.

Commanding the host of the tribe of the children of Benjamin   10:24
was Abidan, son of Gideoni.

Then the standard of the camp of the children of Dan set forward, last of   10:25
all the camps. Commanding their host was Ahiezer, son of Ammishaddai.

Commanding the host of the tribe of the children of Asher   10:26
was Pagiel, son of Ocran.

Commanding the host of the tribe of the children of Naphtali   10:27
was Ahira, son of Enan.

Thus was the order of departure of the Israelites, when they set forward.   10:28

Moses said to Hobab, son of Raguel the Midianite, Moses' father-in-law,   10:29
“We are journeying to the place Yahweh said, ‘I give it you.’ Come with us,
and we will treat you well, for Yahweh has promised good to Israel.”

Hobab said, “I will not go. I will go to my own land, and to my kindred.”   10:30

Moses said, "Leave us not, I pray you. You know where   10:31
we should camp in the wilderness, and you can be our eyes.
Come with us, and what good Yahweh gives unto us, we shall give to you."   10:32
Thus they departed from the mount of Yahweh on a three days' journey.   10:33
The ark of the covenant of Yahweh went before them,
to search out a resting place for them.
The cloud of Yahweh was over them by day as they went from the camp.   10:34
When the ark set forward, Moses said, "Rise up, O Lord.   10:35
Let your enemies be scattered. Let them who hate you flee before you."
When the ark came to rest, Moses said,   10:36
"Return, O Lord, to the many thousands of Israel."

Chapter 11

When the people complained, it displeased Yahweh. When he heard   11:1
them his anger was kindled, and his fire burnt among them,
and consumed the outskirts of the camp.
The people cried out to Moses, and when Moses   11:2
prayed to Yahweh, the fire was quenched.
And it was named Taberah, where the fire of Yahweh burnt among them.   11:3
The mixed multitude that was among them fell a-lusting, and the Israelites   11:4
also complained, saying, "Who shall give us food to eat?
We remember the fish that we ate freely in Egypt,   11:5
and the cucumbers, and melons, and leeks, and onions and garlic.
Now are lives are wasting away. There is nothing here but this manna."   11:6
The manna was like coriander seed, with the color of bdellium.   11:7
The people gathered it, and ground it in mills or beat it in a mortar,   11:8
and baked it in pans and made cakes of it. It tasted like fresh oil.
When the dew fell upon the camp in the night, the manna fell upon it.   11:9

Moses heard the people weeping, every man in the door of his tent,   11:10
and the anger of Yahweh was kindled greatly. Moses was also displeased.
Moses said to Yahweh, "Why have you afflicted your servant? Have I not   11:11
found favor in your sight, that you lay the burden of these people on me?
Am I the father of all these people? Have I begotten them, that you should   11:12
say to me, 'Carry them in your bosom as a nurse bears a sucking child
into the land you promised to their ancestors?'
Where am I to get meat for all these people?   11:13
They cry out to me, 'Give us flesh, that we may eat.'
I am not able to bear all these people alone. It is too heavy for me.   11:14
If you would deal with me thus, just kill me now, I pray you. But if I   11:15
have found favor in your sight, let me not endure this wretchedness."

Yahweh said to Moses, "Gather before me seventy elders of Israel,   11:16
men you know to be authorities and officers over the people.
Bring them into the tabernacle, that they may stand there with you.
I will come down and talk with you there. I will take of the spirit   11:17
that is upon you and put it upon them. They shall bear
the burden of the people with you, that you not bear it alone.

Say to the people, 'Sanctify yourselves, for tomorrow $\qquad$ 11:18
you shall eat meat. You have wept in the ears of Yahweh, saying,
"Who shall give us meat to eat, for it was well with us in Egypt?"
Therefore Yahweh will give you meat, and you shall eat.
You shall not eat one day, nor two days, nor five nor ten nor twenty days, $\qquad$ 11:19
but for a whole month, until it comes out of your nostrils and is loathsome $\qquad$ 11:20
to you. For you have despised Yahweh, who is among you, and have
wept before him, saying, "Why did we come forth out of Egypt?"'

Moses said, "There are six hundred thousand people on foot. I am among $\qquad$ 11:21
them. You say, 'I will give them meat, that they may eat a whole month.'
Shall the flocks and the herds be slain to suffice them? $\qquad$ 11:22
Shall all the fish of the sea be gathered together to suffice them?"
Yahweh said to Moses, "Has Yahweh's hand waxed short? $\qquad$ 11:23
You shall see whether or not my word comes to pass."
Moses went out and told the people the words of Yahweh, and gathered $\qquad$ 11:24
the seventy elders of the people, and set them round about the tabernacle.
Yahweh came down in a cloud, and spoke to him, and took of the spirit $\qquad$ 11:25
that was upon him and gave it unto the seventy elders. And when the
spirit rested upon them, they prophesied, but not again afterwards.
Two of the seventy elders, named Eldad and Medad, $\qquad$ 11:26
remained in camp and did not enter the sanctuary.
The spirit rested upon them there, and they prophesied in the camp.
A young man ran to Moses and said, "Eldad and Medad prophesy in camp." $\qquad$ 11:27
Joshua, son of Nun, a servant to Moses since his youth, $\qquad$ 11:28
said, "My lord Moses, forbid them."
Moses said, "Are you jealous for my sake? Would that all Yahweh's people $\qquad$ 11:29
were prophets, and that Yahweh would put his spirit upon them!"
Moses and the elders of Israel went back into the camp. $\qquad$ 11:30
And there went forth a wind from Yahweh that drove masses of birds $\qquad$ 11:31
from the sea, and made them fall on the camp, two cubits deep upon
the earth, over an area so wide it was a day's journey all around.
All that day, all that night, and all the next day, the people gathered $\qquad$ 11:32
the multitude of birds—he that gathered least gathered ten homers—
and spread out feasts for themselves around the camp.
But while the flesh was yet between their teeth—while it was still $\qquad$ 11:33
being chewed—the wrath of Yahweh was kindled against the people,
and Yahweh smote the people with a very great plague.
He named that place Kibroth-Hattaavah, $\qquad$ 11:34
because there they buried the people who lusted.
The people journeyed from Kibroth-Hattaavah to Hazeroth, $\qquad$ 11:35
and abided in Hazeroth.

Chapter 12

Miriam and Aaron spoke against Moses $\qquad$ 12:1
because he had married an Ethiopian woman.
They said, "Has Yahweh indeed spoken only by Moses? $\qquad$ 12:2
Has he not spoken also by us?" And Yahweh heard it.

Now, Moses was very humble, above all men upon the face of the earth.   12:3
Yahweh spoke suddenly to Moses, and to Aaron and Miriam: "Come out   12:4
unto the tabernacle of the congregation." And the three of them came out.
Yahweh came down in the pillar of the cloud and stood in the door   12:5
of the tabernacle and called Aaron and Miriam, and they both came forth.
He said, "Hear my words. If there be a prophet among you, I, Yahweh, will   12:6
make myself known to him in a vision, and will speak to him in a dream.
It is not so with my servant Moses, who is faithful in all my house.   12:7
With him I speak clearly, mouth to mouth, not in dark speeches. He has   12:8
seen my form. Why are you unafraid to speak against my servant Moses?"

The anger of Yahweh was kindled against them, and he left.   12:9
The cloud departed from the tabernacle, and behold, Miriam became   12:10
leprous, white as snow. Aaron looked upon her and saw she was leprous.
Aaron said to Moses, "My lord, I beseech you, do not punish us   12:11
for our foolish acts, wherein we have sinned.
Let her not be as a stillborn, whose flesh is half-rotted   12:12
when it comes out of its mother's womb."
Moses cried unto Yahweh, saying, "Heal her now, O Lord, I beseech you."   12:13
Yahweh said to Moses, "If her father had spit in her face and shamed her,   12:14
should she not be shamed for seven days? Let her be shut out from
the camp seven days. After that, let her be received in again."
So Miriam was shut out from the camp seven days,   12:15
and the people did not journey until Miriam was brought in again.
Then the people left Hazeroth and pitched in the wilderness of Paran.   12:16

Chapter 13

Yahweh spoke to Moses, saying,   13:1
"Send men to explore the land of Canaan, which I give unto the children   13:2
of Israel. Send one man from every tribe, each a chief among them."
So Moses, by the commandment of Yahweh, sent out from the   13:3
wilderness of Paran men who were heads of the children of Israel.
These were their names: 13:4
Of the tribe of Reuben: Shammua, son of Zaccur.
Of the tribe of Simeon: Shaphat, son of Hori.   13:5
Of the tribe of Judah: Caleb, son of Jephunneh.   13:6
Of the tribe of Issachar: Igal, son of Joseph.   13:7
Of the tribe of Ephraim: Oshea, son of Nun.   13:8
Of the tribe of Benjamin: Palti, son of Raphu.   13:9
Of the tribe of Zebulun: Gaddiel, son of Sodi.   13:10
Of the tribe of Joseph, namely, of the tribe of Manasseh: Gaddi, son of Susi.   13:11
Of the tribe of Dan: Ammiel, son of Gemalli.   13:12
Of the tribe of Asher: Sethur, son of Michael.   13:13
Of the tribe of Naphtali: Nahbi, son of Vophsi.   13:14
Of the tribe of Gad: Geuel, son of Machi.   13:15
These are the names of the men Moses sent to explore the land.   13:16
Moses changed the name of Oshea, son of Nun, to Jehoshua.

Moses sent them to explore the land of Canaan, and said to them, 13:17
"Enter the land from the south, and go up into the mountains.
See what the land is like. See whether the people 13:18
who dwell there are strong or weak, few or many.
See what the land they dwell in is like, whether it is good or bad, 13:19
and what their cities are like, whether tents or strongholds.
See whether the land is fertile or lean, and if there is wood. Be of good 13:20
courage. Bring back the land's fruits. Now is the time of the first grapes."

So they searched from the wilderness of Zin to Rehob, by way of Hamath. 13:21
They ascended from the south, and came into Hebron, 13:22
where Ahiman, Sheshai and Talmai, the children of Anak were.
Now, Hebron was built seven years before Zoan in Egypt.
When they came to the valley of Eshcol, they cut down a branch 13:23
with a single cluster of grapes that had to be carried on a pole
between two men. They also took pomegranates and figs.
The place was called the valley of Eshcol, because of the 13:24
cluster of grapes the children of Israel cut down there.

They returned from searching the land after forty days. 13:25
They returned to the camp of the Israelites in the wilderness of Paran, 13:26
in Kadesh, and they gave an account to Moses and Aaron
and the chiefs, and showed them the fruit of the land.
They said, "We went into the land wherein you sent us, 13:27
and it surely flows with milk and honey. This is the fruit of it.
Nevertheless, the people who dwell in the land are strong, and the cities 13:28
are walled and very great. Moreover, we saw the children of Anak there.
The Amalekites dwell in the land of the south. The Hittites, 13:29
the Jebusites, and the Amorites dwell in the mountains.
The Canaanites dwell by the sea, and along the banks of Jordan."

Caleb said to Moses, "Let us go at once and take this land, 13:30
for we are well able to overcome it."
But the men who had been there said, "We be not able 13:31
to go up against these people, for they are stronger than we."
So they gave a bad account to the Israelites of the land they explored, 13:32
saying, "The land we searched devours its inhabitants,
and the people we saw there are huge men.
We saw the Nephilim giants, and the sons of Anak, who come from 13:33
the giants. We felt like grasshoppers, and so we were in their sight."

Chapter 14

That night all the congregation lifted up their voices and the people wept. 14:1
And all the children of Israel murmured against Moses and Aaron. 14:2
The whole congregation said, "Would God that we had died
in the land of Egypt! Or would God we had died in this wilderness!
Why has Yahweh brought us into this land, to fall by the sword, 14:3
and our wives and children become prey?
Would it not be better for us to return to Egypt?"

They said one to another, "Let us choose a leader and return to Egypt."   14:4
And Moses and Aaron fell on their faces before all the assembly   14:5
of the congregation of the children of Israel.

Then Joshua the son of Nun, and Caleb the son of Jephunneh,   14:6
who were among those who explored the land, rent their clothes.
and spoke unto all the company of the children of Israel, saying,   14:7
"The land we searched is an exceeding good land.
If Yahweh delights in us, he will bring us into this land,   14:8
and give it to us. It is a land that flows with milk and honey.
Only, do not rebel against Yahweh, nor fear the people of that land.   14:9
We will eat them up. Their protection has left them,
and Yahweh is with us. Fear them not."

But all the congregation wanted to stone them to death. Then did the glory   14:10
of Yahweh appeared in the tabernacle before all the children of Israel.
And Yahweh said to Moses, "How long will this people provoke me?   14:11
How long before they believe in me, after all the signs I have shown them?
I will smite them with pestilence, and disown them,   14:12
and I will make of you a greater nation, mightier than they."
Moses said to Yahweh, "But then the Egyptians shall hear of it,   14:13
for by your power you brought this people up from among them.
And they will tell it to the inhabitants of the land, for they have heard   14:14
that you, Lord, are among this people, that you, Lord, are seen face-to-face,
and that your cloud stands over them, and that you go before them,
by day in a pillar of cloud, and by night in a pillar of fire.
If you kill all this people as one, the nations   14:15
that have heard of your fame will speak out, saying,
'Because Yahweh was not able to bring this people into the land   14:16
he promised them, he has therefore slain them in the wilderness.'
I beseech you, let the power of my Lord be great,   14:17
according to the words you have spoken, saying,
'Yahweh is longsuffering and merciful, forgiving iniquity and   14:18
transgression. Yet he by no means clears the guilty, but visits the iniquity
of the fathers upon the children, unto the third and fourth generation.'
Please, I beseech you, pardon the iniquity of this people in the greatness   14:19
of your mercy, as you have forgiven them from Egypt until now."

Yahweh said, "I have pardoned them according to your word.   14:20
But as truly as I live, all the earth shall be filled with the glory of Yahweh.   14:21
Because all those men who have seen my glory, and the miracles   14:22
I did in Egypt and in the wilderness, yet have tempted me now
these ten times, and have not hearkened unto my voice,
shall surely not see the land I promised to their fathers,   14:23
neither shall any of them who provoked me see it.
But my servant Caleb, because he has a different spirit with him,   14:24
and has followed me fully, him I will bring into the land
wherein he went, and his children shall possess it.

The Amalekites and the Canaanites now dwell in the valley. 14:25
Tomorrow, turn and go into the wilderness by the way of the Red Sea."

Yahweh spoke to Moses and to Aaron, saying, 14:26
"How long shall I bear with this evil congregation that murmurs 14:27
against me? I have heard the murmurings of the Israelites against me.
Tell them, 'As truly as I live,' saith Yahweh, 14:28
'as you have spoken in my ears, so will I do to you.
Your carcasses shall fall in this wilderness, and all that were numbered, 14:29
from twenty years old and upward, who have murmured against me,
shall surely shall not come into the land I promised, 14:30
except for Caleb the son of Jephunneh, and Joshua the son of Nun.
But your little ones, who you said would be prey, them will I bring in, 14:31
and they shall know the land you rejected.
As for you, your carcasses shall fall in this wilderness. 14:32
And your children shall wander in the wilderness forty years, 14:33
and bear your unfaithfulness until your bodies turn to dust.
After the number of the days you searched the land, forty days, 14:34
shall be the number of years you shall bear your iniquities,
forty years, and you shall know my rejection.'
I, Yahweh, have said, 'This I will surely do to all this evil congregation 14:35
that are gathered together against me. In this wilderness
they shall be consumed, and there they shall die.'"

And the men Moses sent to search the land who returned and made 14:36
the congregation murmur against him by speaking evil about the land—
those who gave the land a bad report—died of the plague before Yahweh. 14:37
But Joshua the son of Nun, and Caleb the son of Jephunneh, 14:38
who were among the men who went to search the land, lived.
Moses told all this to the children of Israel, and they mourned greatly. 14:39
And they rose up early in the morning, and went to Moses and said, 14:40
"Lo, we are here, and we will go into the land
Yahweh has promised, for we have sinned."
But Moses said, "Why would you transgress 14:41
the commandment of Yahweh? It shall not prosper.
Do not go there, for Yahweh is not with you. Your enemies will defeat you. 14:42
The Amalekites and the Canaanites are there before you, 14:43
and you shall fall by the sword, because you have turned away
from Yahweh, and therefore Yahweh will not be with you."
Yet they still dared to go into the hills of that land, though the 14:44
ark of the covenant of Yahweh, and Moses, did not leave the camp.
And the Amalekites and the Canaanites who dwelt in the hills, 14:45
defeated them, and drove them all the way to Hormah.

Chapter 15

Yahweh spoke to Moses, telling him to 15:1
speak unto the children of Israel, and say to them, 15:2
"When you come into the land of your habitations, which I give to you,

and make an offering of the herd or flock by fire, to make a sweet savor 15:3
unto Yahweh—a burnt offering, or a sacrifice in performing a vow,
or a freewill offering, or in your solemn feasts—
if your offering unto Yahweh is lambs, you shall also bring a grain offering 15:4
of a tenth part of a deal of fine flour mixed with a fourth part of a hin of oil,
and for a drink offering, the fourth part of an hin of wine for each lamb. 15:5
For a ram, you shall prepare for a grain offering two-tenths deal 15:6
of fine flour mixed with the third part of a hin of oil.
And for a drink offering you shall offer the third part 15:7
of a hin of wine, for a sweet savor unto Yahweh.
When you prepare a bull for a burnt offering, or for a sacrifice 15:8
in performing a vow, or as a peace offering unto Yahweh,
you shall bring with the bull a grain offering 15:9
of three-tenth deals of flour mixed with half a hin of oil.
And for a drink offering, you shall bring half a hin of wine, 15:10
for an offering made by fire, of a sweet savor unto Yahweh.
Thus shall it be done for one bull, or one ram, or for a lamb or a kid. 15:11
According to the number you offer, so shall you do for each. 15:12

"All who are born of the country shall do these things after this manner 15:13
when offering an offering made by fire, of a sweet savor unto Yahweh.
If a stranger sojourns with you, or whoever is among you 15:14
in your families, and would offer an offering made by fire,
of a sweet savor unto Yahweh, as you do, so shall he do.
One ordinance shall be for both—for the congregation, 15:15
and for the stranger—an ordinance forever in your generations.
As you are, so shall the stranger be before Yahweh.
One law and one manner shall be for you, 15:16
and for the stranger who sojourns with you."

Yahweh spoke to Moses, telling him to 15:17
speak to the children of Israel, and say, 15:18
"When you come into the land whither I bring you,
it shall be that, when you eat of the bread of the land, 15:19
you shall offer up a heave offering unto Yahweh.
You shall offer up a cake of the first dough for a heave offering, 15:20
just as you do the heave offering of the threshing floor.
Of the first of your dough you shall give unto Yahweh 15:21
a heave offering in your generations.
If you have erred, and have not observed all these 15:22
commandments Yahweh has spoken unto Moses—
all that Yahweh has commanded you by the hand of Moses, from the day 15:23
Yahweh first commanded Moses, henceforth among your generations—
then it shall be, if it is committed by ignorance without the knowledge of 15:24
the congregation, that all the congregation shall offer one young bull for a
burnt offering, for a sweet savor unto Yahweh, with its grain offering and
drink offering according to law, and one kid of the goats for a sin offering.
The priest shall make an atonement for all the congregation of the 15:25
children of Israel, and it shall be forgiven them, for it is ignorance.

They shall bring their offering, a sacrifice made by fire unto Yahweh,
and their sin offering before Yahweh, for their ignorance.
And it shall be forgiven all the congregation, and the strangers 15:26
who sojourn among them, since all the people were in ignorance.
If anyone sins through ignorance, he shall bring 15:27
a she-goat of the first year for a sin offering.
And the priest shall make an atonement for the one who 15:28
sinned by ignorance before Yahweh, and it shall be forgiven him.
You shall have one law for him who sinned through ignorance, 15:29
for both him who is born among the children of Israel,
and for the stranger who sojourns among them.
But the person who sins deliberately—whether born in the land 15:30
or a stranger—insults Yahweh, and he shall be cut off from the people.
He has despised the word of Yahweh, and has broken Yahweh's 15:31
commandment. He shall be utterly cut off. His iniquity shall be upon him."

While the children of Israel were in the wilderness, 15:32
they found a man who gathered sticks on the sabbath day.
They who found him gathering sticks brought him 15:33
to Moses and Aaron, and to all the congregation.
They did not know what was to be done to him so they put him in custody. 15:34
Yahweh said to Moses, "That man shall surely be put to death. 15:35
All the congregation shall stone him with stones outside the camp."
So the congregation took him outside the camp 15:36
and killed him with stones, as Yahweh commanded Moses.

Yahweh spoke to Moses, telling him to 15:37
speak to the children of Israel, and say, 15:38
"Make fringes on the borders of your garments, throughout your
generations, and make the fringe of the borders a cord of blue.
It shall be for you a fringe that you look upon and remember all the 15:39
commandments of Yahweh, and do them. And that you seek not after
your own heart and your own eyes, which you use to follow your lusts.
You shall remember and do my commandments, and be holy to your God. 15:40
I am Yahweh, your God, who brought you out of Egypt to be your God. 15:41
I am Yahweh, your God."

Chapter 16

Now, Korah son of Izhar, and the son of Kohath, 16:1
and the son of Levi, and Dathan and Abiram, the sons of Eliab,
and On the son of Peleth, and the sons of Reuben, took men
and rose up before Moses with some of the children of Israel— 16:2
250 princes, famous in the congregation, men of renown—
and they gathered themselves together against Moses and against Aaron, 16:3
and said to them, "You take too much upon yourselves. All the
congregation are holy, every one of them, and Yahweh is among them.
Why do you lift yourselves up above the congregation of Yahweh?"
When Moses heard this, he fell upon his face. 16:4

And he said to Korah and to all his company, "Tomorrow Yahweh will   16:5
show who are his, and who is holy, and will cause him to come near.
Whom he has chosen he will cause to come near unto him.
Do this, Korah, and all of you: Take censers   16:6
and put fire therein, and put incense in them before Yahweh tomorrow.   16:7
And it shall be that the man Yahweh chooses shall be holy.
You take too much upon you, you sons of Levi."

Moses said to Korah, "Hear, I pray you, you sons of Levi: 16:8
Does it seem but a small thing to you that the God of Israel has separated   16:9
you from the congregation of Israel, to bring you near to himself
to do the service of the tabernacle of Yahweh, and to stand
before the congregation to minister unto them?
He has brought you near to him, and all the brethren of the sons   16:10
of Levi with you. Do you now seek the priesthood also?
For this reason you and your company have assembled against Yahweh?   16:11
And what is Aaron, that you murmur against him?"
Then Moses sent for Dathan and Abiram, the sons of Eliab,   16:12
but they said, "We will not come.
Is it not enough that you took us from a land flowing with milk and honey   16:13
to kill us in the wilderness? Now you make yourself a prince over us?
Moreover, you have not brought us into a land of milk and honey,   16:14
or given us an inheritance of fields and vineyards.
Do you think you can deceive these men? We will not come!"

Moses became angry, and said to Yahweh, "Do not respect their offering.   16:15
I have not taken one ass from them, neither have I hurt any of them."
And Moses said to Korah, "You and your company be here tomorrow   16:16
before Yahweh—you, and they, and Aaron.
Every man shall bring his censer—two hundred and fifty censers—   16:17
and burn incense in them before Yahweh, you and Aaron, and every man."
So every man brought his censer, and put fire in it, and laid incense   16:18
thereon, and came to the door of the tabernacle with Moses and Aaron.
Korah and his company stood facing Moses and Aaron at the door of the   16:19
tabernacle, and the glory of Yahweh appeared to all the congregation.
Yahweh spoke to Moses and Aaron, saying,   16:20
"Move away from these men, that I may destroy them in a moment."   16:21
Moses and Aaron fell on their faces, and said, "O God, the God of the spirits   16:22
of all flesh, if one man sins, would you be angry with all the congregation?"

Yahweh said to Moses,   16:23
"Speak to the congregation and tell them, 'Move away from   16:24
the dwellings of Korah, Dathan, and Abiram.'"
Moses went to Dathan and Abiram, and the elders of Israel followed him.   16:25
And he spoke to the congregation, saying, "Depart, I pray you,   16:26
from the tents of these wicked men, and touch nothing of theirs,
lest you be consumed in all their sins."
So they moved away from the dwellings of Korah, Dathan and Abiram.   16:27
Dathan and Abiram came out, and stood in the door of their tents,

with their wives, and their sons, and their little children.
Moses said, "By this you shall know that Yahweh has sent me 16:28
to do all these works. I have not done them of mine own mind.
If these men die a natural death, common to all humanity, 16:29
then Yahweh has not sent me.
But if Yahweh creates anew, and the earth opens her mouth, and swallows 16:30
them up, with all that belongs to them, and they descend alive to the
world of the dead, you shall know that these men provoked Yahweh."
And it came to pass, that as soon as he finished speaking these words, 16:31
the ground clave asunder under them.
And the earth opened her mouth, and swallowed them up, and their 16:32
houses, and all the men who sided with Korah, and all their goods.
They, and all who had joined them, went down alive into the pit, and the 16:33
earth closed upon them, and they perished from among the congregation.
And all Israel that were round about them fled at their cries, saying, 16:34
"The earth may swallow us up also!"
Then there came out a fire from Yahweh 16:35
that consumed the 250 men who offered incense.

Yahweh spoke to Moses, saying, 16:36
"Tell Eleazar, son of Aaron the priest, to take up the censers from out 16:37
of the burning, and scatter their fire yonder, for they are hallowed.
Let the censers of these sinners who died be hammered into broad plates 16:38
for a covering of the altar, for they offered them before Yahweh, therefore
they are hallowed. They shall be a sign unto the children of Israel."
Eleazar the priest took the brass censers that those who were burnt had 16:39
offered, and they were made into broad plates for a covering of the altar,
to be a memorial to the children of Israel, that no one who is not of the 16:40
seed of Aaron come near to offer incense before Yahweh—that no one be
as Korah and his company—as Yahweh told him, by the hand of Moses.

But the next day the congregation of the children of Israel murmured 16:41
against Moses and Aaron, saying, "You have killed the people of Yahweh."
And when the congregation was gathered against Moses and Aaron, 16:42
they looked toward the tabernacle of the congregation and, behold,
the cloud covered it, and the glory of Yahweh appeared.
Moses and Aaron came to the front the tabernacle of the congregation, 16:43
and Yahweh spoke unto Moses, saying, 16:44
"Get away from this congregation, that I may 16:45
consume them in a moment." And they fell upon their faces.
Moses said to Aaron, "Take a censer and put in fire from the altar, 16:46
and incense. Go quickly unto the congregation and make an atonement
for them, for wrath has gone out from Yahweh. The plague has begun."
Aaron did as Moses commanded, and ran into the midst of the 16:47
congregation, and behold, the plague was begun among the people,
and he put on incense, and made an atonement for the people.
He stood between the dead and the living, and the plague was stayed. 16:48
Those who died in the plague were 14,700, 16:49
besides those who died because of the matter of Korah.

Aaron returned to Moses in the door of the tabernacle, 16:50
and the plague was stayed.

Chapter 17

Yahweh spoke unto Moses, saying, 17:1
"Speak to the children of Israel, and take of them a rod from each tribe— 17:2
twelve rods, one from each of the princes of the house of their fathers—
and write every man's name on his rod.
Write Aaron's name on the rod of Levi, 17:3
for there shall be one rod for the head of the each tribe.
Lay them up in the tabernacle before the ark, where I will meet with you. 17:4
And it shall come to pass that the rod of the man I choose will sprout buds, 17:5
and I will rid myself of the murmurings of the Israelites against you."
Moses spoke to the children of Israel, and every prince gave him a rod, 17:6
twelve rods, one for each tribe, and the rod of Aaron was one of the rods.
Moses laid up the rods before Yahweh in the tabernacle of witness. 17:7
And it came to pass, that on the morrow Moses went into the tabernacle, 17:8
and behold, the rod of Aaron for the house of Levi had budded,
and brought forth sprouts, and bloomed blossoms, and yielded almonds.
Moses brought out all the rods, and all the Israelites looked, 17:9
and every man took his rod.
Yahweh said to Moses, "Bring Aaron's rod again before the ark, 17:10
to be kept for a sign to warn other rebels to stop
their murmurings about me, lest they be killed."
Moses did so. As Yahweh commanded him, so he did. 17:11
The Israelites said to Moses, "Behold, we die, we perish, we all perish. 17:12
Whoever comes near the tabernacle of Yahweh is killed. 17:13
Shall we be consumed with dying?"

Chapter 18

Yahweh said to Aaron, "You and your sons, and your father's house 18:1
with you, shall bear the iniquity of the sanctuary.
You and your sons shall bear the iniquity of your priesthood.
You and your sons shall minister before the tabernacle of witness. 18:2
Bring with you your brethren of the tribe of Levi, the tribe of your father,
that they may be joined unto you, and minister unto you.
They shall keep your charge, and the charge of all the tabernacle. 18:3
But they shall not come near the vessels of the sanctuary
and the altar, lest they, and you also, be killed.
They shall be joined unto you, and keep the charge of the tabernacle, 18:4
and a stranger shall not come nigh unto you.
You shall keep the charge of the sanctuary and the charge of the altar, 18:5
that there be no wrath anymore upon the children of Israel.
Behold, I have taken your brethren the Levites from among 18:6
the children of Israel. They are given to you as a gift for Yahweh,
to do the service of the tabernacle of the congregation.
Therefore you and your sons shall keep your priest's office 18:7

for everything of the altar, and within the veil, and you shall serve.
I have given your priest's office to you as a gift of service.
Any stranger who comes near shall be put to death."

Yahweh said to Aaron: "I have also given you charge of my heave   18:8
offerings, of all the hallowed things of the Israelites, because of your
anointing. I give them to you and your sons by an ordinance forever.
Every oblation of theirs, of the most holy things reserved from the fire,   18:9
shall be yours. Every grain offering, every sin offering, and every trespass
offering they render unto me, shall be holy for you and your sons.
In the most holy place, you shall eat it.   18:10
Every male shall eat it. It shall be holy unto you.
This is yours, the heave offering of their gift, with all the wave offerings   18:11
of the Israelites. I have given them to you, and to your sons and daughters
by a statute forever. Everyone who is clean in your house shall eat of it.
All the best of the oil, and of the wine, and of the wheat—   18:12
the first fruits they offer unto Yahweh—I have given you.
Whatsoever is first ripe in the land, which they bring unto Yahweh,   18:13
shall be yours. Everyone who is clean in your house shall eat of it.
Everything devoted in Israel shall be yours.   18:14

"Everything that opens the matrix in all flesh, which they bring   18:15
unto Yahweh, whether it be of men or beasts, shall be yours.
Nevertheless, the firstborn of man you shall surely redeem,
and the firstling of unclean beasts you shall redeem.
Firstborn children are to be redeemed at the age of one month for a price   18:16
of five shekels, after the shekel of the sanctuary, which is twenty gerahs.
The firstling of a cow, or of a sheep, or of a goat, you shall not redeem.   18:17
They are holy. You shall sprinkle their blood upon the altar, and burn
their fat for an offering made by fire, for a sweet savor unto Yahweh.
Their flesh—the wave breast and the right shoulder—are yours.   18:18
All the heave offerings of the holy things, which the children of Israel   18:19
offer unto Yahweh, I have given to you, and to your sons and daughters,
by a statute forever. It is a covenant of salt forever before Yahweh,
unto you, and unto your seed."

Yahweh said to Aaron, "You shall have no inheritance   18:20
in their land, nor will you have any share among them.
I am your share and your inheritance among the Israelites.
I have given the children of Levi all the one-tenth portions   18:21
in Israel for an inheritance, for their service of the tabernacle.
Henceforth, the children of Israel shall not come near   18:22
the tabernacle, lest they bear sin, and be killed.
The Levites shall do the service of the tabernacle, and they shall bear   18:23
their iniquity. It shall be a statute forever throughout your generations,
that among the children of Israel, they have no inheritance.
But the tithes of the Israelites, which they offer as a heave offering unto   18:24
Yahweh, I have given to the Levites to inherit. Therefore I have said to
them, that among the children of Israel they shall have no inheritance."

Yahweh spoke to Moses, saying to   18:25
tell the Levites, "When you take the tithes of the Israelites,   18:26
which I have given you for your inheritance, you shall offer up
a tenth part of their tithes as a heave offering for Yahweh.
This will be counted as your heave offering, as though it were   18:27
the corn of the threshing floor and the fullness of the winepress.
Thus shall you offer a heave offering unto Yahweh from the tithes   18:28
you receive from the Israelites, and you shall give
Yahweh's heave offering to Aaron the priest.
Out of all your gifts you shall offer the best of them,   18:29
the most holy, as a heave offering unto Yahweh."
Therefore say to them, "When you have heaved the best of the tithes,   18:30
it shall be counted for the Levites as the equivalent
of the threshing floor and the winepress.
And you and your families may eat it anywhere. It is your reward   18:31
for your service in the tabernacle of the congregation.
You shall bear no sin because of it, when you have heaved the best.   18:32
But do not profane the holy gifts of the Israelites, lest you be killed."

Chapter 19

Yahweh spoke to Moses and to Aaron, saying,   19:1
"This is the ordinance of the law that Yahweh has commanded: 19:2
Tell the children of Israel to bring you a red cow
with no spots or blemishes, and which has never been yoked.
Give her to Eleazar the priest, that he may take her   19:3
outside the camp, and have her killed before him.
Eleazar the priest shall take of her blood with his finger, and sprinkle   19:4
her blood directly before the tabernacle of the congregation seven times.
He shall have the cow burned in his sight—her skin, her flesh,   19:5
her blood, and her dung—all of her he shall burn.
The priest shall take cedar wood, and hyssop, and scarlet,   19:6
and cast it into the midst of the burning cow.
Then the priest shall wash his clothes, and bathe his flesh in water.   19:7
Afterward, he shall come into camp, and he shall be unclean until evening.

"He that burns the cow shall wash his clothes,   19:8
and bathe his flesh in water, and be unclean until evening.
A man who is clean shall gather up the ashes of the cow, and lay them up   19:9
outside the camp in a clean place, and they shall be kept for the children
of Israel for a water of separation. It is a purification for sin.
He that gathers the ashes of the cow shall wash his clothes,   19:10
and be unclean until evening. So it shall be for the children of Israel,
and for the stranger who sojourns among them, for a statute forever.
He that touches the dead body of any man shall be unclean for seven days.   19:11
He shall purify himself on the third and seventh day, and be clean. If he   19:12
does not purify himself on the third and seventh day, he shall not be clean.
Whoever touches the body of any dead man, and does not purify himself,   19:13
defiles the tabernacle of Yahweh. That person shall be cut off from Israel

because the water of separation was not sprinkled upon him.
He is unclean, for his uncleanness is yet upon him.

"When a man dies in a tent, all who come into the tent, and all | 19:14
that is in the tent, shall be unclean for seven days. This is the law.
Every open vessel that has no covering bound upon it, is unclean. | 19:15
Whoever touches one who is slain with a sword in the fields, or a | 19:16
dead body, or a bone of a man, or a grave, shall be unclean seven days.
An unclean person shall take some of the ashes of the burnt cow | 19:17
of purification for sin, and put them in a vessel with fresh water.
A clean person shall take hyssop, dip it in the water, and sprinkle it | 19:18
upon the tent, and all the vessels, and on the persons who were there,
and on him who touched a bone, or one slain, or one dead, or a grave.
The clean person shall sprinkle upon the unclean person on the third | 19:19
and seventh day. On the seventh day he shall purify himself, and wash
his clothes and bathe himself in water, and he shall be clean at evening.
But a man who becomes unclean, and does not purify himself, shall be cut | 19:20
off from among the congregation. He has defiled the sanctuary of Yahweh.
The water of separation has not been sprinkled upon him. He is unclean.
It shall be a perpetual statute that he who sprinkles the water | 19:21
of separation shall wash his clothes, and anyone who touches
the water of separation shall be unclean until evening.
Whatever an unclean person touches shall be unclean. | 19:22
Anyone who touches that thing shall be unclean until evening."

Chapter 20

In the first month all the children of Israel came into the desert | 20:1
of Zin and pitched in Kadesh. Miriam died there, and was buried.
There was no water for the people, and they gathered | 20:2
themselves together against Moses and Aaron.
The people quarreled with Moses, and said, | 20:3
"Would God that we had died when our brethren died before Yahweh!
Why have you brought the congregation of Yahweh into this wilderness, | 20:4
that we and our cattle should die here?
Why have you made us come out of Egypt, to bring us to this evil place? | 20:5
It is a place of no seed, or figs, or vines, or pomegranates,
and there is no water to drink!"
Moses and Aaron went from the presence of the assembly to the door | 20:6
of the tabernacle of the congregation and fell upon their faces.
The glory of Yahweh appeared unto them,
and Yahweh spoke to Moses, saying, | 20:7
"Take the rod, you and Aaron, and gather the assembly together. Speak to | 20:8
the rock before their eyes, and it shall give forth water. You shall bring
forth water out of the rock, that they and their beasts shall drink."
Moses took the rod from before Yahweh, as he commanded him. | 20:9
Moses and Aaron gathered the congregation before the rock, and said | 20:10
to them, "Hear now, you rebels. Must we fetch you water out of this rock?"
Moses smote the rock twice with his rod, and water came out abundantly, | 20:11

and the congregation drank, and their beasts drank.
Yahweh said to Moses and Aaron, "Because you did not believe I would   20:12
sanctify myself in the eyes of the children of Israel, you shall not bring
this congregation into the land that I have given them."
These are the waters of Meribah, where the Israelites   20:13
strove with Yahweh, and he was sanctified in them.

Moses sent messengers from Kadesh to the king of Edom: 20:14
"Your brother Israel says you know all the travail that has befallen us—
how our fathers went into Egypt, and how we dwelt in Egypt a long time,   20:15
and how the Egyptians vexed us and our fathers.
And how when we cried unto Yahweh he heard our voice,   20:16
and sent an angel, and how he brought us forth out of Egypt.
Now we are in Kadesh, a place on the outskirts of your border.
I pray you, let us pass through your country. We will not pass through   20:17
the fields or vineyards, nor will we drink the water of the wells.
We will go by the king's highway, and we will turn
neither right nor left until we have passed your borders."
Edom said unto him, "You shall not pass by me,   20:18
lest I come out against you with the sword."
The children of Israel said to him, "We will go only by the highway,   20:19
and if our cattle drink your water, we will pay for it.
It is a small request. We only ask to pass through on foot."
But Edom said, "You shall not go through." And Edom   20:20
confronted them with many people, and with a strong hand.
Thus Edom refused to give Israel passage through his country,   20:21
so the Israelites went another way.

The Israelites journeyed from Kadesh to Mount Hor.   20:22
Yahweh spoke to Moses and Aaron in Mount Hor,   20:23
by the coast of the land of Edom, saying,
"Aaron shall join his ancestors, for he shall not enter   20:24
the land I have given to the children of Israel,
because you rebelled against my word at the water of Meribah.
Take Aaron and Eleazar his son, and bring them unto Mount Hor.   20:25
Strip Aaron of his garments and put them on Eleazar.   20:26
Aaron shall die there and join his ancestors."
Moses did as Yahweh commanded. They went   20:27
unto Mount Hor in the sight of all the congregation.
Moses stripped Aaron of his garments, and put them upon Eleazar his son.   20:28
Aaron died there on the top of the mount. Moses and Eleazar came down.
When the people saw that Aaron was dead,   20:29
all the house of Israel mourned him for thirty days.

Chapter 21

When King Arad the Canaanite, who dwelt in the south,   21:1
heard tell from spies that Israel came by way of Atharim,
he fought them, and took some of them prisoner.

Israel vowed a vow unto Yahweh, and said, "If you will deliver   21:2
these people into my hand, I will utterly destroy their cities."
Yahweh hearkened to the voice of Israel, and delivered up the Canaanites.   21:3
And Israel destroyed them and their cities, and named the place Hormah.
They journeyed from Mount Hor by way of the Red Sea, to avoid the land   21:4
of Edom, and the people were discouraged because of the long route.
And the people spoke against Yahweh, and against Moses: 21:5
"Why have you brought us out of Egypt to die in the wilderness?
There is no bread or water, and we detest this scarce food."
So Yahweh sent fiery serpents among the people,   21:6
and they bit the people, and many of the people of Israel died.
Therefore the people came to Moses, and said, "We have sinned,   21:7
for we have spoken against Yahweh, and against you. Pray unto Yahweh,
that he take away the serpents from us." And Moses prayed for the people.
Yahweh said to Moses, "Make a fiery serpent and set it upon a pole.   21:8
Everyone who was bitten, when he looks upon it, shall live."
Moses made a serpent of brass, and put it on a pole. And so it was   21:9
that when anyone bitten by a serpent beheld the brass serpent, he lived.

The children of Israel set forth and pitched in Oboth.   21:10
They journeyed from Oboth, and pitched at Ije-Abarim,   21:11
in the wilderness before Moab, toward the rising sun.
From there they removed, and pitched in the valley of Zared.   21:12
From there they removed, and pitched on the other side of Arnon,   21:13
which is in the wilderness that comes out of the coasts of the Amorites.
Arnon is the border of Moab, between Moab and the Amorites.
Wherefore it is written in the book of the wars of Yahweh,   21:14
what he did in the Red Sea, and in the valleys of Arnon,
and on the slopes of the valleys that go down   21:15
to the settlement of Ar, along the border of Moab.

From there they went to Beer, the well where Yahweh said to Moses,   21:16
"Gather the people together, and I will give them water."
Then Israel sang this song: "Spring up, O well, and sing you unto it."   21:17
The princes dug the well—the nobles of the people dug it—   21:18
by the direction of the lawgiver they dug it with their staves.
And from the wilderness they went to Mattanah.
And from Mattanah to Nahaliel. And from Nahaliel to Bamoth.   21:19
And from Bamoth to the valley in the open country of Moab,   21:20
to the top of Pisgah, which looks toward Jeshimon.
Israel sent messengers to Sihon, king of the Amorites, saying,   21:21
"Let us pass through your land. We will not go into the fields   21:22
or vineyards, or drink water from your wells. We will go along
by the king's highway until we are beyond your borders."
But Sihon would not let Israel to pass through his border.   21:23
He gathered all his people and went out against Israel into
the wilderness, and he came to Jahaz, where he fought against Israel.
But Israel defeated him by the sword, and took all his land from Arnon 21:24
to Jabbok. But not Ammon, for the children of Ammon were strong.

Israel took all these cities, and dwelt in all the cities of the Amorites,   21:25
in Heshbon, and in all the villages around it.

Heshbon was the city of Sihon, king of the Amorites, who had fought   21:26
against the former king of Moab and taken all his land, even unto Arnon.
Wherefore they who speak in proverbs say, "Come into Heshbon.   21:27
Let the city of Sihon be built and prepared.
For there is a fire gone out of Heshbon, a flame from the city of Sihon.   21:28
It has consumed Ar of Moab, and the lords of the high places of Arnon.
Woe to you, Moab! You are undone, O people of Chemosh. Your sons are   21:29
fugitives and your daughters are prisoners of Sihon, king of the Amorites.
Yet we shot them down. Heshbon has been destroyed as far as Dibon, and   21:30
we have laid them waste even unto Nophah, which reaches unto Medeba."
Thus Israel came to dwell in the land of the Amorites.   21:31

Moses sent spies to find out how to attack Jaazer. Then Israel took   21:32
all their villages, and drove out the Amorites who were there.
Then they turned and went up by the way of Bashan. Og, king of Bashan,   21:33
went out against them, he and all his people, to the battle at Edrei.
Yahweh said to Moses, "Fear him not. I have delivered him into your hand,   21:34
and all his people, and all his land. You shall do to him
as you did to Sihon, king of the Amorites, who dwelt at Heshbon."
So they killed him, and his sons and his people.   21:35
There was none left alive. And they possessed his land.

Chapter 22

The children of Israel went forward, and pitched   22:1
in the plains of Moab, on the side of Jordan by Jericho.
Balak, son of Zippor, saw all that Israel had done to the Amorites.   22:2
The Moabites were sore afraid of Israel because of their   22:3
great numbers, and they were bitter against the children of Israel.
Moab said to the elders of Midian, "This horde will devour   22:4
everything around us, as the ox chews up the grass of the field."
Balak, son of Zippor, was king of the Moabites at that time.
He decided to send messengers to Balaam, son of Beor, at Pethor, which is   22:5
by the river of the land of his people, to say, "A people have come out from
Egypt who cover the face of the earth, and they have settled next to me.
Therefore, I pray you, put a curse on this people, for they are too mighty   22:6
for me. Peradventure, I shall then overcome them and drive them
out of the land. For I know that he whom you bless is blessed,
and he whom you curse is cursed."

So the elders of Moab and Midian departed with the payment   22:7
for divination, and went to Balaam, and told him the words of Balak.
Balaam said to them, "Lodge here this night, and I will bring you the   22:8
words my God speaks to me." So the elders of Moab abode with Balaam.
And God came unto Balaam, and said, "Who are these men with you?"   22:9
Balaam said, "Balak son of Zippor, king of Moab, sent them to me, saying,   22:10
"There is a people come out of Egypt who cover the face of the earth.   22:11

Come now, and curse them for me. Peradventure I shall be able
to overcome them, and drive them out.”
God said to Balaam, “You shall not go with them.   22:12
You shall not curse the people, for they are blessed.”
Balaam rose up in the morning, and said to the elders of Balak,   22:13
“Go back to your land. God refuses to give me leave to go with you.”
The elders of Moab went to Balak, and said,   22:14
“Balaam refuses to come with us.”

So Balak sent other elders, more honorable and numerous than the first.   22:15
They went to Balaam, and said, “Balak son of Zippor, says,   22:16
‘I pray you, let nothing hinder you from coming to me.
I will promote you unto great honor, and I will do whatever   22:17
you ask of me. Please come and curse this people for me.’”
Balaam said to the servants of Balak, “Even if Balak gave me his house   22:18
full of silver and gold, I could not do other than the word of my God.
Therefore, I pray you, tarry here also this night,   22:19
that I may hear more of what God will say to me.”
And God came unto Balaam that night, and said to him, “If these men   22:20
come to call you, go with them, but do only what I shall say unto you.”
So the next day, Balaam saddled his ass and went with the elders of Moab.   22:21

Now, Yahweh’s anger was kindled because Balaam came,   22:22
riding upon his ass, his two servants with him. So the angel
of Yahweh stood in the way as an adversary against him.
The ass saw the angel of Yahweh standing in the way, his sword drawn   22:23
in his hand, and the ass turned out of the way and went into a field.
Balaam struck the ass, to turn her back onto the way.
The angel then came to stand on a narrow walled path in the vineyards.   22:24
When the ass saw the angel, she thrust herself into the wall   22:25
and crushed Balaam's foot against it. Balaam struck her again.
The angel of Yahweh went further, and stood in a narrow place   22:26
where was no way to turn, either right or left.
When the ass saw the angel, she fell down under Balaam.   22:27
Balaam's anger was kindled, and he hit the ass with his staff.

Yahweh opened the mouth of the ass, and she said to Balaam,   22:28
“What have I done to you, that you have struck me these three times?”
Balaam said to the ass, “You have tormented me.   22:29
If there were a sword in my hand, I would kill you.”
The ass said to Balaam, “Am not I your ass, upon which you have ridden   22:30
all my life to this day? Have I ever done this before?” And he said, “No.”
Then Yahweh opened the eyes of Balaam, and he saw the angel,   22:31
his sword in hand, and he bowed his head, and fell on his face.
The angel of Yahweh said, “Why have you struck your ass three times?   22:32
I came to stand against you because your purpose is perverse to me.
The ass saw me, and turned from me three times.   22:33
If she had not, I surely would have slain you but left her alive.”
Balaam said to the angel of Yahweh, “I have done wrong. I knew not   22:34

that you stood against me. But if it displeases you, I will go back again."
The angel said, "No, go ahead with these men. But speak only the words   22:35
Yahweh shall give to you." So Balaam went with the elders of Balak.

When Balak heard that Balaam had come, he went out to meet him   22:36
in the city of Moab, which is at the furthest point on the border of Arnon.
Balak said to Balaam, "Did I not earnestly send princes to call you?   22:37
Why did you not come? Am I indeed not able to honor you?"
Balaam said to Balak, "Lo, I have come you. But do I have the power   22:38
to say anything? Only the words God puts in my mouth shall I speak."
Balaam went with Balak, and they came unto Kirjath-Huzoth.   22:39
Balak offered sacrifices of oxen and sheep,   22:40
and gave them to Balaam, and to the princes who were with him.
The next day, Balak took Balaam up into the high places of Baal,   22:41
so that he might see the outermost edges of Israel's camps.

Chapter 23

Balaam said to Balak, "Build me here seven altars,   23:1
and prepare for me seven bulls and seven rams."
Balak did as Balaam had spoken. And Balak and Balaam   23:2
offered a bull and a ram on each altar.
Balaam said to Balak, "Stay by your burnt offering. I will go see   23:3
if the Lord comes to meet me. Whatever he shows me, I will tell you."
And he went to a high place.
Yahweh met Balaam there, and Balaam said to him, "I have prepared   23:4
seven altars, and I have offered upon every altar a bull and a ram.
Yahweh put words in Balaam's mouth, and said,   23:5
"Return unto Balak, and speak what I have given you."
So Balaam returned to Balak, and, lo, he still stood   23:6
by his burnt sacrifice, he, and all the princes of Moab.
Balaam recited his message, saying, "Balak the king of Moab   23:7
has brought me from Aram, out of the mountains of the east,
and said, 'Come, curse Jacob for me. Come, defy Israel.'
How shall I curse whom God has not cursed?   23:8
How shall I defy whom God has not defied?
From the top of the rocks I see them. From the hills I behold them.   23:9
These people dwell alone, and do not reckon themselves among nations.
Who can count the dust of Jacob, or number even the fourth part of Israel?   23:10
Let me die the death of the righteous, and let my end be like his!"

Balak said to Balaam, "What have you done to me? I asked you   23:11
to curse my enemies, but now you have blessed them!"
Balaam said, "Shall I not speak that which the Lord has put in my mouth?"   23:12
Balak said, "Come with me, I pray you, to another place from whence   23:13
you may see but a small part of them, and there curse them for me."
So Balak brought Balaam into the field of Zophim, to the top of Pisgah,   23:14
and they built seven altars, and offered a bull and a ram on every altar.
Balaam said to Balak, "Stand here by your burnt offering,   23:15

while I go yonder to meet the Lord."
And the Lord met Balaam, and put words in his mouth, 23:16
and said, "Go again unto Balak, and say these things."
When he came to Balak, he still stood by his burnt offering, along with 23:17
the princes of Moab. Balak asked him, "What has the Lord spoken?"
Balaam recited his message, saying, "Rise up, Balak, and listen. 23:18
Hearken unto me, you son of Zippor.
God is not a man, that he would lie, nor is he born of woman 23:19
that he would change his mind. What he has said, will he not then do?
What he has spoken, shall he not make it so?

"I have been commanded to bless, and I have blessed. I cannot reverse it. 23:20
He has not beheld iniquity in Jacob, nor has he seen perverseness 23:21
in Israel. Yahweh, his God, is with him, and is proclaimed as his king.
Yahweh brought them out of Egypt. He has the strength of a wild ox. 23:22
No curses affect Jacob, no magic works against Israel. In this time 23:23
it shall be said of Jacob and Israel, 'What greatness God has wrought!'
Behold, Israel rises up as a great lion, and is lifted up as a lion. He shall 23:24
not lie down until he eats of the prey, and drinks the blood of the slain."
Balak said to Balaam, "Then neither curse them, nor bless them at all." 23:25
Balaam answered, "Did I not tell you that all the Lord speaks I must do?" 23:26
But Balak said to Balaam, "Come, I pray you. I will bring you to another 23:27
place. Perhaps it will please God that you curse them for me from there."
So Balak brought Balaam to the top of Peor, that looks toward Jeshimon. 23:28
And Balaam said to Balak, "Build me here seven altars, 23:29
and prepare for me seven bulls and seven rams."
Balak did as Balaam said, and offered a bull and a ram on every altar. 23:30

Chapter 24

When Balaam saw that it pleased Yahweh to bless Israel, he did not, as at 24:1
other times, seek enchantments, but set his face toward the wilderness.
Balaam lifted up his eyes, and saw Israel abiding in their tents, 24:2
according to their tribes, and the spirit of God came upon him.
And he took up his parable, saying, 24:3
"Balaam, son of Beor, the man whose eyes are open,
who heard the words of God, who saw the vision of the Almighty 24:4
while in a trance with his eyes open, saith:
'How goodly are your tents, O Jacob, and your tabernacles, O Israel! 24:5
Like valleys they spread forth, like gardens by the riverside, 24:6
like flowering trees planted by God, like cedar trees beside the waters.
Water shall overflow your buckets, your seeds shall receive rain, 24:7
and your king shall be higher than Agag. Your kingdom shall be exalted.
Yahweh brought you forth out of Egypt. He has the strength of a wild ox. 24:8
He shall devour the nations of his enemies. He shall break
their bones, and pierce them with his arrows.
He pounces like a lion, and lays down like a lion. Who shall disturb him? 24:9
Blessed is he that blesses you, and cursed is he that curses you.'"

Balak's anger was kindled against Balaam. He threw up his hands 24:10
and said to Balaam, "I called you to curse my enemies,
and instead you have blessed them three times.
Therefore now flee to your place. I thought to promote 24:11
you to great honor, but Yahweh has held you back from honor."
Balaam said to Balak, "Did I not say to your messengers, 24:12
'Even if Balak gave me his house full of silver and gold, I could not 24:13
go against the commandment of my God, to do either good or bad
of my own mind, but only what my God says, will I speak?'
Now I go back to my people. But first, let me tell you 24:14
what Israel will do to your people in the latter days."

And he took up his parable, saying, 24:15
"Balaam, son of Beor, the man whose eyes are open,
who heard the words of God, who saw the vision of the Almighty 24:16
while in a trance with his eyes open, saith:
'I see him, but not now. I behold him, but not near. There shall come 24:17
a star out of Jacob, and a scepter shall rise out of Israel. He shall
crush all the corners of Moab, and destroy all the children of Sheth.
Edom shall be his possession. Seir, a possession of his enemies, 24:18
shall be conquered and become his possession. Israel shall fight valiantly.
Out of Jacob shall come he who has dominion, 24:19
and he shall destroy what remains of the city.'"
When Balaam looked upon Amalek he took up his parable, and said, 24:20
"Amalek was the first of the nations, but in the end it shall perish forever."
He looked on the Kenites and took up his parable, and said, 24:21
"Strong is your dwelling place, for you built your nest in cliffs of rock.
Nevertheless, the Kenites shall be wasted when Asshur takes you captive." 24:22
He took up his parable, and said, "Alas, who can live when God does this? 24:23
Ships shall come from the coast of Chittim, and shall afflict 24:24
Asshur, and Eber, and they also shall perish forever."
Then Balaam rose up and returned to his place. Balak also went his way. 24:25

Chapter 25

Israel abode in Shittim, and the people began 25:1
to commit whoredom with the daughters of Moab.
For they called the Israelites to the sacrifices to their gods, 25:2
and the people did eat, and bowed down to their gods.
Israel joined itself unto Baal-Peor, 25:3
and the anger of Yahweh was kindled against Israel.
Yahweh said to Moses, "Take all the heads of the people, 25:4
and hang them up before Yahweh in broad daylight,
that the fierce anger of Yahweh may be turned away from Israel."
Moses said to the judges of Israel, "Kill every one of your men 25:5
who joined himself unto Baal-Peor."
Then an Israelite brought to his brethren a Midianite woman, 25:6
in the sight of Moses and all the congregation of Israel,
who were weeping before the door of the tabernacle.

When Phinehas, son of Eleazar, the son of Aaron the priest, saw this,   25:7
he rose up from among the congregation and took a javelin in his hand.
And he went after the man of Israel into the tent, and thrust both   25:8
of them through, the man of Israel and the woman, through her belly.
So the plague was stayed from the children of Israel.
Those who died in the plague were 24,000.   25:9

Yahweh spoke to Moses, saying,   25:10
"Phinehas son of Eleazar, the son of Aaron the priest, has turned my wrath   25:11
away from the children of Israel, for he was zealous for my sake,
and I did not consume the children of Israel in my jealousy.
Therefore I give him my covenant of peace.   25:12
And he shall have it, and his sons after him, my covenant   25:13
of an everlasting priesthood, because he was zealous for his God,
and made an atonement for the children of Israel."
The name of the Israelite who was slain with the Midianite woman,   25:14
was Zimri, the son of Salu, chief of a house among the Simeonites.
The name of the Midianite woman who was slain was Cozbi,   25:15
the daughter of Zur, who was head of a house in Midian.
Yahweh spoke to Moses, saying,   25:16
"Go after the Midianites and destroy them.   25:17
They deceive you with their wiles. They beguiled you in the matter   25:18
of Peor, and in the matter of Cozbi, their sister, daughter of a chief
of Midian, who was slain in the day of the plague for Peor's sake."

Chapter 26

After the plague, Yahweh spoke to Moses   26:1
and to Eleazar, son of Aaron the priest, saying,
"Take a census of all the congregation of Israel, from twenty   26:2
years old upward, all in Israel who are able to go to war."
Moses and Eleazar the priest spoke with the people   26:3
on the plains of Moab by Jordan, near Jericho, telling them
to take a census of all the congregation of Israel,   26:4
from twenty years old upward, as Yahweh commanded Moses
and the Israelites, who went forth out of the land of Egypt.
The children of Reuben: Hanoch of the Hanochites, Pallu of the Palluites,   26:5
Hezron of the Hezronites, Carmi of the Carmites.   26:6
These are the families Reuben. Those numbered were 43,730.   26:7
The sons of Pallu: Eliab.   26:8
The sons of Eliab: Nemuel, Dathan and Abiram. This is the Dathan and   26:9
Abiram who were famous in the congregation, who strove against Moses
and Aaron in the company of Korah when they stood against Yahweh.
The earth opened her mouth and swallowed them along with Korah,   26:10
when his band died, when fire devoured 250 men and they became a sign.
Notwithstanding, the children of Korah did not die.   26:11

The sons of Simeon: Nemuel of the Nemuelites,   26:12
Jamin of the Jaminites, Jachin of the Jachinites,

Zerah of the Zarhites, Shaul of the Shaulites.	26:13
The families of the Simeonites numbered 22,200.	26:14
The children of Gad: Zephon of the Zephonites,	26:15
Haggi of the Haggites, Shuni of the Shunites,	
Ozni of the Oznites, Eri of the Erites,	26:16
Arod of the Arodites, Areli of the Arelites.	26:17
These are the families of Gad. Those numbered were 40,500.	26:18
The sons of Judah: Er and Onan, who died in the land of Canaan,	26:19
Shelah of the Shelanites, Pharez of the Pharzites, Zerah of the Zarhites.	26:20
The sons of Pharez: Hezron of the Hezronites, Hamul of the Hamulites.	26:21
These are the families of Judah. Those numbered were 76,500.	26:22
The sons of Issachar: Tola of the Tolaites, Pua of the Punites,	26:23
Jashub of the Jashubites, Shimron of the Shimronites.	26:24
These are the families of Issachar. Those numbered were 64,300.	26:25

The sons of Zebulun: Sered of the Sardites, — 26:26
Elon of the Elonites, Jahleel of the Jahleelites.
These are the families Zebulun. Those numbered were 60,500. — 26:27
The sons of Joseph: Manasseh and Ephraim. — 26:28
The sons of Manasseh: Machir of the Machirites. — 26:29
Machir begat Gilead of the Gileadites.
The sons of Gilead: Jeezer of the Jeezerites, Helek of the Helekites, — 26:30
Asriel of the Asrielites, Shechem of the Shechemites, — 26:31
Shemida of the Shemidaites, Hepher of the Hepherites. — 26:32
Zelophehad son of Hepher had no sons, only daughters. — 26:33
Their names were Mahlah, Noah, Hoglah, Milcah and Tirzah.
These are the families of Manasseh. Those numbered were 52,700. — 26:34
The sons of Ephraim: Shuthelah of the Shuthalhites, — 26:35
Becher of the Bachrites, Tahan of the Tahanites.
The son of Shuthelah: Eran of the Eranites. — 26:36
These are the families of Ephraim. Those numbered were 32,500. — 26:37
These are the sons of Joseph after their families.

The sons of Benjamin: Bela of the Belaites, — 26:38
Ashbel of the Ashbelites, Ahiram of the Ahiramites,
Shupham of the Shuphamites, Hupham of the Huphamites. — 26:39
The sons of Bela: Ard of the Ardites, Naaman of the Naamites. — 26:40
These are the sons of Benjamin. Those numbered were 45,600. — 26:41
The sons of Dan: Shuham of the Shuhamites. — 26:42
These are the families of Dan.
All the families of the Shuhamites numbered 64,400. — 26:43
The children of Asher: Jimna of the Jimnites, — 26:44
Jesui of the Jesuites, Beriah of the Beriites.
The sons of Beriah: Heber of the Heberites, Malchiel of the Malchielites. — 26:45
The name of the daughter of Asher was Sarah. — 26:46
These are the families of Asher. Those numbered were 53,400. — 26:47
The sons of Naphtali: Jahzeel of the Jahzeelites, Guni of the Gunites, — 26:48
Jezer of the Jezerites, Shillem of the Shillemites. — 26:49

These are the families of Naphtali. Those numbered were 45,400.   26:50
The numbered children of Israel were 607,730.   26:51

Yahweh spoke to Moses, saying,   26:52
"Unto these the land shall be divided   26:53
for an inheritance, according their numbers.
To the many you shall give more inheritance, to the few   26:54
you shall give less inheritance. Everyone's inheritance
shall be given according to the numbers in his families.
However, the land shall be divided by lot. They shall inherit   26:55
according to the names of their ancestral tribes.
Possession of the land, for the many and the few, shall be decided by lot."   26:56

These are they who were numbered of the Levites: Gershon   26:57
of the Gershonites, Kohath of the Kohathites, Merari of the Merarites.
These are the families of the Levites: the Libnites, the Hebronites,   26:58
the Mahlites, the Mushites, and the Korathites. Kohath begat Amram.
Amram's wife was Jochebed, daughter of Levi, who was born to Levi   26:59
in Egypt. Unto Amram she bore Aaron, Moses, and Miriam, their sister.
Unto Aaron was born Nadab, Abihu, Eleazar and Ithamar.   26:60
Nadab and Abihu died because they offered strange fire before Yahweh.   26:61
Those who were numbered of them were 23,000—all males from   26:62
a month old upward. They were not counted among the Israelites,
because they had no heritage among the children of Israel.
These are they who were numbered by Moses and Eleazar the priest,   26:63
who numbered the Israelites in the plains of Moab by Jordan near Jericho.
But there was not a man among them whom Moses and Aaron the priest   26:64
numbered when they counted the Israelites in the wilderness of Sinai.
For Yahweh said, "They shall die in the wilderness," and there was not   26:65
a man left of them, save Caleb, son of Jephunneh, and Joshua, son of Nun.

Chapter 27

Then these people came forward: The daughters of Zelophehad,   27:1
the son of Hepher, the son of Gilead, the son of Machir,
the son of Manasseh, and the son of Joseph. The names of Zelophehad's
daughters were Mahlah, Noah, Hoglah, Milcah and Tirzah.
They stood by the door of the tabernacle, before Moses and Eleazar   27:2
the priest, and before the princes and all the congregation, and said,
"Our father died in the wilderness, and he was not in the company   27:3
of those who gathered themselves together against Yahweh in the
company of Korah. He died in his own sin and had no sons.
Why should the name of our father be taken away from his family   27:4
because he has no son? Give us a heritage among our father's brothers."
Moses brought their cause before Yahweh.   27:5
Yahweh spoke to Moses, saying,   27:6
"The daughters of Zelophehad speak right. You shall give them   27:7
an inheritance among their father's brethren, and you shall
cause the inheritance of their father to pass on to them.

And you shall speak to the children of Israel, saying, 'If a man dies   27:8
and has no son, his inheritance shall pass unto his daughter.
If he has no daughter, his inheritance shall be given to his brethren.   27:9
If he has no brethren, his inheritance shall pass on to his father's brethren.   27:10
If his father has no brethren, you shall give his inheritance to his closest   27:11
kinsman, and he shall possess it.' This shall be a statute of judgment
unto the children of Israel, as Yahweh commanded Moses."

Yahweh said to Moses, "Go up into this mountain of Abarim,   27:12
and see the land I have given to the children of Israel.
And when you have seen it, you also shall be gathered   27:13
unto your ancestors, as Aaron your brother was gathered.
For you rebelled against my commandment in the desert of Zin   27:14
when the people were angry, and did not sanctify me before their eyes
at the water— the water of Meribah, in Kadesh, in the wilderness of Zin."
Moses spoke to Yahweh, saying,   27:15
"Let Yahweh, the God of the spirits of all flesh,   27:16
appoint a man over the congregation,
who may go out before them, and who may go in before them,   27:17
and who may lead them out, and who may bring them in, so that
the congregation of Yahweh be not as sheep that have no shepherd."
Yahweh said to Moses, "Take Joshua the son of Nun,   27:18
a man in whom is the spirit, and lay your hands upon him.
Set him before Eleazar the priest, and before all   27:19
the congregation, and give him a charge in their sight.
Put some of your honor upon him, that all the people may be obedient.   27:20
He shall stand before Eleazar the priest, who shall ask guidance for him,   27:21
after the judgment of Urim, before Yahweh. At his word shall they go out,
and at his word they shall come in, both he and all the children of Israel."
Moses did as Yahweh commanded him. He set Joshua   27:22
before Eleazar the priest, and before all the congregation.
And he laid his hands upon him, and gave him a charge in their sight,   27:23
as Yahweh commanded by the hand of Moses.

Chapter 28

Yahweh spoke to Moses, telling him to   28:1
command the children of Israel, and say to them, "You shall observe   28:2
my offerings, and my bread for my sacrifices made by fire,
for a sweet savor unto Yahweh, in their due season.
This is the offering made by fire that you shall offer unto Yahweh: 28:3
Two lambs of the first year without blemish every day,
for a continual burnt offering.
One lamb you shall offer in the morning. The other you shall offer   28:4
at evening with a tenth part of an ephah of flour, mixed with   28:5
the fourth part of a hin of beaten oil, for a grain offering.
It is a continual burnt offering, which was ordained on Mount Sinai,   28:6
a sacrifice made by fire for a sweet savor unto Yahweh.
The drink offering shall be the fourth part of a hin of wine for each lamb.   28:7

The wine shall be poured in the holy place, a drink offering unto Yahweh.
The lamb you offer at evening is with a grain offering, as in the morning, **28:8**
and also with a drink offering. You shall offer these as a sacrifice
made by fire, for a sweet savor unto Yahweh.

"On the sabbath day you shall offer two lambs of the first year **28:9**
without blemish, and two-tenths deal of flour mixed with oil
for a grain offering, along with the drink offering.
This is the burnt offering of every sabbath, **28:10**
beside the continual burnt offering, and the drink offering.
On the first of the month you shall offer to Yahweh a burnt offering of two **28:11**
young bulls, one ram, and seven lambs of the first year without blemish.
For each bull, three-tenths deal of flour mixed with oil for a grain offering. **28:12**
For the ram, two-tenths deal of flour mixed with oil for a grain offering.
For each lamb, a tenth deal of flour mixed with oil for a grain offering— **28:13**
a burnt offering, a sacrifice made by fire for a sweet savor unto Yahweh.
The drink offerings shall be half a hin of wine for a bull, the third part **28:14**
of a hin for a ram, and a fourth part of a hin for a lamb. This is the burnt
offering of every month throughout the months of the year.
One kid of the goats shall be offered for a sin offering unto Yahweh, **28:15**
beside the continual burnt offering and the drink offering.

"The fourteenth day of the first month is the Passover of Yahweh. **28:16**
The fifteenth day of this month is the feast. **28:17**
For seven days unleavened bread shall be eaten.
On the first day shall be a holy convocation. **28:18**
You shall do no manner of servile work this day.
You shall offer a sacrifice of two young bulls, one ram, **28:19**
and seven lambs of the first year—a burnt offering unto Yahweh.
They shall be without blemish.
The grain offering shall be of flour mixed with oil. You shall offer **28:20**
three-tenths deal for a bull, and two-tenths deal for a ram.
A tenth deal shall you offer for each lamb. **28:21**
You shall offer one goat for a sin offering, to make an atonement for you. **28:22**
You shall offer these beside the burnt offering in the morning, **28:23**
which is for a continual burnt offering.

"After this manner you shall offer daily, throughout the seven days— **28:24**
a sacrifice made by fire for a sweet savor unto Yahweh. It shall be
offered beside the continual burnt offering and the drink offering.
On the seventh day you shall have a holy convocation. **28:25**
You shall do no servile work.
On the day of the first fruits, when you bring a new grain offering **28:26**
unto Yahweh after your feast of weeks, you shall have
a holy convocation. You shall do no servile work.
You shall offer a burnt offering of two young bulls, one ram, **28:27**
and seven lambs of the first year for a sweet savor unto Yahweh.
The grain offerings shall be flour mixed with oil— **28:28**
three-tenths deal for a bull, two-tenths deal for a ram,

and a tenth deal for each lamb.	28:29
And you shall offer one kid of the goats, to make an atonement for you.	28:30
You shall offer them beside the continual burnt offering, which shall	28:31
be without blemish, and the grain offering, and the drink offerings."	

Chapter 29

"On the first day of the seventh month, you shall have a holy convocation. — 29:1
You shall do no servile work. Let the trumpets be blown that day.
You shall offer as a burnt offering unto Yahweh, one young bull, — 29:2
one ram, and seven lambs of the first year without blemish.
The grain offering shall be of flour mixed with oil— — 29:3
three-tenths deal for a bull, two-tenths deal for a ram,
and one-tenth deal for each lamb. — 29:4
You shall also offer one kid of the goats for a sin offering, — 29:5
to make an atonement for you.
This is in addition to the burnt offering each month, with its grain offering, — 29:6
and the daily burnt offering with its grain offering, and their drink
offerings. It is a sacrifice made by fire for a sweet savor unto Yahweh.

"On the tenth day of the seventh month you shall have a holy convocation. — 29:7
You shall deny yourselves, and shall not do any work.
You shall offer one young bull, one ram, and seven lambs of the first year — 29:8
without blemish as a burnt offering, for a sweet savor unto Yahweh.
The grain offering shall be of flour mixed with oil— — 29:9
three-tenths deal for a bull, two-tenths deal for a ram,
and one-tenth deal for each lamb. — 29:10
You shall offer one kid of the goats for a sin offering— — 29:11
beside the sin offering of atonement, and the continual
burnt offering, and the grain and drink offerings.

"On the fifteenth day of the seventh month you shall have — 29:12
a holy convocation. You shall do no servile work,
and you shall keep a feast unto Yahweh for seven days.
You shall offer thirteen young bulls, two rams, and fourteen lambs — 29:13
of the first year without blemish as a burnt offering—
a sacrifice made by fire, for a sweet savor unto Yahweh.
The grain offering shall be of flour mixed with oil—three-tenths deal — 29:14
for each of the thirteen bulls, two-tenths deal for each of the two rams,
and one-tenth deal for each of the fourteen lambs. — 29:15
And you shall offer one kid of the goats for a sin offering— — 29:16
beside the continual burnt offering, with its grain and drink offerings.

"On the second day you shall offer twelve young bulls, — 29:17
two rams, and fourteen lambs of the first year without blemish.
The grain and drink offerings for the bulls, rams, and lambs — 29:18
shall be according to their number, after the same manner.
And you shall offer one kid of the goats for a sin offering— — 29:19
beside the continual burnt offering, with its grain and drink offerings.
On the third day, eleven bulls, two rams, — 29:20

and fourteen lambs of the first year without blemish.
The grain and drink offerings for the bulls, rams, and lambs   29:21
shall be according to their number, after the same manner.
And you shall offer one kid of the goats for a sin offering—   29:22
beside the continual burnt offering, with its grain and drink offerings.

"On the fourth day, ten bulls, two rams,   29:23
and fourteen lambs of the first year without blemish.
The grain and drink offerings for the bulls, rams, and lambs   29:24
shall be according to their number, after the same manner.
And you shall offer one kid of the goats for a sin offering—   29:25
beside the continual burnt offering, with its grain and drink offerings.
On the fifth day, nine bulls, two rams,   29:26
and fourteen lambs of the first year without blemish.
The grain and drink offerings for the bulls, rams, and lambs   29:27
shall be according to their number, after the same manner.
And you shall offer one kid of the goats for a sin offering—   29:28
beside the continual burnt offering, with its grain and drink offerings.

"On the sixth day, eight bulls, two rams,   29:29
and fourteen lambs of the first year without blemish.
The grain and drink offerings for the bulls, rams, and lambs   29:30
shall be according to their number, after the same manner.
And you shall offer one kid of the goats for a sin offering—   29:31
beside the continual burnt offering, with its grain and drink offerings.
On the seventh day, seven bulls, two rams,   29:32
and fourteen lambs of the first year without blemish.
The grain and drink offerings for the bulls, rams, and lambs   29:33
shall be according to their number, after the same manner.
And you shall offer one kid of the goats for a sin offering—   29:34
beside the continual burnt offering, with its grain and drink offerings.

"On the eighth day you shall have a solemn assembly.   29:35
You shall do no servile work this day.
You shall offer one bull, one ram, and seven lambs of the first year without   29:36
blemish as a sacrifice made by fire, for a sweet savor unto Yahweh.
The grain and drink offerings for the bull, ram, and lambs   29:37
shall be according to their number, after the same manner.
And you shall offer one kid of the goats for a sin offering—   29:38
beside the continual burnt offering, with its grain and drink offerings.
These things you shall do unto Yahweh in your set feasts—   29:39
beside your vows, your freewill offerings, your burnt offerings,
your grain offerings, your drink offerings, and your peace offerings."
Moses told the children of Israel all that Yahweh commanded him.   29:40

Chapter 30

Moses spoke to the heads of the tribes concerning   30:1
the Israelites, saying, "This is what Yahweh has commanded:
If a man vows an oath unto Yahweh, or swears a promise to bind himself,   30:2

he shall not break his word. He must do what he says he will do.

If a woman living in her father's house in her youth,   30:3
vows an oath unto Yahweh, or binds herself by a bond,
and her father hears her vow or her bond yet says nothing, then all   30:4
her vows shall stand, and every bond she has bound to herself shall stand.
But if her father disallows when he hears them, none of her vows or bonds   30:5
shall stand. Yahweh shall forgive her, because her father disallowed her.
If she is married when she vows or utters and oath that binds her,   30:6
and her husband hears it, yet holds his peace, then her vows shall stand,   30:7
and the bonds she bound to herself shall stand.
But if her husband disallows when he hears them, he can make   30:8
her vows and bonds have no effect, and Yahweh shall forgive her.
Every vow or oath of a widow, or of a divorced woman, shall stand.   30:9

"If a woman vows in her husband's house, or binds herself with an oath,   30:10
and her husband hears it, yet holds his peace and does not disallow her,   30:11
then all her vows shall stand, and every bond shall stand.
But if her husband made them void on the day he heard them,   30:12
then whatever vows or bonds proceeded from her lips shall not stand.
Her husband has made them void, and Yahweh shall forgive her.
Every vow or oath a woman makes can either be established   30:13
or made void by her husband.
If her husband holds his peace with her each day, he establishes her vows.   30:14
He confirms them because he says nothing when he hears them.
And if he later makes them void after he first heard them,   30:15
he shall bear her iniquity."
These are the statutes Yahweh commanded Moses, between a man   30:16
and his wife, and between a father and his daughter living in his house.

Chapter 31

Yahweh spoke to Moses, saying,   31:1
"Avenge the children of Israel against the Midianites.   31:2
Afterward shall you be gathered unto your ancestors.
Moses spoke to the people, saying, "Arm some of yourselves   31:3
for war. Go against the Midianites, and avenge Yahweh of Midian.
Every tribe of Israel shall send a thousand men to the war."   31:4
So out of the thousands of Israel were delivered a thousand   31:5
men from every tribe, armed for war—twelve thousand men in all.
Moses sent the twelve thousand men to war, along Phinehas, son of   31:6
Eleazar the priest, carrying the holy instruments and the signal trumpets.
And they warred against the Midianites, as Yahweh   31:7
commanded Moses, and they killed all the males.
They killed the kings of Midian along with the rest of the men,   31:8
namely, Evi, Rekem, Zur, Hur and Reba—the five kings of Midian.
They also killed Balaam the son of Beor with the sword.
The Israelites took all the women of Midian captives, with their little ones,   31:9
and took the spoil of all their cattle, and all their flocks, and all their goods,
and they burned all their cities and encampments with fire.   31:10

They took all the spoil and prey, both human and animal,   31:11
and they brought the captives, the prey and the spoil to Moses   31:12
and Eleazar the priest, and unto all the congregation of Israel,
in their camp on the plains of Moab, by Jordan, near Jericho.
Moses and Eleazar the priest, and all the princes of Israel,   31:13
went forth to meet them outside the camp.
Moses was angry with the officers of the host—with the captains over   31:14
thousands and captains over hundreds—who came from the battle.
Moses said to them, "Why have you saved all the women alive?   31:15
They caused the Israelites, through the counsel of Balaam,   31:16
to commit trespass against Yahweh in the matter of Peor,
and there was a plague among the congregation of Yahweh.
Now, therefore, kill every male among the little ones,   31:17
and kill every woman who has known a man by lying with him.
But all the female children, who have not known a man   31:18
by lying with him, keep alive for yourselves.
You will remain outside the camp for seven days. Whoever among   31:19
you or your captives has killed any person, or touched a dead body,
must purify themselves on the third day and the seventh day, and
purify their garments, and anything made of skins or goat hair or wood."   31:20

Eleazar the priest said to the men who went into battle,   31:21
"This is the ordinance of law that Yahweh commanded Moses:
The gold, silver, brass, iron, tin and lead—   31:22
everything that can withstand the fire—you shall heat with fire and it   31:23
shall be clean, but it also shall be purified with the water of separation.
Anything that cannot go through the fire shall be purified with the water.
You shall wash your clothes, and on the seventh day you shall be clean.   31:24
Afterward you shall come into the camp."

Yahweh spoke to Moses, saying,   31:25
"Take inventory of the spoil that was taken, both of man and beast—   31:26
you and Eleazar the priest, and the chief fathers of the congregation—
and divide the spoil into two parts, one part for those who took the war   31:27
upon them and went into battle, and one part for all the congregation.
And levy a tribute unto Yahweh from the men who went out to battle—   31:28
one out of every five hundred persons, oxen, asses and sheep.
Take these from the warriors share and give it to Eleazar the priest,   31:29
for a heave offering before Yahweh.
And from the children of Israel's half, take one out of every fifty persons,   31:30
oxen, asses, flocks—of all manner of beasts—and give them to
the Levites, who keep the charge of the tabernacle of Yahweh."

Moses and Eleazar the priest did as Yahweh commanded Moses.   31:31
The booty was 675,000 sheep,   31:32
72,000 oxen,   31:33
61,000 asses,   31:34
and 32,000 virgins.   31:35
The half that went to the warriors was 337,500 sheep,   31:36

of which Yahweh's tribute was 675,	31:37
36,000 oxen, of which Yahweh's tribute was 72,	31:38
30,500 asses, of which Yahweh's tribute was 61,	31:39
and 16,000 virgins, of which Yahweh's tribute was 32 virgins.	31:40
Moses gave the tribute, which was Yahweh's heave offering,	31:41
to Eleazar the priest, as Yahweh commanded Moses.	

The children of Israel's half was	31:42
337,500 sheep,	31:43
36,000 oxen,	31:44
30,500 asses,	31:45
and 16,000 virgins.	31:46
From the Israelites' half, Moses took one out of fifty, both of man	31:47
and beast, and gave them to the Levites, who kept the charge	
of the tabernacle of Yahweh, as Yahweh commanded Moses.	
The officers who were over thousands of the host, the captains	31:48
of thousands and the captains of hundreds, came unto Moses.	
They said to him, "Your servants counted the warriors	31:49
under our charge, and not one of us is missing.	
We have therefore brought an oblation for Yahweh, from what every man	31:50
has gotten—jewels, gold, chains, bracelets, rings, earrings and tablets—	
to make an atonement for ourselves before Yahweh.	
Moses and Eleazar the priest took the gold and jewelry from them.	31:51
All the gold of the offering unto Yahweh, from the captains	31:52
of thousands and the captains of hundreds, was 16,750 shekels—	
for the men of war had taken spoil for themselves.	31:53
Moses and Eleazar the priest took the gold from the captains of thousands	31:54
and of hundreds, and brought it into the tabernacle of the congregation,	
for a memorial for the children of Israel before Yahweh.	

Chapter 32

The children of Reuben and the children of Gad had a multitude of cattle.	32:1
When they that saw the land of Jazer and Gilead was good for cattle,	
they came and spoke to Moses and Eleazar the priest,	32:2
and to the princes of the congregation, saying,	
"Ataroth, Dibon, Jazer, Nimrah, Heshbon, Elealeh, Shebam, Nebo and Beon,	32:3
the country that Yahweh consumed before the congregation of Israel,	32:4
is good land for cattle, and your servants have cattle.	
If we have found grace in your sight, let this land be given	32:5
unto your servants for a possession, and take us not over Jordan."	

Moses said to the children of Reuben and of Gad,	32:6
"Shall your brethren go to war while you sit here?	
Why discourage them from going into the land Yahweh has given them?	32:7
So did your fathers, when I sent them from Kadesh-Barnea to see the land.	32:8
For they went into the valley of Eshcol and saw that the land was good,	32:9
yet they discouraged the hearts of the children of Israel,	
saying that they should not go into the land Yahweh had given them.	

Yahweh's anger was kindled at that time, and he swore, saying,   32:10
'Surely none of the men twenty years old and upward who came out   32:11
of Egypt shall see the land that I swore unto Abraham, Isaac and Jacob,
because they have not wholly followed me,
except for Caleb the son of Jephunneh the Kenezite, and Joshua   32:12
the son of Nun, who have wholly followed Yahweh.'
Yahweh's anger was kindled against Israel, and he made them   32:13
wander in the wilderness forty years, until all the generation
that had done evil in the sight of Yahweh, was consumed.
Now you rise up in your fathers' stead, another generation   32:14
of sinful men, to increase the fierce anger of Yahweh toward Israel.
For if you turn away from him, he will yet again abandon Israel   32:15
in the wilderness, and you shall destroy all this people."

They came nearer to Moses, and said, "We will build   32:16
sheepfolds here for our cattle, and cities for our little ones,
but we ourselves will go armed before the children of Israel,   32:17
until we have brought them into their place. Our children will
dwell in the fenced cities because of the inhabitants of the land, but
we will not return to our houses until every Israelite has his inheritance.   32:18
We shall not inherit with them over Jordan and beyond, because our   32:19
inheritance has fallen to us on this side of Jordan eastward."
Moses said to them, "If you will do this thing,   32:20
if you will go armed before Yahweh to war,
and all of you will go armed over Jordan before Yahweh,   32:21
until he has driven out his enemies from before him,
and the land is subdued before Yahweh, then afterward   32:22
you may return and be guiltless before Yahweh, and before Israel.
And this land shall be your possession before Yahweh.
But if you will not do so, you have sinned against Yahweh,   32:23
and your sin will surely find you out.
Build cities for your families and folds for the sheep. Do as you have said."   32:24

The children of Reuben and of Gad said to Moses,   32:25
"Your servants will do as my lord commands.
Our little ones, wives, flocks, and cattle shall be in the cities of Gilead,   32:26
but your servants will go over, every man armed for war   32:27
before Yahweh, to do battle as my lord says."
So concerning them, Moses commanded Eleazar the priest,   32:28
and Joshua the son of Nun, and the chief fathers of the tribes of Israel,
and said to them, "If the children of Gad and of Reuben go with you   32:29
over Jordan, every man armed for battle, then when the land is subdued,
you shall give them the land of Gilead for a possession.
But if they will not pass over with you armed,   32:30
they must take their possessions among you in the land of Canaan."

The children of Gad and of Reuben answered, saying,   32:31
"As Yahweh has said unto your servants, so will we do.
We will pass over armed before Yahweh into the land of Canaan,   32:32

that the possession of our inheritance on this side of Jordan may be ours."

So Moses gave to them—to the children of Gad, and the children of 32:33
Reuben, and to the half-tribe of Manasseh son of Joseph—the kingdom of
Sihon, king of the Amorites, and the kingdom of Og, king of Bashan,
all the land, and cities, and territories round about.

The children of Gad built Dibon, and Ataroth, and Aroer, 32:34
and Atroth, and Shophan, and Jaazer, and Jogbehah, 32:35
and Beth-Nimrah, and Beth-Haran—fenced cities, and folds for sheep. 32:36
The children of Reuben built Heshbon, and Elealeh, and Kirjathaim, 32:37
and Nebo, and Baal-Meon—whose names they changed—and Shibmah. 32:38
And they gave other names to the cities they built.

The children of Machir the son of Manasseh went to Gilead, 32:39
and took it, and dispossessed the Amorites who were there.

Moses gave Gilead to Machir the son of Manasseh, and he dwelt there. 32:40
Jair the son of Manasseh took the small towns 32:41
around Gilead and called them Havoth-Jair.

Nobah took Kenath and its villages. He called it Nobah, after his name. 32:42

Chapter 33

These are the journeys of the Israelites, who went forth out of the land 33:1
of Egypt with their armies, under the hand of Moses and Aaron.

Moses recorded the stages of their journeys, according to the 33:2
commandment of Yahweh. These are the stages of their journeys:

They departed from Rameses in the first month, on the fifteenth day 33:3
of the month. The day after the Passover the Israelites went out
with a high hand in the sight of all Egyptians.

For the Egyptians had buried all their firstborn, which Yahweh had killed. 33:4
Yahweh had also executed judgments upon their gods.

The children of Israel left Rameses and pitched in Succoth. 33:5
They departed from Succoth and pitched in Etham, 33:6
which is on the edge of the wilderness.

They removed from Etham and turned again unto Pi-Hahiroth, 33:7
which is before Baal-Zephon, and they pitched before Migdol.

They departed from Pi-Hahiroth, and passed through the midst 33:8
of the sea into the wilderness. They journeyed three days
in the wilderness of Etham, then pitched in Marah.

They removed from Marah, and came unto Elim. In Elim were 33:9
twelve fountains of water and seventy palm trees. They pitched there.

They removed from Elim and encamped by the Red Sea. 33:10

They removed from the Red Sea and encamped in the wilderness of Sin. 33:11
They journeyed out of the wilderness of Sin and encamped in Dophkah. 33:12
They departed from Dophkah and encamped in Alush. 33:13
They removed from Alush and encamped at Rephidim, 33:14
where there was no water for the people to drink.

They departed from Rephidim and pitched in the wilderness of Sinai. 33:15
They removed from the desert of Sinai and pitched at Kibroth-Hattaavah. 33:16
They departed from Kibroth-Hattaavah and encamped at Hazeroth. 33:17

They departed from Hazeroth and pitched in Rithmah. 33:18
They departed from Rithmah and pitched at Rimmon-Parez. 33:19
They departed from Rimmon-Parez and pitched in Libnah. 33:20
They removed from Libnah and pitched at Rissah. 33:21
They journeyed from Rissah and pitched in Kehelathah. 33:22
They went from Kehelathah and pitched in Mount Shapher. 33:23
They removed from Mount Shapher and encamped in Haradah. 33:24
They removed from Haradah and pitched in Makheloth. 33:25
They removed from Makheloth and encamped at Tahath. 33:26
They departed from Tahath and pitched at Tarah. 33:27
They removed from Tarah and pitched in Mithcah. 33:28
They went from Mithcah and pitched in Hashmonah. 33:29
They departed from Hashmonah and encamped at Moseroth. 33:30
They departed from Moseroth and pitched in Bene-Jaakan. 33:31
They removed from Bene-Jaakan and encamped at Hor-Hagidgad. 33:32
They went from Hor-Hagidgad and pitched in Jotbathah. 33:33
They removed from Jotbathah and encamped at Ebronah. 33:34
They departed from Ebronah and encamped at Ezion-Gaber. 33:35
They removed from Ezion-Gaber and pitched 33:36
in the wilderness of Zin, which is Kadesh.

They removed from Kadesh, and pitched in Mount Hor, 33:37
on the edge of the land of Edom.
Aaron the priest went up Mount Hor at the commandment of Yahweh 33:38
and died there, in the fortieth year after the Israelites came out of Egypt.
Aaron was 123 years old when he died on Mount Hor. 33:39
King Arad the Canaanite, who dwelt in the south of the land of Canaan, 33:40
heard of the coming of the Israelites.
They departed from Mount Hor and pitched in Zalmonah. 33:41
They departed from Zalmonah and pitched in Punon. 33:42
They departed from Punon and pitched in Oboth. 33:43
They departed from Oboth and pitched in Ije-Abarim, 33:44
on the border of Moab.
They departed from Ije-Abarim and pitched in Dibon-Gad. 33:45
They removed from Dibon-Gad and encamped in Almon-Diblathaim. 33:46
They removed from Almon-Diblathaim and pitched 33:47
in the mountains of Abarim, before Nebo.
They departed from the mountains of Abarim 33:48
and pitched in the plains of Moab, by Jordan, near Jericho.
They pitched by Jordan, from Beth-Jesimoth to as far as 33:49
Abel-Shittim in the plains of Moab.

Yahweh spoke to Moses on the plains of Moab, telling him to 33:50
speak to the children of Israel, and say to them, 33:51
"When you have passed over Jordan into the land of Canaan,
you shall drive out all the inhabitants of the land from before you, 33:52
and you shall destroy all their pictures and their molten images,
and tear down all their high places.
You shall dispossess the inhabitants of the land, and dwell there, 33:53

for I have given you the land to possess it.

You shall divide the land by lot for an inheritance among your families.   33:54
To the more, you shall give more inheritance, and to the fewer you shall
give less inheritance. Every man's inheritance shall be in the place where
his lot falls. According to the tribes of your fathers, you shall inherit.
If you do not drive out the inhabitants of the land from before you, then it   33:55
shall come to pass that those you let remain shall be pricks in your eyes
and thorns in your sides, and shall vex you in the land wherein you dwell.
Moreover, I shall do unto you as I intended you do unto them."   33:56

Chapter 34

Yahweh spoke to Moses, telling him to   34:1
command the children of Israel, and say to them,   34:2
"When you come into the land of Canaan—the land that is your
inheritance, the land within the borders of Canaan—
your southern boundary shall be from the wilderness of Zin along   34:3
the border of Edom, eastward to the outermost coast of the Dead Sea.
Your border shall go from there to the slopes of Akrabbim,   34:4
and pass on to Zin. Going forth, it shall be from the south
of Kadesh-Barnea, then to Hazar-Addar, and pass on to Azmon.
The border shall go round from Azmon to the river of Egypt,   34:5
and follow it to the Mediterranean Sea.
Your western border shall be the Mediterranean Sea.   34:6
The Great Sea shall be your western limits.
From the Great Sea your boundary shall be unto Mount Hor.   34:7
This shall be your northern border.
From Mount Hor your border is in the direction of Hamath, unto Zedad.   34:8
The border shall go on to Ziphron, and end at Hazar-Enan.   34:9
This shall be your northern border.
You shall mark your east border from Hazar-Enan to Shepham,   34:10
and from Shepham to Riblah, on the east side of Ain. The border   34:11
shall descend eastward from there unto the Sea of Chinnereth.
The border shall then go down to Jordan, and end at the Dead Sea.   34:12
These shall be the boundaries of your land."

Moses commanded the children of Israel, saying,   34:13
"This is the land you shall inherit by lot, which Yahweh
commanded to give to the nine tribes, and to the half-tribe.
The tribe of Reuben, and the tribe of Gad, and the half-tribe   34:14
of Manasseh have received their inheritance.
These two tribes and the half-tribe have received their inheritance   34:15
on this side of Jordan, near Jericho eastward, toward the rising sun."
Yahweh spoke to Moses, saying,   34:16
"These are the names of the men who shall divide the land unto you: 34:17
Eleazar the priest, and Joshua the son of Nun.
You shall take one prince of every tribe, to divide the land by inheritance.   34:18
These are the names of those men: 34:19
The prince of the tribe of Judah, Caleb the son of Jephunneh.

The prince of the tribe of Simeon, Shemuel the son of Ammihud.	34:20
The prince of the tribe of Benjamin, Elidad the son of Chislon.	34:21
The prince of the tribe of Dan, Bukki the son of Jogli.	34:22
The prince of the tribe of Joseph, for the other half-tribe of Manasseh, Hanniel the son of Ephod.	34:23
The prince of the tribe of Ephraim, Kemuel the son of Shiphtan.	34:24
The prince of the tribe of Zebulun, Elizaphan the son of Parnach.	34:25
The prince of the tribe of Issachar, Paltiel the son of Azzan.	34:26
The prince of the tribe of Asher, Ahihud the son of Shelomi.	34:27
The prince of the tribe of Naphtali, Pedahel the son of Ammihud.	34:28
These are they whom Yahweh commanded to divide the inheritance unto the children of Israel in the land of Canaan.	34:29

Chapter 35

Yahweh spoke unto Moses on the plains of Moab by Jordan, saying, 35:1
"Command the Israelites to give the Levites, from their inheritance, 35:2
cities to dwell in. They shall also give the Levites land around the cities.
The Levites shall dwell in the cities, and the surrounding land 35:3
shall be for their cattle, and for their goods, and for all their beasts.
The land around the cities, which you shall give to the Levites, 35:4
shall reach a thousand cubits from the wall of the city outward.
You shall measure from without the city on the east side two thousand 35:5
cubits, and on the south side two thousand cubits, and on the west side
two thousand cubits, and on the north side two thousand cubits.
This shall be the land of the city. The city shall be in the middle.
Among the cities you shall give to the Levites, there shall be six cities 35:6
for refuge, to which a manslayer may flee, and forty-two other cities.
So all the cities you shall give to the Levites 35:7
shall be forty-eight cities, along with their surrounding lands.
The cities you give shall be from the possession of the Israelites. 35:8
From them who have many, you shall give many. From them
who have few, you shall give few. Everyone shall give
of his cities unto the Levites according to his inheritance."

Yahweh spoke unto Moses, telling him to 35:9
speak to the children of Israel, and say to them, 35:10
"When you come over Jordan into the land of Canaan,
you shall have cities of refuge, where one who kills by accident may flee. 35:11
They shall be for you cities of refuge from the avenger, that the manslayer 35:12
is not killed before he stands before the congregation in judgment.
You shall have six cities for refuge, 35:13
three cities on this side of Jordan, and three cities in the land of Canaan. 35:14
These six cities shall be a refuge, both for the Israelites and for the 35:15
stranger, that anyone who kills a person accidentally may flee there.
If he strikes him with an instrument of iron so that he dies, 35:16
he is a murderer, and a murderer shall surely be put to death.
If he strikes him with a thrown stone so that he dies, he is a murderer, 35:17
and a murderer shall surely be put to death.

If he strikes him with a hand weapon of wood so that he dies,   35:18
he is a murderer, and a murderer shall surely be put to death.

"The avenger of blood himself shall slay the murderer.   35:19
When he meets him, he shall slay him.
If in hatred someone thrusts a man with his sword,   35:20
or lays in wait and hurls a stone or spear, causing his death,
or in enmity strikes him with his hand and kills him,   35:21
he who kills him shall surely be put to death, for he is a murderer.
The avenger of blood shall slay the murderer when he meets him.
But if he thrusts him suddenly without enmity,   35:22
or hurls upon him anything without laying in wait,
or seeing him not casts upon him a stone, and he dies,   35:23
though he was not his enemy, and neither did he seek to harm him,
then the congregation shall judge between the slayer   35:24
and the avenger of blood according to these factors.
The congregation shall deliver the slayer from the hands of the avenger,   35:25
and restore him to the city of refuge where he fled, and he shall abide
there until the death of the high priest who was anointed with holy oil.
But if the slayer at any time comes outside the border of the refuge city,   35:26
and the avenger of blood finds him outside the city of his refuge,   35:27
and kills the slayer, the avenger shall not be guilty of blood.
Because he should have remained in the city of his refuge until   35:28
the death of the high priest. After the death of the high priest,
the slayer can return to the land of his possession.
These things shall be a statute of judgment unto you,   35:29
throughout your generations, in all your dwellings.

"Anyone who kills another person shall be put to death by the word   35:30
of witnesses, but one witness alone is not enough to cause his death.
You shall take no satisfaction for the killing of a person   35:31
who is guilty of murder, but he shall be surely put to death.
You shall take no satisfaction for him who flees to the city of his refuge,   35:32
that he should again dwell in the land before the death of the priest.
You shall not pollute the land wherein you abide, for blood defiles   35:33
the land. The land cannot be cleansed of the blood shed upon it,
except by the blood of him who shed it.
Therefore, do not defile the land you shall inhabit, wherein I dwell.   35:34
I am Yahweh, who dwells among the children of Israel."

Chapter 36

The chiefs of the families of Gilead, son of Machir and grandson   36:1
of Manasseh, and of the families of Joseph, came near
and spoke to Moses, before the other chiefs of the Israelites.
They said, "Yahweh commanded my lord to give the land for an   36:2
inheritance by lot to the children of Israel, and my lord was commanded
by Yahweh to give the inheritance of Zelophehad unto his daughters.
But if they marry any of the sons of the other tribes of the Israelites,   36:3

shall their inheritance be taken from the inheritance of our fathers,
and put to the inheritance of the tribe into which they marry?
And in the Jubilee year, shall their inheritance be put into
the inheritance of the tribe of their marriage, and so be taken
from the inheritance of the tribe of our fathers?"

Moses commanded the children of Israel according to the word
of Yahweh, saying, "The tribe of the sons of Joseph has said well.
This is what Yahweh commands concerning the daughters of Zelophehad:
'Let them marry whomever they think best, but only
within the family of the tribe of their father shall they marry.
No inheritance of the Israelites shall move from tribe to tribe. Every
Israelite shall keep for himself the inheritance of the tribe of his fathers.
Every daughter who possesses an inheritance in any tribe of Israel,
shall be wife unto one of the family of the tribe of her father,
that every man of Israel may enjoy the inheritance of his fathers.
The inheritance shall not move from one tribe to another.
Every tribe of Israel shall keep to its own inheritance.'"

As Yahweh commanded Moses, so did the daughters of Zelophehad do.
Mahlal, Tirzah, Hoglah, Milcah and Noah, the daughters of Zelophehad,
were married unto their father's brothers' sons.
They were married into the families of Manasseh, the son of Joseph,
and their inheritance remained in the tribe of their father.
These are the commandments and the judgments that Yahweh
commanded by the hand of Moses unto the children of Israel,
in the plains of Moab, by Jordan, near Jericho.

The Fifth Book of Moses Called
Deuteronomy

Chapter 1

These are the words Moses spoke to all of Israel in the wilderness	1:1

These are the words Moses spoke to all of Israel in the wilderness beside Jordan, in the plain against the Red Sea,
between Paran, Tophel, Laban, Hazeroth and Dizahab.
It is eleven days' journey from Horeb to Kadesh by way of Mount Seir.   1:2
And it came to pass in the fortieth year, in the eleventh month,   1:3
on the first day of the month, that Moses spoke
to the Israelites all that Yahweh had commanded them,
after he had slain Sihon the king of the Amorites, who dwelt in Heshbon,   1:4
and Og the king of Bashan, who dwelt at Astaroth in Edrei.
Beside Jordan, in the land of Moab, Moses declared to them,   1:5
"Yahweh, our God, spoke unto us in Horeb, saying,   1:6
'You have dwelt long enough in these mountains.
Journey to the mountains of the Amorites, and to all places therein—   1:7
the plains, and hills, and valleys—to the south, and to the sea, and to
the land of the Canaanites, and to Lebanon and the great river Euphrates.
I have set the land before you. Go possess the land Yahweh swore to your   1:8
fathers, Abraham, Isaac and Jacob, to give to them and their descendants.'

"I spoke to you at that time, saying, 'I am not able to carry you alone.   1:9
Yahweh has multiplied you, and you are as many as the stars of heaven—   1:10
and may Yahweh, God of your fathers, make you a thousand times   1:11
as many more, and bless you as he has promised!
But how can I bear your cumbrance, your burden, and your strife alone?   1:12
Choose wise men of understanding, respected among your tribes,   1:13
and I will make them your leaders.'
You answered me, saying 'What you have spoken is good for us to do.'   1:14
So I took men of your tribes who are wise and respected, and made them   1:15
chiefs over you—captains over thousands, captains over hundreds,
captains over fifties, and captains over tens—officers among your tribes.
I charged your judges at that time to hear the causes between   1:16
your brethren, and judge righteously between every man
and his brother, and the strangers who are among you.
Do not respect the persons in judgment, but hear the small as well as   1:17
the great. Do not fear the face of a man, for the judgment is God's.
If the cause is too hard for you, bring it to me, and I will hear it.
I commanded you at that time all the things you should do.   1:18

"When we departed from Horeb, as Yahweh commanded us, we went   1:19
through that great and terrible wilderness, which you saw on the way
to the mountains of the Amorites, and we came to Kadesh-Barnea.
And I said to you then, 'You have come unto the mountain   1:20

of the Amorites, which Yahweh our God gives to us.
Yahweh has set the land before you. Go and possess it, as Yahweh,   1:21
God of your fathers, has said unto you. Do not be afraid or discouraged.'
And you came near unto me, every one of you, and said,   1:22
'We will send men before us to explore the land, and bring us word
about which way we should go, and what cities we will come unto.'
The idea seemed good, so I sent twelve men, one from each tribe.   1:23
They went into the mountains and the valley of Eshcol, and searched.   1:24
They took of the fruit of the land, and brought it back us, and said,   1:25
'It is a good land that Yahweh our God gives to us.'
But you would not go. You rebelled against Yahweh.   1:26
You murmured, saying, 'Because Yahweh hated us, he brought us   1:27
out of Egypt to deliver us into the hands of the Amorites and destroy us.
What shall we do? Our brethren have discouraged our hearts, saying   1:28
"The people are bigger and stronger than we. Their cities are great and
walled up to heaven, and we have seen the sons of the Anakims there."'

"Then I said to you, 'Do not be fearful. Do not be afraid of them.   1:29
Yahweh shall go before you, and he shall fight for you,   1:30
just as you saw him do for you in Egypt, and in the wilderness.
You have seen how Yahweh carries you like a man carries his son,   1:31
in all your journeys, until you have come to this very place.'
Yet for all this, you did not believe in Yahweh your God,   1:32
who went before you—in a cloud by day and in fire by night—to search   1:33
out a place for you to pitch your tents, and to show you which way to go.
And Yahweh heard your words, and became angry, and swore an oath: 1:34
'No man of this evil generation shall see the land I swore to their fathers, 1:35
save Caleb, son of Jephunneh. He shall see it. To him I will give the land he 1:36
trod upon, and to his children, because he has wholly followed Yahweh.'

"Yahweh was angry with me because of you, saying, 'Moses shall not go in.   1:37
But Joshua the son of Nun, who stands before you, he shall go in   1:38
before you. Strengthen him, for he shall cause Israel to inherit.
Moreover, your little ones, who you feared would become prey,   1:39
and your children, who on that day had no knowledge of good and evil,
they shall go in, and to them will I give the land, and they shall possess it.
But as for you, go back into the wilderness by the way of the Red Sea.'   1:40
Then you answered and said to me, 'We have sinned against Yahweh.   1:41
We will go and fight, according to all that Yahweh commanded us.'
And you girded on your weapons, and were ready to go to war.
But Yahweh said to me, 'Tell them not to go, lest they be destroyed   1:42
by their enemies, for I will not be with them.'
So I spoke to you, but you would not hear. You rebelled against the   1:43
commandment of Yahweh, and went presumptuously up into the hills.
And the Amorites who dwelt there came out against you, and destroyed   1:44
you in Seir, and chased you, as bees do, all the way to Hormah.
You returned and wept before Yahweh. But Yahweh   1:45
would not hearken unto your voice, nor give ear unto you.
So you abided in Kadesh for many days."   1:46

226

Chapter 2

"Then we journeyed into the wilderness by the way of the Red Sea,   2:1
as Yahweh told me, and travelled around Mount Seir for many days.
Yahweh spoke to me, saying,   2:2
'You have compassed this mountain long enough. Turn northward,   2:3
and command the people, saying, "You are about to pass through   2:4
the land of your brethren, the children of Esau, who dwell in Seir.
They will be afraid of you, so take care how you act.
Do not meddle with them. I will not give you any of their land—not so   2:5
much as a foot's width. I have given Mount Seir to Esau for a possession.
You shall buy food from them so that you may eat,   2:6
and buy water from them so you may drink.
Yahweh has blessed you in all the works of your hand. He knows   2:7
you have walked through this great wilderness these forty years.
Yahweh has been with you. You have lacked nothing.'

"So we passed by our brethren, the children of Esau,   2:8
who dwelt in Seir, by way of the plain from Elath and Ezion-Gaber.
Then we passed by the way of the wilderness of Moab.
Yahweh said to me, 'Do not trouble the Moabites, nor contend   2:9
with them in battle, for I will not give you any of their land.
I have given Ar unto the children of Lot for a possession.
The Emims dwelt there in times past,   2:10
a great and numerous people, and as tall as the Anakims.
They were giants like the Anakims, but the Moabites call them Emims.   2:11
The Horims also dwelt in Seir in the past, but the children of Esau   2:12
destroyed them, and dwelt there in their stead—as Israel did
unto the land of his possession, which Yahweh gave unto them.
Now rise up and cross over the Zered ravine!'   2:13
And we crossed over the Zered ravine.

"The time between our leaving of Kadesh-Barnea until we crossed   2:14
over the Zered ravine lasted thirty-eight years—until all the generation
of men who first explored Canaan had died, as Yahweh swore unto them.
For the hand of Yahweh was indeed against them,   2:15
destroying them from among the host until all were consumed.
When all the men who explored were dead,   2:16
Yahweh spoke to me, saying,   2:17
'Today you shall pass through Ar, on the border of Moab.   2:18
When you come near the Ammonites, do not trouble them or contend   2:19
with them in battle, for I will not give you any of their land.
I have given it unto the children of Lot for a possession.
This also was a land of giants in the past.   2:20
The Ammonites call them Zamzummims.
They were a great and numerous people, and as tall as the Anakims.   2:21
But Yahweh destroyed them, and the Ammonites succeeded them,
just as he did with the children of Esau, who now dwell in Seir.   2:22
He destroyed the Horims, and the children of Esau dwell there to this day.

The Avims who dwelt in Hazerim as far as Azzah, were destroyed by the   2:23
Caphtorims, who came forth out of Caphtor to dwell there in their stead.

"'Now rise up and cross the river Arnon! I have given into your hand   2:24
Sihon the Amorite, king of Heshbon, and all his land.
Contend with him in battle and take possession of it!
From now on I will make all nations under heaven fear you, and dread   2:25
your coming. Whoever hears news of you shall tremble and shake.'
So I sent messengers out of the wilderness of Kedemoth   2:26
unto Sihon, king of Heshbon, with words of peace, saying,
'Let us pass through your land. We will go along by the highway,   2:27
turning neither turn right nor left.
Sell us food, that we may eat, and sell us water   2:28
that we may drink. Only let us pass through on foot,
as the children of Esau in Seir, and the Moabites in Ar, did for us.   2:29
Let us pass over Jordan into the land that Yahweh our God gives us.'

"But Sihon king of Heshbon would not let us pass through,   2:30
for Yahweh hardened his spirit, and made his heart obstinate,
so that we might defeat him and take his land, as has come to pass.
Yahweh said to me, 'Behold, I have already begun to give Sihon   2:31
and his land to you. Take possession of it, that you may inherit his land.'
Then Sihon came out against us, he and all his people, to fight at Jahaz.   2:32
And Yahweh delivered him unto us, and we destroyed him,   2:33
and his sons, and all his people.
We took all his cities, and utterly destroyed the men,   2:34
women and children of every city. We left none alive.
The cattle we took for as prey for ourselves,   2:35
and we took the spoil of the cities we conquered.
From Aroer on the banks of the river of Arnon, as far as Gilead,   2:36
there was no city too strong for us. Yahweh delivered all unto us.
But we did not go into the land of the Ammonites, nor into any place   2:37
near the river Jabbok, nor into the cities in the mountains,
nor anywhere else Yahweh our God forbade us to enter."

Chapter 3

"Then we turned, and went up the way to Bashan. Og the king of   3:1
Bashan came out against us, he and all his people, to battle at Edrei.
Yahweh said to me, 'Do not fear him. I will deliver him, and all his people,   3:2
and his land into your hand, and you shall do to him as you
did to Sihon king of the Amorites, who dwelt at Heshbon.'
So Yahweh also delivered into our hands Og the king of Bashan   3:3
and all his people, and we destroyed them until none were left alive.
And we took all his cities. There was not a city we did not take from   3:4
them—sixty cities—the entire region of Argob, kingdom of Og in Bashan.
All these cities were fenced with high walls, gates and bars.   3:5
We also took a great many unwalled towns.
We utterly destroyed them, as we did to Sihon, king of Heshbon.   3:6

We utterly destroyed the men, women and children of every city.

All the cattle and the spoil of the cities, we took as booty for ourselves. 3:7

We took all the land on this side of Jordan—from the river of Arnon to 3:8
Mount Hermon—out of the hands of the two kings of the Amorites.

Hermon is called Sirion by the Sidonians. The Amorites call it Shenir. 3:9

We took all the cities of the plains, and of all Gilead, and of all Bashan 3:10
unto Salchah and Edrei—all the cities of the kingdom of Og in Bashan.

"Og king of Bashan was the last of the giants. His bedstead 3:11
was made of iron. It was nine cubits long and four cubits wide.
It remains in the Ammonite city of Rabbath.

The land we took then—Aroer by the river Arnon, and half Mount Gilead, 3:12
and all their cities—I gave to the Reubenites and to the Gadites.

The rest of Gilead, and all of Bashan, the kingdom of Og, 3:13
I gave to the half-tribe of Manasseh—all the region of Argob,
and all Bashan, which was called the land of giants.

Jair, son of Manasseh took all the country of Argob unto Geshuri 3:14
and Maachathi, and called it Bashan-Havoth-Jair, after his name.

I gave Gilead to Machir. 3:15

To the Reubenites and to the Gadites I gave the land from Gilead to the 3:16
river Arnon—half the valley, with mid-river as boundary—all the way
to the river Jabbok, which is the border of the Ammonites,

and also the plain unto Jordan, from Chinnereth to the Dead Sea, 3:17
along the mountains of Ashdoth-Pisgah eastward.

"I commanded you at that time, saying, 'Yahweh has given you this land 3:18
to possess. Your armed men, all that are fit for war, shall cross
over before your brethren, the children of Israel.

Your wives, your little ones, and your cattle—I know you 3:19
have many cattle—shall remain in the cities I have given you,

until Yahweh gives rest to your armed brothers, as well as to you, 3:20
after they possess the land Yahweh has given them beyond Jordan.
Then every man shall return unto his possession, which I have given you.'

I commanded Joshua at that time, saying, 'Your eyes have seen 3:21
all that Yahweh has done unto these two kings.
So shall Yahweh do unto all the kingdoms in your path.

Do not fear them, for Yahweh shall fight for you.' 3:22

"Then I beseeched Yahweh, saying, 3:23

'O Lord God, you have begun to show your servant your greatness 3:24
and your mighty hand. For what God is there in heaven or on earth,
that can do according to your works, and according to your might?

I pray you, let me go over, and see the good land 3:25
that is beyond Jordan, that good mountain, and Lebanon.'

But Yahweh was angry with me because of you, and would not hear me. 3:26
He said to me, 'That's enough! Speak no more to me of this matter.

Go to the top of Pisgah and lift up your eyes westward, and northward, 3:27
and southward, and eastward, and behold the land with your eyes.
For you shall not go over Jordan.

Charge Joshua, and encourage him, and strengthen him. He shall go over 3:28
before this people, and he shall cause them to inherit the land you see.'
So we abode in the valley near Beth-Peor." 3:29

Chapter 4

"Hearken, O Israel, unto the laws and judgments I teach you, and do them, 4:1
that you may live, and go in and possess the land Yahweh gives to you.
You shall not add unto the words I command you, nor shall you 4:2
take from them, that you may keep the commandments of Yahweh.
Your eyes have seen what Yahweh did because of Baal-Peor. 4:3
Yahweh destroyed all the men who followed Baal-Peor.
But you who stayed true to Yahweh are alive today, every one of you. 4:4
I have taught you laws and judgments, as Yahweh commanded me, 4:5
that you should keep them in the land you go to possess.
Therefore keep them, and do them, for this is your wisdom and your 4:6
understanding in the eyes of other nations, which shall hear these laws,
and say, 'Surely this great nation is a wise and understanding people.'
For what nation is there so great, who has its God so near to them, 4:7
as is Yahweh, our God, when we call upon him?
What nation is there so great, that has statutes and judgments 4:8
so righteous as all this law I set before you this day?

"But take heed, and keep your soul diligently, all the days of your life, 4:9
lest you forget the things you have seen, lest they depart from your heart.
Teach them to your sons, and your sons' sons.
Remember the day you stood before Yahweh your God in Horeb, 4:10
when Yahweh said to me, 'Gather the people together and I will make
them hear my words, that they may learn to fear me all the days
they shall live upon the earth, and that they may teach their children.'
And you came near and stood under the mountain, and the mountain 4:11
burned with fire unto the midst of heaven, with clouds and thick darkness.
And Yahweh spoke to you out of the midst of the fire. 4:12
You heard the words, but saw no form. You only heard a voice.
He declared unto you his covenant, which he commanded you to obey, 4:13
and upon two tablets of stone he wrote his ten commandments.
Yahweh commanded me to teach you statutes and judgments, 4:14
that you might do them in the land you go to possess.

"Therefore take good heed for yourselves. You saw no form 4:15
on the day Yahweh spoke to you in Horeb out of the midst of the fire,
therefore do not corrupt yourselves by making a graven image, 4:16
or the form of any figure, or the likeness of a male or female,
or the likeness of any beast on earth, 4:17
or the likeness of any winged fowl that flies in the air,
or the likeness of anything that creeps on the ground, 4:18
or the likeness of any fish in the waters.
And when you lift up your eyes to heaven, and you see the sun, 4:19
and the moon, and the stars, and all the hosts of heaven,

do not worship them and serve them, for God has given
these equally to all the nations under the whole of heaven.
Yahweh has brought you forth out of the iron furnace, out of Egypt,   4:20
to be unto him a people of inheritance, as you are this day.

"Yahweh was angry with me because of you, and swore that I should   4:21
not go over Jordan, that I should not go into that good land he gives you.
I must die in this land. I must not go over Jordan.   4:22
But you shall go over, and possess that good land.
Take heed unto yourself, lest you forget the covenant   4:23
Yahweh made with you, and make for yourself a graven image,
or the likeness of anything—which Yahweh has forbidden you.
Yahweh is a consuming fire, a jealous God.   4:24
When you have begat children, and children's children,   4:25
and have remained long in the land, then corrupt yourselves
by making a graven image or the likeness of anything,
thus doing evil in the sight of Yahweh and provoking him to anger,
I call upon heaven and earth this day to witness against you,   4:26
that you shall soon perish from the land over Jordan. Your days
shall not be prolonged upon it, but you shall be utterly destroyed.
And Yahweh shall scatter you among the nations, and you shall be   4:27
left few in number among the heathen, where Yahweh shall lead you.
There you shall serve gods that are the work of men's hands,   4:28
of wood and stone, that neither see, nor hear, nor eat, nor smell.

"But if from there you seek Yahweh your God, you shall find him—   4:29
if you seek him with all your heart, and with all your soul.
When you are in tribulation, and all these things come upon you   4:30
in the latter days, turn to Yahweh your God, and be obedient to his voice.
Yahweh is a merciful God. He will not forsake you, nor destroy you,   4:31
nor forget the covenant of your fathers that he swore unto them.
Think of the days past, that were before you—since the day God created   4:32
man upon the earth—and ask from one side of heaven to the other if
there has ever been anything like this greatness, or even heard of before?
Did a people ever hear the voice of God speaking   4:33
out of the midst of fire, as you have heard, and live?
Has any God ever taken a nation from the midst of another nation   4:34
by signs, and wonders, and temptations, and war—
by a mighty hand and great terrors, with an outstretched arm—
as Yahweh did for you in Egypt before your very eyes?

"Unto you this was shown, that you might know Yahweh is God.   4:35
There is none else beside him.
Out of heaven he made you hear his voice,   4:36
that he might instruct you. Upon earth he showed you
his great fire, and out of the midst of the fire you heard his words.
Because he loved your fathers, he chose their seed after them,   4:37
and brought you out of Egypt with his power,
to drive out nations greater and mightier than you, to bring you in,   4:38

and to give you their land for an inheritance, as it is this day.
Remember therefore this day, and know in your heart that Yahweh 4:39
is God—in heaven above, and upon the earth below. There is none else.
Therefore keep his statutes and his commandments, which I command 4:40
you this day, that it may go well with you, and with your children, and that
you may prolong your days upon the earth, which God gives you, forever."

Then Moses set aside three cities on this side Jordan toward the east, 4:41
that a manslayer might flee to if he should kill his neighbor accidentally, 4:42
whom he did not hate, and by fleeing to one of these cities he might live.
These were: Bezer in the plains of the Reubenites; Ramoth in Gilead 4:43
of the Gadites; and Golan in Bashan of the Manassites.
This is the law Moses set before the Israelites. 4:44
These are the testimonies, the statutes, and the judgments Moses 4:45
spoke unto the children of Israel after they came forth out of Egypt,
on this side of Jordan, in the valley against Beth-Peor, 4:46
in the land of Sihon king of the Amorites who dwelt at Heshbon,
and whom Moses and the children of Israel destroyed.
And they possessed his land, and the land of Og king of Bashan— 4:47
two kings of the Amorites that were on this side Jordan toward the east—
from Aroer on the bank of the river Arnon, to Mount Sion, 4:48
and all the plain on this side of Jordan eastward, 4:49
even unto the Dead Sea beneath the slopes of Mount Pisgah.

Chapter 5

Moses called all Israel, and said unto them, 5:1
"Hear, O Israel, the statutes and judgments I speak in your ears
this day, that you may learn them, and keep, and do them.
Yahweh our God made a covenant with us in Horeb. 5:2
Yahweh did not make this covenant with our fathers, 5:3
but with us, even us, all of us who are alive here this day.
Yahweh talked with you face-to-face on the mount, out of the midst of fire. 5:4
I stood between you and Yahweh, for you were afraid of the fire. 5:5
At that time, Yahweh said,
'I am Yahweh, that brought you out of Egypt, from the house of bondage. 5:6
You shall have no other gods before me. 5:7
You shall not make any graven image, or any likeness of anything 5:8
in heaven above, or on earth below, or in the waters of the earth.
You shall not bow down to them, nor serve them. For I, Yahweh, 5:9
am a jealous God, visiting the iniquity of the fathers upon the children
unto the third and fourth generation of those who hate me,
and showing mercy to thousands of those who love me 5:10
and keep my commandments.

"'You shall not take the name of Yahweh, your God, in vain. 5:11
Yahweh will not hold him guiltless who takes his name in vain.
Keep the sabbath day to sanctify it, as Yahweh your God has commanded. 5:12
For six days you shall labor, and do all your work. 5:13

But the seventh day is the sabbath of Yahweh your God. On that day | 5:14
you shall not do any work—not you, nor your son, nor your daughter,
nor your manservant, nor your maidservant, nor your ox, nor your ass,
nor any of your cattle, nor the stranger who is within your gates—
that all these may rest as well as you.
Remember that you were a servant in the land of Egypt, and that Yahweh | 5:15
your God brought you out by a mighty hand and with outstretched arms.
Therefore Yahweh commanded you to keep the sabbath day.
Honor your father and your mother, as Yahweh has commanded you, that | 5:16
your days may be many, and that it may go well with you
in the land Yahweh gives you.
You shall not kill. | 5:17
You shall not commit adultery. | 5:18
You shall not steal. | 5:19
You shall not bear false witness against your neighbor. | 5:20
You shall not desire your neighbor's wife, nor shall you covet your | 5:21
neighbor's house, or his field, or his manservant, or his maidservant,
or his ox, or his ass, or anything belonging to your neighbor.'

"With a great voice Yahweh spoke these words to all your assembly, | 5:22
out of the midst of fire, out of the cloud and the thick darkness.
Then he said no more. He wrote these words on two tablets of stone,
and delivered them unto me.
When you heard the voice out of the midst of the darkness— | 5:23
for the mountain did burn with fire— your elders
and all the heads of your tribes came near unto me,
and said, 'Yahweh our God has shown us his glory and his greatness. | 5:24
We have heard his voice out of the midst of the fire. We have seen
this day that God does talk with man, and that man may yet live.
But why should we risk death again? This great fire shall consume us. | 5:25
If we anymore hear the voice of Yahweh our God, we shall die.
Who is there among all flesh, who has heard the voice of a living God | 5:26
speak out of the midst of fire, as we have, and lived?
Moses, you shall go near and hear all that Yahweh our God speaks, | 5:27
then tell us all that he says. We will hear it, and do it.'

"Yahweh heard your words and said unto me, 'I have heard the voice | 5:28
of this people, the words they have spoken to you. They have said well.
O that there were such heart in them that they would fear me, | 5:29
and always keep my commandments, that it might
be well with them, and with their children, forever!
Tell them to go back to their tents. | 5:30
You stand here by me, and I will speak unto you all the commandments, | 5:31
and the statutes, and the judgments, which you shall teach them,
that they may do them in the land I give them to possess.
Be careful to do exactly as Yahweh your God commands you. | 5:32
Do not turn aside to the right or to the left.
Walk in the way Yahweh commands you, that you may live, and that it | 5:33
may be well with you, and that your days be many in the land I give you.'"

Chapter 6

"These are the commandments, statutes and judgments Yahweh   6:1
commanded I teach you, that you might do them in the land you go to,
that you might fear Yahweh your God, and keep all his statutes   6:2
and commandments—you, and your son, and your son's son—
all the days of your life, and that your days may be prolonged.
Hear therefore, O Israel, and be careful to do them, that it may be well   6:3
with you, and that you may increase mightily in the land that flows with
milk and honey, as Yahweh, God of your fathers, has promised you.
Hear, O Israel: Yahweh your God is one God.   6:4
You shall love Yahweh your God with all your heart,   6:5
and with all your soul, and with all your might.
These words, which I command you this day, shall be in your heart.   6:6
You shall teach them diligently to your children, and you shall talk   6:7
of them when you sit in your house, and when you walk by the way,
and when you lie down, and when you rise up.
You shall bind them for a sign upon your hand,   6:8
and wear them on the bands upon your foreheads.
You shall write them on the posts of your houses, and on your gates.   6:9

"When Yahweh brings you into the land he swore unto your fathers,   6:10
to Abraham, Isaac and Jacob, and gives you great cities you did not build,
and houses full of good things you did not make, and wells you did not dig,   6:11
and vineyards and olive trees you did not plant,
and when you have eaten and are full,
beware, lest you forget Yahweh, who brought you forth   6:12
out of the land of Egypt, out from the house of bondage.
You shall fear Yahweh your God, and serve him, and swear by his name.   6:13
You shall not go after other gods, the gods of the people around you,   6:14
lest the anger of Yahweh be kindled against you, and remove you   6:15
from the face of the earth. For Yahweh your God is a jealous God.
You shall not tempt Yahweh your God, as you tempted him in Massah.   6:16
You shall diligently keep the commandments of Yahweh your God,   6:17
and his testimonies, and his statutes, which he has commanded you.
You shall do what is right and good in the sight of Yahweh,   6:18
that it may be well with you, and that you may possess
the good land Yahweh swore unto your fathers,
and cast out all your enemies from before you, as Yahweh has spoken.   6:19

"When your son asks you in times to come, 'What is the meaning of all   6:20
the testimonies, and statutes and judgments Yahweh has commanded?'
You shall say to your son, 'We were Pharaoh's slaves in Egypt,   6:21
and Yahweh brought us out of Egypt with a mighty hand.
Yahweh showed signs and wonders, and brought great tribulations   6:22
upon Egypt, upon Pharaoh and all his household, before our eyes.
He brought us out from there, that he might bring us here,   6:23
to give us the land he swore unto our fathers.
And he commanded us to do all these statutes, to fear Yahweh our God,   6:24

for our good always, that he might let us live, as it is to this day.
We shall be righteousness in Yahweh's eyes if we are careful   6:25
to do all his commandments, as he has commanded us.'"

Chapter 7

"When Yahweh brings you into the land you go to possess, and casts out   7:1
many nations before you—the Hittites, Girgashites, Amorites, Canaanites,
Perizzites, Hivites and Jebusites, nations greater and mightier than you—
when he delivers them to you, you shall defeat and utterly destroy them.   7:2
You shall make no covenant with them, nor show them mercy.
Do not make marriages with them. Do not give your daughters to   7:3
their sons, and do not let your sons take their daughters for wives.
For they will turn your sons away from me to serve other gods,   7:4
and the anger of Yahweh will be kindled, and I will quickly destroy you.
Instead, you shall smash their altars, break down their images,   7:5
cut down their sacred groves, and burn their graven images with fire.
For you are a holy people unto Yahweh. Yahweh your God has chosen you   7:6
as a special people unto him, above all people on the face of the earth.
Yahweh did not set his love upon you and choose you because you were   7:7
more in number than any people, for you were the fewest of all people.
But because Yahweh loved you, and because he would keep the oath   7:8
he swore unto your fathers, he brought you out with a mighty hand,
and redeemed you from bondage at the hand of Pharaoh, king of Egypt.

"Know therefore that Yahweh is your God, a faithful God,   7:9
who keeps covenant and mercy to a thousand generations
with those who love him and keep his commandments.
But he personally repays those who hate him, and he destroys them.   7:10
He is not slack to him who hates him, but repays him to his face.
Therefore keep the commandments, and the statutes and judgments,   7:11
which I command you this day, and do them.
If you hearken to these judgments, and keep, and do them, Yahweh shall   7:12
keep unto you the covenant and the mercy he swore unto your fathers.
He will love you, and bless you, and multiply you. He will bless the fruit   7:13
of your wombs, and of your land—your corn, your wine, your oil, the
increase of your cattle and sheep—in the land he swore unto your fathers.
You shall be blessed above all people. There shall not be   7:14
a barren male or female among you, or among your cattle.
Yahweh will take away all your sickness, and will put none of the evil   7:15
diseases of Egypt upon you, but will lay them upon all who hate you.
You shall destroy all the people Yahweh delivers to you. You shall have   7:16
no pity on them, nor shall you serve their gods, for that is a snare for you.

"You may think, 'These nations are more numerous than us,   7:17
how can we dispossess them?'
But do not be afraid of them. Remember well   7:18
what Yahweh did unto Pharaoh, and unto all Egypt.
The great tribulations you witnessed, and the signs and wonders,   7:19

and the mighty hand, and the outstretched arm, whereby Yahweh
brought you out, so shall Yahweh do to all those of whom you are afraid.
Yahweh will send panic among them until they flee as from hornets.   7:20
Even those who are left and hide themselves from you shall be destroyed.
Do not be afraid, for Yahweh—a terrible and mighty God— is among you.   7:21
Yahweh your God will put out those nations little by little. You may not   7:22
destroy them all at once, lest the wild beasts become too numerous.
Yahweh shall deliver them unto you, and you shall   7:23
consume them one by one until all are destroyed.
He shall deliver their kings into your hand. You shall erase their names   7:24
from heaven. None shall withstand you, and you shall destroy them all.
You shall burn the graven images of their gods with fire.   7:25
You shall not desire the silver or gold on their gods, nor take it
unto you, lest you be snared. It is an abomination to Yahweh your God.
Do not bring any abomination into your house, and so be cursed like it.   7:26
You shall utterly detest it, and abhor it, for it is a cursed thing.”

Chapter 8

“You shall observe and do all the commandments I give you, that you may   8:1
live, and multiply, and possess the land Yahweh swore unto your fathers.
Remember how Yahweh led you these forty years in the wilderness,   8:2
to humble you, to test you, to know what was in your heart,
and to see whether or not you would keep his commandments.
He humbled you, and suffered you to hunger, and fed you with manna—   8:3
which you did not know of, nor did your fathers know—that you might
learn that man does not live by bread alone, but by every word
that proceeds out of the mouth of God does man live.
These forty years your clothing did not wear out, nor did your feet swell.   8:4
Think how a man chastens his son. So does Yahweh chasten you.   8:5
Therefore keep the commandments of Yahweh your God.   8:6
Walk in his ways, and fear him.
For Yahweh brings you into a good land, a land of steams,   8:7
and waterfalls, and springs that gush from the valleys and hills,
a land of wheat and barley, and vines, and fig trees, and pomegranates—   8:8
a land of olive oil, milk and honey—
a land where you shall eat food in abundance, and shall not lack   8:9
for anything, a land whose stones are iron, and whose hills hold brass.

“When you have eaten and are full, you shall bless Yahweh   8:10
for the good land he has given you.
Be careful you do not forget Yahweh your God, and keep not his   8:11
commandments and judgments and statutes I command you this day—
lest when you have eaten, and built good houses, and dwelt therein,   8:12
and when your herds and flocks have multiplied, and your silver   8:13
and gold has multiplied, and all that you have has multiplied,
your heart becomes arrogant, and you forget Yahweh your God,   8:14
who brought you forth out of Egypt from the house of bondage,

who led you through that great and terrible wilderness,   8:15
where there were serpents and scorpions, and drought and no water,
who brought forth water out of a rock for you,
who fed you in the wilderness with manna, that he might   8:16
humble you and test you for your own good in the end—
lest then you forget all this and say in your heart, 'My own power,   8:17
and the might of my own hand, has gotten me this wealth.'

Remember Yahweh your God. Remember it is he who gives you power to   8:18
get wealth, that he may establish the covenant he swore unto your fathers.
If you forget Yahweh your God, and walk with other gods, and serve them,   8:19
and worship them, I swear to you this day, that you shall surely perish.
As the nations before you are destroyed by Yahweh, so shall you be   8:20
destroyed, for you were not obedient to the voice of Yahweh, your God."

Chapter 9

"Hear, O Israel. You are to pass over Jordan this day, to go against nations   9:1
greater and mightier than yourself with cities fenced up to heaven,
a people great and tall, the children of the Anakims,   9:2
of whom people say, 'Who can stand up to the sons of Anak?!'
Know that Yahweh goes before you this day. As a consuming fire he shall   9:3
destroy them, and he shall bring them down before your eyes. You shall
drive them out and destroy them quickly, as Yahweh has told you.
After Yahweh has cast them out, say not in your heart, 'Because of my   9:4
righteousness Yahweh has given me this land.' It is because of
the wickedness of these nations that Yahweh drives them out.
Not for your righteousness or the uprightness of your heart   9:5
do you go to possess their land. It is because of the wickedness
of these nations that Yahweh destroys them, that he may perform
the word he swore unto your fathers, Abraham, Isaac and Jacob.
Know that Yahweh does not give you this good land because   9:6
of your righteousness, for you are a stiff-necked, stubborn people.
Remember, and never forget, how you provoked Yahweh your God   9:7
to anger in the wilderness. From the day you departed Egypt until
you came to this place, you have been rebellious against Yahweh.
You also provoked Yahweh to anger in Horeb,   9:8
and in his anger he threatened to wipe you out.

"When I went into the mount to receive the tablets of stone— the tablets   9:9
of the covenant Yahweh made with you—I abode on the mount
forty days and forty nights. I ate no bread and drank no water.
Yahweh delivered unto me two tablets of stone, written with the finger   9:10
of God. On them was written all the words Yahweh spoke to you
on the day of the assembly, from atop the mount, out of the midst of fire.
At the end of forty days and forty nights, Yahweh gave me   9:11
the two tablets of stone, the tablets of the covenant.
And he said to me, 'Arise, and go down quickly from here, for the people   9:12
you brought out of Egypt have corrupted themselves. They have turned

aside from the way I commanded them, and have made a molten image.'
Yahweh spoke further, saying, 'I have seen this people, 9:13
and beheld what a stiff-necked, stubborn people they are.
Leave me alone so that I can destroy them, and blot out their name from 9:14
under heaven. I will make of you a nation mightier and greater than they.'

"So I came down from the mount, and the mount burned with fire, 9:15
and the two tablets of the covenant were in my two hands.
And I beheld you had sinned against Yahweh your God, and had made 9:16
a molten calf. You had turned aside from way Yahweh commanded you.
So I cast down the two tablets, and broke them before your eyes. 9:17
And I fell down before Yahweh, as I first did. For forty days and forty 9:18
nights I neither ate bread nor drank water, because of all your sins
and wickedness in the sight of Yahweh, provoking him to anger.
I was afraid of the anger and rage of Yahweh. He was going to destroy you! 9:19
But Yahweh hearkened unto me at that time also.
Yahweh was very angry with Aaron and was going to kill him, 9:20
so I also prayed for Aaron.
I took your sin, the calf you had made, and burned it with fire, 9:21
and stamped it, and ground it to dust. And I cast the dust
into the waters that descended out of the mount.
At Taberah, and Massah, and Kibroth-Hattaavah, 9:22
you also provoked Yahweh to wrath.
Likewise, when Yahweh sent you from Kadesh-Barnea, saying, 9:23
'Go and possess the land I have given you,' in that day you did not
trust him or hearken to his voice, but rebelled against him.
You have been rebellious against Yahweh from the first day I knew you. 9:24

"Thus I fell down before Yahweh forty days and forty nights, 9:25
as I fell down at the first, because Yahweh said he would destroy you.
I prayed unto Yahweh, and said, 'O Lord, do not destroy your people 9:26
and your inheritance, which you have redeemed through your greatness,
which you have brought forth out of Egypt with a mighty hand.
Remember your servants, Abraham, Isaac and Jacob. Look not unto the 9:27
stubbornness of this people, nor to their wickedness, nor to their sin,
lest the land from whence you brought us out say, "Because Yahweh 9:28
was not able to bring them into the land he promised them,
and because he hated them, he has slain them in the wilderness."
They are yet your people, and your inheritance, who you 9:29
brought out by your mighty power and by your outstretched arm.'"

Chapter 10

"At that time Yahweh said unto me, 'Hew two tablets of stone like the first, 10:1
and come unto me on the mount. Also make an ark of wood.
I will write on the tablets the words that were on the first tablets, 10:2
which you broke, and you shall put them in the ark.'
So I made an ark of shittim wood, and hewed two tablets of stone, 10:3
like the first, and went up the mount with the two tablets in my hand.

Yahweh wrote on the tablets, according to the first writing, 10:4
the ten commandments he spoke to you on the mount out of the midst
of fire on the day of the assembly. And he gave them to me.
I came down from the mount and put the tablets in the ark I had made, 10:5
as Yahweh commanded me, and there they are to this day."

Now, the children of Israel journeyed from Beeroth, of the children 10:6
of Jaakan, to Mosera. There Aaron died, and there he was buried.
Eleazar his son ministered in the priest's office in his stead.
From there they journeyed to Gudgodah, 10:7
and from Gudgodah to Jotbath, a land of flowing rivers.
At that time Yahweh separated the tribe of Levi, 10:8
to carry the ark of the covenant, to minister unto Yahweh,
and to bless in his name—as it is to this day.
Therefore Levi has no part nor inheritance with his brethren. 10:9
Yahweh is his inheritance, as Yahweh promised him.

Moses said, "I stayed on the mount forty days and forty nights, as I did the 10:10
first time, and Yahweh again hearkened unto me, and did not destroy you.
Yahweh said to me, 'Arise, take your journey before the people, 10:11
that they may go and possess the land I swore unto their fathers.'
Yet now, Israel, what does Yahweh your God require of you? 10:12
Only to fear him, to walk in all his ways, and to love him
and serve him with all your heart and with all your soul,
and to keep his commandments, which he commands for your good. 10:13
Yahweh your God rules heaven, and the heaven of heavens, 10:14
and the earth also, and all therein.
Yahweh delighted in your fathers and loved them, and he chose 10:15
their seed after them—you above all people—as it is to this day.

"Therefore circumcise the foreskin of your heart. Be stubborn no more. 10:16
For Yahweh is God of gods and Lord of lords, a great God, a mighty 10:17
and terrible God that regards not persons, nor takes reward.
He executes judgment of the fatherless and the widow. 10:18
He loves the stranger and gives him food and clothes.
Love you, therefore, the stranger, for you were strangers in Egypt. 10:19
You shall fear Yahweh your God, and him you shall serve. 10:20
To him you shall cleave, and by his name you shall swear.
He is your praise. He is your God. And he has done for you 10:21
great and terrible things, which your eyes have seen.
Your fathers went into Egypt with seventy people. 10:22
Yahweh has made you a multitude, as numerous as the stars of heaven."

Chapter 11

"Therefore you shall love Yahweh your God, and keep his charge, 11:1
and his statutes, and his judgments, and his commandments—always.
You know this. I am not speaking with your children, 11:2
who do not know, who have not known the discipline
and greatness of Yahweh, his mighty hand and his outstretched arm,

and his miracles, and the actions he performed in Egypt — 11:3
unto Pharaoh the king and throughout his land.
And what he did to the army of Egypt, to their horses and their chariots— 11:4
how he made the waters of the Red Sea overflow them
as they pursued after you, and how Yahweh destroyed them.
And what he did unto you in the wilderness until you came to this place, 11:5
and what he did unto Dathan and Abiram, the sons of Eliab and grandsons 11:6
of Reuben, how the earth opened her mouth and swallowed them up—
along with their households, and their tents, and all their possessions—
in the midst of all the congregation of the children of Israel.
But you, your eyes have seen all these great acts of Yahweh. 11:7
Therefore, keep all the commandments I command you this day, 11:8
that you may be strong, and go in and take the land you go to possess,
and that you may prolong your days in the land Yahweh swore unto 11:9
your fathers and their children, a land that flows with milk and honey.

"For the land you go to possess is not like the land of Egypt, where you 11:10
sowed your seed, and watered it by hand like a garden of herbs.
The land you go to possess is a land of hills and valleys, 11:11
watered by the rains of heaven, a land Yahweh your God cares for.
The eyes of Yahweh are always upon it, 11:12
from the beginning of the year to the end.
If you hearken diligently to the commandments I command you this day— 11:13
to love Yahweh, and to serve him with all your heart and all your soul—
he will give you the rain of your land in due season, the first rain and the 11:14
latter rain, that you may gather in your corn, and your wine, and your oil,
and he will grow grass for your cattle, that you may eat and be full. 11:15

"Take heed that your heart is not deceived, 11:16
and you turn aside to serve other gods, and worship them.
For Yahweh's wrath will be kindled against you, and he will shut down 11:17
the heavens that there be no rain, and the land will not yield her fruit,
and you will quickly perish from the good land Yahweh gives you.
Therefore, lay up these words in your heart and soul, and bind them 11:18
as a sign upon your hand, that they may be always before your eyes.
Teach them to your children. Speak of them when you sit in your house, 11:19
when you walk by the way, when you lie down, and when you rise up.
Write them upon the door posts of your house, and upon your gates, 11:20
that your days, and the days of your children, may be multiplied as the 11:21
days of heaven on the earth, in the land Yahweh swore unto your fathers.
If you diligently keep all these commandments and do them— 11:22
love Yahweh your God, walk in all his ways and cleave unto him—
Yahweh will drive out all these nations from before you, 11:23
and you shall possess nations greater and mightier than yourselves.
Every place the soles of your feet tread shall be yours—from the 11:24
wilderness, to Lebanon, to the river Euphrates, to the Mediterranean Sea.
No man shall be able to stand before you. For, as Yahweh has told you, 11:25
he shall lay the fear and dread of you upon all the land wherein you tread.

"Behold, I set before you this day a blessing and a curse— 11:26
a blessing if you obey the commandments of Yahweh your God, 11:27
and a curse if you do not obey them, but turn aside from his way 11:28
to go after other gods, which you have not known.
When Yahweh has brought you into the land, you shall 11:29
put a blessing upon Mount Gerizim, and a curse upon Mount Ebal.
Are they not on the west side of Jordan, in the land of the Canaanites, 11:30
who dwell on the plains over against Gilgal, beside the plains of Moreh?
You shall pass over Jordan and possess the land 11:31
Yahweh gives you, and you shall dwell there,
and you shall observe the commandments I set before you this day." 11:32

Chapter 12

"These are the statutes and judgments you shall observe and do in the 12:1
land Yahweh gives you to possess, for all the days you live upon the earth.
You shall utterly destroy all the places where the nations 12:2
you shall possess served their gods—upon the high mountains,
and upon the hills, and under every green tree.
You shall overthrow their altars, and break their pillars, and burn their 12:3
groves with fire. You shall hew down the graven images of their gods,
and wipe out their names from that place.
Do not do so unto Yahweh, your God. 12:4
Yahweh shall choose out of all your tribes where he will dwell, 12:5
and you shall come into his presence there.
You shall bring your burnt offerings, and your sacrifices, and your tithes, 12:6
and your heave offerings, and your vows, and your freewill offerings,
and the firstlings of your herds and your flocks.
There you and your households shall eat before Yahweh. And you shall 12:7
rejoice in all that you lay your hand to, wherein Yahweh has blessed you.
Do not act the way you do now—everyone doing what seems right to him. 12:8
You have not yet come to the rest, and the inheritance Yahweh gives you. 12:9

"When you go over Jordan and dwell in the land Yahweh gives you, 12:10
when he gives you rest from all your enemies so that you dwell in safety,
there shall be a place Yahweh chooses for his name to dwell, 12:11
and there you shall bring all your burnt offerings, your sacrifices,
your tithes, your heave offerings, and all your vows you vow unto Yahweh.
You shall rejoice before Yahweh your God, you, and your sons, and your 12:12
daughters, and your menservants, and your maidservants, and the Levite
who is within your gates—because he has no part or inheritance with you.
Take heed you do not offer your burnt offerings in every place you see. 12:13
Only in the place Yahweh chooses in one of your tribes shall you offer 12:14
your burnt offerings, and there you shall do all that I command you.
However, you may kill and eat flesh in all your gates, whatever your soul 12:15
desires, according to the blessing Yahweh has given you. The unclean
and the clean both may partake, as if they were eating gazelle or deer.
Only you shall not eat the blood. You shall pour it upon the earth as water. 12:16

"You may not eat within your gates the tithe of your corn, or of your wine,   12:17
or of your oil, or the firstlings of your herds or your flocks, nor any of your
vows you vows, nor your freewill offerings, nor your heave offerings.
You must eat them before Yahweh, in the place Yahweh shall choose—   12:18
you, and your son, and your daughter, and your manservant, and your
maidservant, and the Levite who is within your gates—and you shall
rejoice before Yahweh your God in all that you lay your hand to.
Take heed you do not forsake the Levite, for as long as you live on earth.   12:19
When Yahweh enlarges your borders, as he has promised you,   12:20
and you say, 'I will eat flesh,' because your soul longs to eat flesh,
you may eat flesh, whatever your soul desires.
If the place Yahweh has chosen to put his name is too far from you,   12:21
then you shall kill of your herds and your flocks, which Yahweh has
given you, and you shall eat within your gates whatever your soul desires.
Just as the gazelle and deer are eaten, so you shall eat them.   12:22
The unclean and the clean shall eat of them alike.
Only be sure you do not eat the blood.   12:23
The blood is the life, and you may not eat the life with the flesh.
You shall not eat it. You shall pour it upon the earth as water.   12:24
You shall not eat it, so that it may go well with you, and with your children   12:25
after you, when you do that which is right in the sight of Yahweh.
But your holy things and your vows,   12:26
you shall take to the place Yahweh shall choose.
You shall offer your burnt offerings, the flesh and the blood, upon the altar   12:27
of Yahweh. The blood shall be poured on the altar. The flesh you shall eat.

"Hear and observe all these words I command you. When you   12:28
do that which is good and right in the sight of Yahweh, your God,
it shall go well with you, and with your children after you, forever.
When Yahweh removes the nations from before you, where you   12:29
go to possess their land, and you succeed them and dwell there,
take heed you are not ensnared by following their ways,   12:30
and that you do not inquire after their gods, saying,
'How did these nations serve their gods? I want to do likewise.'
You shall not do so unto Yahweh your God. For every abomination   12:31
to Yahweh, everything he hates, they have done unto their gods.
They have even burned their sons and daughters in the fire to their gods.
Whatever I command, observe and do. Do not add to or diminish from it."   12:32

Chapter 13

"If there arises among you a prophet, or a dreamer of dreams,   13:1
who gives you a sign or a wonder,
and the sign or wonder he spoke comes to pass, and he says, 'Let us go   13:2
after other gods, which you have not known, and let us serve them,'
you shall not hearken unto the words of that prophet, or that dreamer   13:3
of dreams. For Yahweh your God tests you, to know whether
you love him with all your heart and with all your soul.
You shall walk in the way of Yahweh your God, and fear him, and keep his   13:4

commandments, and obey his voice, and serve him and cleave unto him.
And that prophet, or that dreamer of dreams, shall be put to death. 13:5
He has tried to turn you away from Yahweh your God, who brought you
out of the land of Egypt, and redeemed you out of the house of bondage.
He tried to turn you from the way Yahweh commanded you to walk,
and you must purge such evil from your midst.

"If your brother—the son of your mother—or your son, or your daughter, 13:6
or the wife of your bosom, or your friend who is as your own soul,
entices you secretly, saying, 'Let us go and serve other gods,'
which you have not known, neither you nor your fathers—
gods of other people near and far, from one end of the earth to the other— 13:7
you shall not consent to him, nor hearken unto him. 13:8
Neither shall you pity him, nor conceal him, nor spare him.
You shall kill him. Your hand shall be first upon him, 13:9
putting him to death, and afterwards the hands of all the people.
You shall stone him with stones until he dies, because he tried to turn you 13:10
away from Yahweh your God, who brought you out of the land of Egypt.
All Israel shall hear of it, and fear to do any more such wickedness. 13:11

"If you hear tell that in one of your cities Yahweh has given you to dwell, 13:12
wicked men—children of Belial—are tempting the people of their city, 13:13
saying, 'Let us go and serve other gods, which you have not known,'
you shall inquire into it, and do research, and ask diligently of the people. 13:14
And if it is true that such abomination is happening among you,
you shall put the inhabitants of that city to death with the sword. 13:15
Destroy those people, and all their livestock, with the sword.
Then gather all the goods of the city into its midst, and burn the city 13:16
and all its goods with fire, for an offering unto Yahweh, your God.
That city shall remain a heap of ruins forever, and never be built again.
Do not keep any of the cursed goods or animals, so that Yahweh may 13:17
turn from the fierceness of his anger and show you mercy, and have
compassion for you, and multiply you, as he swore unto your fathers.
You shall hearken to the voice of Yahweh and keep all his commandments. 13:18
You shall do that which is right in the eyes of Yahweh, your God."

Chapter 14

"You are the children of Yahweh. 14:1
You shall not cut yourselves nor shave your foreheads for the dead.
You are a holy people to Yahweh your God. He has chosen you 14:2
to be a special people unto himself, above all nations upon the earth.
You shall not eat any abominable thing. 14:3
These are the beasts you shall eat: the ox, the sheep, the goat, the gazelle, 14:4
the deer, the roebuck, the wild goat, the pygarg, the antelope, the chamois. 14:5
Every beast that divides the hoof, and cleaves the cleft into two claws, 14:6
and chews the cud, those beasts you shall eat.
However, you shall not eat the camel, the rabbit, or the rock badger. 14:7
They chew the cud and divide the hoof, but the hoof is not cloven,

therefore they are unclean unto you.
The swine divides the hoof, but does not chew the cud, and so   14:8
is unclean to you. You shall not eat their flesh nor touch their carcasses.
Of that which lives in the waters, you may eat all that have fins and scales.   14:9
Whatever does not have fins and scales you may not eat.   14:10

"All clean birds you may eat.   14:11
But you shall not eat the eagle, the ossifrage, the osprey,   14:12
the glede, the kite, the vulture after his kind,   14:13
the raven after his kind,   14:14
the owl, the night hawk, the cuckow, the hawk after his kind,   14:15
the little owl, the great owl, the swan,   14:16
the pelican, the gier eagle, the cormorant,   14:17
the stork, the heron after her kind, the lapwing, or the bat.   14:18
Every creeping thing that flies is unclean to you. They shall not be eaten.   14:19
All clean fowls you may eat.   14:20
You shall not eat anything that dies of itself. You may give it to the   14:21
stranger in your gates, that he may eat it, or you may sell it to a foreigner.
You are holy unto Yahweh. You shall not boil a kid in his mother's milk.
You shall tithe the yield of your crops every year.   14:22
You shall eat before Yahweh—in the place he shall choose for his name—   14:23
the tithe of your corn, your wine, your oil, and the firstlings of your herds
and your flocks, that you may learn to fear Yahweh always.

"If the way is too long, so that you are not able to carry your tithes—   14:24
if the place Yahweh chooses to set his name is too far from you—
then you shall turn your tithes into money,   14:25
and take it to the place Yahweh shall choose.
There you can use that money to buy whatever you desire—oxen, sheep,   14:26
wine or strong drink—whatever your soul desires, and you shall eat it
before Yahweh, and you shall rejoice, you and your household,
and the Levite who is within your gates. You shall not forsake him,   14:27
for he has no part nor inheritance with you.
Every three years you shall take the tithe of your   14:28
increase that year and lay it up at your city gates.
And the Levite—because he has no part nor inheritance with you—   14:29
and the strangers, and the fatherless, and the widows who are
within your gates, shall come, and shall eat and be satisfied.
Yahweh your God will bless you, and bless all the work of your hand."

Chapter 15

"At the end of every seven years you shall make a release.   15:1
This is the manner of the release: Every creditor who has lent unto his   15:2
neighbor shall release him. He shall not exact it of his neighbor,
or of his neighbor's brother. This is called Yahweh's release.
Of a foreigner you may exact payment, but that which   15:3
is with your brethren, your hand shall release.
However, soon there should be no poor among you, for Yahweh shall   15:4

greatly bless you in the land he gives you to possess for an inheritance—
but only if you carefully hearken unto the voice of Yahweh your God,   15:5
and observe and do all these commandments I command you this day.
Yahweh shall bless you, as he promised. You shall lend to many nations,   15:6
but you shall not borrow from any. You shall reign over many nations,
but none shall reign over you.

"If there is among you a poor brother within any of your gates, you shall   15:7
not harden your heart to him, nor shut your hand to your poor brother.
You shall open your hand wide unto him, and shall surely   15:8
lend him sufficient for his need, in that which he wants.
Beware there is no evil in your heart, saying, 'The seventh year, the year   15:9
of release, is at hand,' and you act coldly with your brother, and give him
nothing, and he cry unto Yahweh against you. It will be a sin unto you.
You shall give to him, and your heart shall not grieve, because for this   15:10
Yahweh shall bless you in all your works, in all that you lay your hand to.
The poor shall never disappear from the earth. Therefore I say to you   15:11
that you shall open your hand wide unto your brother,
to your poor, and to your needy in your land.

"If your brother, a Hebrew man or Hebrew woman, is sold to you,   15:12
he shall serve you six years. In the seventh year you shall let him go free.
And when you set him free, you shall not let him go away empty.   15:13
You shall furnish him liberally from your flock, and your grains, and your   15:14
winepress. From that which Yahweh has blessed you, you shall give him.
Remember, you were a bondman in Egypt, and Yahweh redeemed you.   15:15
Therefore I command you in this way today.
But if your bondman says he will not go away from you,   15:16
because he loves you and your house, and he is happy in your service,
then you shall pierce his ear with an awl, and he shall be your   15:17
servant forever. Do likewise to your maidservant who wants to stay.
Let it not be difficult for you to set him free, for he has served you   15:18
six years at half the cost of a hired servant. Set him free with a glad heart,
and Yahweh shall bless you in all that you do.

"All the firstling males of your herd and your flock you shall sanctify   15:19
unto Yahweh your God. You shall do no work with the firstling
of your oxen, nor shear the firstling of your sheep.
You shall eat it before Yahweh your God, year after year,   15:20
you and your household, in the place Yahweh shall choose.
If it has any blemish, like being lame or blind, or has any   15:21
blemish whatever, you shall not sacrifice it unto Yahweh your God.
You shall eat it within your gates. The clean and the unclean   15:22
person alike shall eat it, as if it were a gazelle or deer.
Only do not eat its blood. You shall pour it on the ground as water."   15:23

Chapter 16

"Observe the month of Abib, and keep the Passover unto Yahweh.   16:1
For in the month of Abib, Yahweh brought you forth out of Egypt by night.

On the Passover you shall sacrifice unto Yahweh from your flocks 16:2
and herds, in the place Yahweh shall choose to place his name.
You shall eat no leavened bread with it. For seven days shall you eat 16:3
unleavened bread, the bread of affliction, that you may remember
all the days of your life, the night you came forth out of Egypt in haste.
For seven days there shall be no leavened bread seen in all your land. 16:4
Nor shall any of the flesh you sacrificed
the first day at evening remain overnight until morning.
You may not sacrifice the Passover offering within any of your gates, 16:5
but only in the place Yahweh your God shall choose for his name to dwell. 16:6
There you shall sacrifice the Passover at evening,
at the setting of the sun, in the season you came forth out of Egypt.
You shall roast it, and eat it in the place Yahweh shall choose. 16:7
The next morning you shall return to your tents.
For six days you shall eat unleavened bread. On the seventh day there 16:8
shall be a solemn assembly to Yahweh. You shall do no work that day.

"Count seven weeks from the time you first put the sickle to your grain, 16:9
then begin to keep the Feast of Weeks unto Yahweh, with a freewill 16:10
offering from the wealth Yahweh has blessed unto you.
Rejoice before Yahweh your God, you, and your son, and your daughter, 16:11
and your manservant, and your maidservant, and the Levite who
is within your gates, and the stranger, and the fatherless, and the widow
among you, in the place Yahweh has chosen to place his name.
Remember, you were a bondman in Egypt. Observe and do these statutes. 16:12
After you have gathered in your grains, and pressed your wine, 16:13
observe the Feast of Tabernacles for seven days.
Rejoice in your feast, you, and your son, and your daughter, and your 16:14
manservant, and your maidservant, and the Levite, and the stranger,
and the fatherless, and the widow who are within your gates.
For seven days you shall keep a solemn feast unto Yahweh, in the place 16:15
Yahweh shall choose. Yahweh shall bless you in all your increase,
and in all the works of your hand, therefore you shall surely rejoice.
Three times a year all your males shall appear before Yahweh— 16:16
at the Passover, at the Feast of Weeks, and at the Feast of Tabernacles.
And they shall not appear before Yahweh empty-handed.
Every man shall give as he is able, from the blessings Yahweh has given. 16:17

"You shall appoint judges and officers in all your gates, throughout 16:18
your tribes, and they shall judge the people with just judgment.
Do not be unjust. You shall not respect persons, nor take gifts. For a gift 16:19
blinds the eyes of the wise, and perverts the words of the righteous.
You shall follow that which is altogether just, that you may live, 16:20
and inherit the land Yahweh your God gives you.
You shall not plant any grove of trees near the altar of Yahweh your God, 16:21
nor set up stone pillars or images, which Yahweh your God hates." 16:22

Chapter 17

"You shall not sacrifice unto Yahweh any bull or sheep 17:1
with a blemish or defect, for that is an abomination to Yahweh.
If there is found among you, within any of your gates, a man or woman 17:2
who has done evil in the sight of Yahweh by transgressing his covenant,
and has served other gods, and worshipped them—either the sun, 17:3
or moon, or any of the host of heaven that I have commanded against—
and you have heard of it, and inquired diligently, and found 17:4
it is true and certain that such abomination is done in Israel,
then shall you bring the man or woman who has committed that 17:5
wickedness to your city gates and stone them with stones until they die.
At the mouth of two witnesses, or three witnesses, 17:6
he that is worthy of death shall be put to death,
but at the mouth of one witness he shall not be put to death.
The witnesses shall be the first to stone him, and afterward all the people. 17:7
And so shall you remove such evil from among you.

"If there arises a matter too hard for you to judge, between blood 17:8
and blood, between plea and plea, between stroke and stroke—
matters of controversy within your gates—you shall go into
the place Yahweh your God shall choose,
and take the matter to the Levitical priests and the judge 17:9
who is serving at the time. They shall pass judgment for you.
And you shall do according to their sentence. 17:10
You must follow their instructions exactly.
You shall act according to the judgment and the sentence they tell you. 17:11
You shall not deviate from the sentence, nor turn to the right or left.
Anyone who acts arrogantly and does not hearken unto the priest 17:12
or judge, shall be put to death. You shall remove that evil from Israel.
The people will hear of it and be afraid to act arrogantly anymore. 17:13

"When you have come into the land Yahweh gives you, and dwell there, 17:14
and say, 'Let us set a king over us, like the nations nearby,'
you shall appoint a king whom Yahweh shall choose, one from 17:15
among your brethren. You may not set a stranger over you.
And he shall not acquire many horses for himself, nor cause 17:16
the people to return to Egypt so that he can acquire horses,
for Yahweh has told you never to go back there again.
Neither shall he acquire many wives, lest his heart turn from God, 17:17
nor greatly multiply gold and silver for himself.
And when he takes the throne of his kingdom, he shall write for himself 17:18
a copy of this book of law, which is in the care of the Levitical priests,
and he shall read it all the days of his life, that he may learn to fear 17:19
Yahweh his God, and to keep and do all the words of this law,
so that his heart is not lifted up above his brethren, and he does not 17:20
turn aside from the commandments, neither right nor left, and that
he and his children may prolong their days in the kingdom of Israel."

Chapter 18

"The Levitical priests, and all the tribe of Levi, shall have no   18:1
part nor inheritance with Israel. They shall eat the offerings
to Yahweh made by fire, which are their portion.
They shall have no inheritance among their brethren.   18:2
Yahweh is their inheritance, as he has said unto them.
The priest's due from they who offer a sacrifice, whether it be   18:3
ox or sheep, shall be the shoulder, the two cheeks, and the maw.
The first fruit of your corn, your wine, and your oil,   18:4
and the first fleece of your sheep, you shall also give to him.
For Yahweh your God has chosen him out of all your tribes   18:5
to minister in the name of Yahweh, him and his sons, forever.
If a Levite comes from any city in Israel where he has been living,   18:6
and desires to come unto the place Yahweh shall choose,
he may minister in the name of Yahweh, as his brethren do.   18:7
He shall be given like portions to eat,   18:8
even if he has money from the sale of family property.

"When you come into the land Yahweh gives you,   18:9
do not follow after the abominations of those nations.
No one among you shall make his son or daughter pass through the fire,   18:10
or use divination, or become a soothsayer, or an enchanter, or a witch,
or a charmer, or a consulter of spirits, or a wizard, or a necromancer.   18:11
For all who do these things are an abomination to Yahweh, and because   18:12
of these abominations, Yahweh drives these nations out from before you.
You shall be perfect with Yahweh, your God.   18:13
These nations that you shall possess hearkened unto sign readers   18:14
and diviners. But Yahweh does not permit you to do the same.
Yahweh will raise up unto you a prophet like me from your midst,   18:15
of your own brethren, and you shall listen to him.

"This is what you requested of Yahweh in Horeb, in the assembly, saying,   18:16
'Let me not hear again the voice of Yahweh or see his great fire, lest I die.'
And Yahweh said to me, 'They have spoken well.   18:17
I will raise them up a prophet from among them, like you. I will put my   18:18
words in his mouth, and he shall speak to them all that I command him.'
Whoever does not hearken to the words   18:19
he speaks in my name, I will hold accountable.
But any prophet who presumes to speak in my name   18:20
a word I have not commanded him to speak—or who speaks
in the name of other gods—shall be put to death.
You might ask, 'How shall we know if the word is not from Yahweh?'   18:21
If what a prophet speaks in the name of Yahweh   18:22
does not follow or come to pass, it is not from Yahweh.
The prophet has spoken arrogantly. You shall not fear him."

Chapter 19

"When Yahweh has cut off the nations whose land he gives you,   19:1
and you succeed them, and dwell in their cities and in their houses,
you shall set apart three cities in the midst of your land,   19:2
which Yahweh your God gives you to possess.
You shall divide your land into three regions, with one   19:3
of these cities in each, to which any manslayer may flee.
A manslayer is one who kills his neighbor accidentally,   19:4
whom he hated not in time past.
As when a man goes into the forest with his neighbor to hew wood,   19:5
and swings a stroke with his axe to cut down a tree, and the head
slips from the shaft and hits his neighbor, killing him.
He shall be able to flee unto one of those cities, and live.
Otherwise, the rightful avenger of blood might pursue the slayer while   19:6
his heart is hot, and overtake him because the way is long, and kill him,
whereas he did not deserve death, since he hated him not in time past.
Therefore I command you, saying, 'You shall separate three cities for this.'   19:7

"If Yahweh enlarges your territory,   19:8
and gives you all the land he swore unto your fathers,
if you keep these commandments I command you this day, and do them—   19:9
to love Yahweh your God, and to walk ever in his ways—
then you shall add three more sanctuary cities beside these,
that innocent blood not be shed in your land, and blood be not upon you.   19:10
But if a man hates his neighbor, and lies in wait for him, and strikes him   19:11
mortally so that he dies, then flees into one of these cities,
the elders of that city shall fetch him, and deliver him   19:12
into the hand of the avenger of blood, that he may be killed.
Your eye shall not pity him. You shall remove from Israel   19:13
the takers of innocent blood, that it may go well with you.
You shall not remove your neighbor's landmark,   19:14
which they of old times have set in the land Yahweh gives you.

"One witness is not enough against a man for any iniquity or sin.   19:15
On the word of two or three witnesses shall the matter be judged.
If a witness comes forward to testify falsely against a man,   19:16
then both the accused and the witness shall stand before Yahweh,   19:17
before the priests and the judges in that day,
and the judges shall make diligent inquisition.   19:18
If the witness has testified falsely against his brother,
then you shall do to him, as he sought to have done unto his brother.   19:19
Put away such evil from among you.
The rest of the people shall hear of it, and fear,   19:20
and henceforth commit no more such evil among you.
Your eye shall not pity him. Life shall go for life, eye for eye,   19:21
tooth for tooth, hand for hand, foot for foot."

Chapter 20

"When you go into battle against your enemies and see horses, 20:1
and chariots, and an army larger yours, be not afraid of them.
Yahweh your God is with you, who brought you out of the land of Egypt.
Before the battle, the priest shall speak unto the people, 20:2
and say to them, 'Hear, O Israel. You go this day into battle 20:3
against your enemies. Let not your hearts be faint. Do not fear.
Do not tremble. Do not be terrified of them.
For Yahweh your God goes with you, to fight for you 20:4
against your enemies, and to save you.'
And the officers shall speak unto the people, saying, 'What man is there 20:5
who has built a new house, and has not dedicated it? Let him return
to his house, lest he die in the battle, and another man dedicate it.
What man has planted a vineyard, and has not yet eaten of it? Let him 20:6
return to his house, lest he die in the battle, and another man eat of it.
What man has betrothed a wife and has not taken her? Let him return 20:7
to his house, lest he die in the battle, and another man take her.'
What man is there who is fearful and fainthearted? Let him return 20:8
to his house, lest his brethren's heart become faint as well.'
When the officers have finished speaking thus unto the people, 20:9
they shall appoint captains to lead the armies of the people.

"When you draw nigh unto a city to do battle, first offer it terms of peace. 20:10
If it surrenders, and opens its gates unto you, then all its people 20:11
shall be slaves unto you, and they shall serve you.
If it will not make peace, but will war against you, you shall besiege it. 20:12
And when Yahweh your God has delivered it into your hands, 20:13
you shall kill every male thereof with the edge of the sword.
But the women, the little ones, the cattle—all the spoil of the city— 20:14
you shall take to yourself, and you shall feast on the spoil of your enemies.
Thus shall you do unto all the cities that are far off from you— 20:15
cities not of these nations.
But in the cities of the land Yahweh gives you for an inheritance, 20:16
you shall leave nothing alive that breathes.
You shall utterly destroy them, namely, the Hittites, the Amorites, 20:17
the Canaanites, the Perizzites, the Hivites, and the Jebusites,
so that they do not teach you all their abominations, which they have done 20:18
unto their gods, and you thereby sin against Yahweh, your God.
When you besiege a city a long time in war, do not cut down the trees 20:19
to employ them in the siege. You can eat from those trees. Do not cut
them down. Trees that produce are man's life. They are not your enemies.
Only if you are sure a tree does not produce food shall you cut it down, 20:20
and use it to besiege against the city, until it falls."

Chapter 21

"If someone is found slain in the land Yahweh gives you to possess, 21:1
lying in the field, and it is not known who has slain him,

your elders and judges shall come forth, and measure   21:2
the distance from the corpse to the cities around it.
And it shall be that the elders of the city closest to the slain man,   21:3
shall take a heifer that has never been worked or yoked,
and bring the heifer into a valley that has never been plowed or planted,   21:4
and there shall break the heifer's neck.
Then the priests, the sons of Levi, shall come near—for Yahweh has   21:5
chosen them to minister unto him—and bless in the name of Yahweh.
And by their word shall every controversy and every blow be judged.
All the elders of that city closest to the corpse,   21:6
shall wash their hands over the heifer whose neck was broken.
And they shall say, 'Our hands have not shed this blood,   21:7
and neither have our eyes seen it.
Be merciful, O Lord, unto your people of Israel, whom you have redeemed,   21:8
and lay not innocent blood unto your people's charge.'
And the blood shall be forgiven them.
So it is that you put away the guilt of innocent blood from among you,   21:9
that you do what is right in the sight of Yahweh.

"When you go forth to war against your enemies, and Yahweh   21:10
has delivered them into your hands, and you have taken them captive,
and you see among the captives a beautiful woman,   21:11
and have a desire to have her for a wife,
you shall bring her to your house. She shall shave her head, cut her nails   21:12
and take off the clothes she was captured in. She shall remain in your   21:13
house and mourn her father and her mother a full month. After that
you shall go unto her and be her husband, and she shall be your wife.
If you have no delight in her, you shall let her go whither she will.   21:14
You shall not sell her. You shall not make merchandise of her
because you have humbled her.
If a man has two wives, one beloved and another hated,   21:15
and they have born him children, both the beloved and the hated,
and if his firstborn son is of her who was hated,
that man shall not give the son of the beloved wife the firstborn's   21:16
inheritance before the son of the hated wife, who is the true firstborn.
He shall acknowledge the son of the hated wife as the firstborn,   21:17
by giving him a double portion of all that he is due, for he is
the first fruits of his strength. The right of the firstborn is his.

"If a man has a stubborn and rebellious son,   21:18
who will not obey the voice of his father, or of his mother,
and who, when they have chastened him, will not hearken unto them,
his father and his mother shall take hold of him, and bring him   21:19
to the elders of his city, at the city gates.
They shall say to the elders, 'Our son is stubborn and rebellious.   21:20
He will not obey our voice. He is a glutton and a drunkard.'
And all the men of his city shall stone him with stones until he dies.   21:21
Put away such evil from among you. All Israel shall hear, and fear.
If a man commits a sin worthy of death, and he is hung to death on a tree,   21:22

his body shall not remain on the tree all night. You shall bury him that day 21:2
so that your land is not defiled. For he that is hanged is accursed of God."

Chapter 22

"If you see your brother's ox or sheep has gone astray, do not pretend 22:
you have not seen. You shall bring it again unto your brother.
If your brother is not near you, or if you do not know him, 22:
bring it to your own house, and keep it with you until
your brother seeks after it, then you can restore it to him.
You shall do the same if it is an ass, or a coat, or anything 22:
your brother has lost that you have found. You may not ignore it.
If your brother's ass or ox falls down by the way, do not walk on past him. 22:
You shall surely help him lift his animal up again.
A woman shall not wear men's clothes, nor shall a man put on a woman's 22:
garment. All who do so are an abomination to Yahweh your God.
If you happen upon a bird's nest in a tree, or on the ground, 22:
where there are eggs or young ones, and the mother
is sitting upon them, you shall not take the mother bird.
The eggs or young ones you may take, but you shall let the mother go, 22:
so that it may be well with you, and that you may prolong your days.
When you build a new house, you shall make a railing for your roof, 22:8
so that no man falls from it and bring blood upon your house.
Do not sow your vineyard with more than one kind of seed, 22:9
lest the fruit of your vineyard be defiled.
Do not plow with an ox and an ass together. 22:10
Do not wear a garment made of both linen and wool. 22:11
Make fringes for the four corners of your coat. 22:12

"If a man takes a wife, and goes unto her, and takes no delight in her, 22:13
and speaks against her, giving her a bad reputation, saying, 22:14
'When I came unto this woman I found no evidence of her virginity,'
the father and mother of the damsel shall bring the tokens 22:15
of the damsel's virginity unto the elders of the city.
The damsel's father shall say to the elders, 'I gave my daughter 22:16
unto this man to be his wife, and he hates her.
He has spoken against her, saying, "I found your daughter 22:17
not a maid," and yet these are the tokens of my daughter's virginity.'
And he shall spread the cloth before the elders of the city as proof.
And the elders of that city shall punish that husband. 22:18
They shall fine him a hundred shekels of silver, and give them to the 22:19
father of the damsel, because he has given a virgin of Isracl a bad name.
And the damsel shall be his wife, and he may never divorce her.
But if the husband is right, and the tokens of virginity are not found, 22:20
they shall bring the damsel to the door of her father's house, and the men 22:21
of her city shall stone her to death. She has brought shame to Israel by
playing the whore in her father's house. So shall you deal with such evil.

"If a man is found lying with a married woman, 22:22
both shall be put to death. So shall you put away such evil from Israel.
If a damsel who is a virgin is betrothed unto a husband, 22:23
and another man of the city takes her and lies with her,
you shall bring both unto the gate of that city and stone them to death. 22:24
The damsel because she did not cry out for help, though being in the city,
and the man because he shamed his neighbor's future wife.
So shall you put away such evil from among you.
But if a man finds a betrothed damsel in the field, and forces her to lie 22:25
with him though she cries out for help, then only the man shall be killed.
You shall do nothing to the damsel. In her there is no sin worthy of death. 22:26
It is the same as if a man attacked his neighbor and killed him.
For he found her in the field, and the betrothed damsel cried out, 22:27
yet there were none to save her.
If a man sees a young virgin who is not betrothed, 22:28
and takes hold of her, and lies with her, and they are found out,
the man who lay with her shall give her father fifty shekels of silver, 22:29
and she shall be his wife, because he has humbled her.
And he can never divorce her, for all his days.
A man shall not dishonor his father by taking his father's wives unto him." 22:30

Chapter 23

"He who is wounded in his stones, or has his privy member cut off, 23:1
shall not enter into the congregation of Yahweh, your God.
A bastard shall not enter into the congregation of Yahweh. Even to his 23:2
tenth generation he shall not enter into the congregation of Yahweh.
An Ammonite or Moabite shall not enter into the congregation 23:3
of Yahweh, even to their tenth generation, forever,
because they would not give you bread and water on the way, 23:4
when you came out of Egypt, and because they hired Balaam,
son of Beor of Pethor of Mesopotamia, to curse you.
But Yahweh would not hearken unto Balaam. Yahweh turned the curse 23:5
into a blessing unto you, because Yahweh your God loves you.
You shall not seek their peace nor their prosperity all your days, forever. 23:6
You shall not hate an Edomite, for he is your brother. 23:7
You shall not hate an Egyptian, for you were a stranger in his land.
Beginning with the children of their third generations, 23:8
they shall be allowed to enter into the congregation of Yahweh.

"When your armies are encamped against your enemies, 23:9
guard yourself from every possible evil.
If a man among you becomes unclean by an emission in the night, 23:10
he shall leave the camp and stay outside it for a day.
When evening comes he shall wash himself with water, 23:11
and when the sun is down, he may come again into the camp.
You shall have a place outside the camp where you go to relieve yourself. 23:12
Carry a spade among your gear to dig a hole where you shall 23:13
relieve yourself, and refill it to cover that which comes from you.

For Yahweh walks in the midst of your camp, to deliver you, and to   23:14
give up your enemies before you. Therefore your camp shall be holy,
so that he sees no unclean thing among you, and turns not away from you.

"If a slave escapes from his master and takes refuge with you,   23:15
you shall not return him to his master.
He shall dwell with you in one of your cities, in a place he chooses,   23:16
wherever he likes best. You shall not oppress him.
There shall be no whore among the daughters of Israel.   23:17
Neither shall any son of Israel give himself to a man.
No money earned from a female's whoring, or a male selling himself   23:18
to a man, shall be brought into the house of Yahweh for any vow.
For these are surely abominations unto Yahweh, your God.
Do not charge interest to Israelites when you lend money,   23:19
food or anything that may be lent with interest.
You may lend with usury to strangers, but unto your brother   23:20
you shall not charge interest, so that Yahweh may bless you
in all you lay your hand to in the land you go to possess.
When you vow an oath unto Yahweh, do not be slack making good on it,   23:21
for Yahweh will surely require it of you, and delaying would be a sin.
If you do not vow, there is no sin.   23:22
But that which freely comes from your lips, you shall keep and perform   23:23
exactly as you vowed it, for you spoke it aloud with your mouth.
When you go into your neighbor's vineyard you may eat your fill of grapes   23:24
while you are there, but you shall not take any away in a basket or vessel.
When you go into your neighbor's field you may pick the ears   23:25
with your hand, but you shall not take a sickle unto his standing grain."

Chapter 24

"When a man takes a wife and it comes to pass that she is no longer   24:1
pleasing to him because there is something he does not like about her,
he shall give her papers of divorce and send her out of his house.
When she has departed from his house, she may be another man's wife.   24:2
If the second husband does not like her, and gives her divorce papers,   24:3
and sends her out of his house, or if the second husband dies,
her first husband may not take her again to be his wife, for she is defiled,   24:4
and that is abomination before Yahweh. You shall not be the cause of sin
in the land Yahweh your God gives you for an inheritance.
When a man takes a new wife, he shall not go out to war nor undertake   24:5
any business for one year, so that he may bring comfort and joy to her.
Do not take a pair of millstones, or an upper millstone, as collateral for   24:6
a debt, for they are his means of sustenance, liken to a pledge of his life.
If a man kidnaps any of his brethren of Israel, to make them slaves or   24:7
sell them, that thief shall die. You shall remove such evil from among you.
Be on guard against the plague of leprosy. Diligently observe and do   24:8
all that the Levitical priests shall teach you, as I commanded them.
Remember what Yahweh did to Miriam after you came forth from Egypt.   24:9

"When you lend to your brother, do not go into his house to get his pledge. 24:10
Wait outside and let the man to whom you lent bring the pledge to you. 24:11
If the man is poor and has pledged his coat, do not keep it overnight. 24:12
Return the pledge to him at sunset, that he may sleep in his own coat, 24:13
and bless you, and that you shall be righteousness before Yahweh.
You shall not oppress a hired servant who is poor and needy, 24:14
whether he be of your brethren, or a stranger within your gates.
Pay him each day for his work. Do not keep it overnight, lest he cry out to 24:15
Yahweh, and it be sin unto you. For he is poor, and sets his heart upon it.
Fathers shall not be put to death for their children, nor shall the children 24:16
be put to death for their fathers. Everyone shall die for his own sin.
Do not deny justice to the stranger, or to the fatherless. 24:17
Do not take a widow's coat for a pledge.
Remember that you were a bondman in Egypt, and that Yahweh 24:18
redeemed you. Therefore I command you in these things.
When you cut down your harvest and forget a sheaf in the field, do not 24:19
go back to fetch it. It shall be for the stranger, for the fatherless, and for
the widow, that Yahweh may bless you in all the work of your hands.
When you harvest your olives, do not beat the boughs over again. 24:20
Leave the rest for the stranger, for the fatherless, and for the widow.
When you gather the grapes of your vineyard, you shall not glean it twice. 24:21
Leave some for the stranger, for the fatherless, and for the widow.
Remember, you were a bondman in Egypt, so I command you in this way." 24:22

Chapter 25

"If there is a controversy between men, and they take it to the judges for 25:1
judgment, the judges shall justify the righteous and condemn the wicked.
If the wicked man deserves flogging, the judge shall have him lie down 25:2
and be flogged, with the number of stripes determined by his offense.
He may be given no more than forty stripes, lest he be publicly humiliated. 25:3
Do not muzzle the ox while he is treading out your grain. Let him eat of it. 25:4
If two blood brothers live together and one dies having no child, his wife 25:5
shall not marry outside the family. Her husband's brother shall take her as
a wife and go unto her. It is the brother's duty to perform as her husband.
And it shall be that the firstborn she bears shall carry the name 25:6
of his dead brother, that his name not be forgotten in Israel.
If the man will not take his brother's wife, then let his brother's wife 25:7
go to the city elders, and say, 'My husband's brother refuses to keep
his brother's name in Israel. He will not perform as my husband.'
Then the elders of his city shall call him, and speak with him on her behalf. 25:8
But if he stands firm and says, 'I do not want to marry her,'
then his brother's wife shall come to him in the presence of the elders, 25:9
take his shoe off his foot, and spit in his face. And she shall say,
'So shall it be done to the man who will not build up his brother's house.'
And henceforth his family name shall be, 25:10
'The house of him who had his shoe taken off.'

"If two men are fighting, and the wife of one jumps in 25:11
to help her husband by grabbing his attacker's genitals,
you shall cut off her hand. You shall not pity her. 25:12
You shall not carry two different money weights, a great and a small. 25:13
You shall not have in your house two weights, a great and a small. 25:14
You shall have one perfect and just weight, and one perfect and just 25:15
measure, that your days may be lengthened in the land Yahweh gives you.
For all who do such things, and who do business dishonestly, 25:16
are an abomination unto Yahweh, your God.
Remember what Amalek did unto you by the way, 25:17
when you came forth out of Egypt,
how he came upon you, and attacked those who were straggling 25:18
behind because they were feeble or tired. He did not fear God.
Therefore, when Yahweh has given you rest from all your enemies 25:19
in the land he gives you to possess, you must blot out the memory
of the name of Amalek from under heaven. Do not forget!"

Chapter 26

"When you come into the land Yahweh gives you 26:1
for an inheritance, and possesses it, and dwell there,
take some of the first fruits of your land Yahweh gives you, put it in a 26:2
basket, and take it to the place Yahweh shall choose to place his name.
Go to the priest of that time and say unto him, 'I profess this day unto 26:3
Yahweh, that I have come into the land Yahweh swore unto our fathers.'
The priest shall take the basket out of your hand, 26:4
and set it down before the altar of Yahweh, your God.
And you shall say before Yahweh, 'My fathers were wandering Arameans, 26:5
so few in number they were ready to perish. And they went into Egypt,
and sojourned there, and became a great nation, mighty and numerous.
The Egyptians treated us cruelly, and laid upon us hard bondage. 26:6
And we cried unto Yahweh, God of our fathers, and he heard. 26:7
And he looked upon our affliction, and our labor, and our oppression.
And Yahweh brought us out of Egypt, with a mighty hand and an 26:8
outstretched arm, with terrifying power, and signs and wonders.
He brought us to this place and gave us this land, 26:9
a land that flows with milk and honey.
Now I have brought the first fruits of the land, which you have given me.' 26:10
And you shall set it before Yahweh, and worship before Yahweh your God.
You shall rejoice in every good thing Yahweh has given you, 26:11
and to your house—you, and the Levite, and the stranger among you.

"When you have finished setting aside the tenth part of your increase 26:12
in the third year—the year of tithing—and have given it to the Levite,
the stranger, the fatherless, and the widow,
that they may eat within your gates and be filled,
then you shall say before Yahweh your God, 'I have set aside the holy 26:13
portion of my increase, and have given it to the Levite, and the stranger,
and the fatherless and the widow, according to all your commandments.

I have not transgressed your commandments, nor have I forgotten them.
No part of this have I eaten while mourning, nor while unclean, nor used 26:14
as dedication for the dead. I have hearkened to the voice of Yahweh,
and have done according to all that you have commanded me.
Look down, therefore, from your holy habitation, from heaven, and bless 26:15
your people, Israel, and the land you have given us, a land you swore
unto our fathers, a land that flows with milk and honey.'

"In this very moment Yahweh your God commands you to do these 26:16
statutes and judgments. You shall therefore keep them, and do them,
with all your heart, and with all your soul.
You have this day acknowledged Yahweh as your God, and you shall 26:17
walk in his ways, and keep his statutes, and keep his commandments,
and keep his judgments, and hearken unto his voice.
Yahweh has affirmed this day that you are his chosen people, 26:18
as he promised you, and that you shall keep all his commandments,
and that he shall raise you high above all nations, in praise, and in name, 26:19
and in honor, that you may be a holy people unto Yahweh, your God."

Chapter 27

Moses, along with the elders of Israel, commanded the people, saying, 27:1
"Keep all the commandments I command you this day.
When you go over Jordan into the land Yahweh gives you, 27:2
set up great stones, and plaster them with plaster.
Write on them all the words of this law when you have passed over 27:3
into the land Yahweh gives you, a land that flows with milk and honey,
as Yahweh, God of your fathers, promised you.
Therefore, when you go over Jordan, set up these stones 27:4
in Mount Ebal, and plaster them with plaster.
Build an altar unto Yahweh, an altar of stones 27:5
that have not had an iron tool laid upon them.
Build the altar unto Yahweh of whole stones, 27:6
and thereon you shall offer burnt offerings unto Yahweh.
You shall offer peace offerings, and shall eat there, 27:7
and rejoice before Yahweh.
And you shall write upon the stones all the words of this law very plainly." 27:8

Moses and the Levitical priests spoke unto all Israel, saying, "Take heed, 27:9
and hearken, O Israel. Today you have become the people of Yahweh.
You shall therefore obey the voice of Yahweh, your God, and do his 27:10
commandments and his statutes, which I command you this day."
Moses charged the people that same day, saying, 27:11
"These men shall stand upon Mount Gerizim to bless the people 27:12
when you have gone over Jordan: Simeon, and Levi,
and Judah, and Issachar, and Joseph and Benjamin.
These shall stand upon Mount Ebal to curse: 27:13
Reuben, Gad, Asher, Zebulun, Dan and Naphtali.
And the Levites shall speak, and say unto all of Israel with a loud voice, 27:14

'Cursed be he who makes any graven or molten image, an abomination   27:15
unto Yahweh—the work of the hands of the craftsman—and secretly
worships it.' And all the people shall answer and say, 'Amen.'

"'Cursed be he who does not honor his father or his mother.'   27:16
And all the people shall say, 'Amen.'
'Cursed be he who removes his neighbor's landmark.'   27:17
And all the people shall say, 'Amen.'
'Cursed be he who makes the blind wander out of the way.'   27:18
And all the people shall say, 'Amen.'
'Cursed be he who perverts the judgment of the stranger,   27:19
the fatherless, and the widow.' And all the people shall say, 'Amen.'
'Cursed be he who lies with his father's wife, for he uncovers   27:20
his father's privacy.' And all the people shall say, 'Amen.'
'Cursed be he who lies with any manner of beast.'   27:21
And all the people shall say, 'Amen.'
'Cursed be he who lies with his sister—the daughter of his father,   27:22
or the daughter of his mother.' And all the people shall say, 'Amen.'
'Cursed be he who lies with his mother-in-law.'   27:23
And all the people shall say, 'Amen.'
'Cursed be he who kills his neighbor secretly.'   27:24
And all the people shall say, 'Amen.'
'Cursed be he who takes money to kill an innocent person.'   27:25
And all the people shall say, 'Amen.'
'Cursed be he who confirms not all the words of this law, and does them.'   27:26
And all the people shall say, 'Amen.'"

Chapter 28

"If you hearken diligently unto the voice of Yahweh your God,   28:1
and observe and do all his commandments I command you this day,
Yahweh will set you high above all other nations of the earth.
All these blessings shall come upon you, and overtake you,   28:2
if you hearken to the voice of Yahweh:
Blessed shall you be in the city, and blessed shall you be in the field.   28:3
Blessed shall be the fruit of your body, and the fruit of your ground,   28:4
and the fruit of your cattle, and the increase of your herds and flocks.
Blessed shall be your grain basket and your food stores.   28:5
Blessed shall you be when you come in,   28:6
and blessed shall you be when you go out.
Yahweh shall cause your enemies to be defeated before your face.   28:7
They shall come at you from one way, and flee from you seven ways.
Yahweh shall command his blessing upon you in your storehouses,   28:8
and in all you set your hand to. He shall bless you in the land he gives you.
Yahweh shall establish you as a holy people unto himself, as he has   28:9
sworn to you, if you keep his commandments and walk in his ways.
All the people of earth shall see that you are called   28:10
by the name of Yahweh, and they shall fear you.
Yahweh shall make good things abound for you, in the fruit of your body,   28:11

and in the fruit of your cattle, and in the fruit of your ground,
in the land Yahweh swore unto your fathers.
Yahweh shall open unto you his good treasure. The heavens shall send   28:12
rain upon your land in season, and he shall bless the work of your hand.
You shall lend to many nations, and you shall not borrow.
Yahweh shall make you the head, and not the tail. You shall only be above,   28:13
and not be beneath—if you hearken unto the commandments of Yahweh
your God, which I command you this day, and observe and do them.
You shall not go aside from any of the words I command you,   28:14
to the right hand or to the left, to go after other gods to serve them.

"But if you will not hearken to the voice of Yahweh your God, to observe   28:15
and do all his commandments and his statutes, which I command you
this day, then all these curses shall come upon you, and overtake you:
Cursed shall you be in the city, and cursed shall you be in the field.   28:16
Cursed shall be your grain basket and your food stores.   28:17
Cursed shall be the fruit of your body, and the fruit of your land,   28:18
and the increase of your herds and flocks.
Cursed shall you be when you come in,   28:19
and cursed shall you be when you go out.
Yahweh shall send upon you cursing and vexation and rebuke in all that   28:20
you set your hand to, until you are destroyed, until you suddenly perish
because of your wickedness, because you have forsaken me.
Yahweh shall make pestilence cleave unto you, until he has   28:21
utterly wiped you from the face of the land you go to possess.
Yahweh shall strike you with consumption, fever and inflammation,   28:22
and with the sword, and scorching heat, and drought, and crop disease,
and they shall plague you until you perish.
The heaven above your heads shall be brass,   28:23
and the earth under your feet shall be iron.
Yahweh shall make the rain of your land be powder and dust. Dirt shall   28:24
rain down on you from heaven, until you are completely destroyed.

"Yahweh shall cause you to be utterly defeated by your enemies.   28:25
You shall go out one way against them, and flee seven ways before them.
You shall be scattered unto all the kingdoms of the earth.
Your corpses shall be meat for the birds of the air and the beasts   28:26
of the land, and no one shall be left alive to chase them off.
Yahweh will strike you with all the diseases of Egypt—the boils,   28:27
and tumors, and scabs, and lesions—and you shall never heal of them.
Yahweh will strike you with madness, blindness, and panic of heart.   28:28
You shall grope about in daylight as the blind grope in darkness.   28:29
You shall not prosper in your ways. You shall be oppressed
and impoverished forever. You will have no savior.
You shall betroth a wife and another man shall lie with her.   28:30
You shall build a house and never dwell therein.
You shall plant a vineyard, and never gather its grapes.

Your ox will be slain before your eyes, but you shall not be the one who 28:31
eats of it. Your ass shall be violently taken from you, and never given back.
Your sheep shall be given to your enemies. And you will have no savior.

"Your sons and daughters will be given to another people, 28:32
and your eyes shall waste away from longing and weeping for them
all the day long, and you will have no power to do anything about it.
The fruit of your land and all your labors shall eaten by a nation 28:33
of strangers. You will be crushed and downtrodden forever.
The things you shall see and endure will drive you to madness. 28:34
Yahweh shall inflame your knees, inflict your legs, and cover 28:35
your body from head to foot with painful, incurable boils and lesions.
Yahweh shall send you, and the king you shall set over you, 28:36
to a nation neither you nor your fathers have ever known,
and there you shall serve other gods, gods of wood and stone.
You shall become a horror, a laughingstock, a cautionary tale, 28:37
a proverb, among all the nations where Yahweh takes you.
You shall carry much seed into the field, but gather little in. 28:38
Locusts shall consume your harvests.
You shall plant vineyards, and dress them, but shall neither gather 28:39
the grapes nor drink the wine. Worms shall eat your harvests.
You shall have olive trees throughout your land, but you shall 28:40
not anoint yourself with their oil, for the trees shall give no fruit.
You shall beget sons and daughters, but you will not enjoy them, 28:41
for they shall go into captivity.
Locusts shall consume all your trees and the fruit of your land. 28:42
The stranger among you shall be lifted higher and higher. 28:43
You shall sink lower and lower.
He shall lend to you, but you shall not lend to him. 28:44
He shall be the head, and you shall be the tail.

"All these curses shall come upon you, and pursue you, and overtake you, 28:45
and destroy you, because you hearkened not unto the voice of Yahweh,
to keep the commandments and the statutes he commanded you.
They shall be upon you a sign and wonder, and upon your seed forever, 28:46
because you did not serve Yahweh with joyfulness, 28:47
and with gladness of heart for the abundance of all things.
You shall serve your enemies that Yahweh will send against you, 28:48
in hunger, and in thirst, and in nakedness, and in want of all things.
And he shall put a yoke of iron on your neck until he has destroyed you.
Yahweh shall bring a nation against you from afar—from the end of the 28:49
earth, as swift as the eagle flies—a nation whose tongue you do not know,
a nation of fierce countenance, that shall not regard 28:50
the person of the old, nor show favor to the young.
He shall eat your cattle and the fruit of your land, until you are destroyed. 28:51
He shall not leave you any of your grain, or wine, or oil, or the increase of
your herds or flocks, until he has caused you to perish.
He shall besiege your cities until the high fenced walls you trusted in come 28:52
down. He shall surround all your cities in the land Yahweh has given you.

Because of the length and severity of the sieges, you shall come to eat   28:53
the offspring of your own wombs, the flesh of your sons and daughters.
Even the most gentle and refined man shall turn evil toward his brother,   28:54
and toward the wife of his bosom, and toward the last of his children.
He will not give them any of the flesh of his children, whom he shall be   28:55
eating because he has nothing left him in the siege, in the dire
circumstances your enemies shall inflict on all your cities.
The most tender and delicate woman among you, who would not so much   28:56
as stomp her foot in anger, shall cast an evil eye toward the husband
of her bosom, and toward her son, and toward her daughter,
and toward her newborn baby—toward any children she shall bear—   28:57
and she shall eat them secretly for want of food, in the siege and
desperate circumstances your enemy shall bring upon your cities.

"If you will not observe and do all the words of this law, which are written   28:58
in this book, that you may fear the glorious name of YAHWEH, your God,
then Yahweh will send unimaginable plagues upon you and your seed—   28:59
severe untreatable afflictions and terrible chronic ills.
And he will bring upon you all the diseases of Egypt,   28:60
which you were afraid of, and they shall cleave unto you.
Also every other sickness and plague not written in this book of law   28:61
will Yahweh bring upon you, until you are completely destroyed.
You shall be left few in number, whereas you were as numerous as   28:62
the stars of heaven, because you would not obey the voice of Yahweh.
As Yahweh rejoiced over you to do you good, and to multiply you,   28:63
so will Yahweh rejoice in destroying you, and annihilating you.
You shall be plucked from off the land you go to possess.
Yahweh will scatter you among all peoples, from the one end of the earth   28:64
to the other, and there you shall serve other gods, which neither you
nor your fathers have known, gods of wood and stone.

"Among these nations you shall find no rest, nor place of safety.   28:65
Yahweh shall give you a trembling heart, failing eyes, and sorrow of mind.
Your life shall hang in doubt, and you shall live in fear day and night.   28:66
You shall have no assurance of life.
In the morning you will say, 'Would God it were evening!'   28:67
And at evening you will say, 'Would God it were morning!'
because of the fear in your heart, and the sights you shall see.
Yahweh will send you back to Egypt in ships, by the route I told you,   28:68
'You shall not see this way again.' There you shall offer yourselves
as slaves to your enemies, but no man will buy you."

Chapter 29

These are the words of the covenant Yahweh commanded Moses   29:1
to make with the children of Israel in the land of Moab,
beside the covenant he made with them in Horeb.
Moses called unto all Israel, and said to them,   29:2
"You have seen all that Yahweh did before your eyes in Egypt,

unto Pharaoh and all his servants, and unto all his land—
the terrible plagues, wondrous signs, and great miracles.   29:3
Yet to this day, Yahweh has not given your heart to perceive,   29:4
your eyes to see, your ears to hear, or your mind to understand.
I have led you forty years in the wilderness. Your clothes have not   29:5
grown old upon you, and the shoes on your feet have not worn out.
You have not eaten bread, nor drunk wine or strong drink,   29:6
that you might know I am Yahweh, your God.
When you came unto this place, Sihon the king of Heshbon,   29:7
and Og the king of Bashan, came out against us, and we defeated them.
We took their land and gave it for an inheritance to the Reubenites,   29:8
and to the Gadites, and to the half-tribe of Manasseh.
Therefore, keep the words of this covenant, and do them,   29:9
that you may prosper in all that you do.

"You stand this day before Yahweh, all of you, the captains   29:10
of your tribes, your elders, your officers and all the men of Israel,
your little ones, your wives, and the strangers in your camp—   29:11
from the hewer of your wood to he who draws your water—
that you should enter into a covenant with Yahweh your God,   29:12
and into his oath, which he makes with you this day,
that he may establish you for a people unto himself,   29:13
and that he may be unto you a God, as he has said to you,
and as he has sworn unto your fathers, Abraham, Isaac and Jacob.
I make this covenant and this oath not only with you   29:14
who stand here with us this day before Yahweh,   29:15
but also with those who are not here with us today.
You know how we were treated in the land of Egypt,   29:16
and how we passed through nations as we traveled.
You have seen their abominations,   29:17
and their idols of wood, stone, silver and gold.
So let there not be among you a man, or woman, or family, or tribe,   29:18
whose heart turns away from Yahweh to serve the gods of these nations.
Let there not be a root among you that bears gall and wormwood.
Let there not be among you a man who hears the words of this curse,   29:19
yet convinces himself he shall have peace walking in the way of his whims,
lest his stubbornness dry up the waters of the righteous ones.

"Yahweh will not spare him. The anger and jealousy of Yahweh shall burn   29:20
against that man, and all the curses written in this book shall come
upon him, and Yahweh shall blot out his name from under heaven.
And Yahweh shall single out his tribe for an example, and bring upon   29:21
them all the curses of the covenant written in this book of law,
so that the generations of your children who rise up after you,   29:22
and the stranger who comes from a far land, shall see the plagues
of that land, and the sicknesses Yahweh has laid upon it,
and that the whole land is brimstone, and salt and burning,   29:23
and that it is not sown, nor does it bear, nor does any grass grow—
like the destruction of Sodom and Gomorrah, Admah and Zeboim,

which Yahweh overthrew in his anger and his wrath.

They shall say, 'Why has Yahweh done this to this land? 29:24
What is the meaning of his great anger?'

And men shall say, 'Because they have forsaken the covenant of Yahweh, 29:25
God of their fathers, which he made when he brought them out of Egypt.

They went and served other gods, and worshipped them, 29:26
gods whom they knew not, and whom he had not given unto them.

And the anger of Yahweh was kindled against this land, 29:27
to bring upon it all the curses that are written in this book.

And Yahweh rooted them out of their land in anger and great indignation, 29:28
and cast them into another land, as it is to this day.'

The secret things belong to Yahweh. But those things that are revealed, 29:29
belong unto us and to our children forever,
that we may do all the words of this law."

Chapter 30

"When these things are upon you—the blessing and the curse 30:1
I have set before you—and you call them to mind when you
are in the nations where Yahweh your God has driven you,

and you return unto Yahweh, and obey his voice according to all 30:2
that I command you this day, you and your children,
with all your heart, and with all your soul,

Yahweh will overturn your captivity, and have compassion for you, 30:3
and will gather you from all the nations where he has scattered you.

Even if Yahweh has driven you unto the end of heaven, 30:4
from there he will gather you, and take you back.

He will bring you into the land your fathers possessed, and you shall 30:5
possess it. He will do you good, and multiply you beyond your fathers.

He will circumcise your heart, and the heart of your seed, to love Yahweh 30:6
your God with all your heart, and with all your soul, that you may live.

Yahweh will put all these curses upon your enemies, 30:7
and on those who hated you, and persecuted you.

You shall return and obey the voice of Yahweh, 30:8
and do all his commandments, which I command you this day.

Yahweh will make you succeed in all the works of your hand, in the fruits 30:9
of your body, and in the fruits of your cattle, and in the fruits of your land.
Yahweh will rejoice over you as he rejoiced over your fathers,

if you hearken unto his voice, and keep his commandments— 30:10
which are written in this book of the law—and turn unto Yahweh
with all your heart, and with all your soul.

"The commandment I give you this day is not hidden or beyond reach. 30:11
It is not in heaven, that you should say, 'Who shall go up to heaven 30:12
for us, and bring it unto us, that we may hear it, and do it?'

Neither is it beyond the sea, that you should say, 'Who shall go over 30:13
the sea for us, and bring it unto us, that we may hear it, and do it?'

The word is very near unto you—in your mouth, 30:14
and in your heart—that you may hear it, and do it.

I have set before you today: Life, and good, and death, and evil. 30:15
I command you this day to love Yahweh your God, to walk in all his ways, 30:16
and to keep his commandments, and his statutes, and his judgments,
that you may live, and multiply, and so that Yahweh your God
will bless you in the land you go to possess.
But if your heart turns away so that you will not hear, 30:17
and you are drawn away to worship other gods, and to serve them,
I shall denounce you that very day, and you shall surely perish. 30:18
Your days shall not be long in the land over Jordan you go to possess.
Let heaven and earth be my witness, that I have set before you life and 30:19
death, blessing and curse. Choose life, that you and your seed may live.
Love Yahweh your God, and obey his voice, and cleave unto him, 30:20
for he is your life and your length of days. Dwell in peace in the land
Yahweh swore unto your fathers: Abraham, Isaac and Jacob.”

Chapter 31

Moses spoke to all Israel, and said unto them, 31:1
“I am a hundred and twenty years old this day. I can no more go out 31:2
and come in. Also, Yahweh has said to me, ‘You shall not go over Jordan.’
Yahweh will go over before you, and he will destroy those nations, 31:3
and you shall possess them. Joshua shall lead you, as Yahweh has said.
Yahweh shall do unto them as he did to Sihon and Og, 31:4
kings of the Amorites, whom he destroyed.
Yahweh shall give them up before you, that you may do unto them 31:5
according to all the commandments I have commanded you.
Be strong and of a good courage. Fear not. Do not be afraid of them, 31:6
for Yahweh your God goes with you. He will not fail you, nor forsake you.”
Moses called to Joshua, and said to him in the sight of all Israel, 31:7
“Be strong and of good courage. Go with this people into the land Yahweh
swore unto their fathers, and you shall cause them to inherit it.
Yahweh goes before you. He will be with you. He will not fail you. 31:8
He will not forsake you. Fear not, and be not troubled.”

Moses wrote this law and delivered it to the priests, the sons of Levi, 31:9
who bore the ark of the covenant of Yahweh, and to all the elders of Israel.
And Moses commanded them, saying, “At the end of every seven years, 31:10
in the solemnity of the year of release, in the Feast of Tabernacles,
when all Israel has come to appear before Yahweh in the place 31:11
he shall choose, you shall read this law before all Israel in their hearing.
Gather the people together, men, women, children, and the strangers 31:12
within your gates, that they may hear, and learn, and fear Yahweh
your God, and observe and do all the words of this law,
and that their children, who have not known any of this, 31:13
may hear, and learn to fear Yahweh your God,
for as long as you live in the land over Jordan.”

Yahweh said to Moses, “Behold, your days approach that you must die. 31:14
Call Joshua and present yourselves in the tabernacle, that I may give him

a charge." So Moses and Joshua presented themselves in the tabernacle.
Yahweh appeared in the tabernacle as a pillar of cloud.   31:15
And the pillar of cloud stood over the door of the tabernacle.
Yahweh said to Moses, "Behold, you shall sleep with your ancestors,   31:16
and this people will rise up, and go whoring after the gods
of the strangers of the land, and will forsake me, and break my covenant.
And my anger shall be kindled against them, and I will forsake them,   31:17
and I will turn my face from them, and they shall be devoured,
and many evils and troubles shall befall them. And they will say,
'Are not these evils come upon us because our God is not among us?'
I will surely turn my face from them in that day, for all the evil   31:18
they have done because they worshipped other gods.
Now, therefore, write this song, and teach it to the children of Israel.   31:19
Put it in their mouths, that it may be a witness for me against Israel.
For when I have brought them into the land I swore unto their fathers,   31:20
a land that flows with milk and honey, and they have eaten,
and filled themselves, and gotten fat, they will turn to other gods,
and serve them, and provoke me, and break my covenant.
And when many evils and troubles have befallen them, this song shall   31:21
be remembered by their children, and testify against them as a witness.
Yes, I know their thoughts and inclinations even now,
before I have brought them into the land I swore to them."

So Moses wrote the song that same day, and taught it to the Israelites.   31:22
And he gave Joshua the son of Nun a charge, and said,   31:23
"Be strong and of good courage, for you shall bring the children
of Israel into the land I swore unto them, and I will be with you."
When Moses finished writing all the words of this law in a book,   31:24
he commanded the Levites, who bore the ark of the covenant, saying,   31:25
"Take this book of the law, and put it in the side of the ark of the covenant 31:26
of Yahweh your God, that it may be there for a witness against you.
For I know your rebellion and your stubbornness.   31:27
Even while I am yet alive with you this day, you have been
rebellious against Yahweh. How much more so after my death?
Gather all the elders and officers of your tribes, that I may speak these   31:28
words in their ears, and call heaven and earth to witness against them.
For I know that after my death you will utterly corrupt yourselves,   31:29
and turn aside from the way I have commanded you, and evil will befall
you in the latter days because you will do evil in the sight of Yahweh,
and provoke him to anger through the work of your hands."
Then Moses spoke into the ears of all the congregation of the children   31:30
of Israel the words of this song, until they were ended.

Chapter 32

"Hear, O heavens, what I will speak. Hear, O earth, the words of my mouth.   32:1
Let my doctrine fall like rain, let my speech settle like the dew,   32:2
like gentle mist upon the tender herb, like showers upon the grass.
For I proclaim the name of Yahweh, and declare the greatness of our God.   32:3

He is the Rock. His work is perfect, for all his ways are righteous.   32:4
He is a God of truth, and is without iniquity. He is just, and right.
They have corrupted themselves. Their mark is not the mark   32:5
of his children. They are a perverse and crooked generation.
O foolish unwise people. Is this how you thank Yahweh?   32:6
Is he not your father? Has he not brought you, and established you?
Remember the days of old. Consider the years of many generations.   32:7
Ask your father and he will show you. Ask your elders—they will tell you.

"When the Most High divided mankind into nations—   32:8
when he separated the sons of Adam—he set the boundaries
of the nations according to the number of gods in his retinue.
Yahweh's portion is the people of Israel. Jacob is the lot of his inheritance.   32:9
He found him in the desert, a wasteland, a howling wilderness.   32:10
He led him about and instructed him. He kept him as the apple of his eye.
As an eagle stirs her nest and flutters over her young,   32:11
as she takes them up and bears them upon her wings,
so did Yahweh alone lead Jacob. There was no other god with him.   32:12
He brought him to the mounts and valleys of earth, that he might eat   32:13
the crops of the fields. He gave him honey from rock, and oil from flint.
He gave you butter of cows, and milk of sheep, and fat of lambs,   32:14
and rams of the breed of Bashan, and goats, and kernels of wheat,
and you drank the pure blood of the grape.
But Jeshurun grew fat and rebellious, as you have grown fat,   32:15
and thick, and covered with soft flesh. Then Jeshurun forsook
the God who had made him, and rejected the Rock of his salvation.
They provoked Yahweh to jealousy with strange gods,   32:16
and with abominations provoked him to anger.
They sacrificed unto devils, to gods they knew not—   32:17
to strange new gods that your fathers did not revere.
You are unmindful of the Rock that fathered you.   32:18
You have forgotten the God that gave you life.

"When Yahweh saw this he abhorred the provocations of his children.   32:19
He said, 'I will turn my face from them, and see what their end shall be.   32:20
For they are a perverse generation, children in whom there is no faith.
They have moved me to jealousy with that which is not of God. They have   32:21
provoked me to anger with their vanities. I will move them to jealousy
with that which is not of people. I will make them an angry nation of fools.
For the fire of anger is kindled in me, and it burns unto the lowest hells.   32:22
It shall consume the earth and her crops, and set fire under mountains.
I will heap disasters upon them, and spend my arrows against them.   32:23
They shall burn with hunger, and be devoured with scorching heat   32:24
and bitter destruction. I will set the fangs of beasts upon them,
and poison them with the venom of serpents and creatures of the dust.
With the sword without, and terror within, I shall destroy   32:25
young men and virgins, sucklings and gray-haired men.
I thought to scatter them to the far corners of earth,   32:26
and erase the memory of them from among men,

but I feared their adversaries would take credit, and boast,   32:27
"Our hand is mighty. It is we, not Yahweh, that has done all this."

'They are a nation void of wisdom and understanding.   32:28
O that they were wise, and understood, and would consider their future!   32:29
How could one chase a thousand, and two put ten thousand to flight,   32:30
unless their Rock had abandoned them, and Yahweh had given them up?
For our enemy's rock is not as our Rock. Even they themselves know this.   32:31
Their vine is of the vine of Sodom, their fields are the fields of Gomorrah.   32:32
Their grapes are grapes of gall, their clusters are bitter.
Their wine is the poison of dragons and the cruel venom of asps.   32:33
Is this knowledge not secretly stored with me, waiting in my vault?   32:34
Vengeance is mine, and recompense. Their foot shall slip in due time.   32:35
The day of their calamity is at hand, and their destiny is quickening.
Yahweh shall judge his people, and have compassion for his servants   32:36
once he sees their power is gone and there are none left, slave or free.
And he shall say, "Where are their gods, their rock in whom they trusted,   32:37
that ate the fat of their sacrifices, and drank the wine of their offerings?   32:38
Let them rise up and help you, and be your protection."

'See now that I am he, and there is no other god beside me. I kill and I   32:39
make alive. I wound and I heal. Nothing can deliver you from my hand.
I lift up my hand to heaven, and say, "I live forever!"   32:40
When I whet my glittering sword, and my hand takes hold of judgment,   32:41
I render vengeance upon my enemies and punish those who hate me.
I make my arrows drunk with blood, and my sword devours flesh—   32:42
both of those killed fighting and those who surrendered—
and this is but the beginning of my revenge upon the enemy.'
Rejoice, O you nations, and you people. He will avenge the blood   32:43
of his servants, and will render vengeance unto his adversaries.
But he will be merciful unto his land, and unto his people."
Moses spoke all the words of this song   32:44
in the ears of the people, he, and Hoshea the son of Nun.
Then Moses made an end of speaking these words to all Israel.   32:45
And he said to them, "Let these words go deep into your hearts,   32:46
and command your children to observe and do all the words of this law.
It is no small thing for you. It is your life. It is by this alone that you   32:47
shall prolong your days in the land over Jordan you go to possess."

Yahweh spoke unto Moses that same day, saying,   32:48
"Go into the mountains of Abarim, unto Mount Nebo,   32:49
in the land of Moab opposite Jericho, and behold the land of Canaan,
which I give to the children of Israel for a possession.
You will die on that mountain and be gathered unto your ancestors,   32:50
as Aaron died on Mount Hor and was gathered unto his ancestors,
because you trespassed against me among the children of Israel   32:51
at the waters of Meribah-Kadesh, in the wilderness of Zin,
and because you did not sanctify me in the midst of the children of Israel.

You shall see the land before you, but you shall not go in.   32:52
You shall not cross over into the land I give to Israel."

Chapter 33

This is the blessing Moses, the man of God,   33:1
blessed the children of Israel with before his death.
He said, "Yahweh came from Sinai, and rose up from Seir.   33:2
He shined forth from Mount Paran, and came with ten thousand saints.
From his right hand burned a fiery law. He loved the people.
His saints are in your hand. They sit at your feet and receive your words.   33:3
Moses commanded us a law, the inheritance of the congregation of Jacob.   33:4
He was king in Jeshurun, when the heads of the people   33:5
and the tribes of Israel were gathered together:

"Let Reuben live, and not die. Let not his men be few."   33:6
This is the blessing of Judah, "Hear, Lord, the voice of Judah,   33:7
and bring him unto his people. Let his hands be sufficient for his tasks,
and may you help him in the fight against his enemies."
Of Levi he said, "Let your Thummim and your Urim   33:8
be with your holy one, whom you did test at Massah,
and with whom you were angry at the waters of Meribah—
who said unto his father and mother, 'I do not know them.'   33:9
Neither did he acknowledge his brethren, nor his own children.
They have observed your word, and kept your covenant.
They shall teach Jacob your judgments, and Israel your law.   33:10
They shall bring incense before you, and burn sacrifices upon your altar.
Bless, O Lord, Levi's substance, and accept the work of his hands.   33:11
Crush the loins of them who rise against him, that they rise never again."

Of Benjamin he said, "The beloved of Yahweh shall dwell safely with him.   33:12
Yahweh shall shield him all the day long, and he shall rest in his arms."
Of Joseph he said, "Let the blessing of Yahweh, the good things of heaven,   33:13
be on his land—the dew, and the waters that run beneath,
and the precious fruits brought forth by the sun,   33:14
and the precious things brought forth by the moon,
and the precious things of the ancient mountains,   33:15
and the precious things of the lasting hills,
and the precious things of the earth in its fullness,   33:16
and the goodwill of him who dwells in the bush—
let these blessings come upon the head of Joseph,
upon the head of him who was separated from his brethren.
His majesty is like a firstborn bull. His horns are like a wild ox.   33:17
With them he shall drive peoples to the ends of the earth—
the ten thousands of Ephraim, the thousands of Manasseh."

Of Zebulun he said, "Rejoice, Zebulun, in your going out,"   33:18
and of Issachar, "Rejoice in your tents.
They shall call the people unto the mountain, and there they shall offer   33:19
sacrifices of righteousness. For they shall be nourished by the

abundance of the seas, and by the treasures hidden in the sand."
Of Gad he said, "Blessed is he who enlarges the land of Gad.   33:20
He dwells there like a lion, and tears off arms and the crowns of heads.
He kept the best part for himself, because it was his right as ruler.   33:21
He met with the heads of Israel, and executed the justice of Yahweh."
Of Dan he said, "Dan is a lion's whelp. He shall leap from Bashan."   33:22
Of Naphtali he said, "O Naphtali, satisfied with favor, and full   33:23
with the blessing of Yahweh, possess you the west and the south."
Of Asher he said, "Let Asher be blessed with children.   33:24
Let him be acceptable to his brethren, and let his feet be dipped in oil.
Let his gates be iron and brass, and let his strength last for all his days.   33:25

"There is none like the God of Jeshurun, who comes in the   33:26
cloud of heaven to help you, in all his excellence and majesty.
The eternal God is your refuge. You are held safe in his everlasting arms.   33:27
He shall drive out your enemy before you, and say, 'Destroy them.'
Israel shall then dwell in safety. The fountain of Jacob shall be upon   33:28
a land of bread and wine. His heavens shall give generously of their dew.
Blessed you are, O Israel! Who is like unto you? You are a people saved   33:29
by Yahweh—who is your shield, your help, the sword of your excellency!
Your enemies shall fawn before you, and you shall tread on their backs."

Chapter 34

Moses went up from the plains of Moab into the mountain of Nebo,   34:1
to the top of Pisgah, which is over against Jericho.
And Yahweh showed him all the land of Gilead as far as Dan,
and all Naphtali, and the land of Ephraim and Manasseh,   34:2
and all the land of Judah unto the Mediterranean Sea, and the south,
and the plain of the valley of Jericho, the city of palm trees, unto Zoar.   34:3
And Yahweh said to Moses, "This is the land I swore unto   34:4
Abraham, Isaac and Jacob, saying, 'I will give it to your children.'
I have let you see it with your eyes, but you shall not go into it."
So Moses, the servant of Yahweh, died there in the land of Moab,   34:5
according to the word of Yahweh.
And Yahweh buried him in a valley in the land of Moab,   34:6
over against Beth-Peor, but no man knows of his sepulcher to this day.
Moses was a hundred and twenty years old when he died.   34:7
His eye was not dim, nor his natural force abated.
The children of Israel wept for Moses in the plains of Moab for thirty days,   34:8
then the days of weeping and mourning for Moses ended.
Joshua the son of Nun was full of the spirit of wisdom,   34:9
for Moses had laid his hands upon him. And the children of Israel
hearkened unto him, and did as Yahweh commanded Moses.

There has not since arisen in Israel a prophet like unto Moses,   34:10
whom Yahweh knew face-to-face,
and who performed all the signs and wonders Yahweh commanded   34:11
him to do in Egypt, to Pharaoh and all his servants, and to all his people.

With a fearless and mighty hand, Moses, servant of Yahweh, showed in the sight of all Israel great wonders and terrifying deeds no other prophet has done before or after him.

With a fearless and mighty hand, Moses, servant of Yahweh, showed in the sight of all Israel great wonders and terrifying deeds no other prophet has done before or after him.